Shades of Justice

A Memoir

Paul Krehbiel

Autumn Leaf Press
Altadena, California

Library of Congress Control Number: 2007909689

ISBN: 978-0-9799762-1-6

1. Memoir. 2. United States History.
2. War in Vietnam. 4. US Anti-war Movement.

Autumn Leaf Press
P. O. Box 6528
Altadena, CA 91003
626-398-9984

autumnleafpress.com

shadesofjustice.com

Printed in the United States of America

Dedicated to:
The memory of my father,
and to my mother,
Patty and Alex,
and all who
stand for justice.

Acknowledgements

I would like to thank a number of individuals and organizations for their assistance. First, the members of the Pasadena Writers Group II for their invaluable suggestions and continued support and encouragement: Stephanie Barshefski, Ray Elizondo, Jean Gerard, Linda Ifkheideh, Cindy Chase Marquez, Sylvia Torres Parcella, Delores Ramos, Alyson Ross, and W. Roger Scott.

I also want to thank George and Leslie Cownie, Lee Krehbiel, Jim Krehbiel, Howard Kling, Patricia Margaret, Roger Marheine, Tristine Rainer, Mike Reilly, Jim Rivard, and Mary Ellen Sheehan for helping to jog my memory and/or making excellent suggestions.

I also want to thank the following organizations: Buffalo and Erie County Historical Society, Buffalo and Erie County Library, *Buffalo Courier-Express, Buffalo Evening News,* Buffalo Nine Defense Committee, Saint Paul's Cathedral, State University of New York at Buffalo Archives, State University College at Buffalo Archives, *The National Guardian, The New York Times,* and *The Spectrum,* along with the authors of the books I referred to in writing this book.

Finally, I am responsible for the content of this work, including any errors.

Cover:
1,000 people march in downtown Buffalo, February 20, 1970, to protest the conviction of the "Chicago 8" anti-war organizers.

Cover art and design by Paul Krehbiel.

This is a true story. Some literary license has been used for dramatic purposes and some names have been changed to protect the identity of individuals involved.

Contents

Part 1: The Young Artist

Part 2: Crisis and Awakening

Part 3: The Organizer

Part 4: Commitment

Part 5: Students Strike and Protests Spread

Part 1: The Young Artist

Prologue

The Chase

"Get 'em!" growled a gravelly voice over a squawking radio. A cop car swung toward me and two exploding headlights blinded me in the gray-black night. Rubber burned and screeched on the pavement and the monster jumped the curb. Blazing fireballs blotted out the darkness.

I was standing near Bruce and we took off across the lawn. I slipped on a patch of ice, quickly regained my balance, and dashed between a clump of nearby trees, hoping the car would crash into them. I glanced over my shoulder and saw the wild beast swerve around the barriers and charge us again. They're trying to run us over!

My heart was screaming as we tore toward Main Street. We veered left onto the sidewalk and raced in front of a small building to a driveway. Bruce, and then I, hooked our arms around a pole and boomeranged ourselves 90 degrees up the narrow lane.

I immediately saw a solid wall of buildings on each side of us and a building in front. We're trapped on a dead-end road! Tires squealed so loudly behind me I thought I felt the bumper hit the back of my legs. I leaped between two parked cars on my right and hit the ground. It was pitch black around me.

Bruce was gone. I was alone and had no where to run. I clutched the baseball-sized rock that I pulled from my pocket and turned to face my attackers. If they slammed on their brakes where I ducked in, I would throw the rock at the first cop as hard as I could, and try to escape down the alley to Main Street. If I missed, they could kill me right there.

Two cones of light raced along the pavement in front of me, the roaring engine reverberated off the nearby walls, and the front of their car zoomed into sight. And kept going. I couldn't believe it! I raced down the pavement to Main Street into the glare of the city lights. Beads of steaming sweat rolled down my neck – even in the

1

cold winter night air, and my throat was burning. I looked around quickly and saw no one, felt a moment of relief, and then disappeared into the night. It was March 1970 at the height of the Buffalo riots. It was my closest call yet, but I had escaped again.

Four weeks later the snow had melted. Little green buds appeared on the bony fingers of trees, and red, blue and yellow dollops popped up in nearby fields. Life was reborn. It was quiet and peaceful as women and girls got out their finest dresses and bonnets for Easter. But it was a calm before a much bigger storm. Spring 1970. It changed my life forever.

Chapter 1

Respect

I was born in 1948 in Buffalo, New York and raised in a loving family in the Town of Tonawanda, a northern suburb of workers and professionals. My dad did surveying and engineering jobs in the family business, designing and laying-out roads, water and sewer lines, and residential and commercial property. My mom stayed at home to raise my two younger brothers and me. We had all the basic necessities of life – food, clothing, a comfortable home, access to medical care, and more. We had dinner together as a family every night, went on one or two week summer vacations to the Adirondack Mountains, and celebrated birthdays, Christmas and other special events. My parents took my brother Lee and me to our little league baseball and hockey games, and my brother Jim to his music lessons. By all accounts, we were considered a successful, middle-class family.

My dad, Theodore, was born on a farm in nearby Clarence Center where the first Krehbiels settled and worked when they came to the United States from Germany after the Peasant Revolutions in 1831. Whether they were involved in those upheavals or not, I don't know. My grandmother told me that our ancestors, after getting married in Germany, received money for wedding presents to travel to the "New World." After a frightful boat trip across the Atlantic, where storms cracked wooden planks in the boat and water leaked in and people died from the harsh conditions, they landed in New York Harbor. They went to Grand Central Station, put all their money on the counter and asked for two train tickets as far west as they could afford. They were let off the train about 30 miles east of Buffalo in the small farming community of Clarence Center. They worked on other people's farms for years until they saved enough money to buy their own small farm. That was where my father was born. I remember as a young boy going out to Uncle Emory's farm in Clarence Center and when we pulled into the driveway, hundreds of chickens squawked and jumped out of the way, feathers flying everywhere.

My mom, Nancy, was born and raised in Buffalo. My grandfather was from Ohio, but came to Buffalo and married my

3

grandmother. My mom told me about how they struggled during the Great Depression in the 1930's when my grandfather's income dwindled to almost nothing and they lost their home. But they recovered when it was over. My mom's family was mostly English, with some Irish. But our entire family considered ourselves Americans. Both families worked diligently, and after World War II, they prospered. It was a time when the economy was expanding, and life improved for millions of people.

My mom says I was a happy and fun-loving child, and I have many memories of being jazzed on life. Early childhood photos confirm this. I'm often seen laughing and clowning around. When I was old enough to run, I loved playing baseball, football, basketball and hockey. I liked the New York Yankees because they had Mickey Mantle, Roger Maris and Yogi Berra. I liked the Cleveland Browns because of Jim Brown, and the Montreal Canadians because of Maurice "the Rocket" Richard. In 1962, at age 14, I secretly fell in love with Kathy Young when she sang the very romantic love song, "A Thousand Stars." Well, I fell in love with the song since I didn't know her, but would have liked to. I loved going to the movies, and enjoyed the rock-and-roll music of the Beatles, the Rolling Stones, and Chuck Berry, and the ballads of the Five Satins, the Platters and the Righteous Brothers. When I was in high school I participated in many school activities, enjoyed good friends, and had several girlfriends – but not at the same time.

Both my parents taught my brothers and me the importance of hard work, taking personal responsibility for our actions, honesty, and love for our family and our country. I grew up feeling loved, cared for, and secure – well, secure most of the time. My parents counseled against racial or national discrimination and believed everyone should be treated with respect. They also said we should care about others who have less than we have. I believed all those values and still do. When I was in elementary school, my mother gave my brothers and me and other neighborhood children small cartons to collect money from neighbors to help starving children in other countries for the United Nations International Children's Emergency Fund (UNICEF). I, like many others, was moved hearing of children suffering and wanted to help. To many people, I probably appeared to be the typical, average American youth, in a family living the American Dream.

But things weren't as wonderful as they looked. A series of events, seemingly beneath the radar screen to outsiders, began to change my view of life. I probably became aware of this change sometime in high school, but since it was still in embryo form, it didn't manifest itself in my outward appearance or behavior. When I look back on this process, I believe the seeds were sown as early as six or seven years of age.

One of those seeds was dealing with a neighborhood kid with a Jeckel and Hyde personality. His name was Carlton. He was a few years older than me and considerably bigger. He could be the most charming person in the neighborhood much of the time, and then, for no apparent reason, switch into a madman. Most everyone has had to deal with oppressors and tyrants sometime in their lives, and many challenge and overcome them, or seem to handle or endure them and then move on. To some degree, I did the same thing. But as a child, I didn't understand why some people were so mean, and why society seemed either unable or uninterested in stopping their abusiveness. My interactions with Carlton went on for years and had a big impact on me.

Carlton was one of a half dozen or more kids within a few years of each other in age that lived in our neighborhood and we all played sports and other games and hung out together. We played baseball and football in the street or on a field, shot hoops at my house or at school, and played ice hockey at an artificial rink or on a neighborhood pond. Most of the time we had a lot of fun.

But every so often, usually when Carlton and I just played alone, some switch would flip inside him and the monster would appear. We played a game called kick-off return. I would throw the football to Carlton and he would run toward me and try to get by me while I tried to tackle him. Then he would throw it to me and I would try to get by him. I was fast and agile, so I could often avoid getting crunched hard. We played with no equipment. But once in a while Carlton would line me up and run me over with a hit and punch as vicious as a Mack truck squashing a squirrel on the highway. I would lie on the ground with the wind knocked out of me or writhe in pain, and he would just look at me with a blank expression. I hobbled home fighting back tears. I was seven the first time this happened. It wasn't just the physical pain that bothered me, but also the emotional humiliation of being attacked, and for no reason.

Paul Krehbiel

My parents told me not to play with Carlton anymore and I stayed clear of him for a days or weeks. I don't know if my parents talked to his parents. They might have. I wasn't sure Carlton's parents could control him, so how could my parents? I had seen Carlton's father scold him abusively and often, and with a raised hand. So maybe his dad was part of the problem. After a week or two, Carlton would come over and, as inviting as an ice cream sundae, invite me to come out and play again. The memories of the abuse were still there, but dimmed quickly at the anticipation of playing sports again. After all, I reasoned, we played together for days and even weeks without any problem, so maybe the attack was just a fluke. I went outside, we had fun for a week, and then the attacks happened again.

One summer day we went to a wooded area to play army. I was about ten and Carlton was twelve or thirteen. He explained that playing army was serious business because the real army protected our country from terrible enemies and we needed to act just like our soldiers. He said that he was the Sergeant and I was the Private. We had brought toy army guns and helmets and other gear with us, and he put on his helmet. I put on mine. He pointed to some bushes about fifty feet away and said that's where the enemy was hiding.

"Okay," he whispered urgently, "come over here and duck down behind these bushes. And keep your head low or you'll get it blown off." I ducked down and scurried to where he was.

"Now, when I give the signal, you run over to those bushes and I'll cover you." He pointed to a thick mass of leafy shrubs about twenty feet in front of us. "And keep down low," he said emphatically. He peered over the bushes and whispered: "They're reloading. Go now!"

I crouched down and ran to our new forward position.

"Rat tat tat," I heard the clicking noise from his toy machine-gun. Just as I got to the bushes, he motioned for me to come back. I couldn't figure out why, but I crouched down and ran back.

"I forgot my canteen," he announced. "Run back to my house and get it, Private!" he ordered. I didn't think that was part of the game. "Why don't you go back and get it?" I asked.

"Because you're the Private and I'm the Sergeant. The Sergeant has a higher rank than the Private. When the Sergeant gives an order, the Private has to follow it. If he doesn't, he'll be put in the brig."

6

"What's the brig?" I asked.

"Jail," he said.

I thought about it for a moment. It was true. He was the Sergeant and I was the Private, and if this was the way the real army worked, then I had to do it. I wasn't too worried about the jail threat because we didn't have anything around there that looked like a jail. I got up and headed back to his house. But I started getting a bad feeling in my stomach that something was wrong. I got his canteen and as I started slowly walking back, this feeling got worse. It was *his* canteen. He forgot it. He should have gone to get it. And this wasn't the real army. We were just playing. By the time I got back I was angry. I felt like he was taking advantage of me. I dropped the canteen and announced: "I'm not playing anymore," and turned and went home.

The gaps between our playing together lengthened, but I was a slow learner. One day he suggested that we go over to a new house still under construction in our neighborhood to check it out. It sounded like fun so I went. We played in the house for a while, going from room to room and into the basement. We had a good time.

Then I climbed onto the roof rafters. No plywood had been put down for the roof yet, so I had to balance carefully and hold on. Carlton walked to the driveway where a bed of stones lay, and started throwing them at me. Real hard. If I ducked, I would fall off the rafters. So I crouched down and hung on and got bombarded. I yelled for him to stop but he kept throwing and laughing. And he kept laughing. Finally he quit and left. I climbed down, fought back the tears again, and went home. But this time I was seething with rage. I had had enough. I decided I was going to get even with him. I was 11 years old.

I started thinking of ways to retaliate. Since he was bigger and stronger, I decided to catch him by surprise. I thought of luring him into an alley when it was dark and hitting him with a board. Or getting on a rooftop and smashing him with rocks, like he did to me. But as time went on, my anger subsided and I put these ideas on the back burner.

I never did retaliate physically. I think I was afraid that it would escalate, and he would attack me more brutally. I realized that he was crazy. If I went after him, where would it end? With one or both of us getting seriously hurt or worse? It didn't seem worth it.

Finally, I just tried to stay away from him. I made more friends at school and that helped a lot. I never forgot the abusiveness and how much I hated it, but I tried to put it behind me.

I did get in my share of fights in the neighborhood. Mostly with kids my own age. We'd argue about something, and start calling each other names or put each other down. Then the punches would fly. I didn't start them, especially with bigger kids who seemed like they could whip me. But if someone really angered me, or cornered me and threatened me, I'd come out swinging.

One kid I got into a couple of fights with was, Jay, who lived in our neighborhood. He was my age, about my size and was a friend. We played baseball and football together and hung out with each other. His father was a life-long military man, and he taught boxing and other fighting arts to the troops. Jay learned these skills from his dad and was a tough and skilled fighter. I remember his father asking me one day when I was over at their house if I wanted to box with his son. I said okay. He put boxing gloves on us and turned us loose. Since Jay was trained he got the better of me, and his father clearly enjoyed it, which seemed a little sick to me. But I did get in a couple of licks. Jay and I remained friends but we still got into a couple of fights with each other in the street without boxing gloves.

When I was 13 and in the 8th grade at Herbert Hoover Junior High School, I thought the neighborhood fighting was stupid. There must be a better way to live, I thought, and I made a conscious effort to find that life and the people who lived it. I started making friends with kids who were active in school clubs, went to school dances and had parties at their parents' houses. I was a little nervous at first, because I didn't know if I could fit in with them. But as we got to know each other better, we became friends and soon I was accepted. One attraction was that there were a lot of girls in that group. They were smart, funny and great to be with. It didn't take much to see that it was more fun being with a group of girls than with a group of guys who put each other down and beat each other up. Once I got out of the negative environment in my neighborhood, I gained self-confidence, became more outgoing, and had more fun.

When I started Kenmore West Senior High School, I thought the good times would continue. But, to my surprise, some of the friendly girls from junior high acted like they didn't even know me and many of the other guys from our old group. They were too busy trying to impress the upper classmen. I realized then just how much I hated cliques and hierarchies. I vowed then not to turn my back on my friends.

I got involved in many school activities and made new friends. I ran track and played on the soccer team. I wasn't a star in either sport, but got varsity letters. I also acted in class shows, joined a number of school clubs, went to weekend football games, school dances and parties, and had a girlfriend, Lynn, who I really liked a lot. I enjoyed all of this so much, that the academics seemed boring, difficult or unrelated to my life.

I went to class regularly, but more to socialize than to study. I tried to sit in the back so I could more easily visit with my friends. I sometimes found it hard to get engaged in what the teacher was saying, and occasionally I blurted out a whispered wisecrack because something that we were doing struck me as funny.

It was common for our teachers to give homework every night and sometimes over the weekend. I joined everyone else in writing down the assignment, but I was thinking more about watching a hockey game on TV, or going out if it was Friday night. I tried to do the homework during the week with varying degrees of success, but when Friday afternoon came, school became a distant memory. While many of my classmates were preparing for their future by studying over the weekend, I was preparing for my next beer with my friends. The legal drinking age in New York State then was 18, but we found ways to get beer or wine when we were 15 or 16. My lack of academic motivation showed in my mediocre grades. Basically, I did enough to get by.

All of this was great fun, but as I started my senior year in the fall of 1965 I realized that I didn't know what I wanted to do in life. I was 17, and I had no plans for a job or a future, and wasn't trained for anything. But I had an experience with my guidance counselor that changed this.

Every senior was scheduled to meet with a guidance counselor to help plan our future. When I entered my counselor's office he was looking at a folder on his desk. He motioned for me to take a seat and I did.

"Well, you're not college material," he stated with authority, looking up from my transcript. "You've got all these C's. Do you think any college is going to be interested in marks like these?" I was a little startled. I didn't expect to be humiliated. I thought he was supposed to help me.

9

"I guess not," I answered.

"There are only so many good jobs out there, Paul," he said firmly as he leaned forward in his chair, "and most of them require a college education. You're in competition with everyone else. Some people get left behind. Do you want to be left behind?" He paused for a moment and stared at me. I felt his glare pierce my brain. Humiliation and anger heated up my head and face. I had images of Carlton.

"Are these marks going to impress a prospective employer?" he continued.

"Probably not," I answered. Okay, so I wasn't a good student. So what. He didn't have to keep harping on it. He was disrespecting me and I didn't like it.

"My recommendation is that you join the Army." He looked at me for a moment to see my response. I said nothing. He stood up and shook my hand.

"Good luck," he said, as he directed me toward his door.

Join the Army? There was a war in Vietnam heating up. I didn't understand what it was about, and wasn't paying much attention to it. No one seemed to know much about it. But our government leaders had strong feelings about it. President Johnson said the North Vietnamese Communists had attacked South Vietnam. Our government, the mass media, our schools and even the movies told us that communism was worse than death and our country was threatened by it. The Communists had their world headquarters in Moscow, our leaders told us, which was run by madmen with nuclear weapons. I remembered nuclear war drills in elementary school when a loud siren signaled all of us to duck under our one-inch thick laminated wooden desks in the event of a nuclear attack on our school. When I got older, I realized that was ludicrous. I wasn't interested in politics, but stopping the communists sounded like something we had to do.

But my guidance counselor had gotten under my skin for a different reason. That night when I was in my room waiting for dinner, I began thinking about his comment that I wasn't college material. I also had doubts, but he said it so emphatically that it became a challenge to me.

I was also struck by the similarities between the guidance counselor and Carlton. Both tried to humiliate me. And they weren't the only people I saw disrespecting others. Sometimes, I noticed someone I thought of as a decent person and a friend being abusive to someone else. How could they do that? Maybe I didn't really know them as well as I thought. Or, I would see a friend of mine who was nice, but see his friends mistreat others.

I thought about a couple of guys I was friendly with in school who were like that. They were in fraternities at our high school and fraternity members were seen as "cool" and were often looked up to. Many fraternity guys had a quick wit and a sharp put-down. Some were smart, good athletes, flashy dressers, charismatic, attractive, or good fighters. A few were leaders in student government or in school clubs. There were four fraternities at my high school and it was an honor to be invited to join one.

But I noticed that many of the fraternity guys were arrogant. I saw them harass and bully other kids at school, often singling out the weaker kid, or the one that didn't appear to fit in. That bothered me. I was friends with some of the guys in all four fraternities at our high school, and got rushes to join all of them. But I rejected all of them. They were stunned. You didn't turn down an offer to join a fraternity.

"Why don't you want to join?" Bob asked one day in a surprised tone of voice.

"Look, I like you, Bob, and some of the other guys, but I don't like the way some of your fraternity brothers treat other kids. You know, picking on them in school, making fun of them, flipping their books, and intimidating them."

"But it's only done in fun," Bob responded.

"I don't think it's much fun for them."

"Okay. I agree. Sometimes it gets a little out of control. So don't hang around those guys. But you're friends with the other guys. Come on and join. We'll have a blast together. There's a meeting this weekend for all the new pledges at John's house. Come over. You'll see, the guys aren't so bad. Then you pledge for two months, go through hell night, and then you're in."

"I don't think so, Bob. I'm not pledging to join a fraternity." During pledging, you were assigned to a fraternity brother who ordered you to do silly things, and then they all beat you with wooden paddles on hell night. I saw it as humiliating. It brought back bad memories of Carlton.

"Why not?" Bob asked.

"Because I'm not going to subject myself to that."

"It's not that bad," he responded. "And besides, once you're in, then you can do it to someone else."

"But I don't want to do it to anyone else."

Bob had a dumbfounded look on his face. "Well, it's up to you," he mumbled.

I remained friends with Bob and some of the other guys in all the fraternities and we did have some good times together. But I never joined. I refused to be a part of any group that humiliated or mistreated others. And I started distancing myself from people who were friends of abusers. I didn't think about it at the time, but these experiences were shaping the person I was to become.

Chapter 2

Searching for a Future

After the meeting with my guidance counselor, I had dinner that evening with my family.

"So, how was everyone's day?" my dad asked as he handed me a plate of chicken. My brother, Lee, scooped up some mashed potatoes and plopped them onto his plate. He was three years younger than me, pretty smart, but even less motivated in school than me. No one answered.

"How, about you, Paul?" my dad asked. "How was your day?"

"It was okay," I said, not looking up from my meal.

"You sure? You seem quiet tonight."

"Well, I had a meeting with my guidance counselor today and it didn't go too well."

"Why's that?" he asked.

"He had my transcript and noticed that I had a lot of C's, and he said that no college would be interested in marks like that. He said I wasn't college material and that I should join the Army."

My dad was silent for a moment, probably to see if I was going to say anything else, or to think about what I said. I remained silent, so he began.

"You know your mother and I have always wanted the best for you and your brothers."

"I know, Dad, and I appreciate that."

"And you know that we think education is important. We also believe that serving our country is important." My dad had served in the Navy in the pacific during WWII, and I was proud of him.

"Yes. I believe in service to our country, too," I said.

"I know you haven't always been that interested in school, but if you wanted to go to college, we might be able to help you find one – maybe a junior college. If you did well there, you could transfer to a regular four-year university. But you'll have to work hard. You can't just skate along and think that's okay."

"Yeah, I understand."

"Could you pass the potatoes?" my youngest brother, Jim, asked.

My mom passed him the potatoes.

"Or maybe you would prefer to go into the service," my father continued. "Would you like to do that? You could do your military service and that would give you a little more time to think about your future. Maybe then you would have an idea of what you might like to study in college, or what kind of job you'd like to have."

I appreciated the way my dad handled problems. He looked at the facts, analyzed them, and came to a conclusion. He rarely got emotional or angry. When I was faced with a problem, he didn't tell me what to do, but tried to get me to follow a similar process. He wasn't a big man physically, but in my eyes he was. Perhaps most importantly, he and my mom, were always there for me.

I knew some kids in high school who said they were going to enlist in the military right after high school graduation and volunteer for Vietnam. The year before, my friend, Bill, a year older than me, said we should go in there real heavy with more troops and bombers and get it over with. I knew so little about it that his idea seemed to make sense at the time. Some time after that conversation, I saw terrible scenes of killing in Vietnam on TV, and had a feeling that that wasn't the right thing to do. But the war was far enough away from me that I didn't really think about it much. I was more focused on my immediate world: sports, parties, friends, beer and my girlfriend.

"I'm done," said Jim. "Can I be excused from the table?"

"Wait," said Lee. "What note is this?" He tapped his glass with a fork.

"A," Jim answered. "Can I go now?" He played classical piano and violin and he was still in elementary school.

"Yes," answered my mom. "And please take your dirty dishes to the sink." She said it in such a pleasant tone you didn't mind doing it.

"Another option," my dad continued," is to come to work with me after high school on a surveying crew. You might get drafted then, but you'll have to do your military service sometime." I had worked on a surveying crew for the past two summers and it was fine. I enjoyed being outside and I liked the physical labor, which included pounding stakes in the ground to layout roads, water and sewer lines, and buildings. I didn't work directly with my dad. He was inside lining up jobs and doing other work. But I felt good knowing he was there and we were working together for our family.

"I don't know," I answered. "I'm not sure what I want to do." I paused for a moment. "But I've been thinking about what the guidance counselor said to me today, that I'm not college material. That bothered me. I don't know if I am or not, but I'm going to try to prove him wrong. I'm not sure how, but I'll figure out something."

"That's good," my dad said, his face brightening up. "I'm glad to hear that. I think if you put your mind to it, you can get into college and succeed. But that means working hard. If you want any help from either your mother or I, just ask."

"Thanks, Dad. I will."

When I started high school my dad told me that colleges were looking for kids who majored in math and science. He had been good in math and science in school so I guess he hoped I would be too. This was five years after the Soviet Union had sent up the first sputnik into outer space in 1957, and the US government was frantic. Everyone said we needed more mathematicians and scientists so we could beef up our military to defend our country against the communists. I wasn't very interested in math or science, but I thought if my dad and our country thought it's important, I'll major in math and science. So I did. Algebra was okay. Geometry was interesting. I limped through trigonometry. I took general science, biology, and geology, which they called earth science. So I had majors in math and science, and that's what counted.

But my grades were so lackluster that I didn't see myself as a rocket scientist or much help to our side in the arms race. In my senior year, I signed up for chemistry. But memorizing the Periodic Table seemed too hard and boring, and I didn't know why I should learn it. So, a future as a nuclear weapons designer looked dim too. Actually, going to college as a math or science student didn't appeal to me at all.

What about some other subject, I wondered? Maybe history? I did have one brief moment of academic success in history; unfortunately, it was fleeting. In my junior year, my history teacher was Mr. Mooshie, who was highly respected and popular. We were expected to attend class every day, take notes on his lectures, ask questions and participate in class discussions, read the textbook, do homework and study for weekly tests. We were tested on one chapter each Friday. History seemed like a jumble of disconnected events, dates and the names of a few great people. It didn't make much sense to me. And what about just ordinary people? They were largely ignored. It wasn't very relevant to my life. I attended class, took a few notes, didn't read much of the textbook, faked or skipped the homework, and went through the motions of studying. I was often staring out the window daydreaming, or sleeping.

"Okay class. Here are the results of your first tests," Mr. Mooshie announced one Monday morning early in the semester. "Many of you did well, some did okay and others failed," he said as he handed back our tests. When I received mine, I lifted the front cover and spotted a red F.

"For those of you who got an F, and there were a number of you, you will have to write a five page summary of the next chapter and hand it in before taking next week's chapter test." I felt like groaning out loud, but that would have given me away.

So the night before the next test, I opened the book, read the chapter, and took some notes. I had to actually figure out what the author was saying, no matter how hard or boring it was, so I could write my summary. To my amazement, when I was writing, I understood something about what was in the chapter. I started to see connections between events. I went into class Friday and turned in my paper. Mr. Mooshie handed out the tests and we began. I was pleasantly surprised. I knew some of the answers. Actually, I knew a lot of them.

On Monday, Mr. Mooshie started handing back our tests and gave the same speech about some doing well and others failing, and when he came to me he had a funny little smile on his face. I couldn't figure out why. He seemed like such a nice man. I opened the front cover ever so slowly and peeked apprehensively inside. There was a big red A. I was stunned. I couldn't believe it. I looked up and Mr. Mooshie had a twinkle in his eye, as if to say, 'see, I knew you could do it.'

For me, the best part was that I didn't have to write a summary of the next chapter, so I went back to my old study habits. That Friday, the chapter test seemed harder. But, what the hell, I thought. At least I got through it.

The following Monday, Mr. Mooshie started handing back our tests, and when he got to me he had a slight frown on his face. I didn't know why. I flipped open the front cover and there was a big fat, red F staring at me. I quickly closed the cover and looked around to see if anyone had noticed. Getting an F was not a good feeling.

I got a couple more A's and F's and then one day Mr. Mooshie requested that I stay after class.

After everyone had left, he began.

"What are you doing?" he asked exasperated. "You are alternating between A's and F's every other week. How can you do that?"

"Well, on the week that I have to write the summary of the chapter, I do better on the test," I responded.

"Yes! I know that!" he exclaimed. "Why don't you do that every week?"

"It seems like so much work," I responded lamely. "I figured why should I write the summary if I don't have to?"

"Because it will make the difference between getting an A or an F!" he said astonished. "I've never had a student do this before. You obviously have the ability to be a very good student." I thought that was nice of him to say it, but I didn't believe him.

"Don't you care?" he continued.

"Well. Kind of," I mumbled.

"Well, you should care. Don't you want to go to college and make something of your life?"

"I guess so," I stammered.

He looked at me in stunned silence.

"I'm not going to make you write the summary for every chapter," he said, looking drained. "You have to learn to take personal responsibility for your work. Can you do that? Will you please try to do that?" he pleaded.

"Yes. I'll try," I assured him.

I intended to study more but something always came up to distract me. So, I fluctuated between A's and F's all semester for my C average. I think some of the other students sitting around me knew of my ups and downs in history. The girl who sat next to me was a straight A student, and she wrote in my Yearbook: "To the sleeping mental giant of history..." I guess she saw my chapter test grades.

Why all this competition over grades, I wondered? So somebody could get ahead of someone else? I wasn't interested in "getting ahead" at someone else's expense. Not much danger of that with my record. I did feel, after all, that most of the students were smarter than me. Maybe I could have "gotten ahead" if I wrote summaries of every chapter assigned to us. But why? I felt that it was a little sick to compete with each other.

I look back now and see that it was training us for life in our very competitive society, so we would battle each other over who could get a job or not, who would get the "better" job or a promotion, make the most money, buy the biggest house, own the most expensive car and so on. I felt alienated from this. Competition can help bring out the best in people when one competes to do a great job. When competition is pushed to an extreme, it brings out the worst in people – manipulation, back-stabbing, and degrading others. When this kind of competition is combined with greed, it's deadly.

There was little or no talk about the value of cooperation and working for the common good. That would be more humane, more effective, and more enjoyable, I thought. Very little in school seemed connected to my life or my interests. I didn't want to flunk and have to repeat a grade so I did enough to pass. I knew that everyone had to be productive in society by working, and that was fine with me. I'd get out of school and get a job.

But now I was beginning my senior year. After that challenge thrown down by my guidance counselor, and the ongoing humiliation of my mediocrity and failure, I decided that I had to find something to get serious about. I decided to choose something that I liked, rather than something to please someone else.

I loved sports. Could I get into college through some sports connection? With sports, competition seemed okay, and I was very competitive. When I was younger, I had played Little League baseball and had fantasies of being a pitcher, but was a better second baseman. I also played sandlot football, and since I was not one of the bigger boys, I got pounded pretty good, but I still loved the game. Even though I ran track and played soccer in high school and got varsity letters, I wasn't going to get into college playing any of those sports

Now, hockey – that was a different story. I loved hockey and it was the sport that I was the best at by far. As a boy and teenager I had dreams of making it into the National Hockey League. I loved the speed of the game and improvising plays on the fly – it was like semi-controlled chaos. I usually played center or left wing, was one of the fastest skaters on the ice, and usually one of the top scorers. There was no greater thrill than cutting in front of an opposing team's goalie and deflecting a teammate's shot into the upper corner of the net! We didn't have a varsity hockey team at high school yet, so I played in the town league. I was often on the first place team, and I made the All-Star Team a number of years.

Our All-Star Team traveled to other cities and towns in New York State to play other All-Stars, and it was then that I saw that there were a lot of very good hockey players. Somewhere in my teen years, and after several of these All-Star tours, I realized that it would be tougher than I thought making it into the NHL. Now, in my senior year in high school, if I couldn't make it as a player, how about preparing for a job as a coach, announcer or sports writer, or working in another sports-related job? No. I wasn't interested and didn't give it a second thought.

Since none of this was leading to college, maybe college wasn't in my future. I tried telling myself that there was a difference between not being college material, and deciding not to go. Maybe I would *decide* I didn't want to go to college.

That wasn't so bad. The Buffalo area was a good place to live and work, even without any college. Most people in Buffalo didn't go to college and they seemed to be doing fine. Maybe they had a skill that they parlayed into a job. Did I have such a skill? No. But there was one long shot. I believed I had a knack for making up names for things. That didn't require a college degree. That was a time when McDonald's hamburger stands were opening all over the country and people were standing in long lines for that 15 cent burger. There was a little known contender in Buffalo, called Henry's. Being the underdog, I thought up a new name for their burger, a Hankburger. I'd say to my friends or my brothers: "Hey, let's go out for a Hankburger." The name caught on in our small group. But when I suggested the new name to an employee at the Henry's stand one day he just looked at me with a blank face. Then, Henry's went out of business. So much for that idea.

Maybe I needed to think more about a traditional job. Since I was basically unskilled, how about an unskilled job in one of the many hundreds of Buffalo-area factories or warehouses that dominated our economy. Didn't need college for that. The manufacturing process was kind of fascinating to me. When I was in junior high school our teacher took our class to the big General Motors assembly plant in Tonawanda so we could watch the workers make engines for cars. The school probably thought they should show us early in our young lives what the future had in store for many of us. The work looked hard and dirty, but watching the men make a car engine was interesting.

Also, when I was in high school, I liked the blue-collar guys I worked with on the surveying crew during the summers because they were so down-to-earth. In fact, most of Buffalo was that way. Not too many snobs in a place where so many people made a living pouring steel ingots, or stamping out doors for cars – like they did at the big Ford stamping plant on Buffalo's southern border. With so many unskilled or semi-skilled jobs around, I figured I could find something. And there was always the surveying crew. I never thought about leaving Buffalo. I loved it. It was my home.

Some people complained about the winters, but I liked all the seasons. In the summer it got warm and we went to the beach and I earned money mowing lawns. I loved the fall when it cooled down at night and the leaves turned brilliant shades of red, orange and yellow. In the winter we had tons of snow and got at least three or four days off from school because of it. Then I'd go out and earn money shoveling people's driveways all day. I loved working outside. Maybe there was a career there. Being a snow-plow driver.

We also had the greatest sunsets – ten shades of orange, purple and blue. That was from all the pollution that poured into the sky from the giant steel mills, chemical companies and other factories. Some areas of town were just block after block and acre after acre of factories. Visitors coming to Buffalo from many miles away said they could see a huge orange and brown haze dome on the horizon before they ever saw the tall downtown buildings.

The sounds were comforting too. As you approached the city from the south, you heard the clanging, hissing and banging of Bethlehem Steel, 24 hours a day, seven days a week. The sprawling steel mill towered above anything else in south Buffalo or near-by Lackawanna. You knew Buffalo was pulling its weight. When I was growing up, it seemed like everyone was working. One drawback was the thin layer of fine rust-colored steel dust that covered everything, but, the thought then was, hey, people are employed.

And jobs were plentiful. With over 20,000 people working at Bethlehem Steel, hiring was going on regularly. And these were good paying union jobs, with paid vacations and health insurance and retirement benefits. A worker in a large, unionized mill or factory could make enough money to support himself, his wife and children on his pay alone. And he could own his own house. With so many factories around almost anyone could find a job if they wanted one, even people who didn't have any skills at all. At the beginning of my senior year in high school it seemed like I was headed for some type of blue-collar career.

A couple of weeks after the meeting with my guidance counselor, something happened to change that. One Saturday morning at the breakfast table my mom was reading the newspaper while I was finishing a bowl of cereal.

"There's an exhibition at the Albright-Knox," she said, as she looked up from the paper. That was the major art gallery in town. "It's featuring European art, including many of the Impressionists. Are you interested in going?" I had gone for years to the Albright-Knox and loved it. Both my mom and dad liked art, and they took both my brothers and me.

"Sure, that sounds good," I responded. Impressionism was my favorite genre. I had enjoyed art as a young boy and was taking an art class in school that semester that I was enjoying very much. We got in the car and drove to the gallery.

We looked at the works in the exhibit as well as throughout the gallery. We saw paintings by Van Gogh, Monet, Toulouse-Lautrec, Degas, Pissarro, Renoir, Gauguin and others. I loved them all. There was such humanity, such depth of feeling in their work. Van Gogh was my favorite. I stood in front of one of his paintings, titled *The Old Mill*.

"Look at those bold brush strokes," I commented to my mom. "The earth colors are so alive. It's like the mill has just grown out of the ground. And the blues and greens and splashes of red are so pure – he uses the colors straight out of the tube." I had heard my art teacher say that.

"Yes. It's a wonderful painting," she added.

"And Monet. When you get up close it looks like a smearing of paints," I said. "Then step back here and everything falls into place. And look at the light through the fog – it shimmers."

"I like his water lilies the best," she said. "They're so peaceful."

We viewed watercolors, weavings and sculptures. We looked at etchings and drawings. I studied the shapes, color combinations, shading, brushwork and pen lines, and then moved back to take in the entire composition. We looked at realism, expressionism and abstract art. I loved landscapes and the renderings of people. I was moved by the expressions on their faces, especially their eyes, which were a window into their emotions. I was studying one work intently for several minutes when all of a sudden it dawned on me: "I can do that," I said to my mom. "I believe I can do that. Not as great as these works maybe. But I can do this." I now felt like I had a calling.

When I returned to school on Monday, I went down to the office.

"I want to drop my chemistry class and take another art class," I told the woman behind the counter.

"Are you sure? If you're planning to go to college, chemistry will be much better to have on your transcript than art."

"I am planning on going to college," I told her. "And I believe having another art course on my transcript will be just fine."

"Well, I'll have to ask your guidance counselor to see if this can be approved." She walked to his office and knocked on the door. There was no answer.

Just then he walked in and saw me.

"Mr. Krehbiel, correct?" he asked.

"Yes. That's correct."

"We just talked the other day didn't we?"

"Yes, we did."

"Ah. You're down here to find out about signing up for the Army, right?"

"Not today. Today I'm down here to drop my chemistry class and sign up for another art class."

"Well, I'm not sure we can do that. The semester has already started. You'll be behind."

"I'll catch up. I know what they're doing. I have art first period, and the class I want to add is second period in the same room. I know what they're working on so I can catch up easily."

He called Mr. Fenn, the art teacher for both classes, and Mr. Fenn said okay. I filled out a form to drop my chemistry class and add the second art class. I was ecstatic. I was going to be an art student.

I was doing well in Mr. Fenn's first period class and now with this second art class, I was getting serious. I worked hard, but it wasn't like work at all. I did some interesting things, and Mr. Fenn was pleased. I started developing a pen and ink crosshatching style that had been influenced by the Impressionists.

I designed a record album cover of the famous trumpet player, Louis Armstrong, using this crosshatching technique and won an award for it. It was displayed in one of the art showcases at school. I further refined this style, and did many pen and ink drawings, mostly of people's faces, but also of landscapes and still-lifes.

Students in all the art classes in the school were assigned to design a poster for the upcoming school play. It was "The Diary of Anne Frank," about the inspiring young Jewish girl and her family who were hidden by friends from the Nazis. My poster was chosen to open the play. I wrote her name in white paint on a background that looked like a brick wall, like kids do in their neighborhoods. It was projected onto the stage's backdrop using an overhead projector.

I was also chosen by Mr. Fenn to attend special art classes for "promising" high school art students at the Albright-Knox Art Gallery. It was a good feeling to finally do something well.

I had study hall third period, so I asked Mr. Fenn if I could stay in his class and continue to work on my projects. He said I could. So I had three solid hours of art every morning. I was in heaven.

A new world had opened up for me. I got A's on my art assignments so my plan was to go to college as an art major, and then become an artist. I knew it wouldn't be easy to make a living as an artist. I might have to work in a factory or on the surveying crew while I pursued my art. But I had found a future.

Chapter 3

The Corroding Society

While I was serious about art, not all of my art was serious. In one class we were assigned to make "found art." That meant finding a common, every-day object and turning it into an art piece. One kid brought in popsicle sticks and glued them together in some sort of design. Another kid brought in a door handle and painted it. I asked my teacher if a classmate, George, and I could work together on our project, and he said okay.

George Cownie was one of my best friends. He lived on the next block from me so we also hung around together outside of school. He was smart in practically every subject, and unlike me, didn't have to work hard to get high grades. His mind was like a sponge – it just absorbed information. Which was a good thing, because he didn't seem much interested in school either. He was a little taller than me, had an easy going personality and we both looked forward to having a few beers on the weekends. His hair was brown, except for a clump on top that flopped across his forehead and got bleached light yellow from the summer sun.

George and I had our tall, wooden art desks pushed together facing each other so we had a large working space. We were on the opposite side of the room from Mr. Fenn's desk, right near the door. Mr. Fenn was a pretty easy-going teacher, so this was a great set-up for George and I to visit with each other. Mr. Fenn was tall and lanky, with a round protruding chin, and his face occasionally broke into a weird crooked smile for no apparent reason.

We had no idea what to do about this found art project. We watched the other kids work, and after a few days many were well into their projects. We discussed two ideas briefly, neither of which were very interesting, and spent most of our time discussing our plans for upcoming parties and other social events. Honestly, this assignment seemed like a joke. By the end of the first week, and with absolutely nothing happening on our desks, Mr. Fenn came over to our side of the room.

"What are you guys doin'?" he asked.

"We're discussing our found art project, Mr. Fenn," George replied. Mr. Fenn had been watching us for a week, and the frown on his face had gotten longer by the day.

"Paul, I don't understand. You've done so well in my class from the beginning. And now this. What's going on?"

"Well, we're just having a hard time narrowing down the field of objects that we're considering using," I responded.

"Well, you better pick something pretty fast or you're going to get a poor mark on this project. You guys have been sitting here talking for a week and you haven't done anything," he said with anger rising in his voice. "If you boys don't have your found object in on Monday, you'll lose one letter grade. And if your final project is late, you'll lose another letter grade for each day it's late. Do you understand?"

"Yes, Mr. Fenn," we said in unison. He turned and walked away.

So, we decided we had to do it. Finally, we came up with what we thought was the appropriate object for this project: a garbage can. And we knew where we could get an old one for free. So, on Monday, we walked to school carrying a metal garbage can and a gym bag filled with saws and hammers. We got a few strange looks, but no one said anything.

The garbage can was rusted, bent and bashed. We got to art class and put it on top of our desks. The bell rang and Mr. Fenn stood up. He turned toward us and a look of bewilderment creased his face. He headed in our direction.

"What's that garbage can doing in here?" he asked.

"That's our found art piece," George answered.

He stared for a moment, but said nothing. He turned and walked back to his desk, and everyone went back to work.

We had no idea what we were going to do with this garbage can. George pulled the gym bag out from under his desk and handed me a hammer. He picked up another one and we both started smashing the metal cylinder. Loud crashing noises pierced the air, reverberating off the windows and down the hall.

"What are you doing," Mr. Fenn yelled as he hurried toward us, waving his arms in the air.

Just then, the door burst open.

"Is everyone okay" a woman's voice screeched. It was Mrs. Roberts, the health teacher. "What was that terrible noise? I heard it all the way down the hall in my classroom," she said breathlessly, her panic-stricken eyes darting around the room.

"It's okay, Mrs. Roberts," Mr. Fenn said, as he took her by the shoulders. "Calm down. It was just a couple of my art students working on a project."

"Well, they can't do that in here," she exclaimed indignantly. "They're disturbing the whole school. I can't teach with that racket," she said in a tone that implied that Mr. Fenn was condoning such a practice.

"Yes, I know," responded Mr. Fenn, in a soothing voice. "I know. It won't happen again."

Mrs. Roberts looked around the room, saw us holding our hammers and glared at us. She was beet red. She whirled around and left the room.

"That's it. Down to the office with the both of you," Mr. Fenn sputtered. "And I'm calling Mr. Stark to let him know you're on your way." He scribbled a note to the vice principal in charge of discipline, and gave it to me as we packed up our stuff.

"What should we do with our garbage can?" I asked.

"Leave it there!"

I knew Mr. Stark. Not that well, but a little. I hadn't really gotten in too much trouble in school, but I had been down to Mr. Stark's office maybe once or twice before. In a school of 2,500 students, I was sure he wouldn't remember me.

"Well, what happened this time, Paul?" Mr. Stark asked as we entered his office.

"We were working on our art project and apparently we were a little too loud."

"You were smashing a garbage can with hammers," he said, his voice rising. He looked at us over his glasses. He was a tall, thin guy, with protruding cheekbones and pointy chin. His eyebrows arched up on his forehead making him look like the devil.

"What are you doing with a garbage can in art class?" he demanded.

We explained our found art assignment.

"But why did you pick a garbage can? Couldn't you find something else?" he asked.

"Not for what we're planning," I responded. "The plans we've developed for our art project can only be done with a garbage can."

His face scrunched up as he fiddled with a pencil on his desk. He looked out the window as if he was thinking about what I had said. He appeared to be calming down.

"Certainly there must be some place where we can work on this project," I continued, "where we won't bother anyone."

"Well, let me call Mr. Hennessey down in the metal shop. Maybe you can work down there."

He telephoned Mr. Hennessey and he said okay.

We went back to Mr. Fenn's class and got our garbage can and tools and went to the metal shop.

As we entered we saw a bunch of guys doing professional-looking metal work. One guy near the door was burnishing a nicely rounded copper bowl. I remembered making a wrought iron wall lamp when I took metal shop. The lamp was on my bedroom wall.

"Hi, Mr. Hennessey," I said as he approached us.

"So, you're the guys doing metal work for an art class?" he asked. He then looked down. "What are you doing with that garbage can?"

We explained that it was for our art class assignment.

Furrows crisscrossed his forehead and he squinted his eyes. Then he shook his head and mumbled something under his breath that sounded like "fucking idiots."

"Yeah, it seems weird to us too, but we have to do it," I added.

"Okay. Follow me."

We followed him to a metal bench. "You can work here. Do you need any tools?"

"No. We're all set. We have our own," I answered. He walked away still shaking his head.

We put our garbage can on our workbench, took out our hammers and started hitting it. The crashing noise broke the near silence. Everyone looked up startled and stared at us.

"Whoa! What the hell do you guys think you're doing?" Mr. Hennessey yelled as he rushed up the isle toward us. "You can't do that in here. Are you nuts?! Get out! I'm calling Stark right now."

When we got back to Mr. Stark's office, he was pissed off.

"You've pushed your luck too far this time, Paul," Mr. Stark shot out. "You're getting detention."

"Wait a minute, Mr. Stark," I pleaded. "What did we do? We got an assignment from our teacher, and we're trying to do it. We have a great plan for this garbage can. Isn't there some place we could go to work on it where we won't bother anyone."

"And we'll show you the final project when it's done," George promised.

Mr. Stark looked at us. The muscles in his face relaxed a little and a slight smile came to his lips.

"All right. I think I know of a place where you can work on that. When it's finished, I want to see it."

"Okay, where do we go," I asked.

"You can go to the old coal bin of the school, in the basement. We don't use coal anymore to heat the school, so the area is empty. I'll take you there. Come on."

Mr. Stark led us to a door with a sign on it which read: "Danger: Do Not Enter." He opened the door and we followed him inside. It was dark, dingy and dirty. We walked down a long flight of metal steps. There were dim lights off in the distance. It looked hazy – almost spooky down there. We saw a couple of workmen off in the distance tending to loudly hissing kettles with foggy smoke hovering over them.

"Here you go, boys," Mr. Stark said. "You can work here."

"Ah, Mr. Stark," I raised my voice above the noise. "I have Mr. Fenn's art class second period, and I have a study hall third period. I often use that study hall to work on my art assignments. Could I come down here third period as well to work on this project?"

"If it's okay with Mr. Fenn its okay with me," Mr. Stark replied. "But remember, I want to see your final project." He turned and walked off into the dark haze. Imagine two 17 year old boys, in school but not in class, in the basement with hammers and a metal garbage can. And no supervision.

"What are we going to do with this thing?" George asked.

"Well, we could begin by kicking the shit out of it," I said as I picked it up and threw it against a metal pole."

"Here, let me try it," George exclaimed. He grabbed the can and smashed it against the concrete wall. Then we got out the hammers and started bashing it. We were having a great time! We got in a few more hits before we had to get to our next class.

The next day we told Mr. Fenn that Mr. Stark had assigned us a spot in the basement of the school to work on our project. He said he already knew. So every day at second period, we went down to the coal bin and smashed the garbage can, whopping and hollering each time we hit it. One day, the workmen came a little closer to see what we were doing. They watched for a few minutes and then disappeared. We never saw them again. We heard that they thought we were on drugs.

Soon the word had gotten around school that George and I were in the coal bin working on a special art project. Friends asked if they could see it. Some had study hall second or third period so they got permission to come with us. Our friend, Howard, came down one day.

Howard Kling was about George's height, but skinnier. He was also a good student and had a great sense of humor. He and I and two other friends from the Art Club did a skit for a class show, the old melodrama with Nell and her hero boyfriend, Dudley Doowright. Howard played a pathetic-looking Doowright and got his ass kicked by the much bigger villain, while Nell was saved by our skit narrator who was impersonating the TV host, Ed Sullivan.

As we entered our work area we showed Howard the bashed up garbage can.

"What are you doing with that?" he asked perplexed.

George picked up the garbage can, held it over his head, and said, "I'll show you." He ran about fifteen feet toward the wall and hurled the can at it with a bloodcurdling yell.

A big smile spread across Howard's face. "Can I try it?"

"Sure," said George.

After Howard threw the can against the wall a couple of times, I spoke up.

"That's not all. Want to see something else?"

"Yeah," said Howard.

George picked up the garbage can, and I picked up a hammer. He threw the can in the air in a soft arc toward me and I swung the hammer with all my might. I punched a hole in the side of the can.

"Wow! Let me try it," Howard squealed.

So for the next week we brought a parade of friends down to the coal bin to take some hits on the garbage can. Some could only come down between classes, so they only got one or two hits, and then had to rush off to their next class, sweating and dirty, but exhilarated.

With only several days to go before our project was due, we were in the coal bin with a smashed up garbage can and a few scraps of twisted metal lying around on the ground.

"We've got to do something with this," George announced. "We've got nothing."

It was true. We had nothing. And we still had no plan.

We canceled all the tours of the coal bin, and there were a lot of whispers and smirks among our friends about how we were going to get clobbered by Mr. Fenn, and especially Mr. Stark.

"Maybe we could cut it up with the saws," I suggested.

So we started sawing. We sawed long strips. We brought in heavy workers gloves and grabbed the strips and twisted them. And bent them, and shaped them, and started wiring the strips together. We knew about form and design and soon some interesting things started to happen. We were creating an abstract metal sculpture, where every angle created a different three-dimensional design, yet each part was unified within the entire piece.

The surface was also shaping up. This was an old grey galvanized metal garbage can. Where we had hit the surface with hammers, the galvanizing had chipped off, revealing shiny, silver metal that glistened. Also, the surface was textured from the repeated blows; it was wrinkled and crushed. We put some glossy black enamel paint in a jar and splattered the paint over the metal. The shiny black contrasted nicely with the dull gray and shiny silver.

The base of the garbage can was more or less intact in a circle, and the rest of the metal flowed upward in spirals of twisted metal, which crisscrossed each other and connected to other spirals. It was generally circular in shape and stood about three feet high. The entire sculpture looked enclosed, but there were a lot of negative spaces, which created interesting shapes and forms. Then we mounted it on a mahogany-stained platform. We finished it the day before it was due. It looked pretty good. In fact, it looked real good. We initially called it *The Zero*. But we decided we wanted something with more meaning, so we renamed it *The Corroding Society*.

I'm not sure how we came up with that name. We were becoming more aware of the problems in society – the poverty, racism, the growing gap between rich and poor, and the war in Vietnam. And we saw the hypocrisy. Our society said we were for freedom, peace, democracy, equality and tolerance, yet we saw examples of the opposite. While we lived in an all-white neighborhood with no noticeable poverty, I saw new buildings go up in wealthy neighborhoods, while poorer areas, especially in the black community, deteriorated badly. The war in Vietnam was escalating, and this was after US government leaders said they were winning and peace was at hand.

I remember asking my mom and dad a number of times over the years why these problems existed. They said they didn't know, or gave an answer that seemed unsatisfactory. I apparently asked these questions so often that they finally sent me to a psychiatrist. He listened patiently, said he didn't know either, and then concluded our session by saying: "I wish more people thought like you." That was a nice compliment, but it wasn't much help, so I never went back. I didn't have any bad feelings about my parents for sending me to a psychiatrist, even though back then there was something of a stigma attached to such a visit. They were just doing what they thought was right.

On the day our sculpture was due, George and I got to school early. We went to the cafeteria and moved a lunch table into the main corridor, right across from the front door. Stark's office was down the hall. We put *The Corroding Society* on it as kids started coming into school. Some gathered around the table to look. Howard and the other guys who helped us smash it up were impressed with our final project. Howard hung out with us at the table.

Mr. Stark came in, looked at it, looked at us, and then nodded. A slight smile came across his face.

"Okay boys, you know the cafeteria table doesn't belong in the hall," Mr. Stark said. "Take your sculpture down and put the table back in the cafeteria."

We put the table back and took *The Corroding Society* up to Mr. Fenn's room. He was straightening up some papers on his desk and looked up as we entered the room.

"Here's our found art piece, Mr. Fenn," I announced. "It's called *The Corroding Society*." Mr. Fenn got up from his desk and walked toward us.

"Put it on this table," he motioned. He then walked slowly around it, bending down occasionally, and stopping to look more closely. After a couple of moments, he straightened up and looked at us. That crooked smile crept across his face.

"It's good. It's very good," he said. "Okay. Go to your homeroom now and I'll see you second period."

When second period came, a small group of students came into the class and stood around our sculpture looking at it. The bell rang and everyone took their seats.

"Good morning class," Mr. Fenn said. "Today, as you know, your found art pieces are due. As you can see, we have many of them at the front of the class. I would like each person to tell the class something about your piece: how you selected your object, what you were trying to accomplish with it, and how you did it."

One by one, each student got up and talked about their found art object. When our turn came, George and I got up and went to the front of the class and stood by our sculpture. It towered over the other pieces.

"This is *The Corroding Society*," I began. "It was made from a garbage can. It reflects society in the process of decay." This stuff was just rolling off my lips as I went. I found I wasn't so nervous speaking in front of the class if I was speaking about something that I knew about and had feelings for. "There are still healthy parts, represented by the shiny silver, but also darker, unhealthy spots, represented by the rust, dull gray and black, and the crumpled metal, and dead spots represented by the open spaces. We see much material wealth all around us in society, and it looks shiny and bright. But under the surface, there is injustice, suffering, poverty, and war, and it threatens the whole society."

I rarely talked about these things, but they obviously had an impact on me. It began in 1963 when President Kennedy was assassinated. I was shocked then, along with the rest of the nation. The following year, 1964, and through 1968, riots took place in black communities across the country, including in Buffalo in 1967, in frustration over poverty, racism, unemployment and police brutality. The revolts were suppressed and hundreds of blacks were killed across the nation. That was shocking. I didn't know much about the life of blacks in the inner cities, but based on the dilapidated buildings I saw there, I was sympathetic to the people's plight.

George went on to explain how we made the sculpture. He said that the smashing of the hammers on the metal represented the smashing of people's lives and dreams.

Mr. Fenn loved it and gave us an A.

We were pretty taken with it ourselves, and for the next couple of weeks we paraded *The Corroding Society* around school and into

History and English classes and gave short two-minute talks about the significance of it.

In fact, we thought it was so good that it should be displayed at the Albright-Knox Art Gallery. But how would we get it in? It was unlikely that they would accept it. So we made a plan.

Chapter 4

The Albright-Knox

One Saturday, George and I got up early and dressed up in ties and coats. I borrowed my mom's car, and we drove *The Corroding Society* to the Albright-Knox Art Gallery. We figured if we walked in and acted like we knew what we were doing, maybe we could get our sculpture into the gallery and put it on display.

We pulled into a gallery parking space, picked up our sculpture and headed for the basement door. I knew it would be unlocked because I regularly went in that door to attend special Saturday morning art classes for "promising" Buffalo area high school art students. I also knew that once in the basement, we could go up into the main gallery without going through security. George and I entered the building without any problem. We walked through the basement halls, past rooms where art works of great masters and pedestals were stored, up a flight of stairs and into the gallery. No one saw us. We were surprised that we had gotten that far and hadn't thought about how to display it. So we put it on a bench.

It looked pretty good there, near paintings and sculptures by famous artists. But we thought it would look much better on a white pedestal, like the other sculptures. We went back to the basement and rummaged around in a storage room until we found a big white pedestal that we liked. We carried it upstairs, placed it about five feet in front of a wall with a Picasso painting behind it, and in a row with other sculptures. Then we placed *The Corroding Society* on the pedestal. It looked great!

People were starting to come into the gallery now, and some were headed toward us, stopping to view the paintings and sculptures as they went. When the first couple reached The Corroding Society, they stopped to look at it. We walked over and looked too.

"That's a pretty interesting sculpture," I remarked to the middle aged and stylish woman.

"Yes, it is," she replied.

"But who are the artists?" her husband asked, as he leaned forward to read the nametag. "Krehbiel and Cownie. I've never heard of them."

"Yeah, we don't know either," remarked George, "but it's good, isn't it?"

"Yes, it's very interesting," said the woman.

We couldn't believe it. No security guard had seen us yet, and the public was viewing our sculpture in the Albright-Knox Art Gallery!

"We've got to get a picture of this," I whispered to George.

He agreed. But we didn't have a camera with us so we decided to race home and get one. When we returned, *The Corroding Society* was gone. We went to one of the security guards.

"Excuse me, sir," George began. "We were here a littler earlier this morning, and we saw a very interesting sculpture along this wall called *The Corroding Society*. We don't see it now."

"So you're the guys who brought that in here!" the guard seethed. "Mrs. Smith is furious over this."

"Who is Mrs. Smith?" I asked.

"She's the director of the gallery," he almost shouted.

"Well, where is our sculpture now?" I asked. "If you're not going to show it, we'd like it back."

"You'll be lucky not to go to jail," the guard snapped at us. "Mrs. Smith is calling the police right now. Come with me." He took us through some inner hallways until we got to an office. An older woman was sitting behind a desk, a phone to her ear. Her hair was pulled back in a tight bun, and thick make-up partially filled in the deep wrinkles in her skin. Her teeth were clenched so tight I could see the muscles in her jaw.

"These are the boys who brought that sculpture in, Mrs. Smith," the guard announced.

Her eyes blazed through a horrific scowl on her face. She hung up the phone and glared at us.

"How did you get into the gallery?" she demanded.

"We came in through the basement door," I said.

"How did you know you could get in that way?"

"Because I've come in that door to take Saturday art classes," I answered.

"What? You're one of the students taking those classes."

"Yes," I said.

"I've never been so embarrassed in my life," she exclaimed. She was speechless and her eyes bugged out of her head.

"So, I guess that means you don't want to display it?" I asked.

"Display it?" she said in a loud angry voice. "I was calling the police."

"Well, I think it's better that we brought something in, rather than take something out," George said, trying to lighten her up.

She jerked her head toward him with a look of horror on her face.

"Look, we made the sculpture for an art class in school," I explained. "We're students at Kenmore West High School. Mr. Fenn is our teacher."

She looked at us for a moment and her face softened a bit. "You're Mr. Fenn's students?" she asked, seeming somewhat relieved. "What are your names?"

We told her, and she called Mr. Fenn. He confirmed that we were his students.

"We're sorry if we offended you, Mrs. Smith," George began, "but if you're not going to display it, we'd like it back."

She looked at George for a moment. "Yes. I'll give it back. But don't you ever try to pull a stunt like that again. Do you understand?"

"Yes, ma'am," we said. She instructed the guard to take us to the storage room where *The Corroding Society* was sitting among the paintings and sculptures of Rembrandt, Leonardo da Vinci and Michelangelo. We retrieved our sculpture and left.

But we were undaunted. We still believed our sculpture deserved a wider showing. So, we entered it in the Allentown Art Festival, an outdoor weekend art show held every June in the Allentown section of Buffalo. This is the largest art show in the area, attended by over a hundred thousand people each year. We included some of our other pieces of work, but *The Corroding Society* was our centerpiece.

Within the first two hours on Saturday morning we had an offer to buy it from a couple in their mid-thirties. We had never intended to sell it and told them so. But the same couple came back and asked again. We thanked them for their interest, but told them no again. A photographer from the *Buffalo Courier Express*, the daily morning newspaper, came by and took a picture of *The Corroding Society*. It appeared at the top of the picture page in Sunday morning's edition with me next to it.

On Sunday, the same couple came back again and restated their desire to buy it. We told them we would discuss it and to come back in the afternoon. They did.

"What have you decided," the man asked. "My wife and I have seen everything at the festival, and this is what we want to buy. That's why we keep coming back. We love this sculpture."

"Well, we've talked it over," I said. "You know, we told you we had no intention of selling it. We love it too, and we don't want to part with it. But we've decided to sell it to you on one condition."

"What's that?" the man asked.

"We'll sell it to you if we can come over to your house whenever we want to look at it," I answered.

The man looked at his wife with anticipation, and she nodded. "You've got a deal. How much do you want for it?"

"Well, how about $35," I responded. That seemed a reasonable price back in 1966 for a couple of high school kids selling a garbage can.

The man reached into his wallet and gave us $35. We exchanged names and telephone numbers and got his address. His name was John and he lived in Tonawanda, not far from us.

A couple of weeks later, George and I decided we wanted to see *The Corroding Society*, so we called him up. John invited us over. When we got there, we saw our sculpture displayed on a high narrow table in his living room in front of his picture window.

"This has been a real hit with our friends," John said, with a big smile. "We had a party last Friday, and it was the major topic of conversation. We can't thank you enough for selling it to us."

Over the next several years, George and I would call John and his wife to go over to see *The Corroding Society*. And, occasionally, he'd call us to explain that one of the pieces of metal had come loose and he didn't know where it was supposed to go. So we'd go over with a pair of pliers and look hard at the twisted metal. We had no idea where the loose piece went. But after careful inspection, we'd announce with great confidence: "Of course. It goes right here." Then we'd wrap the loose metal end around whatever part was nearby, and give it a twist with the pliers to hold it in place.

"It's amazing how you guys still remember where those parts go," John said one time, thanking us profusely.

"Yeah. When you get into it as deeply as we have, it's hard to forget," I said.

I learned some important lessons. I learned more about art and creativity, and that it was possible to make something out of almost anything. I also learned to think big and to act boldly, even if obstacles got in my way. And I learned that while you are accomplishing something, if you do it right, you can have fun at the same time.

Chapter 5

Donna

After graduating from high school, I went to work again on the surveying crew. I was to do this for about two months, and then start college in the fall at St. Petersburg Junior College in Clearwater, Florida as an art major. I made this choice because St. Petersburg would take me, and I thought living and going to school at the beach would be fun.

When I first started working on a surveying crew, I was assigned to be the third man on a three-man team. That was two summers earlier. I knew nothing about surveying then, but was told that I would be carrying equipment and supplies, pounding stakes in the ground, and making simple measurements. I guessed that I could handle that and I did. It was interesting work, I liked the physical part of the job and being outdoors, and I started to learn something about surveying.

As the third man on the crew, I sat in the back seat of the van. That was fine except there were no windows back there and it was dark. I noticed the darkness the past two summers and had said something, but no one did anything about it. It wasn't that important, but I couldn't see what was going on in the world as we drove from one job to the next, and when I stepped out of the van my eyes weren't used to the bright sun light. I asked several people, including my dad, why the vans didn't have windows in the back, and was told the company didn't want people looking into the van when it was parked and left unattended for fear that someone might see something to steal. I responded that someone could look into the van through the front windshield, side windows in the front, or in the back windows and see something to steal. I never got a satisfactory reply.

There were about five or six surveying vans that went into the field every day. While the crews waited in the parking lot to go out in the morning, I talked to the other guys who also had to sit in the back seat about the lack of windows. They all agreed windows in the back would be nice, but none of them felt we could do anything about it. Each crew had big thick crayons that we used to mark lines on the road when we were making measurements – red, blue and yellow – the primary colors. Sometimes guys would use these crayons to write things on the inside walls of the vans – girlfriends names and swear words, but usually not together. So, one day while riding to a job, I decided to draw a window in the back of the van on the inside wall. Then I drew a scene that might be outside, with trees, a meadow, a brook and a house.

It was common to switch the men on the crews, so after a week or so, I was assigned to another crew, which meant I rode in a different van. I drew a window and a mountain scene in the back of that van. Sometimes the crews would stop at the same place for lunch, and the guys would visit with each other.

While they talked, I drew windows and outdoor scenes on the inside walls of the other vans until all the vans had them. Yellow crayon over the blue crayon and made green grass, bushes and tree leaves. Soon everyone was talking about the outdoor scenes in their vans and how we should have windows in the back of the trucks so we could see the outside world. People weren't angry about it, but it was something to talk and joke about. A couple of the guys thought I was making a fuss over nothing.

"Why are you making such a big deal out of this?" one of the senior guys asked me one day.

"Well, I agree, it's not that big a deal," I said. "So if it's not a big deal, why not just get vans with windows in the back the next time they get new vans," I responded. The next time the company bought new vans, they got them with windows all the way around. I didn't realize it at the time, but I was learning skills that would become useful to me later.

Overall, I enjoyed the job. Sometimes we had to lay out a road through swampy areas, like on Grand Island which is in the middle of the Niagara River, and the mosquitoes had us for lunch. But we always pushed on and got the job done. It was a good feeling of accomplishment.

The most exciting thing that happened that summer of 1966 was that I met Donna. I was at a beach on Grand Island with George one warm summer day when we noticed two cute girls on a blanket not too far from ours. We were young, trim and we believed athletic looking. George's blond clump of hair was getting even more bleached in the summer sun. They were young, shapely and they looked great in two-piece bathing suits.

We looked at them. They looked at us. Then they looked away. They were talking and laughing, and stole another glance in our direction. These were all good signs.

"Did you see those girls?" I asked George, nodding my head in their direction.

"Yeah, they were looking over here, too," he said.

A couple more glances were exchanged.

"Let's go over and talk to them," I said.

"Okay, but what will we say?" George asked.

"I don't know," I responded as I started getting up. "We'll figure it out when we get there."

They were about 40 feet from us and there weren't too many other people on the beach that morning. As we approached their blanket they were looking at us, and a small smile broke across the face of the dark haired girl.

"Hi. How are you girls doing today?" I asked. They looked great sitting on their blanket.

"Good," the dark-haired girl responded.

"It's a nice day, isn't it?" I continued. There was hardly a cloud in the sky, the sun was warm and bright, and a faint breeze whispered by. That's a good day for Buffalo.

"Yes, it is," the dark-haired girl said.

"Do you come here often?"

"No, not too often."

"Where are you from?"

"Tonawanda."

"We're from Tonawanda, too," I said. "We're neighbors! Do you mind if we sit down?"

"No, here, you can sit here," the dark-haired girl said as she moved over to make room on the blanket.

"My name is Paul," I said as I extended my hand toward hers.

"My name is Donna," she returned, as she put out her hand. I took it and shook it softly noticing the fine details of her fingers. She had long dark hair, sparkling eyes that lit up when she smiled, a deep rich tan, real womanly hips and legs, and silky smooth skin. We had more conversation: What school are you from, do you know so and so, and other talk of that nature. But I couldn't take my eyes off of her. The conversation was going on around me and I was talking, but I was thinking: who is this girl? She's sweet, and friendly, and feminine and exciting. We kept talking, and George

41

and the other girl were talking, and somewhere in my euphoria, I asked her if I could call her. She said yes and gave me her phone number.

A couple days later I called her. We talked several more times, and then I asked her out. We started seeing each on the weekends, and we were talking two or three times a week on the phone. Soon I saw her almost every night after work. I was falling in love.

My friends were happy for me, but also a little perturbed – I hardly ever hung out with George and Howard anymore.

"Hey, I heard there's going to be a party over at Joe's this Friday," said Howard one day. "Why don't you come with us?"

Joe was a little older than us and had been to Vietnam. I heard that he was acting wild and crazy since he came home from the war, challenging people to fight him.

"I'd like to but I'm going over to Donna's," I responded.

"You always go over there," George added. "We hardly see you any more."

"Yeah, I know," I said, "but there's hardly any time."

"So, bring her with you," George said.

"Well, maybe. I'll see."

I knew I wouldn't take Donna over there. They were mostly a bunch of single guys trying to hit on every girl they saw. They wouldn't bother Donna since she was with me. But they would get drunk and act crazy. I had done it too. And, if what people were saying about Joe was true, I didn't want to bring Donna around him.

I was in love now. I had a new purpose in life, and my new world looked a lot better than my old one. Some guys wanted to go out with many girls. But I had always wanted one girlfriend. Now I had one. My life felt fulfilled. There is nothing greater than to love and be loved.

We didn't go to the party at Joe's. We went to a movie, and then back to her house where we watched TV and made out on the couch after her parents went to bed.

Finally, about 1:30 in the morning, I got up to leave. I opened the door, and there was my Volkswagen bug right in front of the door. I could hardly get out. George and Howard had come over and pushed my car from the driveway across the lawn to where I found it. I chuckled to myself as I got in and tried to drive it quietly across the grass, knowing that this was their way of saying, 'Hey, why don't you spend a little more time with us.'

I had had girlfriends before, but Donna was something else. I thought about her all the time. Now the world was aglow. The sun shown brighter, the leaves were greener, the flowers smelled sweeter. Even the mosquitoes at work weren't half-bad, and sloshing through the swamps was taking me one step closer to seeing Donna that night.

That whole summer was kind of a blur. My routine was simple. Get up in the morning and go to work all day. Come home and take a nap for about an hour. Eat dinner. Go over to Donna's house. Then we either went out somewhere, or stayed at her house and watched TV and made out on her couch until midnight or later. Then I'd go home and go to bed and do it all over again.

We went to movies, parties, the beach and to Niagara Falls. A favorite hangout was Sherkston Beach. It's located on the northeastern end of Lake Erie on the Canadian side, about an hour drive from Tonawanda. Lake Erie is so large that you can't see across it. There are great sand dunes 50 to 100 feet high at this beach, and sometimes we would go up there with a group of friends on a warm Saturday afternoon and stay well into the evening. We'd build a bonfire on the beach at night, cook dinner, talk, and listen to music on our radio or George would play his guitar, and we'd drink beer or wine.

One day, after the sun went down and it cooled off, couples cuddled together under blankets around the fire and talked quietly as red and yellow flames danced across the logs. Donna was sitting in front of me, leaning back against my chest, and my arms were around her waist.

"Do you want to go up into the sand dunes?" I whispered in her ear as I pulled our blanket around us and held her tighter.

"Sure," she whispered back, looking up at me with soft smiling eyes. They sparkled in the twinkling light of the fire.

"Ah, we're going up to the sand dunes," I announced quietly to the group as we started getting up. That was met with knowing glances and a few smiles.

The sand dunes were about 30 feet away and pretty steep. I held her hand in mine, and the blanket in the other and we started climbing. Soon we were about 75 feet above the beach, and found a small cozy hollow big enough for our blanket. It was surrounded on three sides by bushes and trees and clumps of sand dune, but the front was completely open to the huge lake. The moon was bright in the sky, casting a dazzling silvery path across the water's ripples all the way from the horizon to us. Down below on the beach, a warm yellow-orange glow radiated from our crackling fire.

"How's this," I whispered, as I kissed her on the lips.

"Yes, this is perfect."

I spread out the blanket and we lay down on it. She was lying on her back looking up at the night sky.

"Look at all the stars," she said quietly.

"Yes, they're spectacular, aren't they?" There were millions of them, some brighter than others, some in faint clusters scattered across the heavens. "Some people think there's other life out there."

"What do you think?" she asked quietly as she snuggled in my arms.

"I don't know," I answered. "Maybe."

"If there are, I wonder if they're like us?" she asked.

"Well, if they've been around longer than us they're probably smarter. But I know one thing. They're not as cute as you." I tickled her and she laughed and I rolled towards her, and kissed her again on the lips. My body pressed against hers, and we made out for hours, transported into a little dream world all our own. Finally, the fire died down, and Howard called up to us.

"It's midnight. We should get going."

We loved Sherkston Beach. In fact, I did a pen and ink drawing of the sand dunes where we made out, done in colored inks.

As the end of summer approached, I began preparing for college with mixed emotions. I knew I had to go, but I didn't want to leave Donna. She still had to complete her senior year of high school. We talked of her coming with me. But that wasn't to be. We both knew she should finish school. We would write, and I would see her when I returned to Buffalo over Christmas vacation. I left for Florida on a journey that changed my life.

Chapter 6

Florida

Both George and Howard were accepted at the State University of New York at Buffalo, a highly respected university in New York and in the nation. I felt lucky just to be going to college. But I was excited about becoming an art major and living in another part of the country.

Tom, a friend of mine from a Buffalo-area Methodist youth group we were both in, was also going to St. Petersburg Junior College in Clearwater. I wasn't a Methodist, but had joined the group long before I met Donna because there were so many cute girls in it. Tom and I decided to get an apartment together in Florida. He arrived a week before me in mid-August and got a great deal on an apartment behind an animal hospital. It was small, with only one bedroom, had a kitchen and bathroom, and every room was painted light blue. A thin wall and door divided the dogs from us. There was no dorm housing at the community college, but I wasn't interested in living in a dorm anyway.

Tom was a wild guy. He was about 5'10", had a round face and long curly hair that was frizzed up like Bob Dylan's. Tom wasn't too much into school. He spent much of his time in the apartment sitting propped up on his bed drinking beer and shooting cockroaches the size of half dollars off the walls with his BB gun.

Cockroaches loved Florida because it is so hot and humid, and the Gulf side of the state is the worst. The hot sweat just poured down my skin everywhere, matting my hair to my forehead and neck, and sticking my shirt to my back and my shorts up my butt. Today, some kids wear stuff that purposely goes up their butts – thongs. Go figure. Anyway, we had no air conditioning, and I had hoped it would cool down at night. It didn't. We went to bed only in shorts, but the heat and humidity were so suffocating I couldn't sleep. I woke in the morning exhausted and drenched in sweat and wrapped in a soggy sheet. Showering was of little help. When I stepped out of the shower and started drying off, I never knew if I was drying off bath water or sweat or both.

One good thing was that we got to live in the apartment for free in exchange for working part-time in the animal hospital, and we

45

earned a little money. Our job consisted of feeding the dogs twice a day, cleaning out their cages, putting them outside on the runs, and doing other minor cleaning up around the place.

I liked dogs and I had a dog for a pet myself growing up, so I thought this would work out fine. We made a plan. We'd get up in the morning and feed the dogs. Then go to school. Then return and do the other chores in the afternoon, and study at night. It didn't work out that way.

First, there were about twenty to thirty dogs in this hospital. Most were being boarded, but some were sick. The first night one or two dogs started barking, and soon every dog in the entire kennel was yapping. The wall was so thin between us and them that you could almost hear their breathing. I couldn't believe it. I'm not a heavy sleeper and noises awaken me easily. Worse, once awake, I have a hard time falling back to sleep. Tom was a sounder sleeper than me, but he was also woken up.

"What are we going to do?" I asked, lying in the pitch black of night listening to a deafening roar of twenty dogs barking about thirty feet from us. Beads of sweat were dripping down my forehead.

"I don't know," Tom responded.

"Well, I've got an idea," I announced.

I turned on the light, got up, opened the door to the kennel and screamed: "Shut up!" A bead of sweat ran down my temple onto my cheek.

There was immediate silence. All the dogs stopped. I closed the door, went back to bed and turned off the light.

I was just drifting off to sleep when the barking started again. At first it was just one dog, then two, then three and then the entire kennel was roaring. I pulled off my single, soaked sheet, turned on the light, stormed to the door, and screamed at them again. Again there was silence. But shorter this time. We didn't get much sleep that night.

In the following days we tried earplugs, whips and what ever else we could think of. We didn't actually whip the dogs, but Tom had a whip and we would go into the kennel when they were barking at night and crack the whip. It made a real loud cracking sound. That scared the shit out of 'em and they shut up. But eventually they learned that nothing more than a loud sound would occur, so the time between when we cracked the whip and when they started barking again became shorter and shorter.

The earplugs didn't work too well either. They were hard plastic and hurt your ears, especially when you slept on one side, and they didn't block out enough of the noise anyway. Tom did better with the earplugs than I did, but neither of us got much sleep. After many restless nights, I felt dead.

The barking dogs were bad enough, but the work added to the misery. Many of the dogs were sick and had diarrhea or were vomiting. They'd lie in their shit and get it all over their sides and backs, then stand up and smear it against the sides and roof of their cages. The smell of shit was everywhere, and it was incredibly overpowering.

In order to clean the cages, we put the dogs outside on the runs – a concrete slab about 30 feet by 30 feet, subdivided into long rows by fences. While the dogs were out there, we would use a strong disinfectant mixed in water to wash down the sides, top and bottom of their cages. The combined smell of disinfectant and shit created an odor that made my stomach retch, and I had to run outside for fresh air to keep from throwing up.

When the cages were clean, we put in clean newspaper, and brought each dog back inside. Then, with a coal shovel and a big bucket, we would go back outside to shovel up steaming piles of shit that the dogs dropped from one end of the run to the other. That wasn't so bad. At least I was outside in the open air. Some dogs were so sick they died. We were told by the doctor to just stuff them into empty dog food bags and throw them out in the garbage. It was a bad feeling knowing that was someone's pet. This was a far cry from the near nirvana I had just left with Donna, friends and family in Buffalo.

I learned two things from this job. First, don't eat until after you've finished doing this type of work. And second, I knew I had to get the hell out of there and find a new place to live. I talked to Tom about moving. He agreed it wasn't much fun there, but he was on a tighter budget so we stayed much longer than I wanted.

This is the way some people live and work, I thought, especially poor people. I had read about miserable living and working conditions in books, with the heat, bugs, noise, odors and crowdedness. But experiencing them firsthand gave me a whole new understanding. This was another world and I sympathized with people who had to put up with these conditions every day.

But I had to look on the bright side. I was an art student in college now, and that was exciting. I had three art classes: drawing, design and art history. In art history I learned that the Impressionists were initially rejected by the official art world and the rulers of European society because the Impressionists defied the conservative and restrictive ideas about art and life in the late 1800s. Instead, the Impressionists painted every day people, workers and farm families, as well as landscapes, using bold and creative colors, shapes and brushstrokes that broke with a realistic style that was often dominated by religious figures. But the Impressionists won over the public and their art predominated. I was also learning more about perspective, proportion, shading, mixing colors, and the elements of good design.

We went to Safety Harbor to draw sponge fishermen, and I did paintings of still-lifes and landscapes. I wanted to excel in art so I took on art projects that were dramatic. For one assignment we had to design a door. I designed one that combined the ornateness of 17th century Baroque art with its sweeping curves, with the more orderly 18th century Greek and Roman Neoclassical architecture. I cut out circles of various sizes from balsa wood, created a relief sculpture on the door, topped with five large gold-colored domes. It was a very labor-intensive project, and while it came out regal, a good painter friend, who spent most every day in art class not working but talking about the finer points of a woman's anatomy – including the "cute little dimples above her butt," simply did a quick painting on his door the day before the project was due and got an A. There was another lesson here. Go with your strengths. I wasn't sure what mine were yet, so I kept experimenting with new things. I thought maybe I should do something big – that would get attention.

One day I was driving in the woods with a friend from school. The trees were huge and I got an idea to make a large wood sculpture. We got a chainsaw and came back and I cut down a forty-foot high tree that was four feet in diameter. It made a huge crash when it fell in the woods and that was exciting. But cutting down the tree was very stupid. That was somebody's property. What we were doing was illegal. I broke the chain saw trying to cut off an eight-foot piece, so we came back the next week with an axe to finish the job. That's when we were arrested. I had not given any thought to how I was going to get a 1,000 pound block of wood home either. Fortunately, we were only convicted of trespassing and not cutting down the tree, and we were sentenced to guard the trees for the next two months each weekend by sitting in those woods all day. That's were I learned about gnats – those tiny little bugs that look like a dot and hover an inch in front of your eyes as if they want to fly into your pupil.

The Sheriff's deputies drove out to where we were to make sure we showed up. One particularly hot and humid day the gnats were as thick as gray curtains hanging in the air. They were driving me nuts when a deputy drove up. He cracked his window just slightly.

"You boys enjoyin' yourselves out there?" he said with a smile.

"Oh yeah. We're havin' a ball," I responded as I swatted a gazillion gnats away from my face, my arms moving like a windmill in fast motion.

"How do you like these gnats?" he asked with a chuckle.

"Personally, I like 'em," I responded. "They keep me busy. And I get my exercise and I don't get bored."

"That's good," he laughed, "because you've got four more hours of 'em today. I'll check back on you a little later." He laughed again, rolled up his window and drove off.

I realized then that there are consequences for the dumb things you do, and those consequences usually aren't much fun. I never made a large wooden sculpture. But I learned that how big or how ornate something is doesn't necessarily make great art. There is something more intrinsic. It has to do with the message and the feelings and how well they are conveyed.

I enjoyed my classes and was doing well. Not only had I proved my high school guidance counselor wrong, but more importantly, I was now becoming a serious student, and in my academic subjects as well.

I was also learning to live on my own, well sort of. My parents paid the college tuition and sent me some money to live on. Their philosophy was simple: 'if you're in school, we'll help you. If you're not, you need to get a full-time job and support yourself.'

It was nice to feel independent. I could come and go as I pleased. I could stay up all night if I wanted. I could get drunk and not worry about sneaking in so my dad wouldn't hear me. But with this newfound freedom, I also learned more about personal responsibility. It was hard getting up in the morning and being productive at school after drinking the night before, so I didn't do it. But on the weekends, Tom and I would go out to bars and clubs and party.

That was the first time I had lived away from home for any length of time, and while I enjoyed being on my own, I missed my family and especially Donna. We didn't have a phone in our apartment, so every Sunday I would go to a pay phone and call my parents. Talking to them reconnected me to my earlier life. Donna and I also wrote to each other at least once or twice a week, and I eagerly looked forward to her letters. I missed her very much and couldn't wait to go home for Christmas break. Unfortunately, that was months away and we had to make something of a new life in Florida. Tom and I wanted to meet people and make some friends, so we decided to go to the first fall school dance. It was held in the gym. We got there early, and not too many other kids were there yet. But we knew the songs they were playing, and asked some of the girls to dance.

There were both blacks and whites at this college, though many more whites, and each group stayed mostly by themselves. I danced with several white girls and talked to them about where they were from and what classes they were taking. They were interesting, but the conversation didn't last much longer than the breaks between one or two songs. So I went back and stood with Tom.

I saw a couple of cute black girls standing by themselves and decided to ask one of them to dance. Society was still pretty segregated in the mid-1960's, though in Buffalo I had gone to the Holland House bar with friends, a racially-mixed club on Michigan Avenue downtown where blacks and whites shared tables, socialized and danced with each other.

"Hi. Would you like to dance," I asked the shorter of the two young women. She was slender with a nice figure accentuated by a thin light blue cashmere sweater and dark skirt that stopped about two inches above her knees.

"Sure," she responded, as a fast popular rock and roll song began. People danced to fast songs facing their partner, but not touching. I tried talking to her a little bit during the song but it was so loud she couldn't hear me. But she smiled and looked at me, and seemed interested in talking. As the song was ending, I decided to try again. We introduced ourselves, and asked each other about our classes.

Then another song started, but this time it was a slow one. I had seen blacks and whites in the same classes and in the cafeteria at school, and while they mostly stayed in their own groups, there was some interaction between them. The Civil Rights Movement was changing society, and I thought, in my own small way, I might push the limits a little bit. I remembered hearing about the March on Washington in 1963 where blacks and whites walked with arms linked to protest discrimination against blacks, and where Martin Luther King made his famous "I have a dream" speech, prophesizing that one day blacks and whites would live in peace with one another.

"Would you like to dance?"

"Okay."

I put my arms around her waist and she put her hands around my neck. And we danced. Suddenly, the people around me stopped dancing and a crowd formed a circle around us. They were all white and more students joined until there were twenty or thirty people there. Some had their arms folded across their chests and they glared. The song kept playing, we kept dancing and the crowd kept glaring. I thought: Uh oh, what's going to happen now. Here I am in the South, I don't know anyone here, and maybe I pushed this a little too far.

Just as the song was ending, a group of about fifteen black students entered the gym and they walked slowly along the edge of the circle in single file. A guy looked at my dance partner.

"Come on. You better come with us, "he said solemnly as he kept walking toward the back of the gym.

"I'd better go," she said uneasily.

"Yes, I guess so," I responded apprehensively, eyeing the crowd that hadn't moved. "Maybe I'll see you around campus," I said as she moved away.

"Maybe," she said, looking back over her shoulder. The white circle was slowly breaking up and all of the black students went to the back of the gym. A friend from my art classes, Tony, walked up to me.

"What the hell are you trying to do, start a race war?"

"What are you talking about?" I asked, trying to feign innocence.

"Dancing with them. Maybe you do that up north, but not down here you don't."

"Nobody's going to tell me who I can dance with," I retorted, anger rising in my voice. "I'll dance with who ever I damn please."

51

"Yeah, you do that again, and you'll be lucky to walk out of here in one piece." He walked away. I noticed another group of about five white guys who kept glaring at me. I wondered if I would get out of there in one piece.

Things eventually calmed down, and Tom and I left without incident. But it made me think. So, this was the South. I thought Florida was different. Up north we heard about northerners going to Florida for winter vacations, and to retire there. They didn't seem like racists, and they talked about all the wonderful things to see and do there. Especially how nice the weather and beaches were. Most of them moved to Miami. I learned first-hand that there was another reality in Florida. Especially when you got into the smaller cities and towns and rural areas, Florida was more like the Deep South.

The racism I witnessed at the school dance was just the tip of the iceberg. Racism was alive and stark in and around Clearwater in 1966. One day I was driving down a beautiful, tree-line paved street and saw whites living in nice houses with lawns. There were street-lights, restaurants, and a movie theater nearby and other amenities. I noticed a little dirt turn-off under some big leafy trees and wondered where that dirt road led. So I pulled off the main highway and drove down a slight but steep dirt road under the low hanging tree branches and all of a sudden I was in a different world. Before me was a small community of the worst poverty I had ever seen. Black people were everywhere. It had rained earlier that morning and the dirt roads had turned into a sea of mud. The houses were dilapidated wooden shanties, patched together with gray, weather-beaten old boards without a speck of paint on them, and covered with rusty, corrugated tin roofs. They were packed one right next to the other, leaning to and fro. It looked like a third world country. One advantage of these shacks being built so close to each other was that if one was about to collapse, it would sag against the wall of the one next to it, which might hold it up. I bumped and slid in shock along one of the muddy roads on the edge of this community. I couldn't take my eyes off the disaster, but I also looked ahead for someplace to turn around so I could go back to the main highway.

Little kids were running around on broken porches and in the dirt and mud in rags. Some had no shirts, some no pants and most had no shoes. This sight was an assault on human dignity. I felt sick to my stomach. Many adults were standing around and it was the middle of the day – I had heard that jobs were hard to come by for blacks. People stared at me as I drove slowly along the edge of their community. I saw no other white people there. The expressions on the faces of some of the older people looked hopeless.

I was shaken. How could a society with such material wealth treat some of its citizens so poorly? I knew something about racism, and the history of slavery and the struggle of blacks to win freedom and equality. And I supported the Civil Rights Movement, from its roots in the south ten years earlier, to its activities in the north, including in Buffalo, and I had thought that some progress had been made. Clearly, not nearly enough. I had never seen the starkness of such racism right in my face.

I talked to Tom about what I'd seen, and asked him if he wanted to see it with me.

"No, not really."

"Why not?" I asked.

"It sounds bad," said Tom, "but I don't want to see it. Anyway, what can we do about it?" I didn't know, but it bothered me deeply. I felt that we should try to do something. Maybe the first step was to learn more about it. I started looking for a book that might help me understand it. One day I found one, but almost by accident.

I was taking American Government and our teacher handed out a long list of books and told us we had to pick one and do a book report on it. I read over the titles: "The Executive Branch: How it Works." "How a Bill is Passed into Law." And other similar titles. None of these seemed to be very interesting or what I was looking for. I wanted to read something that would help me answer the questions I had about racism and poverty.

I went to the library and came across a book that was making quite a stir in society at that time, *The Autobiography of Malcolm X.* I read a few pages there and decided that was what I wanted so I checked it out. I took it home and started reading it and couldn't put it down. It was what I was looking for.

After my next government class, I went up to the teacher.

"Mrs. Lindsay, could I talk to you for a minute?" I asked.

"Yes," she responded as she looked directly at me. She was young and smart. She also seemed kind.

"I was looking over the list of books you gave us for our book report, and I didn't see anything that addresses my major interests," I explained. "What I'm really looking for are the human stories that impact government. What I'd like to do is a book report on something like that. Maybe about a person or social movement that has had an impact on government, and resulted in the passage of a law."

She looked at me as if she was pondering what I had said.

"Do you have something in mind?" she asked.

"Well, I was in the library the other day, and I came across a book that deals with a social movement. And it resulted in the passage of the Civil Rights Act."

"Is that so?" she responded, her eyebrows arching slightly. "What is the book?"

"*The Autobiography of Malcolm X,*" I stated matter of factly.

She stared at me for a moment. Then her face softened and a small smile appeared. "Okay. That's fine. You can do your book report on that."

Wow, what a relief! I didn't have to read a boring government book and could read about Malcolm X. The book was excellent. I learned about how poverty and racism so negatively impacts people's lives. I also learned that through reading and studying and soul-searching and talking with others, as Malcolm X did, that someone headed down an anti-social path can turn his life around. For Malcolm X it was a 180 degree turn, as he committed his life to helping to eradicate racism and poverty in order to make the world a better, fairer place. I was impressed by Malcolm X and reflected that in my book report.

The following week we got our papers back. As I was leaving the class, a friend, Travis, a tall, lanky white southerner who was a nice guy, was walking next to me looking at his grade.

"How dja' do?" he asked, in a thick southern drawl.

"Pretty good," I responded.

"Whadja get, if you don't mind my askin'?"

"No, I don't mind. I got an A. How about you?"

"I got a B," he responded.

"That's good," I returned.

"Whatcha do your report on?" he continued as we walked down the hall.

"*The Autobiography of Malcolm X,*" I responded.

"What?" His voice rose and a startled look came across his face. "I don't remember seein' that on the list."

"It wasn't. I asked the teacher if I could do my report on that book and she said okay."

"Why would you want to do a report on that book? That guy's crazy!" His voice rose another level, and his eyes blazed. "He's a criminal and hates white people and is stirrin' up the coloreds."

"Well, not quite," I responded. "He started out as a rebellious kid who hated racism, and turned to crime and went to prison for burglary."

"See! I told you he was a criminal!" His arm flew up and his hand cut the air to emphasize his point.

"Yeah. But in prison, he started reading and realized that a life of crime is wrong, and he became a Muslim."

"Yeah, but they hate white people!" he continued, as agitated as before.

"The leader of the Muslims in America preaches that, but Malcolm X went to Mecca in the Middle East and saw people of all races working and praying together and he changed his thinking."

Travis was quiet for a minute.

"Well, I don't know about that. But I do know he's stirrin' up the coloreds in this country, and we don't need that!"

"Look, he's saying that racism is wrong, and that we should eradicate it from society," I countered. "I agree with him."

"What, are you crazy too?! Supporting people like that!?

"Look Travis," I said, stopping on the sidewalk outside the building and looking at him in his pale blue eyes. "What if someone said that we're going to build a society and one of the tenets of that society is that we are going treat everyone who has blue eyes like shit. Everyone with blue eyes is going to have a lousy job or no job, the worst housing, and is going to be discriminated against in every other way. Do you think you'd like that?"

"Well, no," he stuttered.

"And don't you think you'd want to do something about it?"

"Well, I guess so," he muttered.

"Well, that's what Malcolm X and the Civil Rights Movement is all about," I said emphatically.

He looked at me with a puzzled look on his face. We were jostled by students passing by, hurrying to get to their next class. He got caught up in the crowd going one way, and I headed to my next class.

Not all southerners were like that. In fact, most of the white kids Tom and I became friends with didn't act like racists, at least not in front of us. I don't know how they would have responded if there had been an active Civil Rights Movement in town – maybe there was but I didn't know about it. But the guys and girls Tom and I hung out with and became friends with were very down-to-earth and friendly. There really was something to the "Southern Hospitality" I'd heard about, at least for us white guys.

After three months living and working at the animal hospital, I decided I had to find another place to live, whether Tom was ready to move or not. I found a small efficiency in a tiny motel and moved in. The first night was like heaven. No barking dogs. No shit or disinfectant smells. And no dead dogs. I finally got a good night's sleep. After three days, I felt like a new man. There was less than a month left in the semester, and I was looking forward to going back to Buffalo for Christmas, especially to see Donna.

The proprietors of the motel were nice people. When they learned that I was an art student at the community college, they asked me if I wanted a job painting a big "Season's Greetings" sign to display in front of the motel. I said sure. We worked out the details of the deal and everything worked out fine. Now, with money in my pocket, I started thinking about what I was going to buy Donna for Christmas.

Chapter 7

War

I flew into the Buffalo airport and my parents were there to pick me up. We went home and I saw my bothers, Lee and Jim, and we all spent some time catching up with each other. It was great to be home, but I couldn't wait to see Donna. I called her and she invited me to come over to her house.

When I got there, she answered the door in a thin sweater and tight pants. My heart soared. She greeted me with a beautiful smile that said 'I missed you,' and we threw our arms around each other. All of a sudden I was in nirvana again. All the thoughts of the bad things I'd seen in Florida vanished, and we were together again, in our own world where no one could bother us.

Donna and I saw each other every day. We went Christmas shopping together, went to movies, and watched TV curled up together on the couch at her house.

After several days, I tried talking to her about the things I saw in Florida. But she didn't want to hear about them, so I didn't bring them up again.

One night I went to a Buffalo Bisons hockey game with my dad and my brother Lee. The Bisons were a minor league team that would be replaced in 1970 when the Buffalo Sabres were formed and came into the National Hockey League and would become our city's major hockey team. As we turned a corner in the hallway to go to our seats I saw a young man sitting in a wheelchair. It was Patrick, a very good athlete from high school who had graduated a year before me and who went to Vietnam. I was stunned. I didn't know him very well but remembered seeing him play school sports. I had heard that he had been wounded in Vietnam. Our eyes met but I couldn't bring myself to go talk to him. I learned from George that Patrick had been shot in the war and was paralyzed from the waist down. I felt terrible for him. What were we doing in Vietnam, I wondered? Seeing him sitting in that wheelchair had a powerful impact on me. He was there for life. There was no do-over. I started thinking more about the war. All sorts of questions came into my mind, like how did we get involved there? After seeing Patrick, I wasn't feeling very good about it.

I saw Donna the next day and told her about Patrick.

"That's horrible," she said. "I feel so sorry for him."

"Yeah, it is terrible," I agreed. "I think there's something wrong with this war," I began tentatively. "The government tells us victory is just around the corner, but the war only gets worse. I wonder if maybe we shouldn't be over there. A lot of Vietnamese don't seem to think so. And a lot of people are getting killed and wounded."

She was silent.

"What do you think?" I asked her

"I don't know," she responded. "All I know is the government thinks we should be there so maybe we should."

"But what if it's wrong?" I asked.

"I don't know. But I don't want to think about it," she said in a gloomy voice. "It's so depressing." She was silent for a moment, and then brightened up. "Let's go to the mall. There's a real cute sweater I want to get."

That evening I brought it up at the dinner table with my family. We started talking about the hockey game we had seen, but then I changed the subject.

"I, ah, saw a guy I knew a little from high school last night at the game," I began.

"Was he sitting near us?" my dad asked. "Do we know him?"

"No. You don't know him. And he wasn't sitting near us. He was in Vietnam and I saw him in the hallway, sitting in a wheelchair. I heard that he is paralyzed."

Everyone was silent. Then my mom spoke.

"I'm so sorry to hear that, Paul." She had a real look of concern on her face. "Did you know him very well?"

"No. Not really. I maybe spoke to him once or twice. Maybe we were in the same gym class. I don't remember. But since seeing him, I've really been thinking about the war. It doesn't make sense to me. I hear what the government says, but it just doesn't add up. All this pain and suffering and deaths, and for what?"

"I know it's hard," my dad said. "War is like that. A lot of times we don't understand all the reasons why we go to war. But the government has a lot more information about it than we do, and they've figured there are good reasons for us to be there. We have to trust them."

"But all the suffering and deaths," I continued. "I can't see how Vietnam is any threat to us, or anyone else. It's not like Hitler marching across Europe and taking over one country after another. That, I can understand."

"Yes, that's true," my dad agreed. "But we want to stop them before that happens." My mom nodded in agreement.

"But how do we know that's what they plan to do?"

"The communists from North Vietnam invaded South Vietnam."

"Well, that's what the government says happened. How do we know that's true?"

"Look. They're our government," my dad said with conviction. "We elected them. I don't think they would have any reasons not to tell us the truth. If they say we have to fight, we fight. We have to serve our country. I did. And if you are called, you will too."

I didn't know what else to say. I loved and respected my mom and dad, and didn't want to argue with them. I just didn't know enough about the war to know what to say. But the killing and suffering, especially of civilians, was wrong and it bothered me. I wished we would have talked more about it, but my dad seemed to think that the government knew best.

I tried to put Patrick and Vietnam out of my mind. When I was with Donna, she occupied my thoughts and feelings. And it was the Christmas season, a time to celebrate the joy of being with family and friends. I spent every day with Donna for two weeks and it was wonderful. And I spent some time with my parents and brothers, sharing our family dinners, and going to a Christmas pageant, complete with many of our favorite Christmas songs.

As my departure day neared, I felt a wave of depression flood over me. I didn't want to leave Donna. I thought of staying in Buffalo. But if I didn't go back to school, I would be eligible to be drafted and sent to Vietnam. That wasn't very appealing. She talked of coming with me to Florida, but we both knew that she should finish high school. We said we would write, and I told her I couldn't wait to get home in the spring to be with her again. "Just four months," I told her as I looked into her sad eyes just before I left. "We can do that." I had my arms around her and she just nodded and a tear ran down her cheek as she buried her head on my shoulder. It was a long and lonely plane flight back to Florida.

When I got to Clearwater, Tom was ready to get out of the animal hospital, so we got a small, run-down apartment together. I quickly got back into the flow of school. In addition to my art classes, I signed up for Introduction to Philosophy, and General Psychology for the 1967 spring semester. I couldn't stop thinking about racism, poverty and war, and thought these academic courses might help me learn answers to these terrible problems.

In my psych class, I met a Vietnam veteran. We talked a few times after class about the readings and the lecture, and then one day I asked him about the war.

"You don't want to know," he said with apprehension. We were standing outside the classroom building under a big palm tree. There was a soft breeze and the sunlight trickled down through the slightly swaying leaves, casting flickering lights and shadows across his face. He looked off in the distance, as if he were deep in thought, and then a look of terror came into his eyes just as the sunlight hit them. He started trembling, and then shook his head quickly from side to side as if to shake something horrible out of his mind. "I can't talk about it," he blurted out.

Later that day, I was in the student lounge and saw on the television a scene of US troops setting fire to grass huts in Vietnam, while women and children were screaming on the ground and others were lying still in pools of blood. The camera quickly turned to the reporter who said that the village was an enemy stronghold. Crying mothers and their babies, enemies? This was sick.

I started reading the newspaper more often and saw almost daily reports of battles where scores of people were killed on both sides. But I also learned about growing opposition to the war, though I didn't see any organized opposition in Clearwater. In the fall of 1966, French President Charles de Gaulle, our ally, urged the withdrawal of all US troops from Vietnam. The media reported it as though an unstable ally had turned on us. Then I read about three soldiers who refused to go to Vietnam and were court-martialed at Ft. Hood. The media reported that they were facing heavy fines and prison time. I think the message was that if any of you young people think of trying to get out of the war, you'll pay a price. But the message for me was that a world leader and some soldiers believed the war was wrong, so maybe *they* were right. And then I heard about a group of US scientists who urged President Johnson to stop using anti-personal and chemical weapons because they were seriously injuring and maiming people and destroying forests and crops. Why was our government doing that, I asked myself? It seemed barbaric. How is that fighting for a good cause?

I also read that our government announced that the war was going well and peace was around the corner, but then news reporters said that the fighting was worse than ever. It seemed like every time I heard something about the war, it made me feel more and more against it. Also, the fact that others were openly against the war, made me think that perhaps I could be openly against it too. I wondered if the people I knew in Clearwater felt the same way, or if they supported the war. I mentioned these things to Tom one day in our apartment while we were fixing dinner.

"It's not just the crops that are being killed," Tom added. "The chemicals are killing the livestock and the people too!" He felt as strongly about it as I did. That was a good feeling.

"It's pretty outrageous," I said. "I feel like I can't trust what the government says about the war. They say the Vietnamese people are opposed to communism and are glad we're over there. But it seems the Vietnamese people are more opposed to us. The war is getting worse. Certainly, someone doesn't want us there."

"That's the way I see it, too," Tom said.

"But what's the big surprise?" I asked. "Our government and military are in *their* country carrying out a war there. How would we feel if some other country invaded ours and went around shooting people and blowing up their houses?"

"I agree," said Tom. "It's sickening."

The images of bombs, burning huts, babies crying, bodies lying in pools of blood, and Patrick paralyzed in a wheelchair for the rest of his life swirled around in my mind, along with the bullying by Carlton and the frat boys from high school.

"Well, I'm not going to participate in it," I exclaimed.

"Me either," Tom said.

If I refused to join a fraternity in high school because I didn't want to be a part of a group that was abusive to others – especially weaker kids, why would I join the US military to commit the ultimate in abusiveness – murder, and mass murder at that, against people in a small, poor country on the other side of the globe who were absolutely no threat to us. I saw my government as a bully, and a feeling of fear and horror gripped me. This was not the country I grew up believing in. These were not the values that my parents taught me. I was shocked and I felt sick to my stomach every time I heard of a new atrocity. It was the worst feeling that I could remember. I loved my country. How could it commit such terrible crimes? My head was spinning. What was I going to do?

Tom and I agreed that we had to talk to our friends about the war, about why it was wrong, tell them that we weren't going, and convince them not to go. To our happy surprise, most of them agreed with our sentiments. The problem was *how* we would refuse to participate, since the government could force us to go by drafting us.

Tom and I were in the school cafeteria one day having this discussion with two of our classmates.

"I don't want to go either," said one, "but if I get drafted, I guess I'll have to."

"Why?" asked Tom.

"Because it's the law. I don't want to break the law."

"Don't you think there is a higher law," I asked, "and that is, thou shall not kill."

"Yes, but if our government says we have to go, we have to."

"No you don't," I answered. "You don't have to go. There are other options."

"Like what? Go to Canada or jail?"

"Yup," said Tom. "The only thing you ever *have* to do is die. No one can make you go to war if you don't want to."

"So what are you guys going to do?" he asked.

"We haven't decided yet," I responded. "But we know we're not going."

Later that evening in our apartment, Tom and I talked about the options.

"What do you think about going to Canada?" Tom asked.

"Well, Canada would be more enjoyable than jail," I quipped. "I've been to Canada many times growing up. It's just like the US, in many ways. And they have more hockey up there." Tom knew I loved hockey. We didn't make any decisions that night, but it got me thinking.

I knew I wanted to spend more time on my art, and I had been thinking about trying to get into a good art school. I told my dad about this on the phone that Sunday, and a week later he sent me a long article about art schools, with descriptions of each one, their standing in the eyes of the art world, and their addresses. I knew some of my art skills were quite good, so I decided to apply to the top art schools in the country. I had heard of some of them, including the Pratt Institute in New York, and the Art Institute of Chicago. But I also learned of other top art schools, such as the Ontario College of Art in Toronto, Canada. An art school in Canada? That was a good idea, I thought. That would resolve two problems at once. I applied to those three schools and others.

While my goal was to become a fine artist, I found myself becoming increasingly interested in my philosophy class. Philosophy seemed to be concerned about all the issues I was thinking about and it tried to get to the root of these issues. Our textbook covered the major branches of philosophy – what is knowledge and how do we know what is true, how do we acquire this knowledge, what is the fundamental nature of reality, what is logical reasoning, what is ethically right or wrong, and what is art, beauty and culture? Another section covered political and social philosophy – how should society be organized? Other sections covered the philosophy of language, science, religion and other topics.

We read short excerpts from the writings of famous philosophers including Socrates, Plato, Descartes, Locke, Hegel, Marx, Mill and others, and discussion pieces from contemporary philosophical writers analyzing the ideas of these great thinkers. I began seeing connections between the ideas of these philosophers and modern day life. I was fascinated by this whole new world of ideas. While many people think of philosophy and philosophers as distant, remote and unconnected to the real world, I saw that many of their ideas were relevant today.

Socrates, from ancient Greece, for example, developed a method of asking questions of someone that helped expose illogical or inconsistent answers in order to arrive at the truth. This led to the methods attorneys use to question people in court. That method could be used to find out the truth about Vietnam, racism and poverty, I thought.

Locke, an English philosopher of the late 1600s, developed ideas about individual rights, democracy and the role of government as a servant of the people, and inspired Thomas Jefferson when he wrote the Declaration of Independence and Bill of Rights. That is where we got our legally protected rights of freedom of speech and freedom to assemble – though a big shortcoming was that these rights weren't afforded to the slaves. None-the-less, these were important rights that I cherished, and I believed they could help us find the truth about our current pressing social problems because, legally, everyone had a right to express his or her ideas and opinions.

I read a selection by a German philosopher from the 1800s, Arthur Schopenhaurer, where he blasted the stupidity of war and humanity for perpetuating it.   While Schopenhauer had a very pessimistic view of people, what he said about war struck a cord with me.

War is insane, but I was immersed in a society and culture that seemed to think that war was perfectly natural, logical, honorable and even heroic and romantic. I couldn't understand what was so romantic about killing someone, being killed, or being slumped into a wheelchair, paralyzed and in pain, for the rest of your life. Schopenhaurer's scathing indictment of war validated my feelings, in part because of his eloquence, but more importantly because he was a world renowned philosopher.

What was disturbing was that I had not heard many other people in positions of authority oppose the war. Was I wrong? Was my reasoning ability faulty? Our US government officials, journalists, professors, and leaders of big organizations were smart people. They held positions of great influence and people looked up to them. Yet, very few of them opposed the war that I knew of, at least not publicly. Why not, I wondered? It was disturbing. I underlined the passages in my textbook from Schopenhauer and showed them to Tom when he came home.   He agreed, as I knew he would. Certainly, I thought, the human race can find better ways to resolve our differences than with war.

I had four hours of free time in the middle of the day three days a week, so I decided to use that time for uninterrupted reading and studying. I found a stretch of a nearly deserted beach one morning during that break-time. It was so quiet that I heard only the rhythmic rolling of the waves onto the shore. That was a perfect place to read and study and reflect and that was what I did for three days a week for several months.   That was a period of significant intellectual growth for me. I actually felt like I was getting smarter, and it felt great. I started answering questions in class and making statements about what we read.   I was beginning to overcome my fear of speaking in class.

During this time I read about the great poverty in the world, and how millions of people were dying of starvation. I was outraged. How could this happen in a world where there was so much material wealth and such high food production? How was it that I was born in America with enough to eat, and not in India or Vietnam, where people were dying by the thousands? It was luck. I tried to imagine what it felt like to starve. I knew many poor people in America were chronically hungry. I fasted for three days to get a small feeling of what millions of people were experiencing that very moment all over the world, and would feel for most of their lives.

As I was developing a social consciousness, I did some art that reflected my emerging philosophical thoughts. In one of my art classes, I turned an assignment into a political statement against the war. I did a pen and ink drawing of a casket with an American flag draped over it. The casket was sitting on a sidewalk next to an Army recruiting sign that hung from a metal display stand. These signs were all over every town in America then. They read: "Join the Army. A Proud Future Could Be Yours." I crossed out the word "Proud" as if someone had written graffiti on it, and then wrote in "Dead." So the sign read: "Join the Army. A Dead Future Could Be Yours."

"What are you trying to say here?" my art teacher asked.

"I'm trying to point out the futility of war. Well, at least this war. And what the government is promising isn't guaranteed. There's no 'proud future' if you come home in a box. Also, that maybe the government doesn't know what's best, but that some kid on the street doing graffiti has the real answer."

"Yes. I can see that," he said. "You might want to make the casket more ornate to emphasize just how bizarre it is. It's as if the military thinks it can entice people to sign up with images of fancy coffins as a good trade off if you're killed." Did my art teacher agree with me about the war? Or was he just helping me to make the strongest statement I could through my art? I didn't know, but I followed his suggestion. I showed it to my friends and everyone like it.

I still wondered about the general public. Where did they stand on the war? The news media, while showing some of the killing, reported the war as something that had to be won. Reporters interviewed generals, political leaders and a select group of so-called experts who all had ideas on how to achieve victory. Since an anti-war voice was hardly ever heard, it appeared that practically everyone was for the war. Tom and I and our friends felt pretty lonely in our beliefs. Fortunately, that changed one day.

I saw a poster for a concert in near-by Tampa by the folk music group, Peter, Paul and Mary. I liked folk music, and knew some of their songs were anti-war. I asked Tom if he wanted to go, and he said he did. We got tickets and headed to Tampa.

When we arrived, I was excited to see thousands of people inside. We weren't alone! Peter, Paul and Mary sang, "Where Have all the Flowers Gone," "If I had a Hammer," "Blowin' in the Wind," and other anti-war songs, and the crowd cheered wildly. It was the first time I saw such a large number of people who felt the same way I did. It was exhilarating. Being among so many others who wanted peace strengthened my opposition to the war and my readiness to be more outspoken against it. I had the feeling that the media purposely ignored this anti-war sentiment. On the few occasions when newspapers or television showed people opposing the war, it was presented as something outside the mainstream of society. I was beginning to change, both politically and personally.

Those changes became apparent after Tom and me, and Tony and two other guys we knew from college, rented a house together. Our new housemates were in a band and that attracted a group of girls. Consequently, we had a lot of wild parties at our house. I had fun, but my growing opposition to the war, poverty and racism, and my longing for Donna, made me a little less of the fun-loving guy I used to be.

Donna and I continued to write to each other. She was my lifeline to a saner world. I tried to keep my letters happy. I talked about the beautiful sunsets on the beach over the Gulf of Mexico and how I wished she were there with me. I reminded her of the great times we had together at Sherkston Beach in Canada. She wrote similar letters to me. I crossed the days off the calendar so I knew exactly how much longer until I went home.

Tom had been skipping many of his classes, and when he was failing most of them, he dropped out of school. He got a job as a ditch digger for the Clearwater water department. Sometimes I'd drive by where he was working and watch him sweat his ass off in a blazing 95 degree sun. The job was hard, and the heat and humidity made it worse. I was glad I wasn't working on that job.

While my parents continued to help me financially, I got some part-time jobs to cover all of my expenses. One job was painting more signs. Some guys who worked as paramedics for the Mercy Ambulance company lived next door to us and they saw a sign I painted on our mailbox in Old English lettering. They asked if I wanted a job painting their company name on the sides of their ambulances and I said I did. I painted "Mercy" in red letters, but not in Old English, on a light blue background. It was a nice feeling to see my neighbors driving around town taking sick people to the hospital with my sign on their vehicles.

The parties at our house were getting out of control and finally there was one too many and we got kicked out. Tom and I moved to a smaller apartment together further towards downtown Clearwater.

One day shortly after moving in, I noticed a black classmate from one of my art classes across the street. I headed over to see him.

"Hey, James," I called out as I crossed the street toward him.

He looked up. "Hi, Paul. How you doin'?" he asked.

He was standing in front of a house and the door was partly open.

"Do you live here?" I asked

"Yeah, right here." He pointed to the open door.

"Hey, we're neighbors," I responded, "I live just across the street. How are you coming on your art project?"

"Pretty good. I'm working on it right now."

"Can I see it?" I asked.

"Sure. Wait here and I'll go in and get it."

I waited on the sidewalk while James went in the house. He came right back out and showed it to me.

"That's good," I responded. "I like the way you used red and yellow here."

"How about you? How are you coming on yours?" he asked.

"Pretty good," I responded. "Come on over and I'll show you." I started to cross the street.

"Ah, wait a minute," James said in a somber voice, the smile gone from his face. "I can't go over there."

"Why not," I asked with a puzzled tone in my voice.

"Because we can't go over there."

Then I understood. Blacks were restricted by the racism of the day to stay in certain areas.

"But you're my guest. I'm inviting you to be my guest in my house," I responded.

"I'd like to, and I appreciate your invitation," James responded, "but I can't."

"Okay, I understand." I wasn't going to push it. "It was nice seeing you," I said. "I'll see you in class." Then I realized that the only blacks I saw on my side of the street were the city garbagemen. It dawned on me that all the garbagemen were black. So, the jobs are segregated too, and those black garbagemen are the lucky ones because they're working. What a sick society, I thought, as I crossed the street to my apartment.

War, racism, poverty. Meanness, selfishness and greed. All these things swirled around in my head and bothered me. Why did they exist? Why couldn't people treat each other with respect? After all, we're all on this planet together. We all face similar problems, and have similar needs: food, clothing, shelter, good health, jobs, education, art, friendship and love. There are enough problems in life that we have little or no control over – like certain diseases, accidents, natural disasters, old age and death. Why did people have to create new ones for each other?

Was it human nature to mistreat others? I didn't think so. There were a lot of good people who treated others with respect. How do you explain the differences? Is it biological or social, or some combination of both? If it's social, could we organize society in a way that brings out the best in people and ensures that everyone is treated fairly? If we built a society that met everyone's needs, would they get along better? Could war become a thing of the past?

What motivates people to go to war, I wondered? Many people believe that another nation is trying to take something from us that we need for our survival and well-being. Certainly, that's worth fighting for, even at the risk of being maimed or killed. And most young people, who will be called to do the fighting, don't believe they will be hurt or killed in war. These were difficult questions. But I knew there must be answers. There must be some way to eradicate racism, poverty, starvation and war.

Soon the end of the semester came and I started packing to go home. My dad came to Clearwater to help share the drive back to Buffalo. That gave us a chance to talk. At first it was small talk, catching up on the news at home. But then I told him about the things I had seen in Florida, the racism and poverty.

We were driving through the Blue Ridge Mountains in eastern Kentucky on winding roads covered with dense patches of fog. The grass was blue – not bright blue, but a blue-green aqua color. It was beautiful and soothing. My dad listened patiently until I finished.

"Maybe you should go into politics," he said.

"Politics?" I asked, somewhat surprised. "No, I want to be an artist. Politics is so corrupt. I don't want to have anything to do with it."

"But that's how you change things," my dad continued. He wasn't trying to push me into it. He was just sharing his thinking.

"Well, that's not for me. I just want to be able to do my art and be left alone. I don't want to get mixed up in all that corruption. All those politicians making deals."

"They're not all corrupt," he continued. "Probably most aren't. Most are honest and they're just trying their best to do what they think is right. Without them, and without government, we'd have chaos."

"Yeah, that's true," I agreed. "I'm sure some are honest. But I'm not interested in politics. I feel art is what is honest. Politics is too dirty and corrupt, and I don't want to get involved in it."

He didn't press it anymore. We didn't have an argument. We just dropped the subject. I couldn't wait to get home to see Donna.

69

Chapter 8

Merrimac Street

I was glad to get back to Buffalo in the spring of 1967 to see everyone. Donna and I had written each other often and now I was able to see her every day. Life was wonderful again.

One big event we were looking forward to was her senior prom. She spent weeks looking at dresses with her girlfriend, until they both picked out just the ones they wanted. The day of the prom, she spent hours getting ready. As she was having the final touches done on her hair, I went to pick up my tuxedo from the rental department of a men's clothing store. I had a couple of hours before the prom and went home to get dressed. I started putting on the pants and something didn't seem right. They were too tight around the waist and they hung a couple of inches above my ankles. I'll fix this, I figured. I pushed them down on my hips to try to cover my ankles, and then put on the cummerbund to cover the low waistband. It still didn't look right. Also, the jacket was too small. My shirt-sleeves stuck out several inches, the coat barely buttoned, and it was so short it looked more like a bib than a jacket. I felt bad because I knew how important the prom was for Donna. She had been preparing for months and wanted everything to be perfect. And now I looked like a clown.

I called the store but they had nothing in my size. I was stuck. I had to call Donna to explain what had happened.

"Hi, babe, how are you doin?' I asked.

"Fine. I'm just about ready," she said. "I hope you like my dress."

"I'll love it," I said. "I'll bet it looks great. And it fits okay?"

"Yes, it fits perfectly," she said. She sounded so happy. "How are you coming? Did you get the tux?"

"Yes, I got the tux. And things are going okay, except I have one little problem."

"Oh. What's that," her voiced dropped slightly.

"Well, the tux is a little small. I called the store to get another one, but they don't have one in my size and they say it's too late to get one from another store."

She was silent for a moment, but then recovered. "Well, don't worry about it. We're going to have a good time whether it fits right or not."

"That's great, babe. I'm so glad to hear you say that. I was worried. I know how much the prom means to you."

I put on the tux and went over to her house. Her girlfriend and her boyfriend were there and we all had a big laugh. Then we had pictures taken of the four of us. We went to the prom and had a great time. In the darkness of the dance floor, I don't know if anyone noticed my tux. If they did, no one seemed to care. I didn't. I was happy just holding Donna in my arms. We danced and danced. During *Misty*, by Johnny Mathis, I pressed her gently against me and my heart skipped. Such a romantic song and one of my favorites. I closed my eyes and felt our bodies move together to the music. It was dreamy as we floated across the dance floor. Her scent was intoxicating and I felt lightheaded and knew again why I fell in love with her. Yes, life was good.

Of course, we couldn't spend every hour of the day in each other's arms, as much as we might like to. We had to work. She got a job as a checker in a grocery store. I went back to work on the surveying crew.

I also hooked up with George and Howard and some other friends and we rented an apartment together on the ground floor of an older two-story house. It was less than a half a block from the University on Merrimac Street. A group of guys lived upstairs. They were students at the university and I learned they were from New York City. The houses in this neighborhood were built in the early 1900's, before there were many cars, so they were tall and very close together, with very small yards and no driveways. We had a big living room with dark wood paneling, half-walls mid-way back with pillars and mirrors set into the cabinets. There was a long hall with three small bedrooms, one right after the other. But best of all was the front porch.

It was big, with a solid two-foot high wooden railing wall that enclosed the area, and a large overhanging roof. We had an old overstuffed couch out there, which had clumps of stuffing sticking out from under a faded green cover. It sagged and creaked in the middle when you sat on it, and slowly groaned over to one side, but everyone loved it. We had a beat-up armchair there too, along with some mismatched metal kitchen chairs with the red vinyl seat covers half ripped off. We'd sit out there every night drinking beer, listening to Bob Dylan and the Rolling Stones on the record player in the living room, and talking.

Well, we didn't actually live there. My mom would have been crushed if I had come home after being away for nine months and then moved out. Same with the other guys. So we mostly lived at our parent's houses, went to work during the day, and went to Merrimac in the evenings and on weekends to hang out and party.

My daily routine was pretty much the same all summer. Get up in the morning and go to work – slopping through swamps and fighting off mosquitoes. Then come home and eat dinner. Then go over to pick up Donna and meet our friends at Merrimac.

Most nights other friends would come by. Some of the other guys had girlfriends and sometimes other girls would stop by, so it was a nice social atmosphere. Usually around ten at night, when things were quieting down, Donna and I would go back to the middle bedroom and make love until midnight or 1:00 am in the morning, and then fall asleep until 2:00 am or 3:00 am. Then we'd wake up, and I'd take her home. Then I'd go home, slip quietly into the house so as not to wake my parents or brothers, and flop into bed. Two or three hours later the loud ring of the alarm clock would jolt me out of my stupor, and I'd drag myself out of bed to go to work. When I got home, I was so exhausted that I'd fall asleep for an hour or two, then eat dinner, and do the whole routine all over again. It was great. I loved it.

Donna and I also went out to movies, the park, art shows, bars where there was music and dancing, out to eat, to the river, Niagara Falls, shopping, or we just watched TV at her house.

One day we were at the mall shopping. "Tommy asked Janie to marry him," Donna told me, looking deeply into my eyes. They were friends from her high school. They had been going together for a couple of years and I had also become friends with them.

"That's great," I answered. "Have they set a date?"

"No, not yet. But they're planning a wedding for later this summer." She looked at me again with her hopeful brown eyes as if to say; 'when are you going to ask me?' I knew she wanted to get married, and so did I. I was wildly in love with her. We had talked about marriage. But I just didn't feel ready yet. I had too many things on my mind, the most pressing of which was, how would I support us and still go to school?

"Are they planning on having kids right away?" I continued.

"Janie wants to, and I think Tommy does too. She and I went out just before you got home and we looked at baby clothes. They're so cute. You know how much I want to have children."

"Yes, I know, honey. I just need to get some things straightened out, and then, well, we'll be following them shortly." She looked up at me and smiled and put her arm through mine and pulled me against her.

"I hope so. You know how much I love you."

"Yes. I know. And I love you. You're the most important person in my life. But I'd like to keep going to college and we have to figure out how we'll support ourselves."

"They're getting ready to give me full-time hours at the supermarket," she explained, "and if you can work part-time, we can make it."

"Yes. Somehow we'll make it happen," I assured her.

Everyone figured we'd get married. When I was at her house, we'd sit on the couch in the living room in front of the TV, and after a little family time together, her parents and younger sister and brother would leave us alone in the living room.

One evening after watching a couple of sit-coms, her parents went to bed. Donna and I snuggled closer together on the couch, and I put my arm around her shoulders and she put her head on my arm. A movie came on and we settled down to watch it. I kissed her softly on the top of her head and she turned toward me and we kissed on the lips. It was heavenly and I didn't want to stop. Soon we were in each other's arms, kissing passionately. We made out some more and soon we were on the floor making love, as quietly as we could. But apparently not quietly enough.

"My Dad heard us last night," Donna said the next day when I picked her up.

"He did?" I asked, with a little concern in my voice. "How do you know?"

"Because he told me."

"What did he say?" I asked.

"He asked me why I give it to you so much."

"What did you say?"

"I told him that I love you."

I leaned over and kissed her on the cheek. "I love you too."

I was a little nervous and embarrassed the next time I saw him, but he never said anything to me about it. He was a construction worker and he was huge. He could have crushed me if he wanted. But her parents and I liked each other and we got along well. They figured we were going to get married, so that helped. I was kind of like family. Her mom mentioned to Donna and me one day that she'd like to have a big painting of some flowers she saw in a magazine, so I offered to do a painting of them for her. I painted them with bright colors on a five-foot tall canvas. The painting turned out okay but I thought I could make it better and told her I would work on it some more. She said no and seemed to like it and hung it in the living room. I don't know if she really did or was just being nice. Anyway, we tried to be quieter during our late night romances.

I also worked on my own art. Sometimes Donna and I would go into the middle bedroom at Merrimac earlier in the evening, or during the day on the weekend, and she would pose for me. I would draw her, but looking at her naked drove me crazy. I was more interested in making love to her than drawing her. So I would draw her for as long as I could, and then these modeling sessions would end in torrid, passionate love-making. Sometimes the drawing got done, sometimes it didn't.

While my main interest was in the fine arts, I did some commercial art. That summer, my dad asked me if I wanted to do two large drawings to be included in the décor of a restaurant he was involved in. I said I would. The restaurant was the Packet Inn, located on the old Erie Canal in the city of Tonawanda, 15 miles north of where I grew up. He gave me photographs of DeWitt Clinton, Governor of New York State in the 1820's when the canal was being dug, and Nathan Roberts, one of the chief engineers on the project. I did two large, 2' X 3' pen and ink drawings of these men, and they hung in the Packet Inn until it closed in the mid 1980's. Those drawings are now at the Erie Canal Discovery Center in nearby Lockport, another major hub on the old Erie Canal.

George, Howard and I got to know the guys who were living upstairs at the Merrimac Street apartment and sometimes we'd party together. They were a year or two ahead of us in school and seemed pretty wise. One guy, Barry, was the editor of the school newspaper, *The Spectrum*. They all were against the war in Vietnam and would explain to me why we shouldn't be there.

One evening at a party at our apartment, Barry was talking to his roommates, Bob and John, and I was standing nearby and overheard their conversation.

"Did you hear? US forces said they killed 1300 Communists in the Central Highlands last week."

"Of course they're all Communists when they're dead," Bob remarked sarcastically. "I wonder how many were old men, women and children? It's sickening."

"Probably a lot," added John. "Did you see the reports from the Stockholm War Crimes Tribunal? They said there was widespread killing of civilians by the US military."

I had heard this before. It was disturbing. Very disturbing.

"How did you get reports from the Stockholm Tribunal?" I asked.

"It was mailed to us at *The Spectrum* office," Barry responded. "*The Spectrum* has been against the war for a couple of years now, so we get on a lot of anti-war mailing lists."

"I heard something about the Stockholm Tribunal," I continued, "but I don't remember seeing much in the news about it."

"No, of course not," Bob chimed in. "Because there was hardly anything in the news about it. Delegates from 100 countries, including elected leaders, top investigators, scientists, historians, journalists and artists testified to firsthand knowledge of US war crimes against civilians in Vietnam!" he said in a loud and angry voice. "Napalming people, bombing and burning down whole villages, killing women and children. And for what? To keep a dictatorial government in power, which is hated by its own people, so corporate America can get what they want from Southeast Asia. The mass media is a part of this corporate ruling class and they purposely didn't report on the Stockholm Tribunal."

"Yeah, they figured it wouldn't be too good for the war effort," John quipped.

I was speechless. I didn't really understand everything Bob was saying, but the killing of innocent people kept coming up again and again. I had a sick feeling in my stomach, like when I saw such blatant racism and poverty in Florida, but worse. If what Bob was saying was true, it was too frightening to contemplate.

Just then George walked up.

"Hey, let's get another beer," he said to me, pointing to the almost empty beer bottle that I was holding in front of my chest. He grabbed my arm and we headed to the kitchen.

As we entered, I saw Howard and Ned standing by the refrigerator talking. Ned was another friend from high school who was also going to the University of Buffalo.

"When I graduate, my goal is to make a lot of money," I heard Ned say.

"Yeah, but what if you get drafted?" Howard asked.

"I'll just go in and get it over with."

"But Ned," I interjected, "what if you get killed? You won't be able to make much money if you're dead."

He looked at me sickly, opened his mouth but nothing came out.

"Why would you want to go into the service and possibly get sent to Vietnam," I continued, "and fight in a war where innocent people on all sides are being killed and maimed? There are all these reports about atrocities. The guy we're supporting is a dictator. So what are we fighting for there anyway? You know this war is wrong." George handed me a cold beer.

Ned regained his composure and looked at me with a slight frown on his face. "That's the way war is." He paused for a moment. "Hey, look, I don't want to rock the boat. I want to do what's easiest. I want to be able to get a good job and be accepted in the community. I'm not going to go to Canada or jail," he said indignantly. "I don't want anything negative on my record."

"Yes, but don't you think you'll have something negative on your record if you go over there and kill innocent people...?"

"Well, hopefully that won't happen," he interrupted. "Look, I love this country, and I'm not going to do anything against our government."

"I love this country too," I responded. "And I want to be accepted in the community too. But I'm not going to go over there and kill innocent people – people that have done nothing against us. And for what? The government over there is hated by its own people. Why should we support it? I'm not going to. If I'm ostracized by the community, then I'll deal with it. Sometimes we have to stand up for what's right, even if we're alone. This is one of those times."

Just then, Donna walked up behind me and put her arms around my waist.

"Hey, I've missed you," she said softly in my ear. "Let's go out on the porch to get some fresh air." The house was filled with cigarette smoke and a noise level that was escalating.

"Hey Ned," a drunken voice called out from the back porch. Ned stuck his head out the back door and yelled something back. We didn't hear it because we had gone into the living room where the record player was turned up full blast. Mick Jagger was singing, "I can't get no, sa tis fac tion."

We moved through the crowd and out the front door.

"What were you guys talking about?" Donna asked when we got onto the porch.

"The war, and how wrong it is. Ned says he'll just go if he gets drafted."

"Why do you keep bringing it up," she asked.

"Because it's important. The government is drafting kids to go over there and fight. And what for? To support an unpopular government in South Vietnam? No one can give a good answer. Meanwhile, innocent people on all sides are being killed and maimed. My dad and many other people risked their lives fighting Hitler in WWII. Someone had to stop Hitler from goose-stepping across the world and putting people in gas chambers. I can understand that. But this war isn't like that. Most kids don't even know why they are going. And some are coming home in wheelchairs and boxes. Remember Patrick, from high school? He went over there and got shot and now he's home paralyzed for life."

"Yes, yes, I remember. But there's nothing we can do about it," she pleaded. "Let's just hope you don't get drafted, and if you do, that nothing happens to you. We have to think about our future. You and me and our family. You know how much I want to have children."

"Yes, but what kind of future will we have if I go over there and fight for the wrong cause? Or kill innocent people? What kind of America are we creating? Not the kind I grew up believing in. And if we have children, and I get killed over there, what will happen to them? They'll grow up without a father."

"Oh please, Paul, let's not talk about it any longer. It's so depressing."

We stood on the porch and looked out into the street. The night air was cool and a lot fresher than inside. The lampposts cast cones of light onto the pavement. We watched silently as a car passed and headed toward the university. Donna stood at the railing facing the street and I stood behind her. I put my arms around her waist and she leaned back against me. I just wanted all the problems and confusion around us to go away.

While most of my friends weren't lining up to enlist in the service, if they got called, they said they'd go. What was worse, few of them wanted to even talk about the war. They were more interested in drinking and partying and pretending the war wasn't there. I couldn't understand that. If the war was wrong, then we had to figure out some way to stop it. Refusing to participate was the right first step. Nazi soldiers didn't get any sympathy at the Nuremberg War Crimes Tribunal by claiming that they were "just following orders." Nuremberg said that people must be accountable to a higher law and that it was the personal responsibility of each person to do the right thing. I didn't learn much in high school, but I remembered that. My parents taught me about personal responsibility and I believed in it.

I wanted to get my mind off this stuff. "Let's go back inside," I said.

A week later I received an envelope from the Ontario College of Art in Toronto. I slowly opened it and took out the letter. I was accepted! OCA was considered among the top one or two art schools in Canada, and stacked up well against the best art schools in the US. Over 300 students applied for 30 openings for the next First Year Class, and I was one of those accepted! I was ecstatic! I would begin that fall. I immediately went over to Donna's house to tell her the good news. Toronto was a good choice for a couple of reasons. It was only a two-hour drive from Buffalo. And it was in Canada. I had been thinking about our future, and the war wasn't in it.

"That's great that you got accepted," she said. "I'm excited for you. You know I think you are really a great artist."

"Thanks, babe, I really appreciate you saying that. And, if they try to draft me, I can just stay there. And you can join me. We'd be together and the war couldn't hurt us. What do you think?"

She hesitated for a moment and the smile dropped from her face. "Yes. Yes. That sounds okay. But would you be able to come back here?"

"As long as I haven't broken any law I can come back here," I explained. "And I haven't, yet. As long as they don't draft me, I can go back and forth whenever I want. But if they try to draft me, and if I stayed in Canada, then if I came back here, they could arrest me."

"What would happen then?" she asked. I could see she wasn't happy thinking about this.

"Well, I could get five years in prison and be fined up to $10,000. That's what the law says. But I don't know if they're prosecuting everyone who refuses to be drafted. It might not come to that," I tried to comfort her.

"Could they do anything to me?" she asked.

"No, I don't think so. You won't have broken any law."

She was silent for a moment. "Well, if it comes to that, I'll move to Canada with you. But I don't like it that I wouldn't be able to come back here without you. My family is here, and it would be hard to live so far apart from them." She looked worried.

"I know. I'm sorry," I said. "I don't know what else to do. I want us to be together and have a future, but this war is not good for us. Look. I'll be going up to Toronto in September. I'll check things out. Canada is a nice place. I've been there a lot as a kid. When I was younger, I didn't even realize that Canada was a different country. It's just like the US in many ways." I was trying to assure her that everything would be all right. "Anyway, it's only a two hour drive from here, so I'll come home to see you every weekend."

The summer went on and we tried to avoid the subject of the war. Donna and I saw each other every day and cherished each moment together. Soon the summer was coming to an end and it was time to pack and get ready to move to Toronto.

Chapter 9

Toronto

Finally the day arrived to leave and I had mixed emotions. It was the fall of 1967. I was excited to be going to a top rated art school, and in Canada where I could put some distance between me and the war, but I didn't want to leave Donna. I packed my suitcase and art supplies into my Volkswagen bug and said good-bye to everyone. Donna and I hugged and a tear ran down her cheek. I felt terrible. I didn't want to leave her again.

After about a 30 minute drive, I approached the Peace Bridge that would take me into Canada. I had crossed this bridge many times before and never thought anything about it, but now I was a little apprehensive. I wondered if my move to Canada would some day become permanent and that I might never be able to go home again. As I drove onto Canadian soil I felt a sense of freedom – freedom from the terrible decision of my government to go to war against a people who posed no threat to us whatsoever.

When I got to Toronto, I went to the area around the art school and looked for a place to stay until I found an apartment. There was a YMCA nearby, so I checked in there. It was okay, but depressing. There were drunks and down-and-outers on the front steps and in the lobby and sitting on the beds of their rooms with their doors open. I wondered what had happened in their lives to land them in a place that was one step from the street. Did they start life with hope and promise, and then fall? I had hope for my future, but seeing them made me wonder if that could happen to me. Sure, I was an art student at a good art school. But many very good artists starve. Van Gogh sold only one or two of his paintings during his lifetime and for very modest amounts. He survived only because his brother sent him money regularly. I tried not to think about that.

Once in my room, I lay on the bed and stared up at the ceiling. An incredible feeling of loneliness gripped me. Suddenly, I had to get out of that room. I lurched forward and went hurriedly out onto the crowded streets. I walked for blocks, looking in store windows and at all the people rushing by. That helped a little, and as dinnertime approached, I stopped at a restaurant and got something to eat. I walked some more after dinner, and when it got dark, I headed back to my dreary little room at the Y. As I entered the square box, the feeling of loneliness gripped me again. What was I getting myself into, I wondered? Will I be here forever, never to return to my home in the United States? It was a bad feeling.

On Monday, I went to school, got my class schedule and started attending classes. I checked a bulletin board where students had posted signs for roommates and called several of the phone numbers. After three days, I hooked up with a couple of guys from Ottawa, Bruce and Ron, who had rented a five bedroom apartment on the upper two floors of an old house on Grace Street in the heart of Little Italy. I went over and looked at the place and moved in. The bedrooms were small and the kitchen was the size of a closet, but I started feeling better immediately.

Bruce and Ron were nice guys. They both were Industrial Design majors, getting training in drafting, product design and other skills to work for manufacturing companies. I told them my feelings about the war in Vietnam, and they were sympathetic. They weren't political, but they couldn't understand why the United States was at war in Vietnam, and they understood why young American boys would move to Canada to avoid it. In fact, I found the majority of Canadians I spoke with sympathetic to Americans who didn't want to go to Vietnam and many welcomed me to their country. I still have a warm spot in my heart for Canadians today for their kindness toward me in 1967.

Of course, all societies have some oddballs. One was Real, a strange guy from Montreal. He moved into our house and took the fourth bedroom. He was an avid supporter of the arch conservative Ayn Rand. Shortly thereafter, a friend of mine from high school, John, an aspiring poet, moved to Toronto after he received his draft notice and he moved in with us. I was happy to help John escape from the clutches of the US military. The four artists in the house got along well, but Real didn't fit in. He kept pushing this nutty philosophy about each individual standing alone and doing everything for himself without any responsibility to others. We all argued with him and soon he left. His room was then taken by a painter from the Art School, Jack. It was a great bunch of guys, all artists, living on the second and third floors of a house together. We cooked in our tiny kitchen on the second floor, and then ate outside on a small balcony where we also sat after dinner in the evening. When I looked across the tiny backyards, most were filled with vegetable gardens, flowers and other growing things. It was life affirming and that felt good.

Our lives revolved around art. We did art all day at the art college, but also well into the night at home. Bruce had a big closet in his room that he converted into a photographic darkroom, and we spent hours in there developing photographs, experimenting with all sorts of artistic developing techniques. We'd go in at 7:00 pm, after dinner, work for what we figured was an hour or two, and come out and learn that it was 11:30 pm.

I had classes in drawing, design, 3-demensional design, advertising, perspective, lettering, and painting. In our class on three-dimensional design, we had to create a completely enclosed three-dimensional form with one sheet of 8 1/2 x 11 card stock by only folding it – we could not cut it, and not allow any portion of the paper to overlap another portion. I folded and refolded a lot of sheets of paper until I finally created an interesting three-dimensional design that met the assignment's criteria. Most of the students arrived at symmetrical enclosed forms: mine was asymmetrical, and looked like an abstract sculpture, which is just what I wanted.

I also enjoyed drawing and painting classes, and worked in charcoal, conte crayon, india ink, watercolor, and oil paints. I experimented with different styles and liked doing landscapes and people. I drew faces using simple lines and different pen and ink techniques to show various human emotions. I used conte crayons to depict the female form from models in life drawing class where my shading expressed softness, motion, harmony and serenity. When I was doing these drawings I was transported to another world. I felt connected to the subjects I was drawing and the feelings they were expressing. If my subject conveyed peace and beauty, those feelings were conveyed to me and then to the drawing.

I was mesmerized by how color, shape, line and shading could evoke emotions. Often, just a slight change in color or shading would change the emotion of a picture. A little more red or yellow, or a hint of orange blended softly into the background made a picture warmer. Blue is normally a cool color, but it can evoke a number of emotions. It can be regal, brilliant, bold, refreshing, cold, chilling, dreary or something else. But the edge can be taken off a dreary blue by adding lighter blues, light grays or bits of warm colors and the initial feeling of melancholy can be cheered up. When a predominately blue painting has hints of red or yellow, the feeling isn't usually a lighthearted happiness, but rather a deeper, more complex feeling, perhaps a reflection of hardship that is being overcome. When I was in my art world, it was my own world and it was wonderful.

But, like most people, I also needed people in my life. Art by itself wasn't enough. When people were nice, it's great, but when they were not, it's not. While I liked practically all of my teachers, my English teacher and I didn't hit it off too well.

Mrs. Jones was middle-aged with jet-black dyed hair and had an arrogant attitude. I probably wouldn't have noticed her frumpy, square-shaped body balancing precariously on two stick legs if she hadn't acted so haughtily, but since she did, I grew to dislike everything about her. I rarely feel that way about anyone, but my distain for her came to the surface one day when she had us read a book out loud in class that was sexually quite explicit. I didn't have that much of a problem with the content of the book. What bothered me was that the teacher had students read especially racy parts out loud in front of the entire class and she seemed to get enjoyment watching the students squirm. This seemed sick to me. By the third class I was angry. I hated to see anyone embarrassed or humiliated so I raised my hand.

"I think this is degrading," I announced with conviction.

"You do," she retorted. "Do you think we shouldn't read it? You're not advocating censorship, are you?"

"Well, no. I'm not for censorship. I just don't think we should be reading something like this – it's degrading to women, and men," I added.

"This is literature. It's art. You should know that. You're all art students. The author is trying to tell us something. *You* may not like it," she said emphasizing the word "you" and looking right at me, "but others may not be offended by it. Who are you to judge? More importantly, the author has a right to express his feelings, and it is incumbent upon us to respect his right of expression and to determine if there is anything we can learn from this."

I didn't really disagree with what she said, but she was mixing up having students read it out loud, and the actual content. If someone wanted to read this stuff by themselves, that was their business. But forcing people to read it out loud in front of others seemed perverse to me. I thought there has to be a line somewhere between freedom of expression and the degradation of others.   But I couldn't put my feelings into words. I was silent and felt humiliated and defeated.

I thought of how I had handled a similar situation back in high school when I was going out with Lynn, my girlfriend before Donna. I went into the boy's bathroom one day, and Jeff, a guy who was a jerk and who I knew a little, was there.

"I heard you're going out with Lynn?" he asked.

"Yeah," I responded.

"Did you get in her pants yet?"

"Fuck you, Jeff!" I blurted out in anger. He quickly left.

I knew I couldn't tell my English teacher to "fuck off." I had to defeat her with good arguments, but I was stumped. I couldn't figure how to do it. I also wondered why some people seemed to get enjoyment out of watching others who are humiliated or embarrassed. I was angry, but this defeat led me to vow that I would learn how to verbally take on those who disrespected and abused anyone.

Other than that incident, my life was art during the week and Donna on the weekends. My body and head were in Toronto, but my heart was in Buffalo. Every Friday afternoon after my last art class, I headed back across the border to be with Donna Friday night, Saturday and Sunday.

In early September 1967, I heard on the news that elections were held in South Vietnam, and that the current leaders, Thieu and Ky, had been re-elected President and Vice President.   Opposition candidates and others charged that the election was rigged. But US election observers said the election was fair. Maybe this election would calm things down, I thought. It didn't. Only days after the election a fierce four-day battle raged south of Danang where nearly 500 American and Vietnamese were killed. The election didn't seem to help at all. A year or two later I read a report by independent election observers who wrote that widespread election fraud had taken place.

In October of 1967, the US anti-war movement made headlines. Major protest demonstrations involving many thousands of people were held in cities across the United States at draft induction centers to protest the draft and the war. In Oakland, 125 people were arrested for trying to shut down the draft center. Later that month, 100,000 people marched in Washington, D.C. against the war, and a week after that, demonstrations took place on college campuses against recruiters for Dow Chemical Company, which manufactured napalm for use in Vietnam. I was riveted by these events. I saw these things reported in the Canadian news, and to a lesser extent in Buffalo newspapers and on TV when I was in Buffalo on the weekends. The US student movement was also growing, with a plethora of activities including student strikes around student empowerment, educational reform, stopping the war in Vietnam, supporting the civil rights movement, and equal rights for women. I watched with interest and sympathy.

The Ontario College of Art was not immune from this social and political turmoil. We had a student strike over the firing of two popular painting instructors. The painting students felt pretty passionate about it, and they got support from many of the other fine art students and a number of the commercial art students. I joined in picketing and in marches and attended forums to learn about the issue.

I felt that fighting to rehire the fired painting teachers was important, and I gladly participated in most of the strike activities. But on the big issues facing society – like the war, poverty, racism and injustice, few students at the art college seemed very interested. I was all for students' rights, but we had to look beyond just fighting for ourselves. Especially when the stakes were so much higher for others. I saw art as a way to humanize society and express human emotions. But many of my fellow art students were so engrossed in their work that it seemed liked they used their art to escape from the outside world. That was troubling to me. Perhaps this was because most of these big issues were convulsing the United States and not Canada. And these were, after all, overwhelmingly Canadian students.

Even though I was living in Canada and could have stayed there indefinitely, I felt drawn to somehow take a stronger stand against the war. The United States was my home, my country, and I felt a personal responsibility to help correct the wrongs that I saw there. I wasn't sure exactly how to do that, other than to keep talking to the people around me.

One weekend night I was sitting in Donna's kitchen after watching the news on TV which included the latest killings, maimings and other horrors.

"The war is so wrong," I began. "We should get out of Vietnam. Innocent people are being killed and it goes on and on. And 18 and

19 year olds are getting drafted and sent over there to fight, supposedly to protect democracy, and we can't even vote for the man who is ordering us to go. It's not fair."

"What are you talking about?" her mother exclaimed with a slight tone of indignation in her voice as she scrubbed vegetables in the sink. "There have always been wars and injustice in the world and there always will be. The world isn't fair. Accept it. There is nothing you can do about it." Donna shrugged her shoulders and kind of nodded in agreement.

I couldn't accept it. I had to talk about these things and wanted someone, especially Donna, to understand me. I would say something about the war and Donna would say lets not talk about that. I became more adamant in wanting to talk about it, and she became more adamant in not wanting to talk about it. Now we had a new issue to deal with. We couldn't talk about something that was important to me. I was being torn between my love for her and my feelings that I had to do something to try an end this terrible war and injustice.

I started to feel that Donna and I were maybe growing apart a little, and it scared me. It was very painful and I didn't know what to do about it. It started slowly, but gradually worsened. I loved her, but I sometimes felt disconnected from her, and she probably did from me. We started having fights over little things that we wouldn't have fought over before. Then we'd make up, then fight again. But there were also really good times. Then, I felt connected to her again and we were back on track. Love was in the air and life was great. As long as the war didn't come up. When we kept focused on each other, our love blossomed, like it did over the Christmas holidays in December of 1967.

In late January 1968 I was listening to the news and heard the latest report from Vietnam. A massive uprising took place throughout South Vietnam that shook the entire country. It was called the Tet offensive. The insurgents, called the Vietcong by our leaders and media, attacked US and South Vietnamese forces in all of South Vietnam's seven largest cities, including Saigon itself, and in 30 provincial capitals from the Mekong Delta in the south to the Demilitarized Zone in the north. Thousands of people were killed, and by early February, President Johnson claimed a military victory for the US. But that's not how I felt, nor did other people I talked with. One weekend evening when I was in Buffalo having dinner with my family, the Tet offensive came up.

"Johnson says that the Vietcong is a small band of terrorists who have no support among the people," I began. "How did they carry off such a massive, nationwide insurrection then during the Tet offensive?" I asked.

"Nobody can predict how a war is going to go," my father responded. "There are ups and downs. But that doesn't mean that we are wrong to be there. We have to stand by our government."

"But the government has been telling us that things were looking up, that they were winning the war and that peace was just around the corner. Now this Tet offensive blew that theory to pieces. It seems that so much of what the government says is hard to believe. They say the South Vietnamese government is for freedom and democracy, but it doesn't seem like they have much support from the people. And Johnson says we are over there to help protect the South Vietnamese people, but a lot of them don't seem to want us to be there. And a lot of people are asking what we're fighting for over there."

"We're there to stop the spread of communism," my dad responded firmly. "You wouldn't want to live in a country where you're told what to do and think, would you?"

"I feel like Johnson is telling us what to do and think right now."

My brother Lee didn't say anything and just kept on eating. My brother Jim was away at a music high school in Michigan.

"Please, let's not talk about this at the dinner table," my mom pleaded. "We don't get to spend much time together as a family anymore, except at dinner, so let's talk about something else." There was a pause and everyone was quiet. "How was your day, Paul?" she asked.

"It was okay," I mumbled. But a pall had descended over the dinner table. No one said much after that.

I felt bad. I didn't want to disagree with my dad. But I couldn't understand why he wasn't more concerned about the war and my feelings about it. I thought that if I spoke with my mom alone she might be more sympathetic to my point of view, but with my dad there she didn't say anything. And I didn't expect Lee to have much to say about the war. He was not even sixteen yet, over two years away from having to register for the draft. The response from my dad bothered me. It didn't seem to fit with the values he and my mom taught us? To respect others and treat them fairly. To talk over problems and not fight. Did our government talk over all the problems first with the Vietnamese? Did we have all the facts before going to war? I didn't think so. Worse yet, I could be forced to go over there and kill someone, maybe someone who was innocent. Or I could be killed. My dad and I had disagreed about the war before, but each disagreement made me feel worse. Why didn't he understand me? And why wasn't my mom saying anything? It was painful. I had had disagreements with my parents about other issues, but it didn't change our relationship. That's part of life. But on this issue, the question of war and peace, the stakes were so much higher. These disagreements depressed me and I started feeling estranged from my family. It was a terrible feeling. I didn't want that to happen, but it was.

Donna and I continued seeing each other but our relationship was strained. We went out and tried doing the things that we had enjoyed before, but too often a big dark cloud hung over our heads. She wasn't as happy as before, and neither was I.

One evening we were out and I brought up Vietnam again. She became so upset that she said she didn't feel she could go on with our relationship. I was in a panic. I didn't want to lose her. Later that night, I took 12 long-stemmed red roses over and left them on her door with a note about how much I loved her. I called the next day and she hesitantly agreed to meet and talk and we tried to put our relationship back together again. But the divide was still there. How could something that was so good for so long between us, go so bad? I went over it again and again in my mind. I was depressed, confused and angry. Injustice, pain and suffering were everywhere, society was unraveling all around me, and so was my relationship with Donna. And now with my family. It was a pretty lonely feeling.

I tried to not say anything to her about the war. But one afternoon it came up again. We were sitting in my car in her driveway.

"I can't take it any more," she exclaimed. "You are so fixated on Vietnam. Where do I fit in?"

"I love you and I want us to be together," I implored, "but I just can't ignore what's going on around us."

"Well, I can," she responded, clearly upset. "And I can't live like this. I can't. I can't go on this way. It's just too painful. I can't see you any more." She broke into tears.

"Please, don't say that," I pleaded. I reached over to put my arm around her shoulder.

"No. We've been over this before. We tried to patch up the problems. But it isn't working. I don't want you to call me anymore," she sobbed. "And no more flowers. It's over." She opened the car door and ran to her front door.

I felt liked I had been kicked in the solar plexus. Tears welled up in my eyes as I pulled out of her driveway. Somehow I made it back to Toronto. I went through the motions of going to school, but I couldn't get Donna out of my mind. The weeks blurred together as the semester went on and I did the best I could. My interest in everything plummeted.

On April 4, 1968, two days before my 20th birthday, I was sitting at the kitchen table with Bruce and Ron in our house on Grace Street when a news report came across the radio. Martin Luther King Jr. had been assassinated in Memphis while helping striking garbage workers. We were stunned. The world was spinning out of control again. I heard on the news that riots broke out in black communities all across the United States, and that tens of thousands of soldiers were dispatched to put down the protests. I learned later that over 150 cities were involved over the next five days, and that 46 people were killed and some 27,000 arrested. I was shocked and angered by the racism and brutality. I limped through the rest of the semester and then headed back to Buffalo for the summer.

Part 2: Crisis and Awakening

Chapter 10

Standard Mirror

I went back to live at my parents' house and started looking for a summer job. My parents had a rule. You either had to be in school or working. No loafing around. I agreed with that. I wanted to pull my weight and make a contribution. It was good to be home again, but I wasn't happy. My parents and I got along okay, or so it seemed on the surface. We shared how our day went, talked about the weather, but we avoided Vietnam. I was afraid we would argue and I didn't want that. I don't think they wanted that either. Underneath, I was in pain. The horror of Vietnam was splashed across the nightly TV screen in blood. Yet, no one said anything about it. I had lost Donna over my concern for this terrible killing. I knew the war pained her, but she wanted to just look the other way and ignore it. It seemed like my mom and dad were doing the same thing.

While my parents and I went through the motions of normalcy, I felt that our relationship had changed. I had lost something with them, especially with my dad. My abhorrence of the war came, in part, from the values *they* taught me as a child. Now, when these values were being ripped to pieces by our government, our family and all other families should have been outraged. Instead, there was almost nothing. In that sense, our family wasn't so different from other families. But why did it seem like hardly anyone cared? I couldn't talk to anyone I knew about the one thing that was devouring me. I felt estranged from the world, like I didn't fit in. Or that I fit in, but no one else did. How could a whole nation be so blind and callous to such brutality? People would get upset about a murder in an American city, but were oblivious to mass murder in another country. The hypocrisy was incomprehensible. I had an ache in my heart and nausea in my stomach that never seemed to go away. It kept eating at me, hour after hour, day after day. Even though I had heard about anti-war protests around the country, I still felt alone. I knew that my closest friends, George and Howard, didn't like the war either, but it seemed that I was usually the one who brought it up. I think what hurt the most was that my parents seemed to be siding with the government and the war, and not with me.

I wanted to get a job as quickly as I could. I had to do something to get my mind off these terrible thoughts. The harder the job the better, I thought. Physical labor would help burn off my frustration and anger. I could have talked to my dad and he could have gotten me back on one of the surveying crews. But that wasn't going to work now. For many reasons. I had met Donna when I was surveying, and going back to that work would bring back all the memories of her and the great times we had together. It would be too painful. I had to get her out of my mind. I also thought it would be good to gain a measure of independence and distance from my parents. An entirely different job would help, I thought. Something new to focus my mind on.

A friend from high school told me about a job at a mirror factory in south Buffalo where his girlfriend's dad worked. I had never done factory work before, but it sounded worth pursuing. I saw several positive things in getting such a job. For one, it would give me an opportunity to see how other people lived and worked. I would also learn first-hand about the manufacturing process, something I had found interesting years ago as a junior high school student when I saw the auto factory. I also figured it would be a hard and dirty job, but that seemed to fit my mood. So I went down and applied and was hired. The company was Standard Mirror. It wasn't General Motors, but I learned that it was part of the auto industry — they made rear-view mirrors for cars and trucks. Furthermore, it was a part of the huge manufacturing sector which dominated our Buffalo area economy, employing hundreds of thousands of people. *That* was impressive.

George was still in school. His semester ended after mine. But we agreed when he finished, we'd get an apartment together, and maybe he'd join me at Standard Mirror.

The company was founded around 1910 and made a name for itself producing rearview mirrors for the early Model-T Fords. Rear-view mirrors for the automotive industry comprised 99% of its business. In 1968, Standard Mirror had all the rear-view mirror contracts for Ford and Chrysler in the nation. That seemed like a pretty big deal. I may have helped make the rear-view mirror for people who drove a Ford or Chrysler car or truck built in the late 1960's.

The company's main building was at the end of Milton Street off Seneca near the railroad tracks. The company owned a smaller plant on the next street, Harrison. This was in the heart of the Irish community, and you could see the pride of the people in their Irish heritage in symbols – like the green shamrock, on the fronts of many Irish-owned bars and restaurants throughout south Buffalo. Many Irish-Americans from the neighborhood worked at Standard Mirror, but there were also a large number of Polish-Americans employed there, as a large Polish section of town was nearby on the east side. There were also some workers of Italian and German descent, and other nationalities. Most all of them were second and third generation Americans, so the ethnic differences weren't that pronounced. The company was never big, employing about 250 people on three shifts at its peak. The buildings were made of red brick and were covered with ivy. They looked nice from the outside. Inside was something else.

When I entered the front door my first day at work I heard a rumbling in the distance that sounded like military jeeps on a cobblestone street. I opened the door into the factory and loud crashing, banging and popping sounds assaulted my ears. Dragon-like machines were spitting fire. Black and green pipes and hoses crisscrossed everywhere, hissing like coiled cobras. The once-white tile walls looked like old teeth, coated in a yellowish-brown film after years of smoking. My nostrils sucked in the stink of sulfur, ammonia, oil and other unhappy smells. I had stepped into another world. *This* took my mind off the war, Donna, and the estrangement from my parents.

I was told to find Harvey and he would show me my work area. I had been hired as a Helper on the 84 line, whatever that was. Harvey was one of the big bosses and when I found him, he took me to the time clock and showed me how to punch-in. I noticed a sticker pasted next to the clock that read: "United Glass and Ceramic Workers, Local 44." Someone had written on it in pen: "We are a union shop and don't forget it." We walked through a room with fine mist in the air, down a wide hallway and into another large room.

"This is the polishing department," he announced. "This is where you'll be working." He introduced me to a lanky, bald-headed man with a black horseshoe shaped fringe around the sides and back of his shiny head. He had a big nose and wore black-rimmed glasses which were resting half-way down his nose. "Hi, Jerry. This is the new guy – how do you say your last name?"

"Krehbiel. Paul Krehbiel," I answered.

"Yes. Okay. This is Jerry Kowalski. He's the second shift supervisor for this area. He'll be your boss. You take orders from him. He'll tell you what to do."

I leaned toward Jerry and we shook hands. "Nice to meet you," I said. He pushed his glasses up over the bridge of his nose.

"I'll get you an apron, rubber boots and gloves. You're going to get wet on your job." It was about 2:45 pm and the day shift was finishing up.

Jerry handed me the rain gear and led me to a big square shallow tub of water about eight feet by eight feet. There were four large round forms about three feet in diameter lying face down on the bottom in about four inches of water. The machines were stopped now and the day shift workers were cleaning up the area.

"These forms are called chucks. You lift up a chuck like this," and he reached across the form and pulled it up until it stood on edge like a wheel, "and remove the mirrors with this pick." A mirror fell softly into the water. "Then put the chuck on that cart, rinse off the mirrors and put them in these racks." He put a wooden rack into the tub to show me. "But be careful not to scrape the back of the mirror or you'll scratch the silver off it. That'll ruin the mirror." He looked at me to emphasize the point. "Then put the racks on that hand-truck and push it over there to inspection. See where those other trucks are?" He pointed to an area about thirty feet away near some long metal tables with bright lights overhead and where racks of rearview mirrors were stacked on hand trucks as tall as an average man. "That's where the inspectors check the glass."

"Yes, I see," I responded.

He explained that our department took out any imperfections on the surface of the glass with the fine grinder, and then polished the surface to make it perfect.

"That's pretty much it. Your polisher operator will be in shortly. His name is Mike. He'll give you a few other instructions. Okay?"

"Yes. Okay. Thanks."

Mike came in about ten minutes before 3:00 pm and I was introduced to him. He was about my age, maybe a couple years older. He told me he lived half-way up Harrison, the street behind our plant, and it took him two minutes to walk to work. He was

Irish-American, about 5'10", had a muscular build, and black hair. "I'm an iron worker," he announced proudly. "I worked on the high rise buildings in downtown Buffalo. I'm just working here temporarily until another job opens up."

"Yeah, right." I heard a sarcastic voice behind me and turned to see a young, wiry guy a little shorter than Mike. "He's been here a year. Ever since those guys fell off the bank building from the 15th floor and almost pulled Mike down with 'em he's stayed right here."

"That's bullshit, Joey," Mike exclaimed defensively. "My name's on the list. I haven't been called back yet. Anyway, I've got to be around here to keep an eye on you guys to make sure you don't fuck up this job."

Joey ignored him and extended his hand toward me. "My name is Joey. I'm the fine grinder operator on this line. You must be the new guy."

"Yeah. My name is Paul." We shook hands.

"I don't know if anybody explained to you what's going on here."

"Well, Jerry told me about my job. About pulling the mirrors out of that tub of water and racking them up for inspection."

"Yeah, that's good. You'll also have to get material for the machine operators. It's over there in that other room." He took me over to show me. "We'll show you what to do until you get the hang of it."

"Thanks. I appreciate that."

We returned just as the buzzer sounded to start our shift. As the machines started up, the loud banging and crashing started again. Soon, there was water and slimy brown polish and broken glass all over the place. I had to sweep the floor and squeegee it periodically so we wouldn't slip and fall. My job was pretty simple but had enough variety to keep it from getting too boring. It was hard physical work, and at the end of the day my arms and back were sore and I was soaked. But it was okay. I was so tired I slept good that night.

After a couple of weeks I was getting adjusted to my new job and environment. I still thought about Donna and missed her, but I was so busy at work that it helped me take my mind off her and the war, at least while I was at work.

I started to notice things that went on in the factory. Everyday I had to walk through the glass-cutting department to get to my department. The glasscutters worked very quickly and constantly cut their fingers. It was common to see them with two, three or more band-aids on their fingers at any given time. One day I saw a glasscutter slice her finger so badly that blood poured onto the mirrors. Someone rushed up and took the bloody mirrors out of the stack, wiped the dripping blood off her finger and slapped on a band-aid, and the cutter kept cutting. A lot of blood went into making those mirrors, I thought. I was glad I didn't work in that department.

I asked Mike why the glasscutters worked so fast.

"It's their quota. The glasscutters got fucked when the company did the time study there." I wasn't sure what that meant.

The worst part was the mist. That came from the beveling department, which was right next to the glass-cutting department. A fog hung in the air that made everything hazy. But it was a deadly fog, because it had fine, ground-up glass in it. One day I was assigned to work there to fill in for a worker who was out sick. After three or four hours, it felt like someone was rubbing sandpaper across my throat.

Mike and Joey showed me how to use the overhead crane to take the mirrors off the polisher and gently drop them into the water tub. I also learned something about the polisher and fine grinder operator's jobs by watching what they did, and then trying it myself. The work was hard and dirty, but the whole process was pretty interesting.

All the workers were members of the union. That meant after your 30-day probationary period you had to join the union in order to keep working there. I don't remember hearing anyone complain about having to join the union. Sometimes you'd hear people gripe about something the union did or didn't do, but they never said, 'I don't want to join the union,' or 'let's get rid of the union here because I don't like what they do.' I heard people make a complaint or suggestion to a union steward or a union officer, and sometimes I'd hear them say they were going to the union meeting to talk about the issue.

I didn't know much about unions, but I learned quickly. One day I heard a supervisor yell at a worker in our department to work faster. They were about thirty feet from me. A big, stocky worker stepped out from behind a machine and went over to them and yelled back at the supervisor, though I couldn't make out what he said over the noise.

"Who is that?' I asked Joey.

95

"That's Ed. He's the union Steward for our department."

"I've heard of a union steward, but what do they do exactly?"

"Well, the steward is our representative," Joey explained. "He speaks up for us to the company. He helps us take care of problems on the job. If you've got a problem, especially with Jerry or any of the other bosses, go talk to Ed."

"Do you guys ever speak up to management, or is it just Ed?"

"No. We speak up too. But we elected Ed steward because he's tough. And he's smart. He gives us a lot of good ideas on what to do to stop the company from fucking with us. And he really tries to protect the people. He's one of the best."

A couple of days later I got to see Ed in action again. The Personnel Manager was walking through our department when Ed spotted her. He left his machine, walked across the department to cut her off in the isle. They were only about ten feet from where I was working.

"What do you mean telling the workers in beveling to do 1,900 mirrors!" he bellowed. "That's not their quota! Their quota is 1,700." I could hear his booming voice over the din of the machines.

The personal manager was stunned and speechless.

"You know that's not right, Noreen," he continued in a loud and angry voice. "We've told them to do 1,700 and no more. That's all they're doing. 1,700. Understand?" He leaned forward and stared at her.

She turned and quickly walked away. People nearby cheered and laughed. A smile crept across Ed's face and he looked over at us and winked. I was impressed. I wanted to find out more about this union so I decided to go to a union meeting.

Chapter 11

United Glass Workers Union

One afternoon I asked Mike when and where the union meetings were held. He said they were held at a near-by tavern an hour after the day shift ended.

"But we're at work then. How can we attend?"

"That's a problem," Mike responded. "Some people just take the time off and go. Ed goes all the time because he's our steward. I wouldn't advise that you take off and go because you're still new here. Wait 'til you've been here a little longer. Or, if you really want to go, try to switch shifts."

A week later I saw a notice on the union bulletin board for an opening for a polisher operator in my department on the graveyard shift. It paid more money and was a better job than the helper's job, so I applied for it and I got it. I would also now be able to go to the union meetings.

Since the meetings were held so close to the plant, some of the guys from the day shift would go over there right after work to pound down some beers before the meeting started. By then they were drunk and the meetings were often raucous affairs. It was only a handful of guys, but that was enough to disrupt things. The union officers frowned on this and made repeated appeals to the members to refrain from drinking before union meetings. I made plans to attend the next one.

The meeting was gaveled to order by Dave, the president. He said he wanted to take up an issue of importance before we started the official agenda.

"We have discussed the problem of drinking before union meetings for the past two meetings," Dave began, "and it's still a problem. Look, we can't get all of our business accomplished when people come in here drunk." Just then, a little skinny guy with a red nose stood up, staggered into the aisle and screamed in a slurred voice: "whada ya mean drunk? I'm not drunk. I can hold my liquor better than any of youse in this place. And if any of youse says I'm drunk again, you can step outside right now.' I asked the guy next to me who that was.

"That's Jimmy. He's a drunk," the guy answered.

Jimmy then grabbed a chair as he was about to fall on his face, swayed to and fro, and was helped back into his seat where he slumped against a near-by post. He looked a little over 5' tall, and maybe 115 pounds. The guy next to me said he was in his fifties, but he looked at least ten years older to me.

People were laughing and hooting. "Hey, Jimmy, I say you're drunk!" one husky young guy yelled across the room. "Ready to go outside?" Everyone laughed again because Jimmy didn't hear a word of it. He'd passed out or fallen asleep with his head propped up against the pole.

"Order! Order!" the president demanded. "We've been over this before. As you can see, we can't have a productive meeting when people have had too much to drink."

"Yeah, yeah, yeah," muttered one of Jimmy's drinking buddies as he chug-a-lugged the remaining third of a bottle of beer. "We're havin' productive meetins' just fine," he burped. Everyone laughed.

"See. That's what I'm talking about," the president continued. "Clarence you're out of order." Clarence wandered off toward the bar.

"I'll entertain a motion to ban all drinking of alcoholic beverages before union meetings," the president announced.

One of the women sitting up front, Helen, raised her hand. "I'll make that motion."

"Thank you, Helen," the president said. "Is there a second?" Her friend Rose raised her hand. "I'll second that."

"Okay. We have a motion and a second," the president announced, confidence rising in his voice. "Any discussion?"

Jimmy had woken up and asked feebly from the back row: "How about just one?"

"No. Not even just one," the president said. He looked at Helen and said: "I don't remember that motion allowing any drinks before a meeting, do you Helen?"

"Nope," Helen said firmly.

The president paused for a moment and looked around the room. "Any further discussion?"

No one else raised their hand.

"Okay. Seeing no more discussion, I'll call for the vote. All in favor say 'aye'."

Most of the room voiced the affirmative.

"All those opposed say 'nay'." There were a few 'nays' but they were outnumbered.

"Abstentions?" Two members raised their hands half way and then let them drop.

"Okay. The 'ayes' have it and so moved. There will be no drinking of alcohol of any kind before union meetings," the president announced.

Jimmy slunk down in his chair looking defeated.

I thought it was interesting that no one suggested moving the meeting away from the bar. I guess that would have been a loser. Hell, there are bars all over south Buffalo – in some neighborhoods there is one on nearly every other corner. I realized it wasn't wise to try to deny a worker a beer after a hard days work in a grubby factory. After the meeting, practically everyone went to the bar anyway, including most of the union officers.

"Okay, now that we've resolved the drinking problem at union meetings, we can get down to business," the president announced. "The first item on the agenda is," he paused to look at the paper in front of him, "is, well, it's a case involving drinking. This is Norm's case," he said, directing his remarks toward the secretary who was taking minutes of the meeting.

"First, let me say that we talked to Norm and he said it's okay to talk about the details of his case at this meeting," the president began. "Norm was fired for missing two weeks of work without calling in for being on a drunk."

I had heard about the case at work. Norm was a polisher operator in our department and on our shift. He was probably ten years older than me, which would have put him in his late 20's or early 30's. He was a big guy, pretty muscular, but real quiet and kept to himself. I tried talking to him a couple of times, but he didn't say too much.

One thing we all noticed about Norm was his routine. Every night on our first 10-minute break at 1:00 am, he would gulp down his lunch, which consisted of a sandwich, potato chips and chocolate milk. Then at our 3:00 am lunch break, he would go to sleep on a bench in the back for 20 minutes. Then he'd take his regular break at 5:00 am. Then at 7:00 am, our quitting time, he'd go out the back door, walk up to Seneca Street and jump onto a garbage truck and work his day job as a garbage man. We couldn't figure out how he did it. We were tired and sore after our eight hours in the glass factory. Then this guy picked up garbage cans all day.

"What we need to decide is if we are going to take his case to arbitration if we can't get it settled with the company," the president continued.

"Why is he working two physically tough jobs?" came a question from the floor.

"You know, he's got a lot of kids and his wife wanted a new washing machine and dryer and other things," the president responded. "He told us he had to work two jobs to pay for all that stuff, and working for the garbage department was all he could get."

"He's got a good work record, doesn't he?" another member asked.

"Yes, his work record is good and he's had many years with the company. And, you all know, Norm is a good union member."

"So, what happened?" someone else asked. "He seemed to be doing fine for as long as I can remember."

"Yeah, Norm seems to be able to handle the two jobs and the pressure at home pretty good. But eventually it just builds up and I guess he can't take it anymore and he goes out and gets drunk and stays that way for a week."

"Did you say he didn't call in sick?" someone else asked.

"Yes. That's the problem," the president continued. "One Friday after his shift on the garbage truck, he never made it home. His wife didn't hear from him, we didn't see him at work and the guys on the garbage truck didn't see him either."

"I know where he was," Jimmy blurted out with pride in a slightly slurred voice. "He was over at O'Brien's." O'Brien's was a popular neighborhood bar near the factory.

"That's right," the president continued. "That's were he was for the better part of last week. Once he got to drinkin', he lost track of time and everything else. He didn't call home and he didn't call work. No one knew where he was until last Wednesday when Jimmy saw him over there and told us about him."

Jimmy straightened up in his chair and a little grin crept across his face. He looked around to see if anyone noticed the contribution he'd made to this case.

"Some other people saw him at O'Brien's too so the company knows he was there. We told management that Norm is sick and that's why he couldn't call, which is true. In fact, he's home sick in bed now."

I didn't know much about alcoholism then, but looking back on it, I guess Norm was an alcoholic. As long as he didn't drink, he was fine. And he'd go for many months, maybe years without drinking, I was told. But once he had one, he was gone. I thought that doing hard, physical labor in a dirty, highly regimented factory could lead people to drink. I rarely heard these guys talk much about the outside world, like Vietnam or anything else. I guess it was because they had enough of their own problems.

"He's done that before," one of the union stewards, Stan, announced solemnly. "Last year we got him back to work after he went on a drunk then. Ever since he took that job with the garbage department he's been under more stress. We've got a meeting set up with the company tomorrow on this. Norm's a good worker and the company knows it, and they also know about his financial and family pressures. So, we'll see what we can do."

"Thanks, Stan," said the president. "So what we need to decide today is that if we can't get Norm back to work, do we take his case to arbitration? We've filed the grievance and have our first step meeting tomorrow. If we can't resolve it, we'll push it through the grievance procedure. But we need to know how the membership feels about taking it to arbitration if we're denied at the other steps."

"I know this isn't a good case," Stan began. "It's hard to defend someone who hasn't called into work for over a week. But when Norm gets to drinking, he really is too sick to do anything else. I think that needs to be our defense. When Norm has a drink, he gets sick – so sick that he can't call or do anything."

"Of course, the company is going to say that he shouldn't drink then," said Pat. "It's his responsibility not to take the drink. After all, no one is forcing him. I feel sorry for him and would like to help him, but this is a bad case. I'm not saying that I'm against taking it to arbitration, but it's going to be a tough one to win, and arbitration costs money."

I was new to all of this and didn't have any idea how I thought it might turn out. But I was interested in the arguments that each person made, and how this discussion might help us come up with a decision.

Ed, our departmental steward, raised his hand.

"I agree that this case may be hard to win at arbitration," Ed began. "But we don't have to wait for arbitration. We all know that Norm is a good worker. And we know he has a problem with the drink. But Norm would never willfully try to cheat the company or break the rules. I don't think a guy should lose his job because he's got a problem that he doesn't have full control over. Let's have a heart for the guy. If we don't get him back in our meetings with the company, I say we file the grievance through to arbitration. But let's continue to talk to the company and put pressure on them to take him back."

Several heads nodded in agreement. That sounded like a good plan to me. After a brief pause, the president spoke.

"Anyone got anything else to say about this?" No one did.

Turning toward Ed, the president asked: "Ed, do you want to make that into a motion?"

"Yes," said Ed. "Put that in the form of a motion."

"Second," said Stan.

"Any discussion?" the president asked.

"Hearing none, all in favor say 'aye.'" Most of the room said 'aye.'

"All opposed?" The room was silent.

"Abstentions? Again, silence.

"The 'ayes' have it and so moved," the president said.

I was impressed with how the union handled business and was I learning a lot by just watching and listening.

"Next item on the agenda is the company's effort to raise the quota in the beveling department. I hear you gave Noreen hell over that," the president said with a smile as he looked at Ed. There were some chuckles in the room. Obviously, word had gotten around about the incident on the shop floor. "Mary, I think you raised this issue."

"Yes. Thank you," said Mary. "As many of you know the company is doing a time study right now in the beveling department. We girls are worried that they're going to raise our quota, and we'd like some help."

Ed's hand went up and his face was getting red from anger. "Yeah, I know management has been trying to force you to do more already. And I've seen 'em over there with their clipboards and stop watches, the bastards! Sorry for the language ladies. But you're right, they do want to raise the quotas! You know what to do. Work at your regular pace."

"But they're bringing the material right over to our machines," exclaimed Daisy. "Normally we have to go get our material and that takes time."

"So tell 'em," Ed shot back. "Tell 'em you have to get your material and that takes extra time. With the material right there beside you, of course you'll be able to do more. But that's not the way it's set up under normal production. So it's not a fair time study. Ask 'em if they're going to supply another roustabout to make sure you have material right by your machine all day long. Keep arguing with them. And you all have to do it. Mary, Joan, Sally, all of you. You all have to speak up. Make their lives miserable. And don't kill yourself on the job. Take whatever time you have to, to do the job right." He had a little twinkle in his eye.

Joan looked around with a devilish smile on her face. I'd heard that she was known as a hellion in that department. "Yeah, we can do that, right girls?" We heard murmurs of agreement from a number of the beveling workers.

The meeting took up a couple of other issues and then adjourned. I was impressed with how people cared about each other.

The following week I came into work and there was Norm. I couldn't believe it. The union got him back.

Things went back to normal at the glass factory. One night just before our shift began, some young guys from a different department were talking about the war in Vietnam. We were in the lunch room getting coffee and sodas.

"I'm enlisting in the Marines," announced one young guy. I heard someone call him Buck. "When I get to Vietnam, I'm really going to kick some ass." I was surprised at such a statement.

"Why?" I asked.

"What do you mean, why?" he responded in an indignant tone of voice.

"Why are you going over there? They didn't do anything to you."

I had a little longer hair then and a beard, and must have looked to him like a hippie or protestor, though I wasn't either one.

"What are you? One of those 'Make Love, Not War' guys?"

"Well, if you get your head blown off over there, you won't be making love anymore." A couple of guys laughed as they looked over at Buck. He stormed away. No one else said they wanted to go. That was reassuring, I thought.

The buzzer sounded for us to begin our shift and a boss came by and told us to knock it off and get to work.

A couple of weeks later, another incident took place involving a young guy, Brian, who was on my line. He clocked in one night at 11:00 pm, and then crawled out a back window about 12:30 to look for a girl at a party in the neighborhood. He was crawling back in about 2:00 am when our supervisor caught him and fired him on the spot. One worker said we should say Brian forgot his lunch and went home to get it, but that didn't get much support. I knew Brian screwed up, but I wondered if the union would try to help him, especially since they helped Norm get back to work. After all, Norm screwed up too. I saw Ed one day shortly after and asked him.

"I know what Brian did was wrong," I began. "But was there any type of defense for him? I suppose there isn't any language in the contact to help him, or Norm for that matter, is there?"

"No. There isn't any language in the contact to help either of them," Ed began. "But a lot of cases don't fall neatly under the contract. Brian's case is a tougher one though." Ed explained. "Brian should have known better that to pull a stunt like that."

"But you guys got Norm back and Norm didn't call in for a week and he was drunk," I said. "And he didn't come in for two weeks. Norm missed a lot more time than Brian did."

"That's true, Norm missed a lot more time than Brian," Ed agreed. "But that's not the only thing the company looks at. In this case, what the company is more concerned about is that Brian willfully tried to deceive them, and get paid for time he wasn't here. Norm didn't willfully try to deceive them. He didn't punch in and then sneak out. Also, Norm has been here for many years and he's a good worker. The company knows that. But Brian just started here. The company doesn't know Brian very well. They figure if he tries to pull something like that already, what will he try later? They figure they don't need that extra headache."

"But the company knows Norm, and his family, and his situation," Ed continued. "They have more sympathy for a guy who is having trouble with alcohol than they do for a young guy who wants to chase a girl at a party – right or wrong," he chuckled. "But, make no mistake about it," he warned, "Norm is on thin ice. If he does this again, it will be very hard for us to do much to help him. We've told Norm that and told him he needs to get some help."

I learned some important things about the union then. If someone is a good worker and is basically trying to do the right thing, the union will give 110% to help him, even if he makes some dumb mistakes. But if someone is perpetually a screw-up, or is flagrantly dishonest or willfully does things that he knows is wrong, then the sympathy drops off. Then there is every possible combination in between, not to mention when the company unfairly goes after someone who did nothing wrong. So, I saw that every case is unique, and each one must be evaluated on its own merits. Many factors go into the final outcome – not just what words exist or don't exist in the contract. At least that was our union.

"So, the union is a pretty complex thing," I asked Ed.

He looked at me with a quizzical smile on his face.

"Well, not really," he responded. "The union is a group of people working together to help each other."

That sounded good to me. I was definitely a union man from that day on.

Chapter 12

The Quota

My routine was the same every day at Standard Mirror. An opening came up for the fine grinder job on the afternoon shift so I applied and got it. It paid a little more than the polisher operator, but more importantly, I was off graveyards. I didn't like the night shift. I couldn't sleep well during the day and was always tired, and I felt even more out of sync with the rest of the world. I realized that it would be harder to attend union meetings now, but figured that I would just call off with some personal business so I could attend some of them.

Ed and the other older guys had taught the younger guys and me a lot about how a union is run. We saw how they handled problems on the shop floor and it was pretty impressive. It wouldn't be long before we would get our chance to try what we learned.

"Hey, Paul," a familiar voice called out over the din when I came into work one afternoon. I looked across a row of machines and saw Joey. He was now the day shift fine grinder operator on the 84 Line, leaving to go home. He moved to days when an opening came up there, and I took over his job on the second shift.

"Hey, Joey. How ya doin?" I shouted back.

"Good," he yelled over his shoulder as he headed for the door. I couldn't make out the rest of it, but it was something about 'gettin' out of this shithole.' Joey was a good guy. He always left my first run in good shape for me. I appreciated that.

I got to my department, grabbed my black rubber apron and big rubber boots and walked over to my machine. My back and arms were still a little sore from yesterday's work. But, what the hell. I was 20 and in good shape and enjoyed the workout – well, at least for the first four hours. As long as I was busy, sweating and burning up calories, I could keep my mind off the war and Donna. Also, I was so busy with work now that I didn't have time to get involved in trying to stop the war. At least that's what I told myself. Work became a convenient excuse to not do anything about the war. But, even if I had made the time, which I could have, I had no idea what I could do to try and stop it.

A loud irritating sound pierced the air, signaling the start of the second shift. It was 3:00 pm.

I went to the overhead crane and looked underneath for broken glass. There wasn't any. I reached up for the control box and steered the forms over the grinder, and gently lowered them onto the black-slate circular table. I released the vacuum pressure on the hydraulic system, and moved the crane out of the way. Then I flipped the switches to lower the four hydraulic heads. They each popped and hissed just like they should when everything is working right. I guided the heavy heads into place over the forms, turned on the lubricant, and punched the start button.

There was a slight crunching noise as the big slate table began revolving, slowly grinding the surface of the glass mirrors pressed against it.

I walked about fifteen feet to the polishing machine next to me. John, the polisher operator, was putting the last head in place. He was a tall, lanky guy about my age and wore a Brooklyn Dodgers baseball cap every day. It didn't matter that the Dodgers had moved to Los Angeles years earlier – John couldn't accept the fact that they had left New York.

"How you doin?" I asked.

"Okay," he said as he turned on the spigot that poured brown polish onto the felt table.

He hit the start button on his machine. A couple of clumps of the chalky polish splashed over the guardrail as the polisher began to revolve.

"I heard they want to increase the quota on our line," John said.

"Yeah, I heard that too," I responded. "Ed said they'll probably try to start it on the graveyard shift – you know, they have all brand new guys there. They figure those guys don't know anything about the union yet, so they'll get it goin' there first." I heard Ed say that, and it made sense. I hadn't been there much longer than the new guys, but I was learning fast.

"Well, fuck 'em," John said. "We're not doin' any more. We're working steady. They're getting their production."

"Yeah, I know," I said. I felt the same way. I felt like we were working hard. I remembered Ed told us that whenever we had a problem on our line to talk to all the guys about it to find out what everyone thought. I thought about how Ed would do it, and then tried to do the same thing.

"You talk to the guys at your end, and I'll talk to Larry and the guys at the other end, and we'll figure out what to do. I'll talk to Harry when he comes on tonight, and Joey in the morning." I don't know why I thought of those things. It just seemed logical. Harry was the fine grinder operator on the graveyard shift. He was new, young, and seemed like a nice guy.

A couple days later, our shift supervisor, Jerry Kowalski, was standing by my machine when I came into work. He pushed his glasses back up over the bridge of his nose and motioned to the guys to come over. I couldn't figure out how his glasses kept sliding down such a big nose, but as I got closer I saw that his nose was covered with sweat.

"Okay, guys, listen up," he yelled over the din of the machines. "As you probably know, we've completed our time study. We've determined that with a few changes in our production process, we can work smarter and increase our production. We'll keep a running score at the end of each shift, and the shift with the highest production at the end of each week will receive a $25 bonus. We'll start it next Monday, on the graveyard shift."

We were making about $2.50 an hour or about 100 a week in 1968, so a $25 bonus was good extra money each week.

Kowalski was smiling now, and added with a twinkle in his eye: "I know you guys are the best shift. You can beat those other guys. I know you can win those bonuses." He stopped and waited for our response. I could see he was trying to pit the workers on each shift against each other. It reminded me of my high school guidance counselor.

There was some whispering and a lot of blank stares. But no one said anything.

"Look, guys," he began again, the smile gone from his face. "We've got to do this to stay competitive. And that will help us all keep our jobs."

"I understand we've got all the contracts with Ford and Chrysler," I said. "So where's the competition?"

"That's true," Kowalski responded, regaining his composure. "But there's a company up in Michigan that's very aggressive. They've got all the contracts with General Motors, and they're trying to get our contracts with Ford and Chrysler." He was sweating harder now and pushed his glasses back into place again.

"What kind of changes are you talkin' about?" John asked.

"We figure we can reduce the running time on the machines and turn up the pressure," Kowalski responded. "We should be able to maintain our quality and get out three more runs a shift."

"What!?" yelled out Mike. "From eighteen runs to twenty-one? No way!"

"Fuck him," Larry whispered in my ear as he glared at Kowalski. Larry was a short, stocky helper on our line with a barrel chest who was about my age.

There was a general grumbling among the crew. Twenty-one runs would be rough. We'd be running our asses off the entire shift.

"Okay, okay guys, quiet down," Kowalski admonished. "Three more runs isn't that much..."

"If we speed up the machines, we'll produce more scrap," I countered, "because we won't be able to get out all the imperfections."

"We're not going to produce more scrap," he said firmly. "We're going to keep our quality up." The anger was rising in his voice.

"I'm telling you, there will be more scrap," Mike responded in a loud voice. "You can't speed the machines up any faster and hold quality. We can't do it. Twenty-one runs are too many."

"Are you refusing?" Kowalski shouted at us. His face was beet-red and the veins on the side of his neck were popping out like an old garden hose with a bubble in it.

"No, we're not refusing," I responded. We didn't want to be charged with insubordination. "We're just telling you it can't be done."

"Well, I'm telling you that it can be done, and you will do it," Kowalski screamed.

"And if anyone doesn't do it, they will be disciplined, up to being fired! Now get to work!"

I wanted to say that we were sore and tired doing eighteen runs, and twenty-one runs would just add to our misery. But the company didn't want to hear that. We were just parts in the production process to them. The quota was the only thing they cared about. The quota and bigger profits. If I had said that, Kolwalski would have responded by saying: 'What's the matter with you guys, you're just a bunch of pussies. If you can't hack it here, there's the door.' We'd all heard that before. When they talked like that, I had even less respect for them. Their disrespect for women was a disgrace. I bet they didn't use that language when they talked about their wives, girlfriends or daughters, I thought.

We talked to Ed later that day and he gave us some ideas. He told us that we had to talk to the guys on the other shifts and that we all had to be together on this. If one shift broke ranks and did the new quota it would prove it could be done. No one suggested filing a grievance. If we filed a grievance and did the new quota, when we got to our first grievance meeting, management would say: 'What do you mean you can't do it – you're already doing it.'

Our union contract was pretty good. I spent several days reading it. We had language that called for time and a half for any work on Saturday and double-time for work on Sunday, regardless of how many regular weekdays you worked. But we didn't have language that would allow us to stop management from raising work quotas. Ed told me that the union tried to get language to put a brake on job speed-up, but couldn't. But that didn't mean our cause wasn't just. We had to figure out how to stop it right then, language or no language. I had never thought about being a union activist, but when I started thinking, planning and speaking up, I was becoming one. It was a little scary at first, but then it seemed fine.

We talked to all the guys on our shift and they all agreed that we shouldn't do the new quota. Joey told me the guys on days were solid too. Our concern was the graveyard shift.

The next day at lunch, Larry began. "I heard a bunch of guys on nights arc going along with the contest."

"Yeah, I heard that too," added John, as he pulled a baloney sandwich out of his lunch bag. I couldn't help staring at a glop of polish that John had on his Dodger's hat. He obviously hadn't seen it yet, or he'd be pissed off. "Has anyone talked to Harry?"

"I talked to him last night when we were leaving," I responded. "Harry says he understands our position, but he said their supervisor's got all the guys cranked up about the $25 and how they're the best shift – you know, the same bullshit that Jerry tried to feed to us. Harry said he tried to talk to those guys, but they all think they're tough and they're just seeing dollar signs in front of their eyes right now."

"Did he explain to 'em that if we start doin' 21 runs now we'll be doin' 21 forever?" asked Larry. "Where will it end? Remember, Charlie had a heart attack on the 48 line when they tried to raise the quota there."

"Yeah, he told 'em all that," I said.

"I say we go in there tonight and tell 'em we're doin' only eighteen runs and if they refuse to stick with eighteen, we kick their asses," Mike retorted, as he popped opened a can of Pepsi.

"No, no, hold on," I said. "Let's go in there and just talk to them. Harry says there are three of them that are gung ho for this contest, but others don't want to do it. And some aren't sure. Let's get four or five guys from our shift, and we'll talk to them. And I'll talk to Joey about getting some of the first shift guys to come in early to talk to them. That way, they'll see that first and second shifts are united on this."

"What if they still refuse to go along?" Larry asked.

"We're going to tell them that the union fought hard for years to get some control over working conditions, and we're not going to give it up now," I responded. I had heard Ed say that many times. "If that doesn't work, we'll go to Ed and ask him what we should do. What do you guys think?"

"Yeah. Let's try that," John said. "What do you think, Mike?"

"I told you what I think. But we'll try it your way first."

I knew if we got Mike on board we'd be together on our shift. Hell, one time he got so pissed off at Kowalski that he suggested blowing up the place. I didn't know if he was kidding or not.

"Okay. How many of you can stay over for ten or fifteen minutes tonight?" I asked. "We can start tonight."

About half the guys said they could stay. The buzzer sounded for us to return to work.

"And, Mike," I said, as people were getting up, "I don't think you should get into a fight tonight. Even if they don't agree, don't start anything. That's just what management wants. If you start a fight, management will fire you, and then we have another problem on our hands. If they're not with us, we'll talk to Joey and see if the first shift guys can come in early the next morning to talk to them. Okay?"

"Yeah, Okay," said Mike. "But if that doesn't work, let's wait until they leave the premises, and then kick their asses."

That night we talked to the guys on the graveyard shift. We gave them all the reasons why we shouldn't go for this contest and the new quota. We told them that the increased production was worth a lot more to the company than $25 a worker, there was no promise of how long they would pay the bonus, and most importantly, it would raise our quota forever.

"Do you want to be doing twenty-one runs every night forever," I asked Donny, a husky young blonde-haired kid who was a polisher operator on the graveyard shift. I saw his supervisor come down the isle so we stepped behind a big rack of glass.

"But I can do it, no sweat man, and it's $25 more bucks in my pocket a week."

"Yeah, but Donny, if you do twenty-one runs now, what's going to stop them from raising it to twenty-three or twenty-five in three or six months? Or more? When will it end? When you're the last man standing and then finally they give you a quota that even you can't handle? You're letting them take advantage of you."

"Naw, I'm not lettin' em' take advantage of me," he responded with some indignation in his voice. But then a funny look appeared on his face like maybe I was right. So I pursued this line of thought.

"Of course they are," I countered. "The question is, are you tough enough to stand up to them and not be pushed around?"

"No one pushes me around," Donny said, puffing out his barrel chest.

"Well, they are trying to push you around," I continued. "They're telling you that you have to produce twenty-one runs. What if you come in some night and don't feel well? Do you think they'll say, 'Okay, Donny, you don't have to do twenty-one runs tonight. No. They're going to tell you that you still have to do twenty-one runs. Look, we're giving them eighteen runs now. That's a full night's work. That's enough. Okay."

He looked at me quizzically, paused for a moment, and then said, "Okay."

I went over to John and Larry. They were talking to two other guys on graveyard. I listened for a minute and it seemed like they were getting through to them.

"How you guys doin'?" I asked the two night shift guys when there was a pause in the conversation.

"Okay," they said.

I looked at John and Larry. "You guys ready?"

"Yeah, we're ready," said John.

I looked around for Mike and the others and motioned toward the door. We met up in the beveling department where the mist was still hanging in the air.

"How did it go?" I asked. "Pretty good," said Larry. "The guy I talked to seemed to go along."

"What did he say?" I continued.

"Not much. He mostly listened."

"But did he say he agreed with us?" John asked.

"Well, not exactly," Larry responded. "But when I told him first and second shifts are going to keep doing 18 runs, he nodded his head and said 'okay'."

"What about you, Paul?" John asked.

"I talked to Donny. You know, he's one of the gung-ho ones. He argued with me at first, but by the end of the conversation he said he agreed." I explained.

"Do you think we can trust him?" Larry asked.

"I don't know. He seemed pretty weak," I answered, "but we'll see."

"How about you Mike?" I asked, turning toward Mike as we rounded the corner toward the door.

"I was talkin' to some asshole who said he was going to do it because he wanted the extra money. He said 'fuck the union.' I told him to fuck himself and step outside right now. Just then the supervisor came up and told us to stop arguing and for him to get to work."

"Well, one guy can't increase the quota by himself," Larry said.

"Yeah, as long as the others go along with us," I said.

We left the plant and went out into the cool night air.

"See you, guys," I said as we headed for our cars. It was Friday night. John, Larry and I headed for a nearby tavern. A cold beer sure tasted good after an evening at the glass factory. It helped wash down the ground up glass in our throats.

When we left the bar, John went to his car and Larry was still talking to me. As John drove off, Larry said he wanted to tell me something. It was late and the parking lot was half empty, so we stood by the side of the building in the shadows.

"Rose talked to me the other day," he began quietly, looking around to see if anyone was watching. No one was around. Rose was one of the secretaries upstairs that Larry was quietly going out with. Donna popped into my mind and I had a little sick feeling in my stomach, reminding me that I still missed her, but I quickly put her out of my mind. I don't think anyone knew that Larry and Rose were seeing each other. "She told me that she had heard the big bosses talking one day recently behind closed doors about how they could get raises if they got out more production. But she also told me not to say anything because she was the only one around then, and they would know she told people."

"Really," I said. "That's interesting." I knew the company was out to make money. But it was disturbing to think they would tell us one thing to get us to work harder and then plan to put most of the increased profits into *their* pockets. That angered me and made me more determined to stop their plan.

"Thanks, Larry. I appreciate you telling me this."

"Don't tell anyone," he pleaded. "Rose is afraid if it gets out she'll get fired."

"No, I won't say anything," I assured him. We both got in our cars and left.

On Sunday, I wondered about how our plan to stop the new quota would work out. The graveyard shift would start at 11 pm that night and I was worried that they might do the new quota. I was pretty sure day shift would stick to the old quota on Monday morning, and then it would be our turn. I could feel butterflies in my stomach. Would the guys stick to our plan, and would I be strong enough to stick to it? When I was coming to work Monday afternoon, I could feel my apprehension increasing. One benefit of this stress was that it took my mind off the war and Donna.

Chapter 13

The Campaign

I pulled up to the factory just as Mike was getting there. We walked in together, punched our time cards and headed for our department.

We approached our work area and saw bosses everywhere. Even bosses that I hadn't seen before. We turned the corner and saw the blackboard.

"Those sons-a-bitches!" Mike shouted.

'Third Shift: 20 runs,' it read in big white chalk letters and numerals.

"I told you we should have kicked their asses!" Mike exploded.

"Hold on," I said, trying to calm him down. "Let's go talk to Joey to see what they did."

Joey was just finishing up his shift.

"Hey, Joey," I called out as we approached him. He looked up as he hosed off the forms of my first run. "How many did you guys do today?"

"We did eighteen but it was tough. There were bosses all over the place. And are they pissed off. Ralph was standing by my machine watching me like a hawk the whole day." Ralph was the first shift supervisor for our department. "I couldn't turn the time back up or the pressure down."

"So how did you do it?" I asked.

"You know, work to rule, slow down, have every problem you could imagine. The key is the helpers – when they go to get material. But it was hard because the bosses were watching us real close. So we had to be careful. You guys better watch out. They know we don't want to do this quota and they're looking to fire anyone who is goofing off or purposely slowing down. They'll probably be here for your entire shift," he said. "The pressure is really on you guys because they're so mad at us, and they figure you're in it with us." He stopped working for a minute and looked up at me. "But you can do it." We can do it? He seemed so flippant about it. I hoped he was right.

"Did you have more scrap?" I asked.

"Some. We made sure we did," Joey responded.

"What about the guys on graveyard, did you talk to them?" I asked.

"Yeah, we talked to them when we came in this morning. We told them that this is a union shop. We told them that the majority of us in this department believe 18 runs are enough so that's what we're going to give the company. I told them, 'if you guys don't like that, then go down the street and find a non-union employer where you can knock yourselves out.' We told them that we would show them how to do eighteen runs, even with the time turned down and the pressure up on their machines. Can any of you guys stay over a little and show them how to do it? Some of us are coming in early tomorrow morning to make sure they do eighteen."

"Yeah, we can stay over for a little while," Mike answered. A wicked smile crept across his face.

Just then I saw most of the rest of our crew come into the department. We had about 15 minutes before the start of our shift.

"C'mon," I said. "Let's go down to material storage. We can talk down there."

"Okay," I began, as everyone huddled in a tight circle between several large crates. "Management is going to be all over our asses today. That's what Joey said." I told them that first shift did our old quota and that management is really pissed off at them. "So we need to be careful. If they catch anyone slowing down, or wrecking a machine or the product, they're going to come down hard on us. We know they have shortened the run time on our machines, and turned up the pressure. That means we have to stretch out the rest of the work. That means work to rule. Walk inside the yellow lines; no cutting across the department. Follow all the safety rules. Take your time getting material. We know what to do. Just like Joey and Ed told us. Okay?"

People nodded their heads in agreement.

"Also, who can stay over a little tonight to talk to the third shift guys again?"

"I will," Mike chimed in with that same evil grin on his face.

The others looked at him and smiled.

"We got about a minute before the buzzer," John reminded us. "We better get back to our department."

We streamed out of material storage and down the aisle toward our work area. Four bosses were standing there watching us.

"Afternoon, Paul," Jerry said to me as I grabbed my apron and boots. "Ready to make 21 runs today? Did you see, graveyard made 20."

"We'll see," I said slowly.

The buzzer sounded. I checked the glass in the forms hanging from the crane. Everything was okay. I took my time, but Jerry was right there watching me. I put the first run on my grinder, did all the prep work and started it up. I was right on schedule. Everything was going smoothly. Jerry was still watching me. The other bosses walked up and down the line watching the other guys. Jerry knew that my machine controlled the pace of the entire line since my machine supplied glass to the polishers. If my machine slowed down, it slowed down the entire process.

It seemed like in no time my grinder stopped. I was worried. I got the overhead crane in position, lowered it over the forms, turned on the hydraulic suction, and picked the forms off the circular slate table. I hosed off the glass and checked for broken mirrors. There was only one and I flipped it out of the pocket with my screwdriver and it made a tiny crash on the floor. That was normal procedure. Jerry was still watching.

John took the crane and transferred the glass onto his polisher. Everything went smoothly. The run times had been reduced on the polishers too. While the machines were running, we machine operators assisted the helpers by pulling the mirrors out of big water tubs, cleaning them off, throwing out any cracked or broken mirrors, and racking the rest. Then they went to inspection. After the first run, we were on schedule to make 21 runs for the day.

As we approached our first break two hours into the shift, we were still on schedule for 21 runs. There was a little more scrap, but not enough, and Jerry hadn't left my machine for the entire time. My worries worsened.

The buzzer sounded for our 5:00 pm break and we headed for the lunchroom. We went to the table where we all normally sat together.

"We're too far ahead," John said under his breath, as he pulled out a chair to sit on.

"We've got to slow it down," Mike added.

"Yeah, I know," I agreed. I turned to the helpers. "When you guys go for material or tools don't rush. Take your time, in fact, take all the time you can. We'll try to take as much time as we can getting the runs on and off the machines, but they're watching us so closely, it's tough. But they can't see you when you leave the area, or any of us when we leave the area. That's where we've got to slow down, when they can't see us. They can't watch all of us all the time, and there are more of us than there are of them. Okay?"

"Sure," said Larry. "We can handle that." The others nodded in agreement.

"Where's Ed," John asked. "I thought he was going to come over to give us some help."

"He said he'd be over before lunch," I answered. Our lunch break was at 7:00 pm. "I think he had a meeting with management about 4:00. He might still be in there with them."

"Remember, we're giving them 18 runs and that's it," Mike added with emphasis.

Right after our first break, Larry got on a tow motor and went for some more material. I watched him between two of the machines. Before he got out of our department, he came up behind another tow motor that Mike had left in the aisle on purpose. Instead of bumping it out of the way, like we usually did, Larry slowly and carefully backed up his tow motor about thirty feet until he found a clearing beside the tow motor path. Then he carefully pulled his tow motor completely off the path and parked it behind another big machine. You could hardly see it.

Then he walked to the other tow motor, got on it, and drove off out of sight into another department.

About five minutes later, I saw Larry come back into the department. By the time he got over to my work area my machine had been stopped for several minutes.

"Where the fuck have you been," Jerry screamed at him. "This material needs to be here *before* his machine stops!" His face puffed up like a beach ball ready to pop.

"One of the tow motors was left in the aisle," Larry responded. "I couldn't get by."

While Jerry was screaming at Larry, I took an extra long time picking real and imaginary pieces of broken glass out of the form with my screwdriver.

Just then I heard Ed's booming voice.

"What's going on here? Don't yell at that man like that!" Ed screamed at Kowalski, while pointing at Larry.

"It's none of your business, Ed," Kowalski yelled back. "Go back to your line."

"It is my business," Ed shot back. "I'm the steward for this department and you're not going to yell at our people like that!"

While they argued, Larry just stood there doing nothing, and I continued fiddling with my machine.

After several minutes, Kowalski looked over at me.

"What the fuck are you doing?" he screamed at me when he saw my machine wasn't running yet. "Since you're not runnin', the polishers aren't runnin' either!"

"Jerry, I told you we aren't going to put up with you abusing our people like that," Ed yelled back, anger rising in his voice.

"Ed, I told you to stay out of this," Kowalski said as he whirled around.

Another boss, who was watching a polishing operator, saw all the commotion, and came over. "What's going on here?" he demanded.

While Kowalski explained the problem, the polishing operator stopped working. Now two-thirds of our line was grinding to a halt.

Finally, Kowalski looked back at me, his eyes blazing with anger and his jaw muscles so tense he looked crazed.

"I had some broken glass that I couldn't get out of this form," I said lamely.

"Well, get that damn thing going," he said pointing at my machine with his outstretched right arm. Even the muscles in his finger were tense.

"Hey, quality work takes time," I mumbled under my breath.

"What did you say?" has asked angrily. His lips were foaming and the words flew out on gobs of spit. "I'm going to write you up for insubordination," he screamed, "for not following my instructions."

"Hey, I'm following your instructions," I yelled back. I was getting angry now. "What have I refused to do? We're doin' everything you've asked!" As I was talking, I was working even slower. My machine still wasn't going.

While I was arguing with Kowalski, Ed walked down the line and started talking to a polisher operator and a helper, so they weren't working either. Now almost the entire line was stopped. Kowalski looked at them and turned to the other boss.

"Go down there and tell Ed to get back to his job or he's goin' to be written up," he yelled, "and tell those other guys to get back to work!"

All of a sudden there was a loud crash. A rack of glass smashed on the floor. Occasionally, accidents like that happened. Today was a good day for it. Guys all over the department were hootin' and hollerin' – something they normally did when a lot of glass broke. Everyone stopped working to look. Since our department was at the end of the production process, any mirrors wrecked in our department ruined the work that everyone did before us.

We developed a pattern. Every time a boss confronted one guy, he argued back, and then the others who weren't being watched slowed down. It was a cat and mouse game.

Everything was falling apart on our line, and it was a good feeling. I felt we were turning the tide in our favor. About 6:45 pm none of the machines were working, and when the bosses rushed up to the guys, they came up with all sorts of excuses to explain why they were having so much trouble.

Finally, the buzzer sounded at 7:00 pm for our lunch break. We streamed into the lunchroom, giddy with excitement.

"Did you see the veins in Jerry's neck?" Larry said as we reached our table. "They looked like they were going to explode."

"Yeah, we did good out there," I said. "We're at nine and a half runs. We should be at ten and a half to reach the new quota. We've got to keep it up." Under our original quota, we would have nine runs done by lunch, so we were pretty close to our old mark.

"How you guys doin'?" we heard a familiar voice say. It was Ed. He just walked into the lunchroom and had a big grin on his face.

"Good," said Mike. "We're close to our old quota."

"Good. Keep doin' what you're doin," Ed said. "The guys on my line are with you. We're ready to raise some hell over there. You need any more help, you give me a holler. Okay?"

"Yeah, thanks, Ed," I said. "Thanks a lot. You were a big help out there."

After our lunch break we went back to our line and did the same thing. Kowalski was still furious, but now he had a look of desperation on his face. We met again at our 9:00 pm break and we were on target to make 18 runs. Things were going just as we planned. It was exhilarating!

When the graveyard shift guys came in at 11:00 pm, they saw that both first and second shifts did 18 runs. We had another talk with them and gave them some pointers.

When we came in the next day, we saw that the graveyard shift did 19 runs. That was an improvement. By the third day, they were down to 18 too. The total number of mirrors we produced was the same as when we did 18 runs, but the total number of *good* mirrors was less because we were producing more scrap and having more accidents. So instead of production going up, it was going down.

The bosses were livid.

"We know you guys are doin' this on purpose!" Kowalski screamed at us at the end of the third day. "When I catch anyone purposely slowing down, or ruining the product, I'll fire 'em!"

Our campaign had gone on much the same every day that week, but neither Jerry nor any of the other bosses could ever quite catch anyone purposely goofing off.

On Thursday, I was picking a broken piece of glass out of one of my forms when I heard a loud scrapping and crunching sound. I looked over at one of the polishers and saw big strips of felt ripping off the table. It was Mike's polisher. He was nowhere to be seen. He had gone to get some tools. So the table kept revolving, and the broken glass busted up all the mirrors on that run and just shredded the felt. One of the bosses ran over and shut off the machine, and Mike hurried over like he was real concerned about the accident.

Kowalski stormed over there too and I could hear both bosses screaming at Mike, though I couldn't make out what they were saying. Mike was screaming back and more time was being lost. That was fine with us because we knew that polisher would be down for a half hour to forty-five minutes while a new felt was put on it. And that meant it would be impossible to reach the new quota, and we wouldn't have to sweat it too much for the rest of the shift. That day we made only sixteen runs.

We heard that some of the bosses suspected sabotage. I know they wanted to blame Mike but he wasn't around his polisher when it happened. But they were sure that someone had thrown a piece of broken glass onto the felt polisher so it would get imbedded in it and break up all the mirrors. I don't know if there was sabotage or not. We did have this type of accident on the polishers occasionally.

What made things worse for the company was that when third shift came in that evening they had a similar accident on the same polisher, and the bosses thought for sure it was planned sabotage. I don't think it was on the third shift. I guess it was just bad luck. Third shift gave them only fourteen runs that night.

121

By the second week, our numbers were all over the place. Some days we made eighteen, but other days just seventeen or sixteen or worse. Overall, everyone was having more accidents than normal; that undoubtedly accounted for our dismal showing. Once we had built up momentum during our campaign, we felt stronger and it was easier to keep it up. It was a great feeling to see management's plans falling apart.

On Thursday of the second week, management stopped recording our scores on the blackboard. It was nice to come in Friday and see blanks on the blackboard for every shift. Even the number of bosses out on the floor dropped back to close to what it used to be, and the screaming, yelling, hair pulling and threats died down.

On Monday of the third week, some genius in the front office thought it wasn't good for morale to have the numbers "16" and "14" from the week before recorded on the blackboard for everyone to see, or blank spaces either, so by Tuesday the blackboard was gone. And we never heard anything more about the contest.

There was so much scrap, that the run-time on our machines was put back to what it had been. That was on Wednesday of the third week. We never heard any more about the new quota. Nor about any quota. And no one got disciplined. What an incredible feeling. We won!

When we went back into work the next Monday, three weeks after this fiasco started, it seemed like everything was back to normal – well, normal for that shithole.

"Afternoon, Paul," Kowlaski said in a strained voice. "How you doin?"

"Okay," I responded. "How you doin?"

"Okay," Kowalski answered. But he didn't look good. His face drooped and his shoulders sagged. He looked defeated. He then turned and went up front to his office. We didn't see him for the rest of the day.

We were ecstatic. We not only stopped the new quota, but we stood up for ourselves. I saw that the all-powerful company wasn't all-powerful, and that people who seemed to have no power really did have some if they were even a little bit organized. It was scary at first, but when everyone stuck together, it worked. We took some control over our lives, and it felt good. I also learned that the union is all of us standing up for each other, just as Ed had taught us.

Right after this campaign George, Howard and I got an apartment on Bailey Avenue in the Kensington District not far from the University at Buffalo. George started working at Standard Mirror on the same shift and same department with me so we drove to work together. One day, by pure chance, I saw Donna at the mall. I had almost put her out of my mind with all the excitement at work. But when I saw her, all the memories rushed back. I was still in love with her. I was with George and Howard, and she was with a girlfriend. My heart started pounding. We talked briefly, but her girlfriend said they had to leave to get her dad's car home on time. Donna and I agreed to meet again – she would come over to our apartment on Saturday at 2:00 pm. I was excited. Maybe we could get back together again, I thought. But, I was also apprehensive. When we split up before, I was confused and I put most of the blame on her. I tried to push that thought from my mind so we could have a fresh start.

When Saturday came, I showered, put on some clean clothes and waited for her. When 2:00 pm came she wasn't there, but that was okay. I figured she was probably just running a little late. At 2:15, I started to get impatient. At 2:20, I was getting angry, but trying to suppress it. By 2:30 pm, I was steaming. So, she screwed me again, I thought. By 2:40, I had had enough. I left the apartment and just then, she came running up the driveway. She was trying to tell me why she was so late, but I was so angry I couldn't hear her. We argued and she left in tears. George came out and tried to calm me down.

"Why don't you call her up and hear what she has to say," he suggested. "You could just apologize for being so angry, and listen to her. Maybe she had a good reason for being late."

I didn't respond. I was too mad. My mind was in a fog and I didn't call. A week later, I started thinking that George was right. Maybe I had made a mistake. Was there a chance of getting her back again, I wondered? I decided to call her. Then I changed my mind. I kept putting it off until it seemed too late. My head was spinning.

Chapter 14

The Buffalo Nine

One evening about 7:00 pm a couple of guys from the factory and I went to a bar nearby to get some dinner and a few beers. We had knocked off early to go to a party. George was off work and out of town that weekend and Howard was going out with his girlfriend that night. When the guys from work and I got to the bar it was about half full. Workers from some other factories in the area had been in there for hours after coming off their day shift. Some were drunk and carrying on at a couple of tables in the back. We ignored them and headed for the bar where we found three empty stools together and sat down. The tavern was mostly dark, except for a row of lights that were strung across the top of the mirror behind the bar that made the place twinkle. I took a stool right next to a couple of guys in work clothes but I didn't pay any attention to them.

A bartender with a thick bushy black moustache and a white apron came up and asked us what we wanted. My friends ordered first. When it came my turn, I asked for a Michelob and an order of their Buffalo Polish sausages. I had Polish sausages in that bar before and they were great.

Just then, the news came on the TV behind the bar.

"Two young men entered the basement of the Buffalo Unitarian Church on Elmwood Avenue earlier today saying they were taking symbolic sanctuary from the draft and the Vietnam War," the announcer said. "Both boys are Buffalo natives. They received their draft notices, but they are refusing to be inducted into the military because of what they say is an immoral war in Vietnam." I was riveted to the TV. The camera showed two young men standing in front of sleeping bags that had been rolled out on the floor of the church. The announcer gave the names of the two young men, Bruce Beyer and Bruce Cline. Beyer was tall and handsome with blond-hair and clean-shaven. Cline was a little shorter and had thick dark brown wavy hair that was combed up and over the top of his head. This was the first time I had heard about this protest. I was immediately sympathetic to the two guys and wondered what was going to happen to them.

Just then a cold Michelob was placed in front of me.

"The sausage will be up in a minute," the bartender said. I could hear it sizzling on the grill nearby and smelled its rich aroma.

"Look at those godamn cowards," I heard the guy next to me say to his friend. I glanced over at him. He was big and real stocky with a neck like a fire hydrant.

"Hidin' out in a church," his skinny friend added. "They ought to arrest their assess and throw 'em in jail."

"Send 'em back to Moscow, that's what I say," the burly one continued.

I could feel myself getting angry.

"But they're from here," I interrupted calmly, glancing toward my right.

The chubby one looked over at me. "What the fuck do you know about it," he blurted out as he turned toward me. "You one of those protesters too?"

"No. But they both grew up here in Buffalo. Why should they go back to Moscow?"

"Cause that's where all them commies belong. We don't want 'em fuckin' up our country."

"Look. These guys don't believe we've been told the truth about the war. They have a right to express their opinion."

The skinny one craned his neck forward to look past his friend and glared at me.

"No they don't. They're un-American. They ain't got no rights."

They gulped down the last swallows of their beers, threw a couple of bucks on the bar and left.

"Assholes," I said loudly to my friends as the pair walked past us.

"Totally," my friend said.

"What the hell is wrong with them?" I asked.

"Who knows?"

"There must be some reason they acted so stupid," I said.

"They're fuckin' idiots, that's why."

"Well, it could be the steady diet of anti-communism that we get every day."

"Maybe. Who cares? Forget 'em. They're jerks. Here. Have some of these fries." He pushed his basket toward me.

"Yeah, I know. But there are others like them. They get it from the media. I read somewhere that a government guy called the Vietnamese 'raggedly little yellow bastards in black pajamas.' That doesn't help."

"That's true, it doesn't. But what can you do about it? Bartender. Another beer for my friend." He pointed to me.

"I got one here," I said. I took a bite out of my sausage. "Man, this sausage is good. You want some?"

"No. No, thanks." He glanced over at my plate and then paused a moment. "Hmm. That does look good. Hey, bartender. Give me an order of that Polish sausage too, okay?"

I took two long swallows of beer. "I think it's the racism," I continued. "You know how they call the Vietnamese 'Gooks?' Once you've dehumanized a whole group of people, then you can treat them like shit. It's like they're no more than animals. When animals get out of control, you just kill 'em."

"Yeah, you're probably right. It's fucked up," my co-worker commented casually. "Hey bartender, don't burn that sausage!"

"Can't they see that the Vietnamese are *people,* with feelings and families, and hopes and dreams, just like us?"

"I guess not."

Just then, two pretty girls walked up to the bar and sat on the stools on the other side of my friends. My buddies both turned away from me and started talking to the girls. Soon they were all laughing. I tried to join in but I was two bar stools away and I couldn't hear over the background noise. What luck. I sat down next to two assholes. My buddies sat next to two attractive girls. And I just blew it with Donna again. Just then, *Sympathy for the Devil* began playing on the jukebox. My second Michelob was put in front of me, and none too soon.

Over the next few days I learned more about the two Bruces from the news. One newspaper article described Bruce Beyer as a leader of the Buffalo Draft Resistance Union. The paper also reported that a group of people, mostly young university students, were going to the church every day to support the boys.

I was taking a summer school course at the university with George. It was an Ethics class in the Philosophy Department. We took the class in the late morning, and then went to work in the afternoon. George, Howard and I had great discussions about the issues raised in that class, and we related the various ethical arguments to the war. I had heard that anti-war students hung out at Norton Hall, the student union, so one day I went there to see for myself. There was a literature table in a large open area inside the building with a sign, "Students for a Democratic Society." A young man and a young woman were taking literature out of a box and putting it on the table. I walked over to them.

"Hi. I saw the case about the draft resisters on the news the other night." I began. "How are things going?"

"Pretty good," the guy said. "We're getting a lot of support. Here, take one of these leaflets," he said, handing me one. "People are coming to the church every day to support the two Bruces. You should join us."

"You mean come to the church?" I asked, a little surprised. I didn't feel like I belonged there. I wasn't a protester or a university student. "I don't know. It's mostly University students there, right? I'm just taking one class this summer, but I'm not a University student."

"That's okay," the young woman said in a reassuring voice. "Sure, there are a lot of students from the University there, but also a lot of other people. You don't have to be a University student to come to the church. Everyone is welcome."

"Oh, okay. Well, thank you. I'll see." I thought about it for a moment and then remembered something I heard about counter-protesters. "I heard there were some counter-demonstrators out there."

"One day a small group of about seven people marched on the sidewalk in front of the church," the woman explained. "They carried signs that read, 'The enemy is Communism,' and 'We protest bearded dirty college students.' That's interesting because neither of the Bruces have beards. And those counter-demonstrators don't know anything about the war."

"They carried signs that said 'Bomb Hanoi,'" The guy added.

"Yes, that was really sickening," the woman continued. "A young girl who looked about nine or ten years old was there with her parents and was given a sign to carry that read, 'Napalm Hanoi.' It was terrible. Have you seen pictures of people who have been hit with napalm? It burns their skin horribly. In some cases it can burn off their fingers or even their arms. I'm a nursing student and burn patients suffer some of the worst pain imaginable. How anyone could produce such a product for war is shocking. And how any parent could give their child a sign like that to carry is unbelievable. Dow Chemical is the company that makes napalm. That's why we had demonstrations against Dow recruiters last year when they tried to come onto campus to recruit students to work for their company."

"Yes, I had heard about those demonstrations." I remembered hearing on the news then about students protesting Dow recruiters on campus. "So, how are people responding to the counter-demonstrators?"

"Mostly, we ignore them. And there are many more of us than them."

"Have there been any threats from them?"

"Well, there was one," she continued reluctantly, trying not to scare me. "Some right-wingers sent a threatening letter to the church telling the congregation that if they didn't kick the two Bruces out of the church they would blow it up."

"Then what happened?" I asked, trying not to show any alarm.

"Reverend Wright read the letter to the congregation and said that if anyone is concerned about their safety they could leave the building and he would understand. No one left."

"That's pretty incredible," I said. "I remember hearing about people who blew up a church a few years ago in – I think it was some place in Alabama, because the congregation was supporting the Civil Rights movement, and four little black girls were killed."

"Yes. That was in Birmingham. It was terrible. The congregation at the church here is pretty strong. It's the Beyer family church so people have been supportive. And nothing has happened so it's been peaceful. People bring guitars and we have food. You should come by."

I think she was trying to play down the threats so as not to discourage me.

"Thanks for the information. I'm pretty busy working, but I'll see if I can make it."

Several days later, I did go to the church. I saw a large crowd of people on the lawn in front. I parked a few houses away on West Ferry and walked to join them. When I approached the gathering, Bruce Beyer was speaking to about 100 people. "They want us to be cogs in the war machine. They've trained us for war, but we won't go. Hell no, we won't go! Hell no, we won't go!" The crowd took up the chant. I listened for a moment and then joined in, hesitatingly at first, but then with more conviction.

When the chanting died down, several people went up to Bruce to talk to him, and others stood in small groups talking. I didn't know anyone there, but noticed a girl about my age standing right near me with her girlfriend.

"Pretty good turn-out," I commented to her.

"Yes, it is good. And it helps that Bruce has a military background. Up until this case, people always tried to dismiss us as a bunch of pacifists who are un-American."

"He does?"

"Yes. Bruce attended Manlius Military School for three years. That's one of the leading prep schools for West Point. He was a Platoon Sergeant there. Then he came home and graduated from Bennett High." My Mom had gone to Bennett many years earlier, I remembered.

"I didn't know that," I said.

"A number of the guys here have military backgrounds," she continued. "Some have been to Vietnam and realized how wrong it is and now they're home protesting against the war. Bruce Cline's older brother, Dave, was in Vietnam and he's speaking out against the war."

"Yeah, that's good."

"We've got to run." She grabbed her girlfriend by the arm and turned toward the street. "It was nice talking to you," she said over her shoulder. I was impressed with how much she knew about this case and the anti-war movement. I stayed for a few more minutes and then left.

I didn't know anything about anti-war protestors, other than what I heard or read in the media. The media often portrayed them as kooks, people outside the mainstream of society, hippies, and even people who were unpatriotic. That's why I hadn't identified with them before. But I didn't see kooks or misfits at the church. Most were students and residents of the community. Many were there with their families and children. And they sounded sane, rational and intelligent. They seemed like ordinary Americans. Suddenly, I didn't feel so alone anymore. My feelings were validated. It was one thing to be against the war, but it was something else to try to do something to help end it. That's what these people at the church were doing, and even though I didn't know any of them, I felt drawn to them. Maybe this was the family that I was missing.

I started thinking differently about anti-war protesters, and that, perhaps, I might be one too. I knew that the refusal of two young men to go to Vietnam wouldn't stop the war, but it set an example for other draft-age youth. If enough youth refused to go, the government wouldn't be able to fight the war. The Bruces refusal also sent a message to the public that some people were willing to make personal sacrifices because they were so strongly opposed to this war. I greatly admired them.

On August 19, 1968, federal marshals came to the church to arrest both Bruces for draft evasion. I wasn't there that day but the events were reported by the media. A large crowd of supporters was at the church, according to news reports. Pushing and shoving broke out. Bruce Beyer was clubbed to the ground and was bleeding from the head, and *he* was charged with assaulting federal officers. Some of his supporters were grabbed by federal agents and the supporters were charged with felony assault of federal officers. I learned later that a number of those who were arrested were leaders of the major anti-war organizations in Buffalo. A public defense committee was formed and the case became known as the Buffalo Nine.

I was angry at these arrests, and my sympathy for these nine people and the anti-war cause deepened. It was clear to me that the government was trying to silence the growing anti-war movement in Buffalo with repression, intimidation, physical violence, serious legal charges, and especially by targeting the anti-war leaders. I felt that I had to get more involved.

Chapter 15

Democratic National Convention

One evening, I was softly playing a song on my guitar as George and I were watching the Democratic National Convention on TV at our apartment. The convention was held in Chicago, and when we saw Mayor Daley's police club and tear-gas anti-war demonstrators outside the convention hall we were outraged.

"Did you see that!" George exclaimed, as he brushed back the blonde clump of hair from his forehead. We saw a swarm of blue-shirted riot-clad police sweep through Grant Park clubbing and arresting unarmed demonstrators. Some were sleeping on the ground and were clubbed as they lay there.

"Unbelievable," I responded, as I put down the guitar. "They're doing all that right in front of hundreds of TV cameras from all over the world."

"The whole world is watching!" the demonstrators chanted, as the TV cameras kept rolling.

"They're trying to break up the demonstrations so the public won't know how many people are there protesting against the war," George continued.

"That's right," I agreed. "That's exactly what they're doing."

We looked at each other.

"We should go," I said.

"It's about an eight hour drive to Chicago," George said.

"If we leave right now, we'll get there early tomorrow morning," I added.

We grabbed our jackets, got in George's little sports car and headed for Chicago. It was 10:00 pm. Both George and I had worked graveyard shifts before, so driving all night should be no problem. We put on a radio station that carried reports from the streets of Chicago as we drove.

"We'll call in sick for tomorrow," George commented. I nodded. We were hardly thinking of work now.

As we entered Chicago, the sun was coming up. We drove as close to Grant Park as we could and parked, then got out and walked. There were police barricades everywhere. It looked like a war zone. Bloody demonstrators were scattered throughout the park. Some had big red-stained white bandages around their heads. The smell of tear-gas stung the air. Park benches were over-turned and busted up and the park was littered with anti-war leaflets and radical newspapers.

The police had tried to clear the park during the night, with limited success. Some people were still there and others were streaming back into the park at daybreak. Anti-war leaders began mounting upside-down trashcans or anything else they could climb onto and started speaking to the crowd through bullhorns.

"Last night we showed the whole world how the anti-war movement is treated by Daley's storm-troopers," one speaker shouted. "But their repressive tactics are backfiring. For every demonstrator they club, thousands – maybe millions of uncommitted people who are watching sympathize with us and our cause."

Loud applause erupted from the crowd. Speeches and marches and demonstrations went on for the next two days straight, from early morning until late into the night, with the police trying to stop the demonstrators however they could.

We heard many anti-war speakers. I learned later they were leaders of the movement. One was Tom Hayden, a founding leader of Students for a Democratic Society – often called 'SDS,' which I learned was the largest student organization in the country. I heard the names Rennie Davis and David Dellinger, though I didn't know anything about them at that time. Some speakers urged support for the anti-war candidates inside the Democratic Convention. Others denounced the Democrats and Republicans alike as "lackeys for capitalism and imperialism," which were cited as the underlying causes of the war.

I didn't really understand what some of the speakers were talking about, and the angry disagreements and charges that some anti-war organizations made against other anti-war organizations was bewildering. But every speaker opposed the war in Vietnam, and that united everyone. I was glad that George and I were a part of this powerful protest against the war. It really was heard around the world because media from all over the world was there covering the Convention.

As the crowd grew in size, and the sun's rays began warming up the cool morning air, rows and rows of helmeted riot police gathered across the street for as far as the eye could see. No shortage of police in this city I thought to myself. It was an eerie feeling.

"This is the Chicago Police Department," we heard boom across the street and into the park over a sound system. It drowned out our speakers, even the ones with bullhorns.

"You are unlawfully congregating in Grant Park. You have five minutes to leave the park. If you do not leave in five minutes, we will clear the park and you will be arrested."

There was an undercurrent of talking and some anguished looks on a few faces around us. I felt apprehensive too.

An anti-war speaker was standing on something that put him about three feet higher than the crowd, but I couldn't see what it was.

He held a bullhorn to his mouth and started shouting:

"Hell no, we won't go! Hell no, we won't go!" That was a chant by anti-war protesters saying they wouldn't go to Vietnam. In this case, we were also saying we weren't leaving the park.

People in the crowd started picking up the chant, and we joined them. Soon our chanting drowned out the police over their sound system. We drowned out the police! The power of the crowd was intoxicating, and my fear left me as I was swept up in this surge of defiant protest.

"Hell no, we won't go! Hell no, we won't go!" It went on and on. The sound was deafening and liberating.

All of a sudden we heard whistling noises and saw small missile-like objects with smoky tails hurtling through the air towards us, landing on the ground all around and hitting some people. The air was filled with a powerful sickening smell and I started choking. My nose and eyes were burning and running. We had been tear-gassed. Smoke engulfed us, people started running, and I couldn't see where I was going. The leaders yelled through the bullhorns, "Don't run. Walk, but don't run." They were afraid people would get trampled. Most everyone slowed down to a fast walk.

I kept an eye on George so we could stay together and could make out his form vaguely even though he was only several feet from me. We were moving along quickly, bumping into other people as we were propelled along by the crowd. I looked up and through blurry eyes saw a blue wall of riot police coming toward us. They wore gasmasks and carried big shields and huge nightsticks. More teargas canisters sailed over our heads. Suddenly, people broke into a run when the police charged into the crowd near us, clubbing people to the ground. Out of the corner of my eye I saw a big blue shape emerge from the smoke and charge right at me. A club was rushing toward my head. I ducked and swerved to the right and it just missed me, and I darted into the mass of humanity and smoke that was surging away from the assault. I lost sight of George momentarily and then saw him ahead of me. We were running, coughing, and wiping our eyes and noses. Finally we got to the far end of the park. The air was clear there and we were out of immediate danger. We stopped and looked back. The park was strewn with bodies and litter. Some people were still on the ground. Others were being pulled up and put into handcuffs and hauled away by the police. It was surreal.

I learned a lot that summer. At Standard Mirror, I learned that the poorer and less skilled you are the worse you are treated. But I also learned that if people organize, they *can* stop their oppressors. The Vietnamese were doing that, and so were the workers at Standard Mirror – even though on a much smaller scale.

When I got back to Buffalo, I thought about everything that had gone on in August of 1968. I remembered reading that the US Department of Defense reported flying over 100,000 bombing runs on North Vietnam over the past three and a half years, dropping over 2.5 million tons of bombs. Hundreds of thousands of people were killed or maimed for life, including men, women and little children. The horror of it was appalling. What made it even more chilling was when I heard Republican Party presidential candidate Richard Nixon state: "In Vietnam they have no reason to end the war. It's hurting us more than it's hurting them." Nixon is insane, I thought. How could any human being make such an unbelievably vicious and bizarre statement? But, Nixon is not human. When I saw his face, I saw horns. He was the devil incarnate. When Nixon appeared before the public, I felt I was watching a horror movie. The audience saw Nixon disguised as a human being, and many cheered for him at campaign rallies. But I could see he was Lucifer, and I wondered with dread: could he fool enough people to become president of the United States?

I grew a lot that summer. I began seeing connections between the suffering and injustices committed against the Vietnamese people, American soldiers, American factory workers, the poor, minorities, myself and everyone else who is a victim of mistreatment. My own personal connections were being threatened by the draft and possibly being forced to fight in Vietnam, witnessing the injustice of racism in Florida, feeling the injustices at Standard Mirror, and recalling my childhood mistreatment at the hands of a neighborhood bully, Carlton. On the other side were the oppressors – the people who were inflicting this pain and exploitation and abuse on others – the Nixons of the world and their backers. They had to be stopped. I instinctively sided with the first group. I felt it in my bones, in my very being. It could be no other way. I was one of them. At that point I began to see myself as more than an observer or sympathizer. I began to see myself as a participant in the movement for peace and justice. I felt that I was becoming a part of it.

I thought about what that might mean. I thought that there might be a price to pay for standing up for justice. Look at what happened to Bruce Beyer and Bruce Cline and their supporters. They were arrested for protesting the war and were now facing federal felony charges. The Vietnamese people and American soldiers were paying the ultimate price every day. Even well known public leaders were not spared. Two months after Dr. King's death, Bobby Kennedy was assassinated in Los Angeles on June 5 while running for the Presidency on a platform to end the war in Vietnam, end discrimination, and for economic and political reforms. It was chilling.

But remaining uninvolved wasn't safe either. I wasn't involved in social or political movements or politics when I was forced to register for the military draft. I could have been drafted and sent to Vietnam to kill or be killed without ever having voiced a word of criticism of our government's policies, just like most everyone else who was sent there. There was no protection from harm or abuse by being quiet. I was coming to the realization that I had to get more involved. I had to add my voice and efforts to help strengthen this movement because it was the only chance we had of ending the abuse, the exploitation, the killing and the madness. But what about my dream of becoming an artist? I was a student at one of the best art schools in North America. Many aspiring artists would give anything to attend the Ontario College of Art. What would happen to my career as an artist? Would that be jeopardized? Or could I do both art and political activism?

One day I went into a small pizza shop on Delaware Avenue in Tonawanda to get a slice of pizza. I saw a man who caught my attention. He was sitting alone in a booth near the front window and he just stared into space as if in trance. He looked to be about 40 and had an expression on his face that contained a mixture of bewilderment, anger and horror. For some reason he looked like a war veteran to me, possibly from another war and another time. Maybe, because of the type of hat that he was wearing. I couldn't stop looking at his eyes. They seemed to be reflecting something terrible that he witnessed or experienced, like a war. Of course, I didn't know his background or what he was thinking, but that idea came to me. I thought that people who witness the killing and maiming of others and who survive themselves, could be seriously harmed emotionally and psychologically. Today, this condition is recognized and called Post Traumatic Stress Syndrome (PSTD), though I knew nothing of it at the time.

I got my pizza and went out to my car. It was parked about fifteen feet in front of the window where the man was sitting. I got behind the driver's seat and looked at him. He was still starring out of the window, but looking beyond me, and he did not notice me. I watched him for several moments and then remembered I had some drawing paper and a pencil in the car. I started to sketch his face, trying to capture his expression, especially his eyes. I went home and did the drawing in pen and ink. The look on his face haunts me even today. I wonder how many millions of people around the world live with the emotional pain of PSTD because of the terrible things they've seen. This drawing reminds me that suffering does not end after the abuse has stopped. I was deepening my art to express powerful human emotions. Maybe I could combine my art with my feelings about the world.

As the summer drew to a close, I prepared to go back to art school in Toronto. But something had changed in me. I knew that I couldn't just go back to my private life and forget everything I had seen and learned. I knew I had to get more involved in the movements for peace and justice, especially to end the war.

Jazzed on life at age one, 1949.

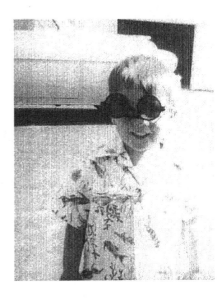

Clowning around with mom's sunglasses, at age 3.

Varsity soccer team at Kenmore West Senior High School, Kenmore, New York, 1966. I am second from left in the front row, next to friend, George Cownie, kneeling.

Paul Krehbiel

The Corroding Society sculpture George and I made for art class, 1966.

High school Yearbook, senior year photo, 1966.

Donna and I at Delaware Park, Buffalo, December 1967.

Going to Donna's Senior Prom, June 1967. My rented tuxedo was too small but it didn't spoil a great evening.

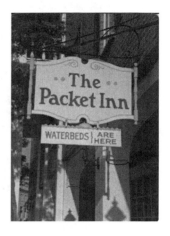

These 2'x 3' drawings that I did in 1967 of New York Governor Dewitt Clinton (top) and Erie Canal engineer Nathan Roberts were part of the décor in the Packet Inn restaurant in the City of Tonawanda, just north of Buffalo. I felt I was on my way to a career as an artist. They are now on display at the Erie Canal Discovery Center in nearby Lockport.

I saw African-Americans living in a poor rural slum in Clearwater, Florida in 1967. The crushing weight of racism and poverty showed on the faces of several older people which I tried to capture in this drawing.

In 1967, as the war worsened in Vietnam, I did this drawing in an art class that year at St. Petersburg Jr. College in Clearwater.

I lived in this duplex with four other art students on Grace St. in Toronto, Canada in 1967-68.

The atrium of the Ontario College of Art in Toronto where I was an art student in 1967-68.

I used various drawing and shading techniques to express emotions in my art. In my sketch of the woman I used a reddish brown contė crayon to convey movement, grace, femininity and softness. The ink drawing of a man with a whimsical expression was done using only vertical lines. I created shading by varying the thickness and spacing of the lines. The man sneaking out of the shadows was done using broad flat strokes with a black contė crayon.

Workers at Standard Mirror remove side mirror assemblies from racks after they were run through the electro-static spray booths and baking ovens. In 1968 I worked in the adjacent department.

Standard Mirror workers lived in these old houses on the same street as the factory. Two, three and more families lived in each house, surrounded by continuous factory noises, day and night.

U.S. soldiers ordered to fight in a war that many
came to oppose.

Young Vietnamese
children terrorized by
massive U. S bombing
campaigns.

The U.S. Military massacred 504 Vietnamese, mostly mothers and their children,
in My Lai, South Vietnam, in 1968. The military suppressed this terrible crime
until 1969 when it came out publically, causing more revulsion against the war,
both in the U.S. and world wide.

Draft resister and anti-war protestor Bruce Beyer after being beaten and arrested by FBI agents at the Unitarian Church in Buffalo in August 1968. Eight other anti-war activists were arrested and all nine were charged with felonies. The case was known as the Buffalo Nine. I became a supporter of the Buffalo Nine Defense Committee.

Police beat up anti-war protestors outside the Democratic Party National Convention in Chicago in August 1968. I was among the protestors and witnessed this brutality.

My depiction of an old veteran, drawn in 1968, revealing the anguish of war.

I put my drawing of two soldiers on Christmas Cards in December 1968. Later, I made it into an anti-war poster.

End the War NOW!

Members of the
Buffalo Draft
Resistance
Union hand out
anti-draft and
anti-war
leaflets at the
Buffalo Draft
Induction
Center on Main
Street, 1969.
I'm on the left.

Over a hundred young men forced by the draft to line up at the Buffalo induction center to prepare to go to war. Here they receive our anti-war leaflets. This size line up took place three days a week. Blacks were drafted in higher numbers than their percentage of the population.

I joined 1,000 students in a College A course at the University of Buffalo in 1969 to do community organizing. Students (left) pack a large assembly room to discuss educational reforms. Black Students (bottom) led fight to establish a Black Studies Program , and free breakfast program for children.

Janis Joplin

I am somewhere in this huge crowd of 500,000 people at the Woodstock Music and Art Fair, August 15-18, 1969. Below, are just a few of the many great artists who performed during this historic weekend.

Richie Havens

Joan Baez

Chapter 16

Felony Charge

I returned to Toronto in September of 1968 in a swirl of emotions. I was still upset about breaking up with Donna and the distance that was growing between my family and me. The war was still raging, anti-war protestors were getting arrested and beaten, a devil was running for president, and most people seemed oblivious to the horrors. I was depressed, angry and confused. My goal was still to become an artist, but also to be someone who stood up for justice. I just wasn't sure how.

When I was battling the lousy working conditions at Standard Mirror, and dodging policemen's clubs in Chicago, I was in the moment and my mind was occupied. But now, back in Canada, I was out of the turmoil, and thoughts of missing Donna flooded my brain. I also wrestled with the feeling that while I had escaped from the dangers in the US, I was shirking my responsibility to try to right the wrongs there. The United States was my home, and my country had been hijacked by a band of rogues who were committing terrible crimes in the name of the American people. How could I turn my back on something I knew to be wrong? Since I was living and going to school in Canada, it seemed harder to help. But the thought of getting more involved stayed in the back of my mind and I mulled it over.

In the meantime, since I had lost Donna, I decided to throw myself into my art. I thought that if I had spent even a fraction of the time that I spent with Donna doing art, I would have something to show for it. I would have a stack of drawings and paintings and sculptures that I could point to and say, 'See, I've done something. Not all is lost.' Of course, all was not lost in my relationship with Donna; in fact, it was an important part of my life and, deep down, I still longed for her.

But I was now a sculpture major and I threw myself into my work. I was in classes where I was doing sculpture every day, all day long. I did clay modeling, mold making, and worked in wood, metal and other materials. I did everything from welding to trying to throw clay pots on a potter's wheel – which I wasn't very good at.

My biggest project was a large semi-abstract sculpture in clay featuring long sweeping curves which slightly resembled human or animal body parts, likes hips, backs and shoulders. The feeling that I was trying to create was one of power and sensuousness. I liked everything about doing this work. Creating something in my head, constructing it in real life, seeing the different shapes that emerged as I moved slowly around it, and feeling the soft clay in my hands as I shaped the forms. I was in another world and it was wonderful.

Yet, the outside world kept crashing in. Every new horror in the escalating war in Vietnam was emblazoned on my brain. I found myself wrestling more and more with my vision of a beautiful world filled with art, human compassion and love, and the injustices and brutality that seemed to be all around me. I was being torn apart.

I started thinking that perhaps I should transfer to a regular university, especially one with an active anti-war movement. I thought about the University of Buffalo. Not this semester, but maybe for the spring 1969 semester, or the fall of 1969. Of course, if I went back to the United States, I would have to deal with the potential of being drafted and sent to Vietnam, but I knew I wouldn't go. I felt I had to continue to do something to protest the war.

Within the first month back at art school, I saw a leaflet for a demonstration against the war in Vietnam to be held in October in downtown Toronto. The leaflet announced that American war resisters living in Canada, including former US soldiers, would be marching. I'd like to meet some of them, I thought. I mentioned it to the guys in our house, but they were either busy or weren't interested. So, I decided to go alone. On the day of the march, people gathered in a park near the start of the march. It seemed like thousands were there. Here were other people, many others, who felt like I did and I was glad I was there. I'm not sure the guys at our house even remembered that this was the day of the march. When I got up that morning they had already left the house, and I left before any of them got home. There were big banners and signs saying; "US Out of Vietnam" and "End the War Now!" I moved toward the front of the march to see what was going on. Someone announced through a bullhorn that the march was about to begin, and a sea of people moved slowly onto a major street and spread out from curb to curb. I found myself unexpectantly at the front.

"Stop the war in Vietnam! Stop the war in Vietnam!" the marchers chanted, and I added my voice to the deafening chorus. A large number of bystanders watched from the sidewalk, and some were applauding and waving. The sound of thousands of people chanting and marching together sent a surge of energy through my body. Together, with this crowd, I felt powerful, and I could see others felt the same way. It was intoxicating.

We had gone several blocks when we saw a line of policemen on horses across the entire width of the street. They were blocking our line of march. As we approached them, the march slowed down and then stopped about 40 feet away.

"This is the police," we heard blaring through a loudspeaker held by a cop atop a huge horse that was clacking his front hoof on the pavement. "You are being ordered to disperse immediately."

"We have a right to be here," said the leader of our march through a much fainter bullhorn. "Everyone stay in line," he instructed.

The police officer repeated his announcement and the horses started forward. The clacking of hooves sounded like an army on the march. Bursts of steam shot from the horse's nostrils in the cool fall air as they approached. Quickly, they loomed above us, and their legs were as tall as people.

"Everyone stay where you are," the march leader repeated. "Don't run." I remembered those same instructions in Chicago.

The horses pushed against our front row. Two women in front of me were knocked to the ground, and two marchers next to them grabbed their arms and dragged them out from under the horses' hooves. I was in the second row and felt the crowd push against me. I was near the curb when suddenly a man in a business suit standing on the sidewalk lunged into the crowd and jumped on the kid next to me and started hitting him. I instinctively jumped on the attacker and grabbed him around his throat with my left arm and started to pull him away.

Immediately *my* air was cut off. I felt an arm squeezing around my neck. I tried to get loose but my head only turned slightly into the crook of an elbow. Out of the corner of my eye saw a uniformed police officer. I was pulled off the attacker and two cops wrestled me to the ground. They handcuffed my hands behind my back and led me to a police paddy wagon. Fighting and rioting and tear gas filled the air, and I was pushed into the back of the empty police van.

The police took my wallet, got my name from my driver's license and wrote it down on a pad.

"Book him for felony assault for attacking a federal agent," one policeman barked to the other.

Suddenly it hit me. I had attacked an undercover law enforcement official. But everything happened so fast that it didn't sink in. The metal door of the paddy wagon slammed shut behind me with a loud bang. Tear gas mist rushed through the little round holes in the grate in the door on narrow streams of light, burning my eyes, nose and throat. It was so dark inside I couldn't see a thing. I heard screaming, feet running on the pavement, thuds, sirens and horses hooves.

Then the door flew open and another protester was thrown inside by two burly cops along with a cloud of tear gas. I was coughing and my eyes and nose were running, but I got a blurry glimpse out of the half-opened door of people running, flying and being clubbed in a white fog. The door slammed shut behind my new companion and it was immediately dark again. I couldn't see him, but it was a comforting knowing that I wasn't alone. The door opened five or six more times as more people were shoved inside. Once our small compartment was packed, the paddy wagon started moving. We were taken to jail and booked.

I was put into a small cell by myself. There was no light in the cell, but a muted glow crept in from the hallway. It was very quiet and I was alone. My mind started going over what had happened. I went to the march by myself and no one there knew me. I wasn't sure my house-mates knew where I had gone, and no one knew I was in jail. I wondered how long I would be there. Then it sunk in. I had been arrested for assaulting a federal officer. I felt a pull in my chest. Assault carries a harsh penalty, including possibly time in prison. A sick feeling gripped my stomach and the euphoria that I experienced in the march drained from my body.

The hallway light shone on some small scratchings on the wall across from my metal bed. I moved closer to look. There were people's names, some profanities and other words I couldn't make out. I had a pen with me and I added my own thoughts: "I was unjustly put in this cell for protesting against the immoral and illegal war in Vietnam." I'm not a criminal, I reminded myself. I did nothing wrong. I felt a little better after I made that statement.

I took solace in knowing that I wasn't the first person to go to jail. I also knew that others who protested the war had gone to prison, some for years, and that the soldiers who were drafted and sent to

Vietnam and the Vietnamese people were suffering much more than I was. I sat quietly and thought about all these things.

After five or six hours, a guard came to my cell and unlocked the door. "Come with me," he instructed.

I got up from my bunk and followed him down a long hallway. Soon we were in a large room with a lot of people scurrying around with file folders and other papers in their hands. I saw a larger crowd of people through a big glass window on the other side of a wall and locked door. Some paperwork was filled out on me, I was given a court date, and then led to the door.

"You're being released," a jail worker told me.

"What?" I asked, not quite understanding what was going on.

"You're being bailed out. You can leave." He opened the door and held it for me as I passed through.

The crowd started clapping, and a leader of the march came up to me and introduced himself. He was a small, wiry guy with dark wavy hair and piercing eyes. I didn't know him but remembered seeing him at the head of the march yelling chants through his bullhorn.

"We've bailed you out, Paul," he told me as he shook my hand. "You were the first of thirty-four people arrested today. You're charged with felony assault but we have lawyers for you. That was a great thing you did today."

"Thanks," I mumbled, wondering what was so great. What's the big deal, I thought. A guy next to me was attacked and I tried to help him.

I was impressed that a group of complete strangers bailed me out of jail. Here they were, well into the night, at the jailhouse, bailing out all of us who were arrested.

"How did you know my name," I asked him.

"We got everyone's names from the police's arrest list. Here, take this," he said, as he handed me a piece of paper. "This is my name and telephone number. If you need to get in touch with me, call. We'll be getting back to you to prepare for your court date. Okay?"

"Yes, yes, that's fine," I said. "Thank you. I really appreciate this. But how much is this going to cost? And the bail. How much do I owe you for that?"

"Don't worry about that," he returned. "We have lawyers taking care of everything."

More people were being released into the crowd, and he moved towards them. People were smiling at me and one guy patted me on the shoulder as I moved toward the door. Before I knew it I was outside in the cool autumn night air. On my way home, I thought about how I had wanted to get more involved in the anti-war movement. And now I was. Of course, getting arrested wasn't part of my plan. But I had no regrets. I felt strongly that I was on the side of what was morally correct and I would deal with whatever punishment might be dealt to me. The fact that I was charged with assault for trying to help someone else who had been assaulted was bizarre to me. Furthermore, we were trying to stop the mass killing in Vietnam, while those giving the orders for those killings – President Johnson and the people around him, were free to continue their criminal murders. The world had turned upside down. Wrong was judged to be right, and good people were being persecuted for trying to stop evil. But I had found the anti-war movement. It's true, I didn't know any of them, but I felt like I had found a home.

Chapter 17

Metal Factory Blues

During the fall of 1968, I was working in a metal factory in Toronto on the afternoon shift. I had left the glass factory in Buffalo at the end of August to return to art school. I finished my art classes around 3 pm, and then left for work. My shift began at 4 pm and ran until 12 midnight. We made primarily metal office furniture. My job was to operate a punch press. It was the most boring job I ever had. I would stick a piece of metal into the machine, activate the press, and it would punch out holes or some other pattern in the end of the metal. Then I would stack the piece on a cart, where it would go to another department to be assembled with other metal parts to make desks, shelves, and other products. There were about twenty other guys in this department doing the same thing that I was doing. The punch presses were lined up in four rows, and you heard the constant pounding of the heavy metal presses over and over again all night long.

It was a terrible job, with low pay and no union. The boredom was unbearable. Pick up a piece of metal, stick it into the machine and punch holes in the end, and stack it on a cart. One after another after another, for hours and hours. We made hundreds and thousands of these parts every night. It was dehumanizing. I felt like a cog in a machine, and a weak cog at that. I got tired, sore and irritable, and my mind began playing tricks on me. But the machine worked on and on.

I was unhappy and angry about my personal life. I was still upset about my breakup with Donna. The horror of Vietnam was still going on, I had a felony assault charge hanging over my head, and I was working at a miserable job.

There was a big round clock on a faded white post in the row in front of me about twenty feet away. From where I worked, I was staring right at it. That clock was deadly. It never moved. After doing four or five pieces of metal, I would look up and the hands on the clock had moved one tick.

Oh shit, I groaned every night to myself, this will never end. With most things that I did, I didn't think about the time too much.

Time just moved along on its own, sometimes faster, sometimes slower, while I was focused on something else.

Not on this job. This job was so simple, there was nothing to focus on. Except time. All I thought about was time, and how it moved at glacial speed. My whole goal was to get the time to pass. I didn't really work toward completing the whole night. That was too steep a mountain to climb. Instead, I worked toward making it to my first 15 minute break. That was two hours away. A very long two hours. Once I made it to the first break, I could breathe a sigh of relief and rest and take a break from the tedium of the machine. I made it. Thank God, I made it, I said to myself. As the buzzer sounded, everyone fled from their machines to go to the coke and coffee and candy machines. Coke never tasted so good after that grinding boredom. Then I worked hard to relish every minute of that 15-minute break. But now time sped up and before long the buzzer sounded and it was back to my machine. Now the goal was to make it another two hours, until lunch break.

One night, when I returned to my machine and started to pick up a piece of metal, I noticed that the clock was staring at me. Taunting me. Daring me to catch it move. I stared back. I fixed my eyes on it. I glared at it. I refused to look away until the big hand moved. We were locked in this staring contest for a long time. And then, finally, it happened. The big hand clicked forward. It moved. I had won! I had beaten the clock. We stared each other down, and the clock blinked first. The big hand had moved one minute.

One minute! Oh my God, I'll never make it to lunch break like this, I thought. I can't look at the clock any more. It doesn't move nearly fast enough. There is something wrong with that clock. I have to do something else. I have to stop thinking about the clock and think about anything else. But what, I wondered as I slid a piece of metal into the machine, keeping my eyes down on my work so I wouldn't look at the clock. I punched out three holes on the end of the metal. I'll think about the newest song by the Rolling Stones. But what is their newest song? I thought for a while and did several more pieces of metal, and couldn't remember. Then I realized that I had gotten my mind off the clock. I kept my eyes on my work and did many more pieces. But then the metal began dancing before my eyes and my mind was spinning. I had to look away. I needed to clear my head. I decided after I completed the next piece I'd look up and check the clock. It certainly would have moved, probably at least 10 or 15 minutes.

As I was punching the next piece, I could feel the clock staring at me. So what, I thought. I know that some real time has passed. That clock is not going to control me; I'm in control here. I finished the piece, put it on the cart next to me and looked up triumphantly at the clock.

Holy shit! It had moved only three minutes! What am I going to do? I started to panic. No, I can't panic, I thought. I've got to calm down and get my mind on something else. Then it hit me. Of course! I'll think about my art projects at school.

So I started working out in my head what I would do next. The big clay sculpture. At one end, there is a part that looks like the strong, long neck of a horse. If I narrow it down a little on each side and put a long smoothly flowing arch into it, it will convey the feeling of a strong horses neck. I pictured the sculpture in my head, and then pictured how I would reshape it. I did this with every part of the piece. Finally, lunch break came. And finally the end of the shift. I was tired after this long day. But I had some good ideas for my art the next day at school.

After finishing one art project in my head, or getting as far as I could, the clock grabbed my attention again. But I knew I just had to think of something else, even if just to daydream, and that helped. Anything that would allow my mind to drift and wander. Daydreaming. That was the mental salvation of many a factory worker. I would dream about girls, relive good times I had in the past, think about upcoming things to do, places I've been or places I would like to visit. Anything. The job was still terrible, but it helped me get through the night.

One evening early in my shift on November 1, 1968, my machine jammed. I went to one of the bosses to tell him about the problem. He was working with someone else, and told me to go back to my machine, and that he would come over to see what the problem was when he finished with the other guy.

I went back to my machine and waited. And waited. He was still busy. I remembered a couple of days earlier, he had told another guy who was standing around and not working, to get to work. He told him in an angry tone of voice, as if something might happen to him if he didn't get to work quickly – like maybe he'd get fired.

The longer I stood there waiting, the more anxious I got. I was afraid a boss would come by and see me doing nothing and want to fire me. So I looked at the machine. Maybe I could see what was causing the jam. As I leaned forward slightly to look into the die area, the machine activated. The huge top part of the press came down and met the bottom plate and I felt a sharp pain in my left hand. The top of the press rose. I looked down at my hand in panic, pulled off my work glove, and saw that my first and second fingers had been crushed.

My head was spinning. I pulled away from my machine and veered into the isle. A boss came running toward me with a big puffy ball of white gauze, which he quickly wrapped around my hand. He had me hold it up to my chest, above my heart, and guided me along by the elbow. Soon we were outside in the parking lot, getting into his car, and heading for the hospital. It was rush hour, and we were hardly moving.

I was in a stunned daze, and thinking repeatedly: can I just play that last few minutes over again. I won't put my hand any where near that machine.

But of course it was too late. In one split second my life was changed forever. Here I was. A 20-year-old sculpture student, distraught over the carnage in Vietnam, depressed over the loss of a girlfriend that I deeply loved, facing a felony assault charge, estranged from my home and family, living in a another country, and working at a terrible job that had maimed me. How could I go on working? How could I continue doing sculpture? Or play the guitar? What would girls think of me now? How would I ever have another girlfriend, or a wife, or family? My life seemed ruined. I wanted to run away. I wanted to get outside of my body and go someplace far away, and pretend this never happened.

Once at the hospital, I was taken into surgery. When I came to, I was lying in a bed with my arm tied up high above my head and wrapped in a huge gauze bandage. I was groggy and in pain and was told I had lost the first finger and half of the second finger on my left hand.

I looked up through blurry eyes and a spinning brain and saw images of soldiers and civilians lying in pools of blood in Vietnam on the TV in my room. Next to me was a man who had been badly burned in an electrical fire while working in the subway system. His face, hands and arms were charred and the skin looked like thick pieces of black and yellow crusts of burnt meat with liquid oozing from cracks in it. Every time he took a breath, his body moved just slightly, and he would let out a quiet but painful groan.

But worst of all was the young 17 year-old unwed girl down the hall who was pregnant and tried to kill herself by jumping in front of a subway train. She didn't succeed, nor did she lose the baby. But she lost both her legs at the knees. It was chilling to see her, with her protruding belly, learning to walk on cold, thin, silver bars that would become her artificial legs.

With all these people in pain and suffering around me, I felt like getting up to help them. My accident gave me a feeling of what the Vietnamese people and American soldiers were experiencing every day, though for many of them, their pain and loss was much worse than mine. But it linked me to them. I remembered something that Schopenhauer had written: "The most effective consolation in every misfortune and every affliction is to observe others who are more unfortunate than we, and everyone can do this. But what does that say for the condition of the whole?"

Chapter 18

University of Buffalo

After my accident, I dropped out of art school and went back to Buffalo to my parent's house. I was taking codeine for the pain and existed in a nether world. I stayed up late at night, drawing or painting or watching TV, and would sleep late in the morning. I really didn't want to get up to face another day. What was I going to do now, I wondered?

During this time I did a number of pen and ink drawings, mostly of people's faces. They were faces full of emotion: mostly sadness, pain and horror. One was of a depressed Black man. Another was of a young Vietnamese girl crying out in pain. I did a drawing of two soldiers, one holding the other on the battlefield. I put that drawing on the cover of Christmas cards that I made that year, 1968, and wrote a poem on the inside:

This is the season that is signified by happiness...
A happiness that is built thru showing concern for
others...
But this season, some will only feel sadness...
A sadness that is pain-filled every season of the year.

I later made the drawing into a poster. Under the two soldiers I wrote in red letters: "End the War NOW!"

The school semester at the University of Buffalo wasn't over yet, so I started sitting in classes with George and Howard in the later half of November 1968. There were about three or four weeks until the end of the semester. One class was a Philosophy course taught by a well-known conservative libertarian, Professor Zimmer, who espoused a philosophy of extreme individualism. His argument was that the only really free man was the man who stood completely on his own, fiercely independent, without ties or obligations to any one else other than those of his own choosing. Therefore, one had to assume personal responsibility for everything in life, and gain as much knowledge as possible in every field in order to be completely free. Government was the embodiment of lack of individual freedom because of all its laws, rules and regulations.

Professor Zimmer was very bright and highly regarded in his field. His classes were filled to capacity. They were composed mostly of conservative and libertarian students who rallied to his defense – though he didn't need it, some left-wing students who wanted to challenge him, and many others who were uncommitted ideologically but who sought the intellectual rigor of his classes. Some, I suspect, were there just to see the fireworks.

Zimmer had an uncanny method of involving his students. He would make a bold statement in class, and when a student challenged him, he would attack the student's arguments with a series of questions. When the student answered his first question, Professor Zimmer would pose a series of other questions. When the student had difficulty presenting a satisfactory explanation to one of Zimmer's questions, the student's arguments appeared to be weakened. Zimmer often asked questions that there wasn't an answer for, or that one wouldn't know the answer unless he had done an exhaustive study of the topic. Working this way, the student's line of thought was thrown into doubt. It then appeared that Professor Zimmer's view had won out.

"A man is free only when he stands alone on his own two feet, apart from duties or responsibilities to others," Professor Zimmer stated one morning. There was silence.

"So, everyone agrees with this?" he asked.

A tall lanky guy in the back with long stringy brown hair mated across his forehead raised his hand.

"Yes. Robert. What do you think?"

"Well, Professor Zimmer, I don't think any one can stand completely alone. We all have ties to other people. For example, we all rely on a variety of social services. We live in houses built by others, and eat food grown by other people," Robert explained.

"But is all that necessary," Zimmer asked. "Don't you have the ability to build your own house and grow your own food?"

"Well, yes," Robert answered somewhat tentatively. "I mean I don't really know how to build a house."

"Yes, but you could learn, couldn't you?"

"Sure, I suppose so."

"And if you learned to build your own house, you would probably save a lot of money and, more importantly, it would be yours. Right now, you're probably paying rent for an apartment, right?" Zimmer asked.

"Yes," Robert responded.

"So, you are unfree because you have to pay rent to someone else for something that is not even yours, and for something that will never be yours. Right?"

"Yes," Robert continued, "but I wouldn't consider myself not being free because I have to pay rent."

"Well, are you free to pay the rent or not pay the rent as you please?" Zimmer pressed on.

"No, I have to pay the rent, or I'll be kicked out."

"So, is that being free? How do you define freedom."?

"Well, freedom is where I have control over my life, where other people aren't trying to control me," Robert continued.

"And do you have control over your life when it comes to paying rent? It sounds like your landlord has control over you when he comes to collect the rent. He's saying, 'pay me the rent, or I'll put you out on the street.' Where is the control over your own life here?"

Robert was silent for a moment.

Professor Zimmer used the pause to continue his attack. "If you built your own house and owned it, no one could tell you that you had to pay rent or would have to move out. In fact no one could tell you anything about your house. They couldn't tell you what color to paint it, or whether or not to remodel it, or what to put on the walls, or even to have walls or not to have walls. You would have control over all of that. Robert, could you knock down the walls in your apartment, if you wanted?"

"No," Robert answered.

"What would happen if you did?" Zimmer pushed on with zeal.

"I would probably be arrested for destroying the property," Robert responded.

"That doesn't sound like much freedom to me," Zimmer announced triumphantly, to snickers and laughter. "Robert, you sound like a condemned and unfree man to me."

Zimmer never proved his bold statement, and likely would have difficulty doing so. Instead, he turned the focus of the discussion onto the weaknesses in the student's argument, defined the terrain of the battle on his terms, set up traps for the student, and then claimed victory. It was infuriating, but also intellectually stimulating. I left Zimmer's class and talked passionately with George and Howard about how to come up with arguments to defeat Zimmer in his next class. At some point I saw that simply poking holes in someone else's position did not automatically "prove" Zimmer's position. But Professor Zimmer forced us to think, to question, to use logical reasoning, and if we were lucky, to recognize the intellectual slight-of-hand that he so successfully employed on a regular basis. His class did a lot to sharpen my skills of critical thinking, analysis, and debate. I loved the intellectual stimulation, and I knew it was good training for battling pro-war, right-wing and conservative students and ideologues, and convincing people that the war was wrong.

I spent a good part of nearly every day on the campus, mostly in Norton Union, the student center, when I wasn't sitting in on a class. I just absorbed everything I could. I saw students in anti-war, liberal and left wing organizations, and many of them set up literature tables in halls and open spaces in Norton Union. They seemed to be the most prominent groups on campus. Members of these groups handed out leaflets every morning inside the main entrance to Norton Union. One leaflet was about a forum on Vietnam. Another announced a meeting to discuss reforms in the University. It was exciting and stimulating and it felt like exactly the place I wanted to be.

Students for a Democratic Society (SDS), a large and militant left-wing student organization with about 100,000 members nationwide, had a literature table in Norton Union. The table held a stack of the SDS newspaper, *New Left Notes*, leaflets and pamphlets about protests against the war in Vietnam, and literature protesting discrimination against racial minorities and women, and for increased rights for workers and unions. Other flyers urged protection of the environment, others exposed and protested the greed of big business and capitalism, and some advocated socialism. I didn't really understand a lot of what the radical and left-wing students were saying at first, especially about capitalism and socialism, but I agreed with SDS in its opposition to the war and on a number of other issues.

The biggest issue for most of the groups was the war. Students stood around the SDS table in the student union discussing the latest bombing in Vietnam and what the anti-war movement was doing to protest it. Others came by the table to pick up stacks of literature to take to other parts of the campus. There was a swirl of activity in Norton Union and it was exciting.

What was intriguing to me was that here was a whole world of ideas, ideals, and action on many issues that I thought about and cared about by a group of some of the brightest young people around, centered in one place. I wanted very much to be a part of it. I had to figure out how I was going to get accepted as a student at UB.

But first I had to deal with the felony assault charge hanging over my head in Canada. During this time I was scheduled to appear in court in Toronto for my arraignment. I arrived on the appointed date and time dressed in a tie and coat and entered the courtroom. I saw some of my fellow defendants and one of the organizers from the anti-war march. I told him I had spoken only briefly with my attorney, over the phone, and that I didn't even know what he looked like. He told me my attorney wasn't there yet, but not to worry. I tried not to, but I couldn't ignore the prospects facing me. If my case went to trial, I could be tied up in court for many months or longer, I thought. And if I was convicted, I might be sentenced to prison. In either case, my dream of going to UB would go up in smoke. The guy from the anti-war movement directed me to take a seat in the dock with the other defendants. Important looking people were entering the courtroom carrying large stacks of files and folders. I asked the guy next to me if he knew who our attorney was. He pointed to a man in a dark suit who had just entered the courtroom and who was carrying a thick briefcase. The judge entered and court was called into session. Some words were spoken by the judge and the attorneys, and then I heard the Judge call out my name and tell me to stand. I was startled to be called so quickly, and without being able to consult with my attorney. I stood up and my heart was thumping. My attorney asked to approach the bench and he, the judge and the prosecutor talked quietly for a couple of minutes. Their conference ended and my attorney returned to his seat. The judge began:

"Mr. Krehbiel. It has come to my attention that the evidence collected on you has been lost. The prosecutor doesn't even know what you were charged with, though he believes you were one of the first persons to be arrested on the date in question. Therefore, there are no charges against you and you are free from any further obligation to this court. You may leave." I couldn't believe it! I was free! I thought that perhaps in all the pandemonium, the officers lost the notes they made on me, or maybe the notes got lost somewhere else in the system. It didn't matter. I was going home to Buffalo.

Chapter 19

Philosophy Student

While I still liked to draw and paint, I decided that I wanted to switch my major to the social sciences. I wanted to become a full-time student at UB. It was much more than proving my high school guidance counselor wrong. My grades had improved after high school to more B's, but would that be good enough to get into UB? The State University of New York at Buffalo is the largest institution in the State University system and is considered a very good university. Bright students from all over the state, the nation and even from other countries come to study at UB. The A students from my high school got into UB. The weak B and C students went elsewhere.

I heard from a friend that it was easier to get into UB's night school, and then, if you did well there, transfer to the day school. After talking to several administrators who felt that I hadn't shown enough academic progress, I found one who reluctantly gave me a chance to prove myself by letting me enroll in night school. I tried to get UB to accept all my credits from St. Petersburg Junior College and the Ontario College of Art, but they only accepted those from St. Pete's. When I asked why the OCA credits were rejected, I was told because OCA wasn't accredited by the proper US accrediting institution. How ironic. My art classes at OCA were much more rigorous and of a higher quality than those at St. Pete's, and I told UB that. But they wouldn't change their mind. So I lost nearly a year and a half of work done at OCA. But I was now a UB student, and that's what counted.

But I was also apprehensive. I didn't know if I could measure up academically. I committed myself then to work as hard as I could. I had to succeed. I switched my major to philosophy, and I enrolled in three philosophy classes, an anthropology class, and a class in College A, an experimental college that combined academic study with involvement in the community. The name of the College A course was Conflict and Change in the Local Community.

I really concentrated in all of my classes. It was difficult at first, since my brain wasn't used to working so hard. But the more I used it, the better it got. It was like exercising a muscle. I actually felt like I was getting smarter. It was exciting to piece bits of information together and gain new insight into things. I found that if I listened in class, took good notes, read the textbook, and then wrote summaries of each topic – like I did in Mr. Mooshie's class in high school, I could understand the material and remember it. I started getting good grades – mostly A's. It was amazing. It felt good to do so well, but it wasn't to "get ahead" of others. My main goal was to learn how society worked, understand why there were wars and poverty and injustice and what could be done to solve those problems. I also think I focused so intently on my studies to help me take my mind off the injury to my hand. As I got smarter, I felt better about myself.

I also started reading a lot more on my own. One book that had a powerful impact on me was *Vietnam! Vietnam!* by Felix Greene. It was given to me by my mom and dad. We still didn't talk much about Vietnam, but they knew the war was an important subject for me. I really appreciated receiving that book. Greene gave a well-documented history of Vietnam and how the United States got involved there. It wasn't a long book. It had about 100 pages of devastating photos with captions and brief descriptions showing the brutal treatment of the Vietnamese by the French and US, and only about 50 pages of text. I was shocked to learn about the lies that our government and the mass media told the American people. The history that was left out by our government turned the truth upside down.

I read and re-read that book. I underlined important sections of it. I took notes. I wrote a summary of the main points. I folded over the corners of pages that contained especially important facts, and put scraps of paper between certain key pages so I could easily find them. Then I rewrote a longer version of the main points. I rewrote it in bullet points. I thought this information was so important that it had to be gotten out to others, so I started writing a leaflet. The more I wrote and rewrote, the clearer the real history became and the more I remembered. I imagined myself arguing with opponents and found that I was memorizing key facts, as well as the arguments opponents would make. I carried the book around with me in my folder. It was as if I had designed a course for myself on that one short 50 page book and I went over it so many times that I knew all the pertinent facts.

One day on campus, I ran into Charles, a bright but very conservative student from one of my classes. He was arrogant and liked to challenge leftist students to debates. He was wearing what looked like a very expensive powder blue Herringbone shirt, embroidered with his initials and he was arguing with a student in Norton Union about Vietnam. I stopped along with several other students to listen. Impromptu discussions and debates like this were common in Norton Union.

"The North Vietnamese Communists and their communist allies in South Vietnam, Russia and China are attempting to overthrow the government in South Vietnam by violence, subvert democracy, and impose a Communist state," Charles charged. "That is not only a threat to the South Vietnamese people, but also to our country. We had to go to Vietnam to defend the South Vietnamese government and democracy."

"That's bullshit," the antiwar student retorted. "The south Vietnamese government is a bunch of lackey's for the US."

"That's your defense?" Charles asked. "What's your proof? Do you deny that the communists are undermining democracy in South Vietnam and trying to take over by force? They have been subverting democracy there for decades."

Our anti-war friend was silent while he was thinking of a response, so I interjected.

"Well, let's get the history straight on this," I said. "There has never been any democracy in South Vietnam. Vietnam was colonized by the French for a hundred years until the French were defeated in 1954 at a battle in Dien Bien Phu. That ended French colonialism in Vietnam. The French tried to hold on to as much power as they could, especially in the southern part of the country, but they were defeated. Then, at the Geneva Conference held that same year, three major points were established: that Vietnam would be temporarily divided at the 17th parallel into a northern and southern zone, that elections would be held in two years to reunite the country, and that neither zone would receive any military aid from outside."

"Yes," said Charles, "but our government didn't sign those provisions."

"The Geneva Accords were agreed to by the principle parties: the Democratic Republic of Vietnam and France," I said. "And the US said it wouldn't interfere with those provisions, and it did. More importantly, the US had no business meddling in their affairs in the first place." I felt very self-confident. The facts were just coming out and I was countering each of Charles' rebuttals. All of my studying and writing was paying off.

"North Vietnam is communist," Charles exclaimed. "It's run by communists who imposed their will on the people by force, including on our allies in South Vietnam. We have an obligation to protect our allies."

"Those so-called allies in south Vietnam are illegitimate," I retorted. "They were imposed on the people of South Vietnam by our government."

"But no one elected the communists to power," Charles responded. "They impose their will on the people by force."

"Just like the American revolutionaries imposed their will on British colonialism by force in 1776," I responded. "There were no elections in the American colonies then. And there were never any elections in Vietnam – ever, and certainly none under French colonialism. But speaking of elections and democracy, when the first national election ever in Vietnam was scheduled for 1956, the US called it off. Do you know why? Because the candidate that the US supported would have lost. In fact, President Eisenhower, certainly no communist, wrote in his book, *Mandate for Change*, that had elections been held in Vietnam in 1956, probably 80% of the people would have voted for the communist Ho Chi Minh!"

The arrogant look dropped from Charles's face. I could hear the wheels turning in his brain as he searched for a response. "Well, I've never heard that," he managed.

"Of course you haven't because you are hearing only one side of the story," I continued. "We're only hearing what our government wants us to hear."

"But the media is over there reporting on the war," Charles returned, "and the government isn't too happy with some of that reporting."

"That's true, to a point," I conceded. "The government doesn't like it when the television news shows American soldiers burning down the grass huts of the people, or showing dead bodies of Americans or Vietnamese. But the media doesn't tell us the whole truth either. Has anyone heard a report on TV or in our newspapers about the Geneva Accords and how they were violated by the US government, or about the Eisenhower quote?"

I looked at Charles and then the other students. A couple students shook their heads no.

"No. And has anyone seen in our media a quote by General Ky, one of the leaders of the south Vietnamese government today that our government is supporting, about who his heroes are?" I asked.

One student said no and the others were silent.

"Well, General Ky was asked who his heroes are, and he said: 'I have only one. Adolph Hitler.' That was reported in the British press, but not in our press. Our media reports the US government line on the war, but not something this damning. It might seriously hurt the war effort if American kids knew they were being forced to fight in South Vietnam to prop up a Hitler-lover. So our government called off the first national elections ever in the history of Vietnam because our candidate couldn't win, and is now supporting someone who admires Hitler. How is that supporting democracy in south Vietnam?" I asked Charles.

I stopped talking to hear his answer. He was silent and looked caught off guard. But he recovered and tried a different line of argument. "So you advocate just letting the communists take over," he asked.

"I'm advocating letting the people of Vietnam decide their own future. If they want to elect a communist to lead their country then that's their choice. And why should we be so surprised? Ho Chi Minh and the communists have been the leaders of the independence movement for decades. The people have been exploited and brutalized by French colonialism for generations, and the communists led the fight to stop it."

"But if we let the communists take over Vietnam, what's next," Charles pleaded. He was repeating exactly the US government line. "Are you going to wait until they get to our doorstep before doing anything about it?"

"Look," I continued. "If people didn't have just grievances, neither communists nor any one else could take over anything. Communists or any other group seeking political power have to have considerable support among significant sections of the population to succeed. I don't hear you or the US government talking about real solutions for the problems facing the Vietnamese people – like eradicating hunger, unemployment, poverty, and repression, or providing quality education, housing and medical care."

Charles just stood there.

"The US government doesn't care about any of those issues," I continued. "They don't give a shit about the Vietnamese people. If they did, why didn't they help them overthrow French colonialism years ago? That was a very brutal, oppressive and undemocratic system. But, in fact, the US government supported French colonialism in Vietnam. And do you know why? Because our American corporations want access to the cheap raw materials there."

"Oh, here comes the Marxist bullshit," Charles retorted, trying to salvage something from this conversation.

"No. You don't have to listen to the Marxists. Just listen to your own anti-communist leaders. Here's President Eisenhower again, in 1953, when we were supporting the French in Vietnam. He's speaking before a conference of US governors in Seattle." I pulled the book *Vietnam! Vietnam!* out of my folder and turned to a page I had marked." Look at this." I showed him the passage, and then I began reading: "'Now let us assume we lost Indochina...The tin and tungsten that we so greatly value from that area would cease coming...so when the United States votes 400 million dollars to help that war, we are not voting a give-away program. We are voting for the cheapest way we can to prevent the occurrence of something that would be of a most terrible significance to the United States of America, our power and ability to get certain things we need from the riches of the Indochinese territory and from southeast Asia.' That's Eisenhower, not the Marxists. Huge American corporations are getting rich off the war and will get richer yet if they succeed in keeping their puppet in power in Vietnam. That's what the war is about. Do you want to risk *your* life Charles, fighting over there so millionaires here can become billionaires? Have you signed up yet to volunteer?"

A pained expression crept over his face. He didn't look well. He glanced at his watch. "I don't have time to argue about this any more," he blurted out and turned and walked away. It was a great feeling defeating pro-war advocates. When their brightest stars couldn't come up with facts or arguments to undermine ours, I felt vindicated. I knew we were right and it made our cause seem just that much more justified.

I didn't encounter many conservative or right-wing students at UB then. I'm sure there were some, but they mostly kept quiet. Liberal and leftist students were the most prevalent by far on campus and the most outspoken, and they set the political tone at UB. There was a very small chapter of the right-wing organization, Young Americans for Freedom (YAF) on campus. I never saw more than two or three of them together, and I saw them only rarely. I don't think Charles was a member of YAF, though he argued like them. One difference was that Charles was more knowledgeable and rational than the YAFers I encountered, so on the few occasions YAF members tried to argue with us we decimated them. We never took them seriously, and usually just ignored them. YAF had no base, no influence and were seen as misfits or a joke on campus.

Little did we know then what we learned years later. That YAF was heavily funded and influenced by right-wing corporations and corporate foundations, such as Mellon bank, Scaife, and Coors, and that their millions of dollars would get some of these right-wingers elected to Congress along with Ronald Reagan and the two Bushes.

But in the late 1960's, on a shoestring budget, the liberals and left were the major political forces at UB and on many other campuses across the country. One example of this influence was seen in our student newspaper, *The Spectrum*. It was filled with articles about protests for more democracy, peace and justice, and against the war, racism, poverty and exploitation. The conservative view was reported in our student newspaper, and even more than the commercial media reported on our anti-war views, but in *The Spectrum,* the anti-war position predominated. It came out Monday, Wednesday and Friday and was piled in stacks in open newspaper boxes in Norton Union, as well as in all the other buildings on campus, and it was free.

I usually picked up a copy every time it came out. I was on campus every day, and on February 17, 1969, I saw that the entire front page contained a feature article titled: "Buffalo Nine: on trial today." That was the case of the anti-war leaders who were arrested while supporting two draft resisters at the Unitarian Church in August of 1968. It was the major anti-war case in Buffalo and a majority of the defendants were UB students. I was glad to see such extensive coverage. The article explained the history of the case and ended by urging support for the Buffalo Nine and announced that buses and car pools were available to take students down to the courthouse for demonstrations to demand their freedom. *The Spectrum* not only informed and educated students, but also helped to build the movement.

The article featured a photograph of Bruce Beyer, a leader of the Buffalo Draft Resistance Union, and Carl Kronberg, a leader of Peace and Freedom Party, both sitting at a Buffalo Nine literature table in Norton Union. I already knew about the demonstration. Defense Committee members had passed out thousands of leaflets on campus, and I was planning to be there. But it was important that this case was covered in the official student newspaper because it lent credibility to our cause, and the paper was available to the entire student body of over 20,000 students. This was just one of many articles *The Spectrum* did on this case, and many other important issues. The student editors also wrote hard-hitting editorials condemning the war and the arrest and trial of the Buffalo Nine.

After I read that article, I flipped through the paper to see what else was going on. There was an article about student and faculty protests over the firing of a popular, left-wing and anti-war Sociology teacher, Marlene Dixon, at the University of Chicago, where 500 students staged a sit-in at the Administration building demanding that she be rehired. I thought it was great that the students in Chicago were protesting this firing, and not just sitting back feeling that they couldn't do anything about it. There was another article about National Guardsmen who were called to the University of Wisconsin in Madison to break-up a militant student strike, begun in support of Black students' demands. The Madison campus also had a very powerful anti-war movement. The article was illustrated with photos of the demonstrating students. Then another article was about student protests at the University of Michigan in Ann Arbor, in part to protest once-secret CIA use of that university as a training ground for US military operations in South Vietnam. This was all in one issue of *The Spectrum*. Practically every issue was similar. I felt right at home in this environment. I had felt so alone in my thoughts and beliefs only six months ago that I loved being a part of this intellectual atmosphere and anti-war activism at UB.

Chapter 20

The Buffalo Nine Trial

Every morning on campus people handed out leaflets to announce demonstrations in support of the Buffalo Nine. Most of the protests were held at the U. S. Courthouse on Court Street in the heart of downtown where the defendants were on trial. On the first day of the trial, George, Howard and I went down and joined 150 other protestors, mostly students, in a picket-line that stretched the entire block in front of the Courthouse. People carried signs that read "Free the Buffalo Nine," "Jail the Warmakers," and "Amnesty for Anti-war Fighters." I carried one that read: "Free the Nine, the Trial's the Crime." As we marched, other people joined us and the picket-line got larger. Organizers handed out leaflets protesting the war and the trial to picketers and the passersby. I took a small bunch to help distribute.

I heard one onlooker comment to a friend just as I walked by: "Where would those clowns be if our country were invaded?"

"We would be defending it," I said loudly as I stepped out of the line. "But this war is wrong. The Vietnamese aren't invading our country, but the US is invading theirs." I looked the man in his eye and then stepped back into the line and kept marching. They said nothing.

I went around a couple more times, and then I stepped out of the line to read the leaflet. A bus driver came over and asked if I had an extra one. I gave him one and he started to read it. "There is a lot of truth in these sheets. I support you guys. Good luck." That was a good feeling. I guessed that a significant number of people opposed the war, but they were afraid to speak out until someone else did. Our demonstration gave them the courage to express their opinion.

On Wednesday, after picketing for about an hour, George, Howard and I went inside to observe the trial. The courtroom was packed with over 100 supporters, and another 150 stayed outside to continue picketing. Herman Erickson, a reporter for the *Buffalo Courier-Express,* the conservative morning newspaper, took the stand. He described what he saw when Federal Marshals approached a crowd of anti-war protestors in front of the church door.

"Mr. Alvin Grossman, a Federal Marshall, led several other Federal Marshals into the church," Erickson testified, "where they were met by a human barricade."

He explained that he saw the Federal Marshals approach the pulpit where both Beyer and Cline were speaking. "I saw Beyer turn," Erickson continued. "He had an object in his hand and he struck FBI Agent Schaller on the nose with it. The agents then forced Beyer against the wall, threw him on the floor and handcuffed him."

When Erickson was questioned about Beyer's bloody condition as he was led from the church, Erickson replied: "The defendant wasn't bleeding. The blood on his shirt was Agent Schaller's." Erickson went on to state emphatically that the agents were not armed.

I had seen photographs of Bruce Beyer being led from the church by federal agents. Beyer was bleeding profusely from the head, had big bloodstains on his white shirt, blood was on his shirt, his clothes looked disheveled, he had no shoes on and he looked dazed. None of the agents looked like they had a hair out of place. I was steaming with anger at what the agents had done to Bruce Beyer, and at Erickson for lying.

During cross-examination, defense attorney Michael Kennedy showed Erickson two photographs of Agent Schaller and Agent Grossman arresting Beyer and escorting him out of the church. They were the photos that I had seen earlier by members of the Buffalo Nine Defense Committee.

"Would you please tell the court what you see Agent Schaller holding?"

Erickson was silent for a moment and looked stunned. "Agent Schaller has a club," he said meekly.

"And how about Agent Grossman? Is he holding anything?"

"Yes. A chain." A surge of adrenalin went through my body and I wanted to scream out, 'yes, Kennedy has caught you lying.' But I didn't. I was certain that testimony would score points for the defendants with the jury.

"Do you see any object in Beyer's hand?"

"No," Erickson admitted.

"Unbelievable," I whispered to Howard. "This guy just lied on the stand." He nodded in agreement.

We then heard chanting from the street below: "2, 4, 6, 8, we don't want a fascist state." "Free the Nine, the trial's a crime." Spectators looked at each other with knowing glances and a low rumbling of whispers could be heard all around us. I was glad the people in the courtroom could hear the chanting because I wanted the jurors to think about the right-ward shift in our country. Is this the kind of society they want, one that is moving toward fascism?

"Silence in the courtroom," Curtin admonished. "We'll have no disruptions in the courtroom."

The *Buffalo Courier-Express* had a reputation for being staunchly pro-war. It reported on the fighting in Vietnam, and regularly quoted generals, politicians and right-wing groups who said we were winning the war. But I rarely saw anything in either the *Courier-Express* or the *Buffalo Evening News* about the anti-war movement and what it believed. I was angry at the obvious bias of the media.

We picketed in front of the courthouse every day, and I saw some of the same faces every day. On the third day, I asked a guy who I had seen there before and who was walking just ahead of us if he knew much about the Buffalo Nine Defense Committee. He said he did. I asked him if the Buffalo Nine had tried to get its side of the story into the two daily newspapers.

"Yes, but they won't cover our side of the story," he explained. "The Buffalo Nine Defense Committee even tried to run a *paid* ad in the both papers and both refused to run it. The ad was a message of support for the Buffalo Nine from 60 professors, students and community leaders and activists." But I had seen ads from Army recruiters and from corporate weapons manufacturers. Another example of the bias in the media, I thought.

I asked him how he got involved in the movement. He said he had been a student at Canisius, a Catholic college in Buffalo, and he had gotten into an argument with some radical members of Students for a Democratic Society from UB. He said he had argued in support of the war, but that the SDS members made some good arguments against the war and won him over. He then transferred to UB and joined SDS. I thanked him and then introduced myself. "Glad to meet you," he said as he stretched out his hand and we shook. "My name is Mike." I saw him at many of the anti-war meetings and rallies, and got to know him a little better. Eventually we became friends.

Mike was from South Buffalo and had also worked in factory, so I felt we had something in common. Factory workers were made out by the media to be pro-war; maybe many of them were given the half-truths and lies they were fed. After all, they were reading the same distorted news reports as everyone else. But they didn't have access to the other side of the story that many of us got through the anti-war newspapers and organizations. It was a good feeling to meet another factory worker who was also against the war.

George, Howard and I continued to go down to the courthouse to picket, and we attended many other sessions of the trial. It was more of the same each time. The prosecution presented witnesses that testified that a defendant attacked a Federal Agent, and then the defense attorneys presented evidence that disproved the allegations. There was virtually no evidence linking Ray Malak, Carl Kronberg or Gerry Gross to anything violent. And the case against Beyer consisted of a witness describing what he called a swinging motion of Beyer's arm – others described it as a flailing motion when Federal Marshals clubbed him from behind. The photographs of Federal marshalls dragging Bruce Beyer from the church with blood from his head dripping onto his shirt clearly showed who was violent.

"With all the conflicting testimony and outright lies by the government's witnesses, I don't see how they could convict these guys," I mentioned to George and Howard one day on the picket-line.

"I agree," said George. "There are so many holes in the government's case that they haven't proven the charges."

"You'd think the jury would see the truth and not convict them, no matter what they thought about the war or anti-war protesters," added Howard.

Toward the end of the trial, George, Howard and I attended a rally to support the Buffalo Nine in the Fillmore Room in Norton Union. Over 800 students were there.

Earlier that day, Gerry Gross, one of the defendants, denounced what he called "the entire power structure and the imperialist nature of the war" in a statement to the jury earlier that day. That was reported to the crowd assembled in the Fillmore Room at UB that evening by Defense Attorney Kennedy. While I was learning about imperialism and agreed with Gerry, I wondered how the jury might react to his revolutionary sounding statements. Would they be so frightened that they might vote to convict, even if they thought the defendants were innocent of the assault charges, I wondered? Ray Malak's comments to the audience soothed my fears: "Even my father, who is at best politically conservative and has attended the trial said: 'I'll never have faith in the FBI again.'" I wished *my* dad could have witnessed what I saw in the courtroom.

Gerald Lefcourt, the other defense attorney, told the crowd: "The courts are not impartial. They have an axe to grind. They are a tool of our government. Anyone who thinks they can walk into an American court and get justice is mistaken." The crowd cheered in agreement, and I joined them, but I hoped he was wrong. However, I too, was worried. I had seen too many people among the general public too willing to believe the government's line and the media slant on the war. Would those people be on this jury? Undoubtedly, they would.

On Wednesday night, I was one of 500 students who staged a sit-in at Norton Union in support of the defendants as we waited for the verdict. As the evening wore on, the crowd swelled to nearly 1,000. Finally, the news came: Bruce Beyer was convicted on two of three counts of assaulting Federal Marshals, and the other three defendants got a hung jury. The government was going to retry two of the defendants who received hung juries. People were furious.

I was angry too, but I also had a sick feeling in my stomach. I was worried about what was happening to our country. The brazen lying, the political frame-ups, the move to the right – some said toward a fascist type of country, was frightening. I thought about the Democratic National Convention. There, I saw policemen beating anti-war demonstrators, but I didn't see any demonstrator beat a cop. I didn't know of any policemen in Chicago who were charged with assault, but leaders of the anti-war movement were arrested on felony charges for committing "conspiracy," what ever that was. And now there was the injustice that was committed against Bruce Beyer and the other anti-war leaders in Buffalo – injustices against all of us, as I saw it. I felt that our system was corrupt and unjust and I had little faith in it.

After the announcement of the verdicts, we heard that campus police were called and were stationed outside Norton Union. I wondered if they might storm the building, beat us and then arrest *us* on assault charges. There was tension in the air and I felt it. But I also felt it was important to be there to take a stand against the injustices. Others felt the same way. Many students were angry. Over 30 young men burned their draft cards at an impromptu rally in an act of defiance. A large meeting was held to discuss our next steps. Several students said we had to publicize the outcome of the trial and Beyer's convictions, and organize students to be ready to protest when Beyer was sentenced. I joined many others in agreeing with this plan. Finally, things calmed down and we left. There was no police assault that night.

In the following days and weeks, anti-war rallies were held in support of Bruce Beyer. Three weeks later, his sentence was announced: he was sentenced to three years in prison. The campus erupted. I was angry and joined the demonstrations. Students surged across campus and destroyed the construction sheds at Project Themis, a Defense Department sponsored military project on campus. I was with a large group of angry students who went into Hayes Hall, the main administration building to continue our protests. Many administrators left their offices, apparently fearing a confrontation. I didn't see any administrator threatened or harmed. But some students loudly criticized administrators for the university's continued support for the war, especially for continuing to train Air Force officers and pilots in the campus ROTC program, and several administrators left their offices and the building.

I saw students sitting at administrator's desks and going through their file cabinets. I had mixed feelings about that. On the one hand, I thought it was really bold – a statement saying 'we're taking over now,' like in a revolution, or 'let's see what these folks are up to.' On the other hand, I thought that perhaps it was going too far, though I wasn't going to say anything. I then heard one student tell another that they had appealed peacefully and reasonably to the administrators for years to take a stand against the war, and the administrators didn't. That was the justification for what the students were doing.

We stayed in the building well into the evening. Growing numbers of students finally left, and I was among them. I learned the next day that some students stayed inside the building over night. Early the next morning the Buffalo police were called onto the campus to clear the building under a court order, and students left Hayes Hall peacefully. While a confrontation was averted, I could feel the tension mounting.

Chapter 21

Conflicting Ideologies

While I was involved in political activities on campus I was also studying political theory in my classes. I could observe the dynamics of social and political movements on campus and in the community, and see how they compared to the theories I was studying in class. Combining theory and practice like this was a unique and exciting learning experience.

George, Howard and I were taking a class, "Conflicting Ideologies," which was taught by a brilliant graduate philosophy student, Robert Cohen. He was a Marxist and a member of SDS. He was of medium height and build, had sharp piercing eyes, and was passionate about his work and beliefs.

Cohen's class had a profound impact on me. We read the writings of Thomas Jefferson on democracy, Adam Smith on capitalism, John Maynard Keynes on regulating capitalism, Mussolini on fascism, Karl Marx on the evils of capitalism and the need for socialism, and the ideas of other writers. We read selections from the major works of these writers and then discussed and debated them in class. Cohen often conducted his class by asking us questions.

"Does capitalism really work the way Adam Smith explained it?" Cohen asked the class one day. "Is it logical to have periods of economic boom and then bust, which is the inherent dynamic of capitalism? Why should people be unemployed when they are ready, able and willing to work, and society has the need for the products and services that they could produce? Isn't war just the most extreme method that capitalism uses for getting cheap raw materials, cheap labor and new markets and military bases? Look at Vietnam, for example. Does the US government and its corporate leaders really care about the well-being of the Vietnamese people? And how about racism? Where did it come from? Is there any viable evidence to prove theories of racial superiority? Or, is there merit in the position of those who say that racism is a way for those in power to divide people, to keep them fighting among themselves, and keep them politically weak and misdirected?" This was a great teaching technique. Cohen made us think and question, and search for the root cause of things. I loved his class.

Outside of class, he switched hats and became the radical organizer. He spoke often at meetings, rallies and demonstrations, and forcefully denounced the inequities and injustices of racism and sexism, and capitalism and its extension abroad – imperialism. He explained in detail the imperial interests of the US and how those interests led our nation into the war. The few opponents who challenged Cohen in public were verbally sliced to pieces.

Many students were attracted to Cohen's class because of his incisive thinking, compelling arguments, and insightful analysis. Most of Cohen's students were against the war and were leftists of one stripe or another. They generally agreed with his explanation of how social problems developed, and they wanted to learn more about how capitalism worked, why we were really in Vietnam, and about socialism.

Other students enrolled because they needed a social sciences elective to graduate and perhaps had an interest in political philosophy. A few students seemed to have signed up for the class not knowing what they were getting into and found the dominant world view presented by the government at odds with Cohen and the leftwing students.

"Can a humane capitalist succeed?" Cohen asked our class one day. "Can he treat his workers fairly when facing a ruthless competitor who slashes the wages of his workers?"

"I think so," said Todd, a husky jock-type guy with short blonde hair. "I think there are other ways to survive in business. One way is to make a better product. Another way is to use more productive machinery and equipment and business methods so you are more efficient. You don't have to exploit your workers to be successful."

"Do people agree with Todd?" Cohen asked the class.

Jerry, a small thin guy who got straight A's and who was also a member of SDS, raised his hand. "How does this business owner get the money to buy more productive machinery?" he asked Todd as he turned toward him. "He had to make a profit in order to get the money to buy the machines," Jerry continued. "That means paying the worker less than the value of what the worker produced. If the capitalist pays the worker less than the value of what the worker produces, then he is exploiting him," Jerry concluded. I loved this interaction between students, and found myself agreeing with Jerry.

181

This discussion went on and other students joined in. One supported Todd, several supported Jerry and two made other points. Some students referred to the writers we were reading to support their argument.

Cohen listened, asked a couple of questions or made a comment to assist the discussion, but allowed the interaction and debate to go on. When it seemed that no one else had anything to say, Cohen continued.

"Let's suppose you are in the furniture business," he said, addressing the entire class. "And you are making tables. You make good tables. You use up-to-date machinery and materials. You have a skilled workforce and you pay your workers what you believe is a fair wage, in keeping with the wages paid to other furniture workers doing similar work. And you are making enough money to pay all your expenses and yourself a decent income."

Images of the metal furniture factory where I had worked came to me, with the crushing boredom, bad working conditions, low wages, pressure to keep up production, and my injury.

"And then you hear that one of your competitors just slashed the prices on his tables," Cohen continued. "And since your tables are of similar quality, customers are going to your competitor to save money. You start losing business and lose money so you inquire as to how he was able to cut his prices. You check around for cheaper materials of the same quality, but find none. You look into getting more efficient machinery and find you have the most up-to-date machinery, just like you're competitor. And then you learn that he had cut the wages of his workers and raised their production quotas."

I thought of Standard Mirror's effort to raise our production quotas, and our campaign to stop them.

"And by slashing wages and forcing the workers to work harder, your competitor was able to reduce the prices of his tables," Cohen went on. "You search for other solutions, because you are a humane capitalist and you don't want to cut your workers wages or force them to work faster when they are already working hard now. But you find no other solution. If you don't slash the prices on your tables, customers will buy from your competitor, your sales and income will drop, and you will be out of business. The only way to cut your prices and stay in business is to slash the wages of your workers or increase their production quotas, or both. What would you do?"

The class was silent. I knew Cohen was right. What he said struck a cord deep inside me.

"There is an inherent contradiction in capitalism," Cohen continued. "On the one hand, each capitalist is driven to produce the best product at the lowest cost. He does this by cutting costs and the key way to do this is to keep wages down, and productivity up. However, when that happens, the workers are forced to work harder for less. If that process continues, it will reach a point where it's intolerable, and the workers will rebel. That's why Marx wrote that capitalism creates its own gravediggers – the working-class. And when the working-class becomes highly organized and politically advanced, it will see that the only real solution to this inherent contradiction of capitalism is socialism – a society where goods and services are produced to meet the needs of the people, not to produce private profits for a small group of capitalists."

I had heard people talk about capitalism and socialism before, but never with such clarity. I had read Marx for this class, and agreed with what I understood of his writings. Cohen made it easy to understand much more. Everything he said made perfect sense. I experienced it first-hand. I was now clearer in my criticism of capitalism, and soon I started reading and studying socialist ideas and models as the way to create a fairer, more just and peaceful society.

When I left Cohen's class that day, I happened to walk out the door beside Todd. He had a look of bewilderment on his face, and seemed agitated. "Did you agree with all that?" he asked me out of the clear blue. I didn't know Todd at all.

"Yeah, I do," I responded. "Cohen is right. That's the way the system works."

"But I still think if someone has a better product they can make a place for themselves in the marketplace."

"Maybe," I allowed. "But it still doesn't change what happens to the workers. Whether they work for one company or another company, they are still exploited."

"But they can go to school, get an education, and get a better job. Or buy stock in the company and have a say in how its run."

"Look, there aren't enough better jobs for everyone. Some people are going to be left behind. And the majority is going to work at jobs where they have little or no say over anything. And as far as buying stock in a company to have a say, how is the average person going to be able to buy enough stock to compete with wealthy stockholders? The owners and major stockholders of these giant corporations and banks have hundreds of thousands and millions of dollars worth of stock. How are you going to compete with them?"

"Just work hard and try to get ahead," he said.

"Did you ever play the board game Monopoly?" I asked.

"Sure." He looked at me a quizzically.

"And do you remember what happened when one player got a couple of hotels on Park Place and Boardwalk and had other property on the board?"

"Yeah. They won the game."

"Right. But not right away. That's just the way capitalism works. At some point in the game it's over – even before the game is over. From that point on it's rigged. That player is going to get richer and own more property and the others are going to lose money and property and go broke and everyone knows it, until the game is finally finished. That's where we are headed now. Sure, there will be some new enterprising individual who will come up with a great idea, or product or service and he will get rich and maybe even have a voice in how society runs. And others may improve their lot. But the general trend is to concentrate more wealth and political power in fewer hands and the growing majority will fall further behind. Maybe not as much in this country as in poor underdeveloped countries, but that's the way things are going."

Todd had a pained look on his face. "I still think," he stuttered, "that there is a place for fair-minded businesses to succeed," and he turned and left.

Chapter 22

The Movement

When we had a break in our schedules, George, Howard and I would sometimes go over to the Beef and Ale restaurant just a half a block down Main Street from the University for lunch. It was a student hangout and was always crowded. We went in one day after one of Cohen's lively classes. There were heavy wooden tables everywhere, thick enough to hold countless pitchers of beer. It was so crowded that you could hardly walk through the place and there was background noise of horseplay, flirting, discussions about upcoming weekend parties, and what went on in school.

We found a vacant table and took it, and shortly a waitress with bright blue eyes came over.

"What can I get you guys?"

"We'll have a pitcher of draft beer," George announced. "And I'll have a Beef-on-Weck."

"I'll have one too," Howard added.

"Me too. And also an order of fries please."

Beef-on-Weck was created in Buffalo. Many decades earlier the German bakeries around town made a large roll called Kimmelweck. It is roundish in shape, like a fat hamburger bun, but is hard on the outside. The top of the roll is covered with black Kimmel seeds and small, square chunks of salt. You cut the roll long-wise, and put slices of roast beef inside and the juice from the meat soaks into the soft inner roll. Some people put horseradish on it. I liked it with ketchup.

"That was a heavy class today," I commented.

"Yeah," Howard agreed.

"You know that quote by Marx about not just studying the world but trying to change it?" I asked. "He's right. I mean, what good is it to know a lot of things, but not use the information to try to make things better."

"Yeah, I agree," George added. "People have tried. Look at all the protests that have taken place against the war. But it just seems to get worse."

"We need to get more people involved," Howard insisted. We have to keep talking to them."

"Yes, but talking to people one by one takes a long time," George said.

"We need to work in an organization," I suggested. "That would allow us to get to a lot more people and more quickly."

The pitcher of beer was put on our table, along with three glasses. "The Beef-on-Weck's are coming up," the waitress said as she moved on to another table.

"Thank you," I said after her.

"Yeah, but which organization are you going to join?" asked Howard. "I agree a lot with what SDS stands for, but I'm not so crazy about how they act sometimes." SDS was in the news more than any other organization. I had heard that it was by far the largest activist anti-war organization on the UB campus and nationally.

"I agree," I continued. "Some of the leaders are pretty arrogant. But some of the others seem pretty decent. A lot of them are smart and they come up with good ideas for organizing around."

"Yeah, but if you join an organization like that and the leaders do something you don't agree with, then you're dragged along with them," George counseled.

"That's true," I said, "but working alone or with just one or two other people is tough. You can't accomplish as much."

Three steaming Beef-on-Weck's were put in front of us along with a large order of fries.

"This looks good," Howard said as he picked up his sandwich.

"You guys want some of these fries?" I asked, pushing the bowl toward the middle of the table. I picked up the ketchup bottle. "You want ketchup on your fries?"

No one answered so I put some on the side of the bowl.

"We could start up our own organization," Howard said with a laugh.

"Yeah. That sounds like a lot of work," George commented.

"But there are other organizations around," I added. "There's Peace and Freedom Party, and Youth Against War and Fascism, the Buffalo Draft Resistance Union, and the Quaker's Anti-Draft Center."

Another friend, Don, came to our table and sat down. "Great. I'm just in time for the beer. Waitress, can we get another glass here?" he yelled as our waitress passed by. "What are you guys talking about? I heard something about the Quaker's Anti-Draft Center."

"Yeah, we're talking about the different organizations that are involved in organizing against the war, and if we want to join any of them," I explained.

"Well, I'm not a Quaker, so I'll pass on that one," said Don.

The waitress came back with another glass and Don poured himself a beer.

"What about Peace and Freedom Party?" I asked. "I don't know too much about them. I guess they started in California to run candidates who opposed the war and to fight against racism. They work with the Black Panther Party. Boy, the Panthers are really under attack. It seems like more of their members are being killed or put in jail all the time."

"Yeah. The Panthers are really being targeted," added Howard. "I don't know much about Peace and Freedom Party either. I don't hear much about what they're doing around Buffalo, except for their involvement in the Buffalo Nine Defense Committee."

"Since they're a political party maybe they don't do as much between elections," George surmised.

"How about Youth Against War and Fascism?" I asked. "They're real active. They're constantly handing out leaflets for different political events, and organizing rallies and picket-lines."

"They also have their literature table set up every day in Norton Union," said Howard. "They're hard workers."

"Yeah, but they're pretty hard-line Marxist-Leninists," said Don after a big gulp of beer. "You'd have to agree with their entire political program to join that group. I'm not signing up for that. Also, YAWF and SDS seem to argue with each other a lot. What's that about?"

"How about the Buffalo Draft Resistance Union," I continued. "They're focused on ending the war and the draft and I hear they have an office off campus and are doing work in the community – I think at the Draft Induction Center."

"That sounds good," said Howard.

"Yeah, I would agree," added George. "But I don't know what other commitments may be involved. Anyway, we can go to the demonstrations and rallies whether we're members of any organization or not."

"I think most of the people in the movement aren't in an organization," added Howard. "That way you can keep your options open. You know, pick and choose the activities you agree with and not be obligated to go to the others. That way, you're not forced into supporting something you don't believe in."

That seemed to make sense. Still, I wanted to do more to build the anti-war movement than just attend demonstrations, and I continued to feel that I could be more effective working in an organization.

About this time, we heard about a forum that was to be held at the University in Norton Union that featured a leader from Students for a Democratic Society from New York City. From Cohen's class and my own reading, I knew that SDS was founded in 1960 to promote greater democracy in society, especially for those with little say in anything, and to challenge the hypocrisy of a society that said it was for peace, equality and justice when war, inequality and injustice were so rampant. They advocated something they called 'participatory democracy," which meant that everyone should have a say in things. That sounded good to me.

SDS got involved in the civil rights movement to end racial discrimination, and gained a national reputation in 1965 when it organized a large demonstration in Washington D. C. against the war. Since then, SDS had organized a growing student movement on campuses all across the country, including militant student strikes and other actions against the war and for student empowerment. Its reputation was huge, though not without controversy.

When the New York SDS leader came to UB, we decided to attend. We entered Norton Union and went to Haas Lounge. It was packed and the SDS leader was in fine form.

"The United States got involved in Vietnam to get cheap raw materials, cheap labor and new markets for giant US corporations, and to stop a popular revolution!" he said to cheers and applause throughout the audience. "It's about capitalism and private profits for a few! They don't give a shit about the Vietnamese people. So we must build a revolutionary movement in this country to overthrow this ruling class and establish socialism and it must be led by revolutionary youth and students. Traditional Marxists-Leninists say we should organize the working-class. But we can't rely on the American working-class. They've got it so easy now that they've sold out to the system. It's the youth that will make the revolution!"

People applauded again and when he finished some went up to talk with the speaker. I went up too. Soon it was my turn.

"I agree with what you said about corporate America trying to control Vietnam. But I didn't understand what you meant about American workers having it so easy and selling out." I was thinking about *my* experiences in the workplace, and the working world seemed none too easy. I thought that this guy must be a lot tougher than me. He hesitated for a moment, so I continued. "Which factories have you worked in?"

He looked at me with a perplexed expression on his face. "I never worked in a factory," he responded, and then turned to talk to someone else.

How could this guy say what he said about workers when he didn't know what he was talking about? It was this kind of irresponsible grandstanding that prevented me from joining such groups.

But his speech presented me with some important questions. Was it *necessary* to overthrow capitalism in order to end the war? Or could we build a strong enough anti-war movement to end the war, even with capitalism still in power? I thought the latter. Of course, then we had to worry about the capitalists starting another war. The student radicals who pushed hard to build a socialist movement argued that if we could establish socialism, that would help end this war and remove the economic incentive to go to war in the future. This could help humanity abolish war. I thought there was much merit to that line of thought. But how do we get to socialism?

I had read a variety of writers on socialism, from the early utopian socialists to Marx to more contemporary writers, and believed that socialism, in theory, was superior to capitalism. But I never heard a very clear explanation of what socialism would look like in the United States, nor how we would achieve it. I also didn't know if any good models of socialism existed in any other countries. At any rate, I thought that if socialism ever came to the United States it would have to develop out of the most progressive, enlightened and democratic institutions and cultural heritage of the American people. In 1969, those progressive ideals and political movements, while developing among students and youth, and among blacks and some others, seemed pretty small within the general US population. SDS and some others in the New Left aspired to lead the battles both to end the war and to establish socialism. And it seemed like growing numbers in SDS were making the fight for socialism the primary fight. I wasn't sure about that.

I didn't feel that fighting for a new nebulous socialist society should be our major focus at that time. In 1969, most Americans didn't seem interested in the subject, and many were hostile to it. However, I believed that it was important to explain to people that it was big businesses' quest for cheap foreign labor, cheap foreign resources, new markets and a higher rate of profit that were the major causes of the war. That would show that the war was not simply a mistake or an error in judgment, but rather someone's desire to profit and a system's desire to expand and increase its influence in the world. When people understood this, I figured they would be angered, and that would move them to make greater efforts to end the war. Our main priority had to be to end the war, but organizing against the war in this way could begin to expose some of the problems of capitalism and start laying the foundation for socialism sometime in the future.

Cohen's class opened my eyes to a new understanding of the world. His class answered a lot of the questions I had asked myself since high school. I now had a good explanation for why there was racism, poverty, exploitation and wars. I understood better why some people were cruel toward others, and what I learned validated many of the things that I believed and had felt for a long time.

I wrote my first serious academic paper ever for this class, titled "A Critique of the New Left." I wrote that "the New Left is composed of people who are dissatisfied with the present human economic, social and political conditions, and want to construct a society that will more adequately fulfill the real needs and desires of all human beings."

I went on to explain why I thought cooperation, rather than competition, was a better way to meet everyone's needs and create a more peaceful and just society. The main focus of capitalism was competition; for socialism it was cooperation. Competition carried to an extreme led to war. Since most wars were fought so one country could get the riches of another country, we should reorganize society – all societies, to be more cooperative. I believed that a new, just society had to ensure real participation and democratic input for all people, so everyone felt that they had a say and some control over their lives. I wrote about how capitalist employers exploited their workers in order to survive and prosper, and that workers would naturally form unions for protection. If conditions became too bad, workers would rebel. I argued that if society produced goods and services to meet the needs of all the people, rather than for the profit of a few, exploitation and wars could end, people would be happier, and they would be free to develop their own interests and talents. Life could be more fulfilling, joyous, and meaningful. It was that vision of the New Left that I identified with and felt a part of. But I ended the paper with a warning: if the New Left created a new society and began to "assume the role of the oppressor, they too will be overthrown by the people." Cohen loved the paper and gave me an A.

After I wrote that paper I saw a reprint of an article from a recent issue of the business magazine, *Fortune,* that reported with alarm that 750,000 college students identified with the New Left. I was surprised and impressed with this figure. It felt good to be a part of that large number. While the progressive political and anti-war movements were strong on many college campuses, I felt we had to broaden our work into the community. I also decided that if I was going to become more effective I had to join an organization. One thing was clear. I didn't feel alone anymore.

Chapter 23

Buffalo Draft Resistance Union

On January 15, 1969, I heard that President Johnson sent his budget request to Congress requesting over $25 *billion* for the fiscal year 1970 for the war in Vietnam. This was just before his term was to expire, as he decided not to run for re-election due the pressure of a growing anti-war movement and the disaster he'd created in Vietnam. The US troop level in Vietnam topped 539,000 soldiers under Johnson, the highest number yet. More money to turn more lives into cannon fodder and corpses, I thought. I wondered how many schools, hospitals, houses, meals and jobs that would pay for. The war was raging and getting worse. I had read that over 1,000 American soldiers were being killed a month! And the Vietnamese were being killed at 10-20 times that number – from 10,000 to 20,000 a month! I was sickened and appalled.

I read articles about the war nearly every day in the newspapers, including both the commercial mass media and in anti-war newspapers, including our anti-war student newspaper, *The Spectrum.* The more I read the more I understood just how terrible the war was. Many people who didn't read or see this news acted as if there wasn't even a war going on. After all, there was no killing on our soil. And reading only the commercial daily newspapers and watching the television stations gave you only a limited picture of the war. You had to read the anti-war press to really understand what was going on and to get a deeper feeling for the gravity of the war.

One of the best anti-war newspapers was the national *Guardian,* published in New York, which I subscribed to and received in the mail every week. SDS sold its newspaper, *New Left Notes,* and radical students brought to campus other New Left and anti-war newspapers from other parts of the country. I remember seeing copies of the *Old Mole* from Boston, *Rat* from New York City, *Great Speckled Bird* from Atlanta, and *Ramparts* magazine from San Francisco. These publications and many others like them were published by anti-war activists and others left of center to tell the story that the commercial media failed to print. Many of these anti-war writers and editors were young people in their 20's. Their papers were completely independent from the business-owned media or other commercial business interests, and were paid for from donations, sales and sometimes ads from small local businesses which had no influence on editorial content. Some of these papers came out weekly, and others bi-monthly or monthly. They were sometimes called "underground" newspapers, in part, because some of their editors, reporters and distributors were harassed by government authorities, including the police. At some of the anti-war newspapers from cities and towns that had a small anti-war movement many of the articles were written anonymously for security reasons. Anti-war reporters had heard stories about other anti-war writers who had used their names in by-lines, and who had been targeted for arrest on phony charges, fired from their regular jobs, or were physically threatened or assaulted. This atmosphere made some of the "underground" newspaper reporters feel like *they* were underground.

The content of these papers was uneven. Some newspapers and articles were very good, and others were quite weak. Some of these writers rejected institutions, practices, customs and laws that, in my view, were fine, such as marriage and family life. Some promoted activities that I didn't agree with, such as the widespread use of drugs and "dropping out" of society, which sometimes meant trying to live off others and not work.

But what was important to me and many others was that virtually all of the anti-war, leftist, and counter-culture newspapers opposed the war in Vietnam, racism, imperialism, sexism, and other forms of discrimination. I had heard that every large city and many medium-size cities had an anti-war newspaper – as did many smaller towns, totaling 250-300 papers with a circulation estimated at 4 - 6 million. In contrast, the commercial newspapers had a circulation of over 60 million, and that was daily.

The differences between the commercial media and the alternative anti-war papers were significant. While both reported on the war, including the deaths, the anti-war papers gave a more detailed and accurate history, reported much more about the impact of the war on ordinary Vietnamese, reported on the anti-war movement, and exposed the lies, corruption, hypocrisy and crimes of the US government. The mass media ignored or downplayed all of these issues. But most mass circulation dailies gave plenty of coverage to the so-called "enemies" that US forces killed. A high "body-count" was reported as a good thing in the commercial press since most Vietnamese were considered enemy combatants, even though old people and young children were often among those killed. The anti-war press reported these killings as the terrible crimes that they were. I learned a great deal from the anti-war newspapers, and I came to rely on them and trust them much more than the mass media for getting the truth about the war.

I read about a huge US military offensive in the anti-war newspapers that began on January 22, 1969 and continued to March 18, called "Dewey Canyon." It was launched by the US Marines in Quangtri Province. At the end of that one campaign the US government announced a big victory, reporting that over 1,330 of the "enemy" were killed, and many more thousands wounded and crippled for life! The US government admitted that 789 American soldiers were killed in the first two weeks of the offensive, and over 4,000 were wounded, many maimed permanently. This massive destruction of American and Vietnamese life was shocking and appalling to me. What did these staggering numbers mean? Each number was a human life. They suffered and died, and their loss brought pain to their family and friends. I remembered reading portions of the book, "All Quiet on the Western Front," written by a World War I German soldier, Erich Remarque. He described soldiers who had their arms and legs blown off, and holes the size of volley balls punched through their stomachs and backs. Many lay for hours screaming, and then days moaning in a tangled mass of blood, shredded muscles and organs, smashed bones and mud until they died.

I had met several Vietnam veterans who were students at the University and became friends with them. One, Al Donohue, became a good friend. He was one of a growing number of veterans who joined Vietnam Veterans Against the War. I told him about the terrible descriptions of death and maimings that I had heard and read about, and asked him what he experienced. Al had been with the 101st Airborne Infantry Unit of the Army, stationed in Vietnam's central highlands.

"I didn't see the worst of it, but I saw enough," he said.

"Like what?" I asked tentatively, thinking maybe I shouldn't have asked. "If you don't want to talk about it, I understand," I added. I thought about veterans I knew who didn't want to talk about what they witnessed.

"It's okay," he responded. "I remember walking by a big brown medic tent once where wounded and dying soldiers were being looked after, and I remember seeing boots, clothing and gear heaped in a big bloody pile outside the tent. That bothered me."

"Yeah. That doesn't sound good," I agreed.

"Then there was a time I walked by some soldiers carrying a dead soldier in a poncho and I could hear the blood sloshing around in the poncho."

"Was it experiences like that that turned you against the war?" I asked.

"That was certainly a big part of it," he responded. "But I also saw that we weren't wanted there by the Vietnamese people. A Lieutenant sent a squad from my company into a village to get some shaving water. When they left, they were shot at and one of my friends was killed. The next morning our company was ordered to attack the village. When we got there, we didn't find any soldiers, but we were told to burn down the people's huts and throw white phosphorous bombs into bunkers dug under some of their homes. A little kid about three or four ran out of one of those bunkers, and that really affected me. I didn't know if there were other people in there that might have been killed or seriously wounded."

"How did you guys deal with this stuff?" I asked.

"At first, we rationalized all of the brutality by saying that we were there to help the Vietnamese. Then, the longer we were there, we saw they hated us even more, so we just shut down to survive. Nobody wanted to be there, but we were stuck there. The military said if anyone went AWOL, when they caught us we would be sent to the brig for six months and then have to serve another six months in Vietnam. Most of the Vietnamese we came in contact with were just ordinary people trying to stay out of it or trying to protect their homes. I saw air strikes on villages, and livestock needlessly killed by US troops. It was a total disregard of human life," Al explained.

I read articles in the anti-war newspapers that confirmed this. Once in a while this information made it into the commercial dailies. One such article quoted a soldier, Dennis Pena, who wrote a letter home to his parents in Ohio. His letter was printed in the *Cleveland Plain Dealer,* and then reprinted in the anti-war press: "What I didn't like was when we burned the village down," Pena wrote. "The women and kids were crying and begging you not to burn them down...Ma, that's not good to see."

I also read news reports of people being napalmed, "enemy" soldiers being pushed out of US planes if they didn't talk, and being pushed out even after they did talk. Thousands of pounds of bombs rained down on Vietnam and the Vietnamese people, along with Agent Orange and other chemical defoliants. Agent Orange caused severe illnesses in adults and horrible birth defects in babies, and illnesses in American soldiers as well.

I was outraged by all of it. How could people be so inhumane to other people? I knew the greed of capitalism was the driving force, but I was shocked at the barbarity of the crimes that our system would commit so the people in power could get what they wanted – more wealth and power. I felt those of us in the anti-war movement were in a race against time to bring this horrible killing to an end.

With all of this going through my mind, I heard on the news that a Federal Grand Jury in Chicago arrested eight anti-war leaders on felony conspiracy charges on March 20 for allegedly inciting the riots at the 1968 Democratic National Convention in Chicago. Conviction on these charges could result in years of imprisonment. I saw these charges as a new set of government crimes to divert public attention from the much worse crimes they were committing in Vietnam and to repress the anti-war movement. The opposite occurred. I and many others were incensed. I had been in Chicago at those demonstrations. While some demonstrators were unruly, the police had been much worse.

It was in this climate of horror, hypocrisy and lies that I joined the Buffalo Draft Resistance Union (BDRU). Neither George nor Howard joined, but they remained involved in the movement, and we spent time together on campus and at demonstrations and political meetings. I choose the BDRU for several reasons. Its goal was to end the war in Vietnam. And it focused on the young men who were being drafted to fight the war. That made a lot of sense to me. When the BDRU was founded its focus was to ask young men to publicly refuse to be inducted into the service and refuse to fight in Vietnam – like Bruce Beyer and Bruce Cline had done. While these activities were good for publicizing and mobilizing opposition to the war and building the anti-war movement, it was difficult to get many people to do what the Bruce's did because of the risk, publicity and personal sacrifice. While many people admired the stand the Bruce's took, many thousands of young men worked quietly to find other ways to get out of military service and Vietnam with as little personal risk as possible. When I joined the BDRU, I wanted to help anyone who resisted the war in every way that I could.

Most of our work consisted of doing draft counseling to help young men get military deferments. They could get deferments for being a college student, for hardship reasons, medical reasons, for being a religious conscious objector and others. But many youth weren't eligible for any deferments, especially working-class youth not in college, so we helped them however we could. We helped some move to Canada. We also assisted AWOL soldiers to escape – by putting them up in safe-houses and helping them get out of the country. It was a felony to aid a soldier to escape, but we took the risk. For those young men who went into the service, we encouraged them to join the anti-war American Servicemen's Union or get support at anti-war GI coffee houses that were springing up around military bases across the country.

The Quaker Anti-Draft Center did many of the same things, but wasn't nearly as involved in actively campaigning against the war. With the BDRU, we put out our own anti-war leaflets, and helped build support for marches, rallies, speeches and other activities to educate people in order to strengthen the anti-war movement. How would we ever end the war by simply helping a relatively small number of young men get out of the service who already opposed the war when hundreds of thousands of others were being lied to daily and duped into going in? We had to reach them too.

The BDRU was started in 1967 by SDS members and other anti-war activists who were predominatcly UB students. As SDS got more radical over the next two years, the BDRU remained focused on reaching draft age young men. The BDRU founders knew that working-class and minority youth made up the bulk of the fighting forces in Vietnam, so the group had to approach these kids where they were at politically. When I joined in early 1969, the BDRU office was at Main and Ferry, a solidly working-class area not far from downtown. On the west side of Main Street was a largely working-class Italian area, and on the east side of Main was the black community.

While the major activity of the BDRU was to reach out to young men who were being drafted, we also worked with high school students throughout the city and suburbs to educate them about the war and let them know there were alternatives to going to Vietnam. We did mass leafleting at most of the Buffalo area high schools.

Another member of the BDRU and I got picked up by the police while handing out anti-draft and anti-war leaflets at Tonawanda High School and we were taken to the police station. They asked us some questions about what we were doing, took our names and addresses and let us go. They didn't arrest us – probably because they knew we weren't breaking any law, but one cop told us to stay away from the high schools. We ignored that advice and leafleted more high schools. Through these and other activities, we developed contacts in many of the area high schools, including at my own high school, Kenmore West, as well as at Kenmore East, Bennett, Amherst, Williamsville, South Park, McKinley, Mt. Saint Mary, Burgard, Akron, Lancaster and others. We had great contacts at the University of Buffalo, and also at other colleges including Buffalo State, Canisius College, Niagara University and Erie Community College. We delivered bundles of leaflets to our contacts and they would distribute them to their fellow students.

A major activity of the BDRU was to go to the Buffalo Draft Induction Center on Main Street at 7:00 am every morning to hand out leaflets to draftees. One leaflet listed the deferments and eligibility requirements to receive them, explained other ways to avoid going to Vietnam, and gave the address and phone number of the BDRU, and that of the Toronto Anti-Draft Program in Canada. After we distributed the leaflets, we returned to our office to receive calls. We got some calls, but I often thought there would be more.

After a month and a half with the BDRU, I had an idea for another leaflet, the one I had been working on at home about the history of US involvement in Vietnam. One day while a group of us were in the BDRU office, I mentioned it.

"What do you think about producing a leaflet that would explain why it's wrong for the US to be in Vietnam?" I asked.

"I don't know," said Chris. "I don't want to get involved in the politics of it. You see what politics has done to the other anti-war groups. It's caused so much infighting in the movement. We don't need that. I think we should just offer draft counseling to those who want it. I don't like the idea of telling people what to do. Let them decide for themselves." Chris was one of the more moderate members of the BDRU. He was a bright and thoughtful UB student. A number of the other members were pretty new to the anti-war movement and I wasn't sure how they would respond to a deeper, more hard-hitting analysis of the war.

"I agree that the factional fighting is a big problem and we should try to avoid it," I said. "But we all agree the war is wrong, don't we?" I asked.

"Sure, we're all against the killing," Chris continued.

"Well, there are many people who believe our government when it says we are in Vietnam to protect the democratic rights of the South Vietnamese people," I continued. "And they sign up for military service thinking they are helping the South Vietnamese people. But I don't believe that's why we are really there, and I believe the facts make it very clear that that isn't the truth."

"I'm not sure anyone knows the whole truth," Chris countered.

"I think we know enough to establish that the US should not be there," I said. "There are well-documented facts, many from the government itself, which prove that we shouldn't be there. Like the violations of the Geneva Agreements. Like the fact that the South Vietnamese government is a creation of the US, is widely hated by the South Vietnamese people, and stays in power only because of massive US military and monetary support. The problem is that very few Americans know this information. The government and the mass media aren't telling people *these* facts. I think we have an obligation to do so. I think we can write a leaflet that would present these facts in an undisputed way. And I think we should get these facts out to as many people as possible, especially draft age kids, so they *can* decide for themselves, based on more information."

"What do you think should go in a leaflet like that?" asked Tom, another UB student and a long-time member of the BDRU.

"Well, I've been reading a lot about Vietnam, so I have some ideas. I think we should include a brief history of how the United States got involved in Vietnam. We should begin with French colonialism in Vietnam, the French defeat at Dien Bien Phu, the Geneva Agreements, how the US violated those Agreements, and something on the economic and political motives of the US."

"That sounds good," Tom continued. "But what sources are you going to use?"

"Well, I've got a bunch of books right here." I reached into my briefcase and brought out five or six books on Vietnam.

"Have you read all of those books?" Beverly asked. She was also a UB student, pretty new to the movement, but smart and eager to learn more.

"Most of them. I'm still finishing a couple of them. Here's one titled *Vietnam! Vietnam!* by Felix Greene. I held it up and handed it to Beverly. "He quotes a lot of US government officials. I also have a book on government Hearings before the US Senate Committee on Foreign Relations on Vietnam." I handed that one to Chris. "Here's one by a Buddhist monk titled *Vietnam: Lotus in a Sea of Fire*, and *Vietnam: The Logic of Withdrawal* by Howard Zinn. He's a professor at Boston University. I also have this pamphlet, *The Vietnam Profiteers*, by Victor Perlo.

"Perlo is a Communist, isn't he?" Chris asked with some alarm in his voice.

"I think so. He's also an economist who worked for the New Deal under Roosevelt."

"But why would you use such a biased writer?" Chris continued.

"He quotes government and corporation sources," I responded, "and he shows the economic motives for being in Vietnam by using the words of government and corporate leaders themselves. He uses their own words to condemn them. What does it matter who writes about the war if they cite undisputed sources? What's interesting about this is that all these writers agree on the basic facts, regardless of where they are on the political spectrum, from left to right and in the middle. I mean, I haven't read any writer who believes that if the elections had been held in 1956 as planned, that the US's candidate would have won. They all know the US-backed candidate would have lost, so the US had the election called off. Those are the facts that I'll use in the leaflet."

"That sounds good," said Tom. "But don't quote any communists, and don't put in any of that SDS rhetoric about capitalism and socialism and revolution either."

"Okay. I agree with that," I said. "I'm proposing to write a leaflet that will be just the facts about the war, in language that people can understand. I'll write a draft of it for everyone to look at, and if people have ideas for changes, I'm open to that. We won't put it out unless people agree with it. What do you think?"

"I think it's a good idea," said Beverly. "Can you write a draft and bring it to the next meeting?"

"Sure," I said. Everyone then looked at Chris.

"I'm not crazy about the idea," said Chris hesitantly. "But if that's what everyone else wants, I'll go along with it. But we have to approve it as a group before it goes out."

"Absolutely," I said. "You've got my word on that."

For the next week I worked on the leaflet. It was one-page, front and back, and very straight-forward and factual, and titled, "America in Vietnam." I included the provisions of the Geneva Agreement, that the US government had violated them, the quote from Eisenhower about how 80% of the people would have voted for Ho Chi Minh, and General Ky's love of Hitler. I brought it in and the group liked it. Even Chris. So we decided to start with an initial print run of several thousand copies. We made the stencil at the BDRU office. Then I took it to the Peace and Freedom office on Elmwood Avenue to use their mimeograph machine to make the leaflets. Then I went to the YAWF office on Main Street near Allen to pick up a bundle of *The Bond* – the American Servicemen's Union newspaper. Then I went to the SDS office on the UB campus to get the latest anti-war flyer. Then we took all of this literature to the Draft Induction Center and passed it out to the hundreds of young men who came in for physicals or induction into the US military two or three days a week.

A couple of months later, I wrote another leaflet titled, "Why the US is Really in Vietnam," also to be handed out to draftees at the Induction Center.

I included in the leaflet a quote from the April 4, 1954 issue of *US News and World Report*, a conservative mass circulation magazine, when the US was supporting a deteriorating French colonialism in Vietnam: "One of the richest areas is open to the winner of Indochina. That's behind the growing US concern...tin, rubber, rice, key strategic raw materials are what the war is really about. The US sees it as a place to hold – at any cost." I got this quote from Felix Greene in *Vietnam! Vietnam!*

"At any cost!" I wrote in the leaflet. "The cost, as of July 1969, has been the killing of over 40,000 Americans and over 570,000 Vietnamese..."

I did research on major companies involved in war production and quoted directly from their corporate documents. I wrote in the leaflet that the top military contractor in 1968 was General Dynamics Corporation, which made over one billion dollars in sales to the government, largely for war production. I also included a quote from the company's 1966 Annual Report to Stockholders: "While 1966 represented a continued increase in both sales and earnings, we are not yet satisfied with our over-all profitability."

From Litton's Annual Report, I included this quote: "The Vietnam conflict also created a strong demand for Hewitt-Robin's transmissions and gearing systems..." And from Dow Chemical Company's 1966 Annual Report I included this quote: "Dow business activities with the U.S. Government continued to increase during 1966. Most of this increase involved the supply of materials to the Department of Defense." Yes. For increased quantities of napalm!

I was angry after reading these reports. I wondered how these corporate executives could look at themselves at the end of the day knowing the horrible pain and suffering they were causing others. Or did they just put it out of their minds? And all for the almighty dollar. Is this what "getting ahead" means in America? I saw them as guilty as the government in these crimes; they lined their pockets with money from misery and deaths of others. I saw them selling themselves, their morals and their very souls in exchange for a fat paycheck so they could buy big houses, big cars, big yachts, expensive clothes and jewelry – all of which was dripping in blood. This was the worst of capitalism, a system that rewarded the captains of industry for producing napalm because there was a "market" for it, created by their allies in government. Certainly, many business owners did not work in the death industry, and many would refuse to do so. But those who did – and there were enough, made a bad name for the business community as a whole.

I wrote about how workers here and in Vietnam were exploited by the war since I knew the people we would be handing these leaflets to were mostly working-class kids who were targeted by the draft. I ended the leaflet by writing that while the owners of these defense contractors "are getting richer and more powerful selling war material to the government, thousands of American soldiers and Vietnamese people suffer and die. Are you going to sacrifice your life so a few greedy profit-seekers can get richer?" The BDRU approved that one too.

Sometimes, two, three or four days a week, buses of draftees came to the Buffalo Induction Center from all over western New York, and as far east as Rochester and as far south as Erie, Pennsylvania. We'd hand out hundreds of leaflets on those days. After leafleting and a stop by the office, we would go to campus to begin our day's classes.

I felt that this was important work, but was struck by two things. Most of the potential draftees took our leaflets, but I was still disappointed by the relatively small number who called us. I wondered if the leaflets had been confiscated by the military authorities before the guys could read them. At one time, the Draft Induction Center demanded that the draftees turn over the leaflets as they entered the building. The BDRU challenged that practice by threatening legal action and writing at the top of our leaflets: "This leaflet is your personal property. It cannot legally be taken from you."

Still, I wondered why the response was less than I expected.

One morning Tom and I were at the Induction Center handing out leaflets and a couple of guys came out about an hour after they went in.

"Are you leaving?" I asked the taller guy. His shiny, slicked down black hair glistened in the sun.

"Yeah, they made a mistake. We're not supposed to be called now. They're going to call us next month."

"Did the Induction Center people take the leaflets away from you?"

"No. I still have mine." He showed me several folded over and crumpled leaflets that had been stuffed in his back pocket.

"Did you read the leaflets," I asked.

"Yeah, we read 'em."

"Are you going in when they call you again? I asked.

"Yeah, probably," the tall guy responded.

"Why?" I asked, surprised. "Didn't you read about how we got involved, and how the US government helped call off elections there, and how big US corporations just want to get the raw materials and profits from over there? And they want *us* to risk our lives for that," I said, emotion rising in my voice. At 21, I was close to their age.

"Yeah, that's fucked up," the tall guy responded somewhat noncommittally. "But what choice do we have?" as he shrugged his shoulders.

"Did you see this leaflet?" I asked, as I walked toward him holding it in front of me. "This one explains the deferments that you might be eligible for, and has an address for the Anti-Draft Program in Toronto."

"Yeah, we saw that one too," he responded. "But we don't qualify for any of the deferments, and I don't want to go to Canada. And I'm not going to jail."

"Were the other guys reading the leaflets?" Tom asked.

"Yeah. Most of the guys did. They got nothin' else to do. We just sit around waitin' for our names to be called to get our physicals."

"Are they talking about what the leaflets say?" I asked.

"Not much. They're mostly just sittin' there quiet."

"So, no one is leaving?" Tom asked.

"No," the shorter guy answered. "I guess they figure they'll just take their chances. That's what we're going to do. Hell, most guys make it back okay. We're trying not to think about it. We're going out to get drunk now to celebrate that we're not going today."

They both laughed and walked away down the street.

"Well, if you go in, join the American Servicemen's Union," I called out after them. "They can help you out."

They didn't respond.

It was disturbing. I couldn't figure out why they didn't take this life and death situation more seriously. I could understand it if the only information they had was what they were getting from the government, but information we were giving them cast a different light on it. I read a study years later that described the powerful impact people in positions of authority have on others in making them do things that they wouldn't choose to do on their own. That probably explained a large part of it, along with the negative ramifications of refusing to be drafted.

The second thing that struck me was that among those who voiced opposition to the war in the Buffalo area, of which there were hundreds and maybe thousands, a relatively small number committed to doing this kind of work. There was a core of about eight to ten members of the BDRU who were active on a regular basis, and a slightly smaller number helped leaflet at the Draft Induction Center. There were thirty to forty members on our roster and others who supported us, but other than coming to some events or contributing some money, most didn't do too much.

I quickly found that I was doing most of the leafleting at the Draft Induction Center, and I had to work to get others to help. For people who knew how wrong the war was, I couldn't figure out why more of them couldn't make even a small commitment to hand out leaflets there once every couple of weeks for an hour or two. There wasn't much glamour in handing out leaflets at the Draft Center, and usually there were little tangible results. But it had to be done. We had to believe that it would have some impact down the road.

No one ever said it, but I suspect that a lot of people thought it wouldn't matter much if we handed out the leaflets or not. I remembered how I felt when I understood what the war was really about. It set my life in a whole new direction. I was so angry that I knew I had to do something about it. But I also knew that it took most people time to change their minds. It took me a while. I tried to avoid the reality of Vietnam, especially when I was trying to keep my relationship with Donna alive. But, finally, I just couldn't avoid it any longer.

Also, I knew it was a lot to expect a large number of young men to openly defy the law and risk going to jail for five years, especially if there were other ways to avoid the draft and Vietnam. I had heard of many creative methods that were used to get out of going, such as guys faking mental illness, or secretly pouring various ingredients into their urine during their physical to show how ill they were.

Others went to Canada. Many in the military went AWOL for days or weeks or longer, and some deserted for good. When I was living and going to art school in Toronto, if I had been drafted then, I would have refused and stayed in Canada. I knew I wasn't going to go. After my industrial accident, I was reclassified 4F – unfit for military service due to medical reasons, and I received a medical deferment.

I knew the anti-war work we were doing in Buffalo at the draft induction center and at high schools was being done in many other cities and towns across the country because we received publications in the mail from many of them, such as the Philadelphia-based American Friends Service Committee publications, *Counterdraft* in Los Angeles, and anti-war newspapers like the *Old Mole* in Boston. We learned of similar activities in New York, Cleveland, Chicago, Detroit, San Francisco and elsewhere.

And we did help a number of young men get out of going into the service and to Vietnam, and we helped some go to Canada – including driving deserters across the border. I hoped the leaflets would have a positive long term impact on the others. Maybe after they got to Vietnam and witnessed the horror first-hand, they would remember one of those leaflets we gave them at the Buffalo Draft

Induction Center. Maybe they would write home to a younger brother – like Dave Cline did to his brother Bruce, or to a friend and tell them that there was something wrong with this war. But I wondered, with all the thousands of kids being drafted in Buffalo, was our leafleting having an impact beyond the small number that we were directly helping?

I learned several months later from Andy Stapp, the leader of the American Servicemen's Union when he came to Buffalo to speak, that some servicemen who joined the ASU told him they had received anti-war leaflets and *The Bond* at the Buffalo Draft Induction Center. We did have a larger impact! We were helping to build the anti-war movement among active duty servicemen. It was a great feeling.

Chapter 24

Back to Nature

While I spent a considerable amount of time working to end the war in Vietnam, I was also a full-time student in the spring of 1969. I hungered for information about different societies, about how people interacted with each other, and about different cultures and political, economic and social systems. I was trying to figure out how we could construct a fair, just and peaceful society. I believed that injustices caused problems in society, and when these problems became serious enough, the result was social upheaval, war, or revolution. George and Howard were reading similar things, and we had great discussions and debates about these ideas that went on for hours.

I was taking four philosophy courses, one anthropology course, and the class "Conflict and Change in the Local Community" in College A. In the College A class, we got credit for doing social and political work in the community. I thought it was important to be involved in and learn from the community, and not just from books. So did many others. Over 500 students took that College A class.

George, Howard and I worked on a project together where we interviewed religious leaders in Buffalo. We asked them questions about their beliefs and if they were active in the community and in social causes. Many were not, but quite a few were. Through this work we met Reverend Ken Sherman, a leading anti-war activist especially in the religious community and a leader of Clergy and Laity Concerned about Vietnam. We made good contacts with other socially and politically active religious leaders which helped build bridges to broaden and strengthen the anti-war movement.

My philosophy courses were, in addition to "Conflicting Ideologies," "Early Modern Philosophy," "Problems in Philosophy," and "Logic and the Scientific Method." My Anthropology course was titled "Man and His Culture." Many other students were also searching for answers to society's problems, and there were advocates of a variety of solutions.

I was handing out leaflets one day for an anti-war rally when Lawrence, a student from my Anthropology class, came by. He had curly brown hair about shoulder length, which was wild and frizzy, and an equally scraggly beard. His loose fitting shirt twinkled in the sunlight from rows of tiny bright red, orange and yellow beads sewn across the front and down the sleeves, and he wore a pair of scruffy blue jeans that were torn at the knees and moccasins with dark brown scuff marks and holes in them. A large silver peace sign hung around his neck on a hand-crafted chain. He was part of the large and growing counter-culture, typified by the hippies. Their solution was to "tune in" to a more humane way to treat one another, and "drop out" of the existing society by not cooperating with it.

"Hey, I dig what you're doing man," Lawrence said as he took a leaflet. "This war is crazy. We got to find some way to stop it."

"Yeah, I agree. Come to the rally on Thursday."

"Ah, I don't know, man. I don't like the vibes at some of those rallies. People get kind of weird."

"Yeah, I know what you mean," I said over my shoulder as I handed out my last leaflet to three girls walking by. He was heading toward Norton Union, the student center, and so was I so we walked together. "I don't always agree with some of what goes on at those rallies, but it's important to make our voices heard. This is one way to do it."

"It's just not my thing. I'm into communes and getting back to nature. People are so materialistic. That's what has screwed up everything. We need to get back to the simple life on the land, when people were at peace and one with the earth, and uncorrupted and unspoiled by the modern world." He looked around, and then pulled his hand out of his pocket and showed me two joints and some pills. "This is what we need. To mellow out and experience life in another dimension."

I didn't know if he was offering this stuff to me or just demonstrating his point with some visuals.

"Ah, no thanks," I said. "I've got to go to a class."

I really didn't want to hear anymore but we were walking in the same direction, so I thought, what the hell, I'll engage him.

"Well, I agree that a lot of people like the material things of modern society, and many get carried away with it. But I'm not so sure things were any better back in the days when the majority of people worked on the land. Mostly, it was hard, back-breaking work, and often in very inhospitable conditions." I thought about my grandparents and aunts and uncles who grew up on farms just outside of Buffalo in Clarence Center.

"Naw, that's just propaganda. People loved and cared for each other then. Look at the Hopi Indians." I had met quite a number of young people who were active in the anti-war movement and in the New Left who romanticized the so-called peaceful, simple life of the old days. Some called themselves hippies and some tried to convince others to follow them. I thought they made some good points, but I wasn't going to join them. I believed that modern science could help make a much better life for all people if it was directed properly.

"I agree that the Hopi's had a pretty special society, at least from what I've read. But I think they were more the exception than the rule."

"No way. All the pastoral people lived like that."

"That's not true," I said. "Have you heard of the Yanomamos?"

"No. Who are they?"

"We don't have to read about them for our Anthro class, but I came across this book when I was doing some research for a paper." I showed him the book I was carrying. "They live in the Amazon in Brazil and Venezuela."

"Cool," he interrupted.

"No, not so cool. Here, look at this part." We stopped walking and I opened the book to a page I had marked. "Go ahead, read this paragraph, out loud. This is what the author, Napolian Chanon, who is an anthropologist, saw when he first came upon the Yanomamo people near their village."

My classmate took the book and began reading: "I looked up and gasped when I saw a dozen burly, naked, sweaty, hideous men staring at us down the shafts of their drawn arrows! Immense wads of green tobacco were stuck between their lower teeth and upper lips making them look even more hideous and strands of dark-green slime dripped or hung from their nostrils – strands so long that they clung to their pectoral muscles or drizzled down their chins."

"This is sick," Lawrence said. He *looked* sick.

"It gets better," I commented. "They like drugs too. Keep reading." Lawrence looked back at the book.

"We arrived at the village while the men were blowing a hallucinogenic drug up their noses. One of the side effects of the drug is a runny nose. The mucus is always saturated with the green powder and they usually let it run freely from their nostrils."

Lawrence raised his eyes and looked sicker than before. "I don't need to read anymore."

"Here's a different section," I said, pointing to another page that I had underlined. He started again, haltingly.

"The stench of the decaying vegetation and filth hit me and I almost got sick."

Lawrence paused for a moment, his chest heaved, and he looked like he might throw up.

"Don't stop now," I instructed. "Read this part." I pointed to another marked page. "It's about how peaceful they are." He continued, choking on Chanon's words:

"We had arrived just after a serious fight. Seven women had been abducted the day before by a neighboring group, and the local men and their guests had just that morning recovered five of them in a brutal club fight that nearly ended in a shooting war." He stopped and looked up, as if he didn't want to continue.

"Not too idyllic or peaceful, is it?" I commented.

"I don't want to read anymore," he said sickly.

"Just this last part, right here," I pointed.

Lawrence looked pale. "I can't." He handed the book back to me.

"Okay. I'll read it," I said.

"I had not eaten all day, I was soaking from perspiration, the bareto were biting me, and I was covered with red pigment, the result of a dozen or so complete examinations I had been given by as many very pushy Yanomamo men. These examinations capped an otherwise grim day. The men would blow their noses into their hands, flick as much of the mucus off that would separate in a snap of the wrist, wipe the residue into their hair and then carefully examine my face, arms, legs, hair and the contents of my pockets. It's hard to blow your nose gracefully when you are stark naked and the invention of hankerchiefs is a millennia away."

"I've got to go," my friend moaned.

"Just this last part," I said.

"No. I've got to go."

"It'll only take a second." I began reading: "The Yanamamo are still conducting intervillage warfare... At least one-fourth of all adult males die violently...'"

"That's enough," he blurted out. He looked ill as he turned and went into Norton Union. I'm not sure I converted him; I wasn't necessarily trying to. And I didn't dislike Lawrence. I agreed with some of his ideas, such as how the focus on material things was wasteful and diverted people's attention from more important things. We did need to spend more time trying to figure out how people could get along with each other, and how we could develop respectful and caring relationships. In that sense, the hippies did make an important contribution, and many of them weren't as far out as Lawrence. They questioned the arbitrary rules of society, the rigidity and hypocrisy, and lived a more mellow, laid-back lifestyle. That was good.

But sometimes they got carried away. Problems can't be resolved by simply turning back the hands of time. I felt that it was important to look back into history, but to study it honestly so we could learn lessons that would help us make better decisions today. I found it difficult to listen to someone romanticize about something they didn't know much about. The good old days usually weren't so good, and often they were considerably worse.

When I saw Lawrence in class later that week, I felt bad for attacking his world, so I apologized. He meekly said "thanks," but I noticed he was quieter after that.

Chapter 25

Molly

In the spring of 1969 I met Molly. I met her through George at his house, which is around the corner from mine. We spoke and I saw immediately that she was warm-hearted, interesting, smart and attractive. Her smile, dimples and the twinkle in her eye lit up my heart.

The night I met her a group of people were there and we all went out to get ice cream. I sat next to Molly in the car and we talked for the entire ride to the ice cream shop. Several days later, George and our friends went out again, and Molly joined us. She and I spent the evening together again. I got her phone number and called the next day and we started going out. The more time I spent with her the more I liked her. Before long, I liked her a lot.

When the weather warmed up in the late spring and early summer, we visited her aging aunt who lived in an old house on Lake Canandaigua. It's one of the five Finger Lakes in a hilly rural area southeast of Rochester that was formed by glaciers over ten thousand years ago. Huge rocks imbedded in the ice carved the lakes into the earth's surface as the glaciers receded and melted. Several of these lakes are thirty miles long and only three to four miles wide, giving the appearance of long fingers from high above. Today the hilly countryside is covered with leafy forests, grassy open fields and colorful wild flowers.

Her aunt's house was built on a rugged embankment about twenty feet above the lake. The back of the house extended over the water and was held up by long stilts. The rear of the house was one big room with huge windows all across the back, so we had a panoramic view of the lake and countryside. It was beautiful, relaxing and romantic.

Molly and I went there with George and our friends, and we'd put up cots and roll out sleeping bags in the evening in that back room. We listened to the water softly lapping the bank beneath us, and the cool evening breeze blew the aroma of wild flowers through the big open windows. When I was lying on my back, I would gaze out the windows at the dark night sky and see millions of stars. Lying next to Molly and sharing all of this was wonderful.

During the day, Molly and I would break away from the group and go for walks in the woods and fields. One warm sunny day in early summer, we took a blanket and picnic lunch with us. We made our way along trails and through tall fields of grass and red, orange and yellow wild flowers and ended up on top of a hill overlooking the lake. It was a large open field with no trees, so we could see a great distance in every direction. No one was around as far as we could see.

We patted down the tall grass and spread out our blanket. When we sat down, we saw four walls of grass at eye level all around us. If we sat up tall, we could just see the lake in the distance over the grass. We ate our lunch and then laid back and looked up at the sky. It was clear blue, with soft white puffy clouds slowly floating by. Sunlight streamed down upon us in a warm glow.

"Look at that cloud," I said. "It looks like a rabbit."

"Yes. Yes, it does," she said slowly. "But where are its ears?"

"Those clouds on top of his head. There's a little separation, but look at the clouds over his head. They look like ears."

"Oh yeah, they do."

Molly was lying right next to me, and our sides were touching. My heart started beating faster. I turned toward her and propped myself up on one elbow. Her light brown curly hair was spread out all over the blanket and she was dazzling. I looked deeply into her blue eyes, leaned forward and kissed her. We spent a heavenly afternoon together in that beautiful setting.

While I was spending my weekends and many evenings with Molly, I kept involved in the anti-war movement. Early in the summer, a guy from Buffalo, David, began talking to some of us about organizing an anti-war march for later in the summer. David was a student at Columbia University in New York City and was active in the anti-war movement there. He was home in Buffalo for the summer. I thought a march was a good idea and brought it up with the Buffalo Draft Resistance Union members. They agreed. David and I contacted other groups and held meetings to plan the march. But I noticed a slight change in my relationship with Molly. As I started spending more time organizing the march, she seemed to pull away a little. She never said she disagreed with what I was doing, so I assumed that she thought it was okay. Maybe it was the amount of time I was spending on the march. I didn't know.

I was over at her house one day and we were sitting on the couch talking, and the phone rang. She got up to answer it.

"Oh hi," she said. "I can't talk right now." She turned her back toward me. She spoke for another minute, but so quietly I couldn't hear what she said. Then she hung up and came back to the couch.

"Who was that?" I asked.

"Oh, just a friend," she responded.

I looked at her to see if she was going to tell me any more.

"It's an old friend I know. He's home on leave from the Army. It's nothing."

I thought for a moment, but then let it go. We spent the rest of the day together and had a nice time.

I called her the next day, and after some small talk, I asked her if she wanted to get together later in the week.

"I'd like to," she began. "But remember that friend I told you about who is in the Army? Well, he's still on leave and I told him I would spend some time with him until he returns to duty."

"When will that be," I asked.

"I don't know. I think just this week."

"Okay. I'll call you early next week then."

"Sure, that's fine," she said. "Call me then."

I was a little concerned. I wondered if something was going on between her and this guy.

I called back on Monday of the following week. He was still in town. She said she'd like to see me, but she had made a commitment to spend time with him until his leave was over.

That was disturbing. What was going on? I thought we were in a relationship with each other. Now I wasn't sure. I was hurt, and threw myself even more into organizing the anti-war march.

I told myself that maybe I just needed to give her a little space. I let another week go by, and then called her again. The Army guy was still around. I was angry. Did this mean she wasn't interested in me anymore and that our relationship was over? I kept working on organizing the march and tried to put Molly out of my mind. In retrospect, that was a mistake. I should have talked to her to find out what was going on with us, but I didn't. Perhaps it was some misguided pride. But I didn't want to lose her. I was in love with her. So, how would I get her back? I wasn't sure, but knew I had to figure out a plan. In the meantime, I plunged into organizing for the march.

Chapter 26

Buffalo Anti-War Coalition

Shortly after I met David, he told me that he was a member of SDS at Columbia and had been involved in the big student strike there earlier in the spring semester. I knew about the Columbia strike because it was reported in the national news after students took over university buildings for days and battled police. David said he felt that the anti-war movement had to broaden out and work with a wide range of community groups. I agreed completely. I also found him to be down-to-earth and easy to work with.

We agreed that we wanted to build a coalition and have the coalition organize the march. So we began by making a list of all the organizations in Buffalo that we thought might be interested in participating in an anti-war march, and then we divided them up and called or visited them. We decided that we would ask all the groups who agreed to be a part of the coalition to decide on the message we wanted to get out to the public. We wanted them to feel that they had real input right from the beginning, and I believed they would feel more committed if they felt they were equal partners.

We got agreement from SDS, YAWF, Peace and Freedom Party, BDRU, Clergy and Laymen Concerned, Quaker Peace Committee, Women's International League for Peace and Freedom, Buffalo Rights Action Group, Urban Action Association, and CAUSE – a community-based social services and civil rights organization. The last three groups were predominately African-American organizations, and it was important to me that we built a working relationship between black and white organizations. One-third of Buffalo's population was African-American, and they along with low income people of all races and nationalities, and workers in general, paid the highest price for the war.

The relationship between blacks and whites was an important issue among a number of activist groups. When the civil rights movement started in the late 1950s, both blacks and whites worked together. It was important for whites to show support for blacks who were fighting against racial discrimination. However, in the early to mid 1960s, some of the blacks felt that certain whites were trying to take-over, and the blacks that felt that way established all-black organizations. The whites who had been working in the civil rights movement were left on their own, and consequently some organizations – like SDS, became all white or predominately white. I understood how and why this happened and I accepted the choices that were made. But it also seemed important to me for whites and blacks to work together, on the basis of mutual respect, in some arenas because that is how we would get to know each other, build trust, and strengthen both the civil rights and anti-war movements.

A couple of representatives from each group attended regular planning meetings, and we adopted the name, "Buffalo Coalition to End the War in Vietnam." David and I were selected to be co-chairmen. It would have been good to have a black person be a co-chair too, but the group said they were fine having David and me coordinate our effort since we had come up with the idea. After discussion among the coalition groups, the march was set for August 23, 1969. Several people asked me if our group was affiliated with the National Mobilization Committee to End the War in Vietnam, the large and diverse national coalition leading protests against the war – usually by holding mass marches in Washington, D. C., since our names were similar. That summer, that group changed its name to the New Mobilization Committee to End the War in Vietnam. I said we were not formally connected, but that I believed in the work of that large national committee and that I saw our coalition in Buffalo as doing the same kind of broad coalition-building work at the local level.

I designed a small poster to advertise the march, featuring a pen and ink drawing I did of a young Vietnamese girl crying, with the date and location of the event, our coalition name and a list of all the member organizations. We passed these out by the thousands and posted them up around town. Each group did outreach to its members and constituents and many of us worked to build this demonstration nearly every day.

David and I went to Delaware Park one Saturday to distribute leaflets to many young people who had gathered there to hear a concert. The park is located near the center of Buffalo and is spread out over miles of rolling hills of open grassy areas surrounded by big leafy maple and oak trees. There is a lake bordered on one side by a large open lawn, and the lake is visited by ducks, birds of all types, boaters and lovers. The Albright-Knox Art Gallery is located along one edge of the park. Nearby are the Buffalo and Erie County

Historical Society and several other beautiful buildings left from the Pan American Exposition of 1901.

As David and I entered the park we headed toward the crowd of concert-goers, handing out leaflets as we went.

"Hi. Here's a leaflet about the anti-war demonstration on August 23rd in downtown Buffalo," I said to a young man and his girlfriend who were slowly walking hand-in-hand under a row of big maple trees. I gave him a leaflet. "It's important that we have a good turn out so we can send a message to our elected leaders in Washington that the people want an end to the war. Think you can come?"

"Oh, I don't know," the guy said. "We'll see." He glanced at the leaflet, and then put his arm around his girlfriend, pulled her close to him and looked into her eyes. He squeezed her and they kept walking.

"They seem a little more interested in each other than an anti-war demonstration," David commented to me.

"Yeah, it looks like it," I responded, as a group of six kids walked towards us.

"Here's a leaflet about the August 23rd anti-war demonstration," I said quickly, before they passed. One guy took it and said 'thanks.'

David was handing out leaflets to others in the group, and we walked with them a short distance.

I mentioned that Nixon was supporting General Ky in South Vietnam, who admired Hitler. "We can't risk our lives and waste our money supporting someone like that, can we?" I asked. "Can you come?"

"Hitler?" the guy with the leaflet responded, somewhat startled. "Yeah, that's sick. We'll be there. Thanks." The group kept walking.

People were generally polite and took the leaflets. Many listened to what we had to say, and many said they agreed with us. But many also seemed caught up in their own world, as if the Vietnam War was a million miles away.

We struck a balance between handing out as many leaflets as we could, and then taking time to talk to people who seemed interested. The more leaflets we handed out, the better chance we had of finding sympathizers who we could talk to and who might actually come to the march. It was also a way to let a broader group of people know that the anti-war movement was here and active, so maybe in the future they would get involved too.

We approached a group sitting along the side of the crowd. There were three guys and three girls. A couple of the girls wore colorful tie-dyed shirts and one wore a necklace with the peace symbol on it. They looked like supporters, and they were. They agreed to take extra leaflets to distribute to their friends. That happened several more times.

Overall, the response was very good and I felt good about what we had accomplished. After we finished leafleting the entire event, we stayed and listened to the concert for a while. Before it was over, we started walking back to our car, and when we got near the edge of the park, behind the Albright-Knox Art Gallery, I handed a leaflet to a couple of guys who were standing under a big tree talking.

"Hi. Here's a leaflet about the August 23rd anti-war demonstration," I said as I extended my hand out toward him.

"Fuck you," the taller guy said, refusing to take the leaflet. "You have some nerve handing out that communist propaganda around here. What's wrong with you? Aren't you a patriotic American?"

"Yes, I am a patriotic American," I returned, as we stopped in front of them. "That's why I'm doing this. The founders of our country fought against tyranny and oppression from Great Britain, and for the right to express their own ideas. That's what I'm doing. I'm expressing my ideas and fighting tyranny and oppression."

"How are you fighting tyranny and oppression by handing out that shit?" he responded, getting angrier.

"Because our country shouldn't be over there," I said firmly. I explained some of the history and mentioned that General Ky was a Hitler supporter. "Do you think we should be supporting someone like that?"

"Well, no," the guy stammered. "But where did you hear that? That's just a bunch of communist propaganda."

I explained it was in the British press and that our government doesn't want us to know that. "Ah, that's bullshit," the guy continued. "We're over there to protect democracy and the right of the people of South Vietnam to decide their own future, free from communist aggression." He took a half step toward me and clenched his fists, seething with anger.

I was nervous but didn't want to back down, so I clenched my fist at my side and tried to talk myself out of what looked like a fight.

"Well, if that's true, then why did the US government call off the elections planned for 1956 to reunite Vietnam?" I asked.

"What?" The guy was clearly in over his head. So I just continued. I talked about the Geneva Conference, Eisenhower's statement about Ho Chi Minh, the quest for raw materials and cheap labor, and the similarity to our own fight for independence from Great Britain.

"But, we have to stop the communists," he finally blurted out.

"Why?" I asked. "If we say we support the right of a nation to choose its own leaders through elections, and they want to choose a communist, what right do we have to go in there and tell them they can't vote for who they want? It would be like some other country coming into the United States and telling us we can't hold our presidential election because some leaders of another country don't like who we might elect! We'd be outraged, and rightly so."

The anger slowly left his face, and tears welled up in his eyes. I was silent now and looked at him. He looked down at the ground, and said quietly: "My brother was killed in Vietnam."

"I'm sorry," I said. "I'm really sorry, I didn't know."

"He was a year older than me. We were really close. We did everything together. I really looked up to him. When he went in the Army, I was so proud of him. I was going to finish high school and then join up too. Then he got killed. I was in shock. Our whole family is in shock. Nothing will ever be the same again." He wiped the tears from his eyes, and looked up.

"I know. It's tough," I said. "I had a friend from high school who was killed in Vietnam. We played on the soccer team together and hung out after school. He wasn't as close to me as it sounds like your brother was to you, but it's tough. That's why we have to stop this war."

He looked me in the eye as if he wanted to say something, but he didn't. I waited for a minute, and then said, "We have to get going."

He just nodded. David and I turned and walked slowly to our car in silence. I felt bad for the guy. But it made me feel that we had to keep working to end this madness.

Chapter 27

Jail and Music

A bright light suddenly shined into my eyes from a distance, momentarily blinding me in the darkness of night. I froze.

"Stop right there," a loud authoritative voice commanded.

I was putting up anti-war posters at Buffalo State College for the march. A few lampposts lit up a nearby street and some buildings but I had been staying in the shadows so as not to be seen by the police who regularly patrolled the college grounds. I was alone and the campus was deserted. I didn't know if it was the police, or some right-wingers, or both, out to beat the shit out of me.

I was carrying a bucket of wheat-paste so I could plaster the posters on walls and they couldn't be torn down. The light was still in my eyes and I could hear footsteps getting closer. I was standing next to a bush and dropped the bucket behind it. I could make out the form of two men with guns. I started sweating.

"What are you doing?" the voice asked, now within a few feet of me. I could make out the outline of two policemen by their hats and gun belts.

"I'm putting up posters for this march," I said, trying to sound nonchalant.

He shined his light on the poster I had just pasted up on a school building wall. "So you're one of those anti-war protesters, huh?"

I remained silent.

"Are you a student here?"

"No."

"Then you're trespassing."

"No, I'm not," I said. "I've been on this campus many times before, and I've never been told I can't be here. Many other people who are not students come onto this campus all the time, and they aren't told to leave either."

"What are you, a wise guy?" the second cop said moving closer to me. "You tryin' to tell us how to do our job?"

I didn't say anything.

They both were standing right in front of me and were silent. I was nervous but tried not to show it.

"We're not going to discuss this any more," the first cop said. "You're under arrest." He took the posters from me, and his buddy turned me around and slapped on the handcuffs.

"What for?"

"Trespassing."

They took me down to the police station and booked me.

"I want to make a telephone call," I told them.

"Yes, yes. You'll get your call."

"Will I be able to get out of here tonight?"

"Nope," the second cop said. "The Judge will have to decide if there is any bail. You'll know tomorrow. So, you'll be spending the night with us," he said with a grin.

I didn't want to call my parents – they'd be upset. I didn't have David's telephone number with me. So I called George. His older brother Jim answered the phone.

"Hi, Jimmy. Is George there?"

"No. He and Greg just left for Europe."

"He did? I thought they were leaving next week."

"No. They just left today."

"Oh, shit," I mumbled.

"What's wrong?"

"Well, I was up at Buff State tonight putting up posters for the anti-war march and a couple of cops arrested me."

"They did? What for?"

"Trespassing."

"How long are they going to hold you?"

"I don't know. Overnight at least. They said they have to check with the Judge tomorrow and maybe I can get out then."

"Well, call me when you find out and I'll come and pick you up."

"Thanks Jimmy, I appreciate it."

I spent the night in jail and nothing happened. I was grateful for that. In the afternoon of the next day I was processed out. I called Jimmy and he came for me.

I called Bill Myers, our movement attorney, and he said he would represent me in court. Since I didn't have any money, Bill didn't charge me anything – after all, it was for the cause. On the big cases, we did fundraising. I really appreciated what Bill did for me and the movement. It was a good feeling knowing we could do what we felt we had to do and not worrying too much about having to pay big legal expenses if we got arrested. When we finally went to court,

Bill proved that I hadn't been trespassing – making the same arguments I had made to the police the night they arrested me, so I was found innocent. This was just another example of how the authorities harassed student and anti-war activists.

About a week after my arrest, I was talking to Howard and some other friends who were working on the march.

"What are you guys doing this weekend?" I asked.

"I think we're going to a concert somewhere near New York City," Howard answered. "Why don't you come with us?"

"How are you getting there?"

"We're going to drive," he responded.

"That's a long drive to go to a concert," I said. "It takes six to eight hours to get to New York."

"Yeah, but this is supposed to be big," Howard continued. "Joan Baez, Jimi Hendrix, Janis Joplin, and a bunch of other groups are supposed to be there."

"Wow. That's great. I like them all. But we've got the anti-war march coming up on the 23rd. I think we should get out more leaflets this weekend," I continued.

"Naw, come with us," Howard implored. "We've handed out tons of leaflets for the march."

"Well, I'll see," I told him.

By the end of the week, I realized that all my friends were going to this concert and I'd be in Buffalo all alone. So, I thought, what the hell, I'll go.

It turned out to be Woodstock.

As we approached the concert site, cars were everywhere. There was a traffic jam that wasn't moving for miles. People just stopped their cars on the edge of the road and started walking. Faintly, off in the distance, we could hear the music. I could just barely make out Richie Havens singing "Handsome Johnny," a popular anti-war song. People were sharing food and water and wine as they walked.

"Where you from?" Howard asked a group walking along side us.

"We're from Ohio," a girl in a tie-dyed hippie-type shirt responded. "Want some wine," she asked and stretched out her slender arm toward us.

"Sure, thanks," said Howard as he took a swig from the bottle.

"Where are you guys from," she asked.

"Buffalo," Tommy replied. He was a friend from high school.

"Oh, I got a cousin who lives in Buffalo," said a guy in front of us who was walking half turned around with another group.

"Where are you guys from?" I asked.

"We're from Michigan – Ann Arbor."

"Cool," I responded. "People are here from all over the country."

"It looks like it," said the first girl. "Here, want some potato chips?"

We saw the people in front of us walk over a trampled down fence so we just followed them. I looked like we may have gotten in for free.

Just then, off to my left I saw two young women walking together about thirty feet away from us. I got a quick glimpse of them between a large group of people walking between us, and the woman on the right looked like Donna. My heart skipped a beat as I strained to look around a big guy wearing a brightly colored serape. I saw glimpses of long brown hair which looked just like Donna's. What if it was her? My heart beat faster. I realized I was still in love with her. I started to go over and talk to her. Maybe I could spend some time with her here and we could reconnect. I could hardly contain my excitement. An opening in the crowd appeared and I saw the back of her head clearly. She turned to her right, and as I saw more of her face I saw that it wasn't her. I felt a slight twinge in my chest.

Faintly, in the distance, we heard an announcement: "This is now a free concert. The promoters will take a bath, but the music is more important than the dollar." Good thing. None of us in our group had tickets and hardly any money.

There was another announcement about an organization called the Hog Farm which was taking care of people who were having bad experiences with drugs. Then we heard the distinctive blues sound of Canned Heat singing "Going Up the Country." We still couldn't see the stage but we were getting closer, and we could hear the music better. We were surrounded by people as far as we could see in every direction.

I then heard the clear voice of Joan Baez.

"My husband, David Harris, is in jail now for draft resistance. He just led a hunger strike involving forty-two prisoners." She dedicated the next song to him and all other war resisters. It was "Joe Hill," about a famous radical union organizer in the early 1900's who was framed on a murder charge but exhorted supporters to keep organizing before he was executed.

We got settled on a small patch of grass, practically touching the people around us, and for three days heard incredible music from the top groups from around the country. I had no idea it would be so big. We heard The Who sing "Summertime Blues," and Joe Cocker's raspy-voiced version of "With A Little Help From My Friends." Janis Joplin wailed "Work Me, Lord," and Jimi Hendrix soared with "Purple Haze." Santana sang "Soul Sacrifice," and the Jefferson Airplane did "Uncle Sam Blues:"

> *"Well Uncle Sam ain't a woman,*
> *but you know he can take your man.*
> *"There's 45,000 guys in the service*
> *and he's got them doing something*
> *they just don't understand."*

Someone near us had a small transistor radio that was reporting on the concert. Then we heard a news report that nearly 1,500 of the "enemy" were killed in Vietnam in the past twenty-four hours during the heaviest fighting in three months, along with hundreds of US and South Vietnamese soldiers, and many hundreds more were wounded. The announcer also said that US troop levels in Vietnam were now over the half million mark.

"That's a downer, man," the guy next to the radio holder said. "I can't believe the death and destruction."

"Yeah. I'll say," said the guy with the radio. "And now there's over a half million GI's over there suffering. That's the same number of people who are here at Woodstock."

"I'm glad I'm with this half million," I said, "and not that half million." They looked at me and nodded. "You got that right," the other guy commented. "Turn that off," he said to his friend. "That's a bummer." The radio was turned off. I thought there were probably two other similarities between us and the troops in Vietnam. One was that most of them probably would have preferred to be with us at Woodstock. The other similarity was that we both were in rain and mud.

A strong wind and rain had come up at Woodstock and people got soaked. They huddled together under blankets or sheets of plastic or other coverings, if they had any. We didn't have anything. But no one seemed to care. Everyone went with the flow. Some people started running down a hill and sliding in the mud. It became a sliding contest.

The differences between Woodstock and the war in Vietnam were stark. The troops and the Vietnamese were living in terror, being killed and maimed in a brutal war. The US soldiers were living in a very regimented society. They were expected to carry out orders without question. Transgressors were punished. We had heard that some soldiers were sent to the brig for refusing to fight. Well, *there* was one more similarity for me personally – I just came from jail for posting anti-war notices.

But Woodstock was so much different. There were no rules, no authorities, no hierarchy, no police. It was a little world of a half million people, who for three days, lived together in an open field in peace, caring for each other, listening to music, sharing wine and food, respecting and applauding the value of each person, and braving the elements with a smile and a hug. No judgments, no negativity. Everyone was accepted simply for who they were. You didn't have to embrace everything that went on at Woodstock, but it was astonishing.

When the rain started picking up, we looked for some shelter. We hadn't thought to bring any rain gear with us, so we tried getting under some trees. That didn't work too well. The rain let up, so we looked for something better. A lot of people brought tents and they pitched them everywhere. We had no tents either, nor blankets, nor any supplies, except for a little food and a lot of beer and wine.

Suddenly the rain picked up again. Tommy and I saw a couple of girls going into a tent and went over to them.

"Do you girls have room in your tent?" I asked. "We're getting soaked out here."

"Sure, come on in," one of the girls said and we did.

"You guys cold?" one girl asked. "You want these blankets to put around you?"

"Sure. Thanks," I said taking a blanket from the girl with long blonde hair that was dancing over her shoulders in ringlet's adorned with white flowers. "We really appreciate this, a lot."

We introduced ourselves. The blonde's name was Veronica.

"Where are you from?" I asked.

"New York City," Veronica answered. She was wearing a thin, white cotton blouse with bright red, orange and yellow flowers embroidered on it. It had a V-cut neck-line that showed the tops and inner sides of her breasts. She looked beautiful. I noticed she wasn't wearing a bra, but I tried not to stare.

"Are you in school?" I continued.

"Yes, we go to NYU."

"What are you studying?"

"I'm an Art major, and Barb is majoring in Sociology. How about you?"

"I began as an art major, but I'm now majoring in philosophy at the University of Buffalo.

Veronica and I talked about art and philosophy and life and death, and how we wanted to help create a better society – one based on love and respect and cooperation. She and Barb offered their food and wine and when it got dark we lit two small candles that illuminated the inside of the tent. We listened to the music to the pitter-patter of the rain on the canvas. As it got colder I put a blanket around Veronica and she leaned into me, so I put my arm around her to keep us warm. We talked quietly and drank more wine and after a couple more hours we blew out the candles and lay back on the soft pillow together. I felt close to Veronica, connected to her in some special way, by the music and the vibes of Woodstock. We started kissing, tentatively at first, and then more passionately. Soon we were making love.

That was unexpected, but wonderful. When we woke up in the morning, I told her I really enjoyed being with her, and that I'd like to see her again. She said she also enjoyed our evening together, but she was still in pain from the break-up of a long-term relationship with her boyfriend. She said she was sorry but she couldn't get involved again with anyone else so soon. I told her I understood. We talked a little longer, and then I left to find my friends.

Woodstock was a unique and magical moment in history. It couldn't have been planned. It just happened. By a half a million people who were on a similar wave-length and instinctively knew something special was unfolding and gravitated to it. For three days, Woodstock created a different world, and showed that people can live in peace, joy, and harmony, caring for one another even in less than optimum conditions. When it was over, we all knew something extraordinary had happened. When the story of Woodstock spread across the land, many who were not there said they wished they had been.

I knew people who wanted to make Woodstock go on forever, like in fairy tales. They "dropped out" of society in varying degrees. Some moved to sparsely-populated rural areas to recreate mini-

Woodstocks, and others tried to live this new life as best they could along side the corruption and decay and pain of the existing society. While I appreciated Woodstock, I knew I had to return to the real world and get on with my work. Not only would it be nearly impossible to create a Woodstock Island in a sea of real-world problems – even if I wanted too, but more importantly, I felt a deep responsibility to work to change the entire society so *everyone* could live happier, fuller lives. I could not go off and try to create a nice little life for myself while so many others continued to face injustice and misery. But Woodstock energized me. It made me see the incredible good in people and that an alternative way of life is possible. I went home with renewed hope that we could build a stronger movement, which could, first and foremost, end the horrible war in Vietnam.

Chapter 28

The March

When I returned to Buffalo we got out more leaflets and made some last minute calls for the anti-war march. On August 23rd, hundreds of people turned out carrying banners and signs, and leaflets were distributed to people passing by or watching from the sidewalks. Some of the banners read: "U.S. Out of Vietnam!" "End the War Now!" "Stop the Draft" and "Big Firms Get Rich, GI's Die!" The last one was a favorite of Youth Against War and Fascism, who brought that message and others on large orange banners.

We marched to a church where a religious leader from Clergy and Laymen Concerned about Vietnam spoke about the moral obligation to end the war. "In the name of God, please stop the killing," the speaker pleaded. Then we marched to the Buffalo Draft Board office where I spoke from the top of the steps to the front door.

I talked about how the US got involved in Vietnam, the violations of the Geneva Agreements, Ky's support for Hitler, the quest for raw materials and markets – all the standard points I always spoke about, and the millions of people who have suffered from the war on all sides. I wanted to connect with the audience so I also talked about the impact on the people of Buffalo.

"Hundreds of Western New Yorkers have been killed and many more wounded in Vietnam. Some were our brothers, neighbors, classmates or co-workers." I saw tears in the eyes of a middle-aged woman standing in front of me at the bottom of the steps and wondered if someone close to her had died in Vietnam. "They received their draft notices from this building behind me. We demand an immediate end to the draft and the closing of this building!" People cheered. "We demand an immediate end to the war in Vietnam!" There was more applause. Then we hung a sign on the front door of the Draft Board which read: "End the Draft."

We then went to the Department of Social Services where a leader of the Buffalo Welfare Rights Organization spoke.

"We are marching today to protest the continuing war in Vietnam," she began. "We have a government that wastes millions of dollars on this war, but can't find the money to provide jobs for the unemployed, decent housing for everyone, good schools for our kids, and affordable health care. Our cities are falling apart, and the government's response is to destroy Vietnam." I joined the crowd in applauding these remarks. Visions of dilapidated slum housing in Buffalo's black and poor white communities came to my mind, in sharp contrast to shiny new office buildings in downtown Buffalo. It brought memories of *The Corroding Society* sculpture George and I made in high school and the speeches we made about it. I didn't realize when we made the sculpture just how accurate a statement it was.

I was glad the Buffalo Welfare Rights Organization was a part of our march because they were making an important connection between the war, the economy and social needs at home. They provided a bridge between the anti-war movement and the majority of people who used these social services. This would help broaden the base of the pro-peace forces. Their involvement also helped link us with the black community. I knew that if we could end the war, billions of dollars could be re-directed to meet human needs both in the US and in Vietnam, under the right political leadership.

We then marched to Manufacturers and Traders Trust bank where a local leader of SDS spoke.

"We are protesting outside M&T today," the SDS leader said, "to expose the connection between this bank and many other banks and corporations and the war in Vietnam, and to UB, where many of us are students. Charles Diebold is a director at M&T Bank. He also sits on the Board of Trustees of UB. M&T is a financial backer of corporations doing business in Vietnam. When M&T lends war profiteers money to conduct their business of death, M&T profits. Charles Diebold's university trains Air Force pilots in its ROTC program for Vietnam. And Charles Diebold doesn't want the students at *his* university protesting against his war, so they arrest us." The crowd cheered. I felt it was important that SDS made those connections because it helped educate people about the causes of the war and the political and economic forces driving it.

Overall, I considered the march a success. Not because I thought this one march would have an impact on the war effort – obviously it wouldn't by itself. But together, with hundreds of other marches and demonstrations and other anti-war activities going on around the country, collectively, all of these activities would help generate greater public opinion against the war and put more pressure on the government to end it. I also felt good about my increasing contribution to the movement to end the war.

The march brought together a diverse group of organizations that worked together for a common cause, and we all learned from each other in the process. That was important to me. I was convinced that building coalitions was absolutely essential for us to create the critical mass needed to move the decision-makers. No one organization had the strength to end the war on its own.

After the march, I spoke to the leaders of the other groups about keeping the coalition together. In theory, they all agreed. But each one had a reason why it wouldn't work.

"We can't work with YAWF," one of the SDS leaders said to me. "We just don't agree with them on a number of issues."

"So. Why don't we just work together on the issues we can agree on," I responded. "Like ending the war, and stopping political repression. We can all agree on those things. Right?"

"Yeah. But YAWF always wants to bring in their own slogans and banners and issues that we don't agree with."

"Why don't we meet with them and talk about the issues that we can agree on, and see if we can get them to stick to just those issues when they're working in the coalition, and when they're not, they can do what ever they want?"

"It won't work. We've tried that before."

"I'm sorry to hear that. But I think we should keep trying. If we can't get agreement on a lot of slogans for a march, let's see if we can get agreement on one or two *main* slogans – like 'End the War Now,' and then let each group bring their own slogans."

"I don't know about that."

"Well, then let's talk to other organizations that we think would be more open to this kind of cooperation."

"We don't have time to convince everyone else that a certain position is correct. We'd get bogged down trying to find the lowest common denominator that everyone could agree on, and then what would we have? Some watered-down, liberal pabulum that wouldn't say anything and wouldn't move anyone. We should just keep building our own organization with our own radical analysis and actions. When there are big demonstrations, that's one thing. But to work in a permanent coalition with them – it just won't work."

When I talked to YAWF, they had the same thing to say about SDS. Some of the people in the religious groups and the Welfare

Rights Organization felt that it would be hard to bring their members and constituents to events where the radical slogans of SDS and YAWF were displayed. Some of the moderate folks were concerned that the radicalism would turn off the moderate mainstream people they were working with. I listened to what people said and then I wrote a paper outlining how I thought we could structure a coalition to make it work. I urged internal democratic decision-making, limiting the focus to one or two broad positions that everyone could support, but allowing each group to raise their own issues on their own. I also said that to make a coalition work, each group had to understand that they weren't going to get everything they wanted, so they would have to "compromise" – a word I knew many hated, but compromise was essential. That didn't mean to compromise one's principles, but it did mean not to fight on every issue because we had to recognize that we had much greater power if we could stay united, even if around only one or two issues. I also felt it was important to bring people together from different backgrounds and political perspectives so we could learn from each and, hopefully, learn how to work together. Unfortunately, most of the other groups were too focused on their own agendas so it didn't happen.

I was disappointed, but not surprised. I had seen this go-it-alone attitude before. It seemed like the leaders of some groups were more interested in competing with each other to be the "leaders" of the movement, instead of building the strongest possible united movement to end the war. Others were so involved in what their group was doing that they didn't make time to try to build a permanent coalition with other groups. Interestingly, most of the organizations that opposed the war felt they could work with the Draft Resistance Union, probably because we focused on just two demands that they all could support: end the war, and end the draft. Also, the BDRU never aspired to be the leader of the movement, nor did we try to push a political position that was controversial among the anti-war groups, and we made an effort to work with everyone. I felt that SDS and YAWF did provide important leadership to the movement and helped propel it forward, with SDS clearly having the broadest influence and following. But both groups also brought some negatives with them, one of which was sometimes being too heavy-handed.

It seemed to me that there should be a way to balance positive leadership qualities with unity-building. I made an effort at it, but I didn't know how to do it. Looking back on this period after many years, I recognize that building a permanent anti-war coalition in Buffalo in 1969, given the disparities and different personalities in the various groups involved, was so difficult it may not have been possible at the time. People have to be ready for it. That means agreeing on a limited number of widely supported progressive principles, with a thoughtful balance of power-sharing, democracy, and mutual respect for each other. I wouldn't want to be part of a coalition that was dominated by one group that others chafed under.

There is also merit to having different groups, or different individuals in an organization, try different organizing strategies because it allows creativity to flourish. Life will show us what works and what doesn't.

I knew that when the march was over, I would have a couple of weeks free before school started. I was still upset about Molly and me breaking up and knew I would feel depressed if I hung around Buffalo with nothing to keep my mind occupied until school started. I had been working day labor jobs to earn money for rent and food. But those boring jobs wouldn't keep my mind off Molly. With Molly out of my life, I thought about Donna again. That made me feel worse. How could I keep screwing up my relationships? Getting out of Buffalo, even briefly, might help.

But there was also a positive reason to get out of Buffalo. I had heard the San Francisco area was considered by many anti-war activists to be the "Mecca" of the movement, the place where it began and where it was strongest and most advanced. Mario Savio had spearheaded the "Free Speech" movement on the University of Berkeley campus in 1964 that helped ignite the movement nation-wide. So I decided to go out there to see it with my own eyes.

Chapter 29

Berkeley

I didn't have much money for my trip across the country so I thought if I could hook up with someone living in the San Francisco Bay area that would be a big help. I still had some money from the accident to my hand which I could use. I also knew that John, one of the guys from the upstairs apartment at Merrimac Street, had moved to San Jose and was one of the leaders of the Draft Resistance Union there. So I called him and told him I was coming out there, and asked if he knew of someplace cheap where I could stay. He told me there was a couch at the Draft Resistance Union office and that I could sleep there for free. I was ecstatic. I scraped together the money for a plane ticket and food and made my plans.

I still thought about Molly and decided to call her one more time. I told her I was going to San Francisco. She seemed surprised, and maybe a little concerned, though I wasn't sure. I figured that I'd show her that I wasn't going to wait around while she went out with a "friend" from the Army. In hindsight, I don't think that was smart. Going on the trip was fine, but I should have tried to talk to her to find out what had happened in our relationship, to learn what she was feeling and thinking. I could have asked her if she romantically liked the guy from the Army. But I didn't. Maybe I couldn't. My ego and hurt and anger overrode everything else. I wondered again, how much of it was my fault? I didn't know.

When I arrived in San Jose, I went to John's house. I arrived there during the day in the middle of the week. John invited me into the living room and I saw a lot of people with long hair sitting around smoking pot, drinking beer and wine, and watching TV or listening to music. Did these people work, I wondered? He apologized that his house was so crowded; otherwise he'd let me stay there. I had mixed feelings about the situation, but deep down I was glad. On the one hand, I wanted to be with other people. But I didn't want to be around people who just wanted to lie around and get high, especially when the war was still raging.

Many of them seemed like hippies, and while I wasn't one, I never had very strong feelings either for or against them. There were some appealing aspects of their philosophy and lifestyle. Many were like Lawrence from my Anthropology class. They were easy going and kind-hearted, rejected the rat race of climbing the social ladder, and shunned the accumulation of wealth and an abundance of material things. That was fine. If someone was working at a job – even if only part-time, or working for a good social cause, or going to school, or doing something constructive, and then wanted to get high or drunk in their free time, who was I to judge them? But when people did nothing socially useful and just got high all the time, I had a problem with that. I didn't know if this was the case with these folks. They seemed like it might be, but maybe I was wrong. But, if they hung out all day and didn't work, how did they buy food and pay the rent?

One of the slogans associated with the hippie lifestyle was "do your own thing." What did that mean? For some, it appeared to be just looking out for themselves and doing whatever they wanted, without much thought for the rest of society. How was that so different from the philosophy of capitalism, which encouraged everyone to look out for themselves, and not care much about others? That philosophy was not for me. I believed people had an obligation to make a contribution to society, to look after the welfare of each other, and the common good.

John took me to the Draft Resistance office and gave me a key, and said I could come and go as I pleased. I thanked him. I was already thinking about how to get up to San Francisco and Berkeley.

"John, I'm a little tight on money. What would be the cheapest way to get to San Francisco?"

"Just go to the freeway entrance and thumb a ride. People hang out there all the time, and people going up there will pick you up and give you a ride for free. People travel all over the Bay Area like that. We often travel like that. When we have a car we pick up people and give them a ride, and when we don't, we thumb a ride. It works out well."

He gave me directions to the freeway entrance to San Francisco, and I was off. Sure enough, there were six or seven people waiting there. Some held up hand-made signs: "San Francisco," "Berkeley," "Marin" and other locations. When I walked up, the guy holding the "San Francisco" sign asked me where I was going.

"San Francisco," I told him. I stood near him and a couple of other people. Most of them had long hair and wore blue jeans.

Some wore sandals and brightly colored shirts. There were both men and women. 'Where you from," he asked.

"Buffalo," I responded. "How about you?"

"St. Louis," the guy responded. "I've been out here for the summer visiting my cousin."

Just then a car pulled up along side us and stopped. The driver called out: "I'm going to San Francisco. Hop in."

My hitchhiker friend shoved his "San Francisco" sign between two trees with other signs, and five of us clamored aboard. People left the signs there for the next person to use. We introduced ourselves as we drove onto the freeway and a guy with a big hat and bushy moustache told us about some of the things going on in San Francisco that week. One event was a play by the San Francisco Mime Troupe that was going to be held in Golden Gate Park. That was great. I had heard of the Mime Troupe and knew they put on plays against the war and in support of good social causes. I felt like I was being transported into a whole new subculture of peace, left-wing politics, kind-hearted people and art.

I went to the University of California at Berkeley, and even though it was a couple of weeks before the fall semester began, there was a lot going on. There were groups handing out leaflets against the war, and others selling books and pamphlets about Marx, the Cuban Revolution, union organizing, ecology, health foods and other things. Vendors sold freshly squeezed orange juice at the entrance of the campus, and the sidewalk along Telegraph Avenue was lined for blocks with craftsmen selling hand-made jewelry, hats, belts, beads, buttons and T-shirts. Some buttons and T-shirts had slogans against the war, but many were about other things too.

I spent days walking around Berkeley and San Francisco. I saw the San Francisco Mime Troupe perform a play attacking the greed of corporations profiting off the killing and misery in Vietnam. I crossed the Golden Gate Bridge and spent one night on Mount Tamilpias. I slept one night on the beach at Big Sur. I spent another night on the beach in San Francisco in front of the big hotels, wondering what kind of work people did to be able to afford to stay in hotels like that. I met people from other parts of the country, as well as native Bay Area residents, most all of whom were friendly and cooperative.

I ran into some guys in San Jose who were against the war and promoting left-wing political ideas and spent part of a day with them.

We were driving around in their car and needed gas so we pulled into a gas station. We got out, and a couple of us went inside to get some soda pop. When we came back out, another guy was opening the trunk of the car. I saw a big box of Red Books by Mao, in English. He took one out and closed the trunk. The driver talked to the gas station attendant as he pumped the gas. I couldn't quite hear what he was saying, but it was something about how corrupt the capitalist system was and how we needed socialism. The gas station attendant stared at him with a blank look on his face.

We paid the gas station man, and were starting to get into the car, when I noticed Mao's Red Book lying on top of the gas pump. Our friend had forgotten his book. I got out of the car and reached for it, and then heard him say in a quiet voice: "No. Leave it there. It's for him," as he nodded toward the gas station attendant.

I got back into the car and we drove off. I thought that was a funny way to organize – leaving copies of "Quotations from Chairman Mao" on gas station pumps around town. It was pretty clear that this proletarian gas station attendant had no idea what the driver was talking about, and he didn't look very interested either. But, who knows, maybe he looked at the book and it got him to thinking. Probably about what nuts we were.

On September 3, 1969, Ho Chi Minh died. Immediately, the anti-war groups put out leaflets announcing a march to commemorate his life and struggles, and to protest continued US involvement in the war.

The march was held in Berkeley near the campus. Upwards of a thousand people showed up. I was among them. Based on what I had read about Ho Chi Minh, I admired his courage and resolve to free the Vietnamese people from foreign domination. I had read that he was seen as the father of an independent Vietnam, by people in both the north and the south. Many people in the memorial march carried candles and pictures of him. Our government and the mass media portrayed Ho Chi Minh as an implacable enemy, so I'm sure most Americans who saw or heard about this march thought we were as nutty as the guys leaving Mao's Red Book on gas station pumps.

But I was impressed at how quickly the anti-war movement could mobilize so many people. And I was impressed at the breadth of the movement in the Bay Area; I saw signs of opposition to the war all around me – even in some store windows. It was a good feeling being around so many like-minded people.

But I also felt like something was missing in my life. Since I had become so involved in the anti-war movement, I felt that I had lost contact with close friends.

Both George and Howard were good personal friends, but it seemed like we had been drifting apart. They were against the war and came to the rallies, demonstrations and meetings. But then it seemed like they went back to their regular lives, going to class, going out for a beer, watching a football game on TV. I still did some of those things, but much less. I found myself constantly thinking abut the pain and suffering that the war was causing, and trying to figure out how to end it. I didn't feel like going out to socialize while this carnage was going on. Maybe it was me. I talked so much about the war that people probably got tired of hearing about it. And maybe I was wrong about Howard and George. Perhaps they did other things against the war that I didn't know about. But too often, I felt alone.

None of my new friends – the ones who were heavily involved in the anti-war movement, were close friends. Maybe because *they* were so busy they didn't have time for anything or anyone else. There had to be a better way.

I wanted close friends and a personal life. I wondered if the large amount of time that I spent on the anti-war movement was a cause of my break-ups with Donna and Molly. I realized years later that it probably was, but I didn't see it clearly at the time. I only saw the predicament that I was in then. Two months earlier, Molly and I were in each other's arms. Now, she was with a guy who was in the Army, and I was in Berkeley marching to commemorate the life of Ho Chi Minh. What was happening to me? I felt like I was being torn between two worlds. My life was changing radically and I didn't seem to have control over it. It certainly wasn't how I had planned it.

Chapter 30

Meeting the Vietnamese

I returned to Buffalo just before school started in the fall of 1969 and the BDRU received an invitation to meet with a group of Vietnamese in Windsor, Canada, just across the border from Detroit. I was now one of the leaders of the BDRU, and I often received and opened the incoming mail. I told other members about the invitation and my interest in attending, and they agreed that I should go. According to the invitation, the North American sponsors of the meeting said the Vietnamese delegation was being organized by the National Liberation Front of South Vietnam, or NLF. I had read about the NLF. It was a broad coalition of organizations composed of intellectuals, students, peasant farmers, workers, religious leaders, and people with a variety of political beliefs including socialists and communists, all united to oppose the Saigon dictatorship and the US war in Vietnam. The US government called the NLF the "Viet Cong," meaning Vietnamese communists, and they were considered "the enemy."

The organizers from the North American side were anti-war activists from both the US and Canada, including some university professors. The invitation explained that the Vietnamese delegation could not meet *inside* the US because the Nixon Administration barred it. The Canadian government had no opposition to the NLF, so the meeting was held there.

There were about ten of us from North American and a slightly smaller number in the Vietnamese delegation. We met in a conference room at the University of Windsor. It was early fall so the grass was green on campus and the flowers were still in bloom. The meeting opened with introductions. A professor from the university looked at the head of the Vietnamese delegation and began.

"We would like to welcome you here today. Thank you for coming to meet with us. We know you had a long trip from Vietnam and we will try to make your stay here as comfortable as possible. We are a group of concerned citizens from both Canada and the United States, who are working to end the war. Some of us are university professors. Others are students, religious leaders, professionals, writers and workers. We are involved in a variety of anti-war activities, from doing research, teaching, and draft counseling, to organizing forums and demonstrations against the war. We have different political beliefs but we are united in our opposition to this illegal and immoral war. Thank you for this opportunity to meet with you and explore how we can work to end this terrible war."

I felt the introduction from our side set a good tone for the meeting: warm, respectful and businesslike.

The leader of the Vietnamese delegation nodded slightly and began speaking in English.

"Thank you for inviting us. We appreciate everything you've done to make our stay comfortable. We are honored to meet with activists in the North American peace movement, some of the finest representatives of your two great countries."

Great country, I thought. He calls the US a great country while our government is bombing the hell out of his country.

"We too are from all walks of life in South Vietnam. We have in our group a leader of a peasant's organization, a student leader, a leader of a women's organization, a religious leader and a trade union leader. We have different political beliefs, but we are completely united in our efforts to end US aggression in our sacred homeland. We value very much the support of peace-loving people in North America."

How can they be so gracious, I wondered, after all the pain and suffering our government has caused them?

We were seated around a large table. Everyone introduced themselves and made brief comments about the work they were involved in.

When it came my turn, I stated my name and began. "I am a student at the University of Buffalo in New York State. I am also one of the leaders of the Buffalo Draft Resistance Union and I am active in the broad anti-war movement, both on campus and in the city. We work with students, workers, civil rights organizations, religious groups and others. I am especially involved in work among young people who have been sent draft notices to report for military service. We explain to them the history of US involvement in Vietnam and why the war is wrong, and we help them find ways to resist military service. I brought some copies of leaflets we give to these draft-age young men which explain the history of the war and why our government and troops should get out of Vietnam immediately. These are copies for you to take with you, if you'd like." I handed the leaflets to a woman who was sitting across the table from me.

The other participants introduced themselves one by one until everyone had spoken.

The young women who I gave the leaflets to introduced herself as a leader of a women's organization. She was beautiful, small and delicate but strong, and had long straight black hair. She was wearing a read, orange and white native Vietnamese dress. Her dark eyes appeared calm, intelligent and warm. She looked at me.

"We have heard about this draft resistance movement that you are building and about the work you are doing among soldiers. This is extremely important work. We want you to know how much we appreciate this because we are certain that once the American youth understand the truth about the war they will not want to fight in it. We know about your American Revolution almost 200 years ago so we know that the American people value independence and freedom. That is what *we* are fighting for today in our country. We want to be able to decide our own future free from outside interference. We want you to understand that we make a clear distinction between the American people and the American government. We want to be friends with the American people, and look forward to the day when our countries can live in peace and friendship with each other."

I was very impressed and moved by what she said. The other Vietnamese spoke in a similar vein. I thought they were considerably more sophisticated politically than many of the activists in our own anti-war movement.

Another radical US student added his thoughts. "The student movement is getting more militant. We've had a number of student strikes and battles with the police. There have been takeovers of University buildings and we're trying to increase the pressure on the Nixon Administration. Do you think increasing these kinds of actions helps?"

"We appreciate everything you are doing," the Vietnamese woman continued. She seemed to be one of the leaders of their delegation. "But only you can decide what activities you think would be most effective. You know the conditions in your country much better than we do. What we especially appreciate are the large public demonstrations that involve people from broad sectors of your society. We are heartened to hear of new, large groups of your people who join these demonstrations, and who speak for millions – such as organizations representing Black Americans, religious organizations, trade unions, professional groups, as well as artists and scientists and what you call your middle-class. We think this is the kind of message that will get the attention of your political leaders. Whether your activities are militant or not – you must be the judge of that. And, of course, your work among youth and soldiers. That is very important."

I thought it was interesting that she emphasized building a very broad anti-war movement that included the middle-class – the very people some of the more radical movement people criticized. This validated my thinking that we had to find a way to move the entire political spectrum, step-by-step, toward an anti-war position. That meant reaching out to the broad middle class, which comprised the majority of the population and was predominately politically moderate. Some groups would be much stronger in their opposition to the war, but it was also important for us to reach out to people who were uncommitted, apolitical, and even pro-war but who we could get to question the war.

Other North Americans asked them about the effect the war was having on their people and the country. Reducing support for the war would also help the anti-war movement.

The Vietnamese trade union leader responded.

"Of course the war is very hard on our people. It has caused much death and suffering. And it is destroying our land and factories and rice fields. But our people are united. We will weather any storm and suffer any hardship to be free and independent. That is something the US government must understand."

"We wish we could make the US government understand that," one of the North American professors added. "What is hard for us to understand is how you can hold up under such bombing." I had heard that the US had dropped more bombs on tiny Vietnam than the total allied bombing in all of World War II. I was shocked and horrified to even think about that.

"There is no question that it is very difficult," the peasant leader answered. "But we have no choice. So we have to be creative. You have probably heard that we have dug many miles of tunnels underground so we can escape from the bombing. And because we have such widespread support from the people, we can go virtually anywhere in Vietnam and be protected. Most of the countryside is in our liberated zones and we have set up a parallel government that plays a predominant role in the life of the people. In some ways, you have a harder job in the US."

"I don't understand how you can say that," one of the US members said. "You are the ones suffering from the war. We haven't suffered like that."

That's true," the Vietnamese peasant leader continued. "But when I say that your job is harder in some respects, I mean it this way. Our people are united against the US aggressors. We are completely one with the people on this issue and we are all of the same mind. But in the US, we know that it is difficult to help the American people understand the truth about the war. You have many forces against you. You must sometimes feel that, even though you are right, that you are in the minority among some groups of people. We know that can be hard."

I thought there was some truth in what he said. I was very moved and humbled to hear him say we had a tougher job when his people were suffering so much.

A middle-aged Canadian woman asked about life in the liberated zones.

"Life is hard everywhere because of the war," the peasant leader continued, "but we do everything we can to create a more normal life for the people. And they participate in this process as well. We have our own mobile factories and workshops, schools and medical centers. When the enemy comes near, we dismantle everything and move it away or hide it underground, or a facility appears on the outside to be in the hands of the South Vietnamese government when really it isn't. And we have our own theater groups, singing groups, and artistic groups. Developing art and culture – this is very important for our people. We have brought you small gifts from our artists." He reached into a bag and brought out small handicrafts and art pieces.

The Vietnamese woman handed me a picture a little larger than 8 1/2 " x 11", done in a light wash depicting a Vietnamese landscape. The artist appeared to be on a mountain looking down into a deep gorge. Far in the distance, you could see a person in a small boat going down a river bordered by large mountains on the far side and cliffs in the foreground. I was moved by this gift. We brought out political buttons and other items from the anti-war movement. I gave them several buttons from the Buffalo Draft Resistance Union. Our button was small, with a red background and the word "Resist" written across it in black letters. Our gifts seemed quite modest next to theirs.

"How can you spend time on art and theater when a war is raging around you?" I asked.

"We think it's important to make time for art and culture," the woman said, "even in the middle of a war. We have to try to make a full life for our people. People can't fight all the time. We need to get away from the war when we can, and we need to feed our souls with art and life."

I was blown away. The war was so terrible that I felt I had to work around the clock to help build the movement to stop it. I was spending very little time on my own art and personal interests because I felt I didn't have time for such things. It had seemed to me that art and music was a luxury during war time. But I came away from this meeting with a profound new understanding of humanity. Even in a terrible war, art and other life-affirming activities are vitally important. Art connects us with our fellow humans, everywhere. It is a universal language with universal messages. It is essential to bring light and entertainment and art and humor to people's lives, including our own. If the Vietnamese could make time for art and rest during war, I could too. Through this small group of Vietnamese, I gained deep respect for Vietnam and its people.

Chapter 31

Students for a Democratic Society

In September of 1969, classes began again at the University, and SDS called its first meeting of the fall semester. Over 700 people came! The left-wing and anti-war groups had been active for years on campus, but general membership meetings drew 20 or 30 of the faithful, and forums drew 50, 100 or maybe 150. If a big name speaker was on hand, then more showed up. But a regular membership meeting had never attracted 700 people. The anti-war movement and left-wing student politics had arrived in force at the University of Buffalo.

I went with Howard and George. It was good to hook up with them again. We crowded into the Fillmore Room of the Student Union in Norton Hall on the Main Street campus.

"This is unbelievable," I commented to Howard as we entered the large room. "I never expected such a large crowd."

"Neither did I," said Howard. "Remember all the leaflets that were handed out to students every week announcing one event or another."

"Yeah, and the same 50 people showed up and that was it," I responded.

We squeezed into a row of chairs that were being occupied quickly. SDS must have expected a larger than normal crowd because they had enough chairs to seat a couple hundred people. The rest had to stand. The room was packed from wall to wall.

A speaker took the podium and the room quieted down.

"I want to thank every one for coming," the young student leader began. It was someone I recognized but I didn't know his name. "This is going to be a very important year for us. Nixon's election last November on a pledge to end the war has seen only an escalation of the war. He pulls out ground troops to appease the American public, but sends in more bombers. We must continue to build the anti-war movement. This October 15, there will be a Vietnam Moratorium in cities and towns all over the country. That means stopping business as usual so we can talk to our fellow citizens about the war. It will be, in part, like a big teach-in, except it will be held all over town, and will include many other activities as well."

Several years earlier, anti-war students and professors began holding "teach-ins" on University campuses all over the country. I remember reading about them in the newspaper and thought it was a great idea. The teach-in organizers invited experts on Vietnam to come onto campus and conduct large classes in auditoriums and large meeting rooms to educate people on the history of Vietnam and US involvement in the war. Often the speakers were University Professors who specialized on this topic.

"They had teach-ins here, the year before you came," George whispered to me.

The SDS leader continued. "Here in Buffalo, we will be participating in a series of activities for the Vietnam Moratorium. We are going to especially focus on the high schools around the city. If you would like to help with this, put your name and phone number on the sign-up sheet being passed around.

"I'm going to sign up for that," I whispered to Howard. I always believed that if we could get the truth out about Vietnam to a large enough percentage of the population, and especially the young men who were expected to fight it, we could end the war.

"On November 15," the SDS leader continued, "there will be a huge demonstration in Washington, D. C. We will be sending buses from Buffalo. If you would like to go, there is another sign-up sheet for that being passed around the room. We need support for both of these activities."

A hand went up in the audience. "Yes," said the SDS leader looking into the crowd. "Do you have a question?"

A girl sitting in the middle toward the back started saying something, but there was murmuring in the audience and I couldn't hear her.

"Go to the microphone in the center isle," the SDS leader said pointing to it. "We can't hear you."

The young woman had long brown hair and wore glasses, but she didn't look nerdy. She was quite attractive and carried herself with great self-confidence.

"How many buses will you have?" she asked.

"We're not sure yet," the SDS leader responded. "It will depend on how many people sign up for the bus."

"Do you have extra sign-up sheets?" the girl asked.

"Yes, we have them right here," he said as he raised his hand about head-high holding a thin stack of papers.

"If you give me some, I'll take them to my dorm and classes and get people to sign-up," she continued.

"Yes, good," the SDS leader continued. "We need others to take sign-up sheets for buses. Come up and see me after the meeting. We have three more items to take up," the SDS leader continued.

"One is stepping up our campaign to get the University to stop its support of the war. We want them to abolish Air Force ROTC on campus." I joined the applause that swept the audience. "This is a national campaign sponsored by SDS so students all over the country are fighting to get ROTC off their campuses. The military counts heavily on ROTC-trained officers. Without them, there would be a lack of military leadership to run the war. Air Force ROTC here at UB trains pilots to fly bombing runs over Vietnam, so this is an important campaign to cripple the war effort and save lives. We also want the University to terminate Project Themis. That's a secret Defense Department sponsored project to study ways for the Navy and Marines to operate under water for military purposes. We must stop Project Themis!" More applause rippled through the audience.

"The biggest issue for us here in Buffalo this year," he said, his voice rising," is to free the Buffalo Nine!" Applause and cheering engulfed the entire room. I agreed completely with the fall program that SDS presented.

"We invite people to support the Buffalo Nine Defense Committee," the SDS leader continued. "This committee was formed by the four major anti-war organizations and other groups and individuals in Buffalo to build a public campaign to demand freedom for the Buffalo Nine. There is another sign-up sheet for people who want to help the Defense Committee."

"One of the major activities this fall is to get as many people as possible to come to the courthouse to join the demonstrations in support of the Buffalo Nine," the SDS leader said. "As many of you know, the trial of four of the defendants – which was held last February, ended in the conviction of Bruce Beyer and a hung jury for the others. The government is going to retry three of the original defendants and has added two others in a second trial of the Buffalo Nine, which will begin this fall."

"Here on campus," he continued, "we are organizing a big conference on Political Repression right before the second trial begins, and there will be a mass march on the courthouse the first day of the trial. The conference will feature nationally-known speakers and was endorsed at the recent national SDS Convention in Chicago. There will be workshops on many of the cases of political repression around the country. This will help build both local and national support for the Buffalo Nine."

"Finally, I'm circulating another form for those who want to sign-up for SDS."

I was impressed. My opinion of SDS was changing. While I had agreed with its basic political principles and often supported its activities, I had kept some distance from it because of the arrogance of some of its leaders. But I also saw that SDS was made up of all sorts of people, just like any large organization. With 100,000 members on campuses across the country, there were bound to be differences.

I also saw that there were many SDS leaders and members who were intelligent, down-to-earth and easy to work with, and that often, SDS came up with brilliant organizing ideas which influenced thousands, perhaps even millions of people. From what I had read and heard, it was clear that SDS was the driving force throughout the 1960's for much of the anti-war movement on the campuses, and often in the cities too. SDS played an important role in fighting racism and helping to build the Civil Rights Movement, and was working to democratize society and empower people to have more control over their lives. SDS wasn't perfect, but what organization was? In Buffalo, SDS was by far the largest and most influential organization in the anti-war movement and on the political left. I wasn't going to allow my dislike of a few individuals keep me from being involved with an organization with this track record.

I didn't know at the time that a bitter internal feud was unfolding inside of SDS at the top. I had heard that it spilled out at the SDS national convention that summer, but I saw few signs of it in Buffalo.

I signed up for everything.

Chapter 32

Reaching Out

Within the next couple of weeks, I attended several meetings of the Buffalo Vietnam Moratorium Committee to plan our involvement in the October 15 Vietnam Moratorium. Some meetings were held in the Student Union at the University. One of the leaders was a young woman in Student Government at UB, Ellen Price, who I knew from high school. On the UB campus, the committee was made up of a variety of groups and individuals, mostly political moderates, including members of Student Government, campus clubs, and various people from the community. I thought the Moratorium was a great idea. What a good way to reach out to large numbers of people who were not yet active.

I learned that the Vietnam Moratorium was conceived by Sam Brown, a former president of the National Student Association, other student government leaders and several non-students including Jerome Grossman, a Boston-area businessman. The initial idea was to develop an organization and a day for politically moderate students to express their anti-war sentiments, apart from the more radical anti-war students and activists. Brown, who had worked on the presidential campaign of the anti-war candidate, Eugene McCarthy, in his failed 1968 bid, believed there was a broad cross-section of moderate but silent Americans who were against the war and who would express their feelings under the right circumstances.

The Vietnam Moratorium leaders sent letters to student government presidents across the country inviting their support. The majority of student government leaders were politically moderate to liberal, though some were active in the anti-war movement and some were in SDS. The response across the country was huge, unleashing a torrent of support beyond the organizers greatest hopes. As many moderate student government presidents signed on to the Moratorium, the national committee sent notices to the press. Here was a new story, about student leaders who had not been involved in protests against the war before, and who were seen as "reasonable" and "moderate" by government leaders and opinion-makers – the kind of American youth leaders the press could embrace. And the media did. News stories were published, and the so-called "silent majority" that Nixon claimed was on his side – or at least a significant portion of them, contacted the Moratorium and said they wanted to join. Religious leaders and housewives, elected officials and community organizations, union leaders and business leaders, and many others called to get on board. Moratorium Committees sprang up all over the country. What started out as a moderate student event, was now being embraced by huge swaths of mainstream America.

People have asked me why I thought the Vietnam Moratorium took off. In my view, the key was that the Moratorium was seen as a day for Americans in the political mainstream of society to express *their* anti-war sentiments in a way that *they* chose and felt comfortable with, without being seen as following the more well-known radical student leaders who were too often viewed as outside the pale of acceptable behavior. That was the genius of the Vietnam Moratorium. Of course, the activist anti-war movement had helped lay the political groundwork for the Moratorium. Growing numbers of the public were turning against the war so the timing was perfect. And without any pressure or preconceived "correct" way to protest the war, any one or any group could organize their own expression for peace on Vietnam Moratorium day. These expressions ranged the gambit, from wearing a small button that said simply "moratorium," to wearing a black armband, to attending a peace tree planting ceremony or religious service, to attending a public forum or marching in a candle-light parade for peace. It was safe, legal, peaceful, and for the most part very respectful. People saw it as within the boundaries of what was considered acceptable American behavior.

Some of the more radical members and supporters of SDS and other more radical groups were initially critical of the Moratorium, believing it to be too moderate politically. But as Moratorium activities mounted, many got involved in planning their own activities or working with others on larger joint projects. I thought the Moratorium was a great idea from the moment I heard about it.

I joined a subcommittee whose goal was to hold educational forums at many of the Buffalo area high schools.

I attended meetings to plan the details. At the first meting, there were a group of eight people in attendance, including several high school teachers. We all introduced ourselves and, Richard, the chair of this loosely formed committee, gave a brief report..

"On Tuesday, I spoke with an administrator at Bennett High about the symposium on October 15," Richard said in his measured, dignified voice. He was an English graduate student and teaching assistant at the University, and worked on a University literary journal. He was also associated with the anti-war movement on campus, but the more intellectual and cultural wing of it. Tall, with thick uncombed tussled black hair and bushy mustache, he clearly enunciated his words. Richard was proper and unflappable.

"The administrator told me that their knowledge of Vietnam is limited and that they do not have adequate expertise in preparing such a symposium," Richard continued. "Therefore, he deferred to our expertise regarding both the content and the organization of it."

Richard kept referring to the Vietnam Moratorium "teach-in" as a symposium. I guess that was to present it in a more dignified, academic and acceptable light.

"I think we should present the history of Vietnam," said Beth, a bright and intense university history student. "That will show how and why the US got involved, and why the war is wrong."

"I agree," I added. "I have a couple of leaflets that we produced at the Buffalo Draft Resistance Union. One goes over the recent history of Vietnam and another one explains the reasons why the US got involved. The facts show clearly why we shouldn't be involved in Vietnam, and they are written in a pretty straight-forward style, without any rhetoric. We could look at those for some ideas." I was a little nervous proposing leaflets written by the Draft Resistance Union, for fear of turning off some of the more moderate subcommittee members.

"I've seen those leaflets," said Harry, a short, pudgy and balding middle-aged man who was a high school history teacher and who also volunteered at his church. "They're factual, and yes, they are free of the radical rhetoric that I've seen in some of the anti-war literature. Maybe we could use them just as they are, that is, if it's okay with the Draft Resistance Union."

"I don't think that would be a problem," I responded in a professional sounding voice, trying hard to contain my excitement. Inside, I was thrilled that a leaflet that I wrote might be adopted by the Buffalo Vietnam Moratorium. "I'll check with the Draft Resistance Union and get back to you, but I think it should be okay." I had just become the Treasurer of the BDRU, and as one of its leaders, I didn't anticipate any opposition.

There was a moment of silence. Then Richard spoke.

"Have people seen the leaflets we're talking about that were written by the Draft Resistance Union?" Several people nodded, but three people said they hadn't seen them. Richard asked me if I had any copies with me. I did and passed them out to the group. Everyone read them for several minutes and then, one by one, each looked up.

"What does the Committee think about using the leaflets from the Buffalo Draft Resistance Union?" he asked. Several people nodded their heads and a few said yes.

"I agree," said Bill, another high school teacher. "They're written in a clear, simple style, and without the strident emotionalism. I think they would be appropriate for our students."

"Any opposition or questions?" Richard asked. There was none.

"Very good," said Richard. Then he turned to me. "Paul, can you see about getting approval from the Draft Resistance Union?" I nodded.

"If they approve, we will need an initial run of 20,000 copies of those leaflets for the participating high schools and other events. We are getting approval from the principals and we are hoping to use the school auditoriums. The symposium will be attended by many hundreds of students at each school."

I was ecstatic. The thought of these informative leaflets being produced in thousands of copies and distributed to high school students at educational assemblies in school auditoriums sanctioned by school administrators was mind-boggling. Getting to 17 year olds with our message *before* they got to the draft induction center was a giant step forward.

We discussed a couple of other matters, made some assignments, and set another meeting date.

Richard and I left the meeting together and headed for the door to leave the building.

"This is huge," I commented to Richard. "Thousands of high school students from all over Buffalo are going to hear the real history of Vietnam and take our literature home to their families."

"Yes, this is a very important new development," Richard added.

"It seems like a new day," I continued. "The broader community now seems open to having an informed discussion about Vietnam. It seems that people are really coming to their senses."

We opened the door and began walking down the steps to the pavement below, and saw two straggly guys with picket signs that read: "The World is Coming to an End in 30 days. Repent Now!"

One tall lanky guy with long stringy yellow hair and unkempt beard and wearing a purple robe approached us carrying a sign.

"It's time to repent and be saved by God," he proclaimed with alarm in his voice.

"How do you know the world is coming to an end?" Richard asked politely as we kept walking.

"Because God has told us," the purple robe responded as he turned to walk along side us.

"How do you know it will be in 30 days?" I asked the man. "We'll miss the Vietnam Moratorium then," I warned Richard as I turned slightly toward him. Richard looked straight ahead and kept walking.

"Because it has been prophesized," the robe said.

I ignored him.

The robe stepped partially in front of Richard and pleaded, "It's still not too late."

Richard stopped walking. "So we have 30 days?"

"Yes," said the man with hope in his voice.

Richard walked around him and looked back over his shoulder.

"That's okay. We'll just wait it out."

The purple robe looked crushed.

"Well. I guess not everyone has come to his senses," I commented.

"No," Richard said.

We kept walking.

Chapter 33

Visiting Home

While I had my own apartment in Buffalo, I visited my parents, usually on weekends. I would go over to have dinner, maybe once every week or two on Sunday evening, maybe less. I remembered the arguments we had about the war and how I felt somewhat estranged from them. So I tried to avoid the war when ever I saw them to keep the peace. But I was learning so many things in school that helped me understand how our society worked that I felt emboldened. I felt I had a good explanation for why we have poverty, injustice and war, so when my parents asked me what I was learning in school, I told them. I talked briefly about how the US got involved in the war in Vietnam and said I thought the war was a result of our system of capitalism and its inherent drive to expand and increase profits. My dad disagreed. He said the war was about stopping communism.

"Communism can't work because a committee can't plan the economy," he said. "And you must reward self initiative, hard work and ingenuity or you'll have mediocrity and failure."

"But what about Sputnik," I asked. "That wasn't mediocre." That was when the Soviet Union put a capsule into space before the US did.

"That's true," he admitted. "That's because they put a lot of money and talent into their space and arms programs."

"So, that proves that it *can* work, if the right resources and skilled people are put on the job."

"Maybe. But that's an exception. Meanwhile, other areas of their society are suffering. And people don't have democratic rights, like we do. I want to be rewarded for what I do, and if I can make more money, I want the right to be able to do that. What's worse is that the communists want to export their way of life to others. Like in Vietnam. We can't stand by and let them impose their rule over South Vietnam. And now these radical students want to tear down the university." I think my dad knew I was around those students, but maybe he wasn't sure if I identified with them or not.

"But that's not what happened in Vietnam," I responded. I had read a lot about Vietnam, and now felt I could hold my own in a discussion about the war with my dad. I went into more detail about the history of Vietnam – the rule of French colonialism, the violation of the Geneva Agreements, the popular support for the liberation movement in Vietnam – which did have communists in it, the exploitation and impoverishment of the Vietnamese people by foreign capitalist corporations, and how when the Vietnamese protested this treatment, fighting broke out that lead to war. "As for the radical students, they are trying to stop the war because it's wrong, and they are the leaders of the anti-war movement," I said.

"Let's not talk about this now," my Mom interjected, trying to make peace at the table. "We're eating dinner." Both my brothers Lee and Jim were away at school.

But my dad and I were too heavily into it and the discussion continued until it ended in a heated argument. I felt bad. I left the kitchen and went into the living room and stared out the window. After about five minutes, my mom came in. She had a big heart for people. Whenever she saw conflict, or someone hurt, she felt bad for them. She wanted the best for everyone, and I deeply admired her for that. I felt close to my mom.

"I hate to see you and your father argue like that."

"Yeah, I know. I don't like it either."

"Why do you have to be involved in such a radical political movement?

"I don't agree with everything the radicals do," I said. "But they are the only people saying what has to be said about a lot of important issues. I know people don't like to hear about the quest for material gain from the war, but that's the truth. The radicals have done the research and they have the courage to say it. And they're the major force trying to stop the war."

"But they're so radical. Can't you work more in the mainstream? Like supporting those Democrats and liberals who oppose the war?"

"Well, I did that to an extent. I was supportive of Senator McCarthy and Bobby Kennedy. McCarthy lost the nomination, and Kennedy got killed. And besides, the Democratic Party isn't talking about the real reasons we're in Vietnam. They're not educating the people about the war, and a lot of them are supporting it. And under Johnson, they escalated it."

"But I think the radicals scare people. The public thinks their ideas are too extreme."

"I don't think most of our ideas are too extreme. I think the radical's ideas are mostly correct, moral and just plain good common sense. The war our government is waging against Vietnam is extreme. It's immoral, it's a national tragedy, it's a crime against humanity, and the American people have been lied to about it. To expose the lies, to protest against the war, and try to stop it isn't radical – it's the only moral thing to do. And I am trying to work more in the mainstream – by taking the real facts about the war to people who haven't heard them before, like young kids getting drafted and high school kids whose draft notices are about to come in the mail."

"But are they ready to hear what you have to say?"

"Some are, some aren't. But we have to keep saying it. It's the truth, and as unpleasant as it is to hear some of it, it must be said."

"Don't you think you could accomplish more by moderating what you say and do? Some of those activities at the university are so extreme, don't you think? Like strikes and violence and talk of revolution?"

"Yes, some of it sounds pretty extreme. But too often, it seems like the public isn't listening. So the students get frustrated, and resort to more radical ideas and tactics."

"I know you care about people and want to stop the wrongs in the world. But why couldn't you do something more practical, like being a social worker? They help people."

"Yes, I know they help people, and I'm glad we have them. But I'm more interested in trying to stop the abuses before they start, not just try to help people after they have been hurt. I want to stop the knife from stabbing, not just put bandages on the wounds. If we don't stop the knife from stabbing, we'll be putting bandages on the wounds forever and the suffering will never end."

My mom was silent for a moment. I could see that she was thinking about what I had said.

"And," I continued, "I'm involved with a new effort called the Vietnam Moratorium, which *is* moderate. Its goal is to reach out to the mainstream of society and ask people to express opposition to the war how ever they want. Maybe attend a special church service or go to an educational forum or what ever else they want to do."

"Yes, that sounds much better," my mom said, her face brightening up. "Are you doing something for this?"

"Yeah, I'm working with a group that is going into high schools to present an educational forum, and we're trying to get approval from the principals of the schools."

"That's wonderful!" she exclaimed. "I'm so glad you are trying to work within the system. That's much better, and I'll bet you'll get a much better response to your message that way."

"I hope so," I responded. I didn't know then just how right my mom would be.

She then changed the subject.

"Now, what about your art? Are you still drawing or painting? You're so talented and have so much to give through your art. It's a good way to bring some beauty into the world. Please don't give that up."

"I'm not giving it up, Mom. It's just hard to find time to concentrate on art when these bad things are going on in the world. But, yes, I'm making the time to do art. I've done some sketches, and want to do more pen and ink drawings." I recalled the meeting with the Vietnamese in Canada and about the importance they placed on doing art and developing culture. I also thought about some of the drawings I had done recently – like the man who looked terrorized from what I guessed to be war. I wasn't sure that drawing would bring much beauty into the world, but hopefully, it would make people think.

"Good. I'm so glad to hear that," she said with a smile. "How about a girlfriend?" she asked with a twinkle in her eye. "Anyone special in your life now? Donna was so sweet."

"Yes, Donna was sweet, Mom," I said, wishing she hadn't reminded me of how much I had loved Donna, and maybe still did. "But, no. I'm not seeing anyone now." I was in such emotional turmoil over the war that I had a hard time thinking about falling in love.

"Well, I'm sure you will meet someone," she said, still smiling.

"Yes. Thanks, Mom," I managed. "Well, I should be going. Thanks for the dinner. It was great. And it was good seeing you and Dad again."

"Will we see you next Sunday, for dinner?"

"Yes, I think that will be fine. I'll call you during the week."

"Good. We always love to see you. But next time, try not to argue with your father so much. Okay?"

"Yeah, I'll try."

I did try not to argue with my father. I loved him and respected him, but on this issue we just didn't agree. Unfortunately, we did argue, again and again. My mom was caught in the middle. I don't think she wanted to challenge my father, so she either quietly mentioned that he made a good point, or remained silent. Finally the arguments between my dad and me became so heated that I didn't visit them for many, many months. I was in pain. I was now estranged from my father, and unintentionally, from my mom too.

Chapter 34

SDS in Crisis

A group of militant activists in the national leadership of SDS steered the organization onto an even more militant path at their fiery convention in Chicago in the summer of 1969. I didn't know much about it when it happened, except what I read in an article in one of our local Buffalo newspapers. I thought it was interesting that the newspapers usually ignored peaceful educational forums that SDS held, but publicized events where there was discord. The article explained that one group in SDS, Progressive Labor Party (PL), was kicked out of SDS by another faction based in the national SDS office called Revolutionary Youth Movement (RYM). I heard later that Progressive Labor Party claimed they had majority support at that convention for their program, so the Revolutionary Youth Movement group suspended the convention, and then reconvened it minus the PL group. But that wasn't the end of it.

I learned later from my friends at UB that shortly after the convention, the Revolutionary Youth Movement then split into two groups. The first one was called Weathermen, named from a line in a Bob Dylan song, "You don't need a weatherman to know which way the wind blows." The other faction called itself Revolutionary Youth Movement II. And there was a third group that wasn't a part of any of the factions. That group was probably the largest, but they weren't organized in any formal organization.

I was in Norton Union one day that fall and saw a group of people around the SDS table. Two students were standing behind the table and four students were in front of it talking loudly in an animated way. I moved closer to hear what they were taking about. They were arguing about the split in SDS.

"They're crazy," one student said emphatically. He was tall and was wearing a green Army jacket. "They've lost faith in the American people. They talk about the American working-class selling out to the ruling class – that's bullshit. They've never worked in a factory, or anywhere else, so they have no idea of how American workers fight against exploitation and oppression every day. Just look at any strike, or the struggles that go on inside the plant daily.

The Weathermen need to get jobs and then they'll wake up to the reality of the class struggle right here in the US."

"What class struggle?" another student with long black curly hair asked sarcastically. He was skinny, with eyes that twitched and darted about. "American workers are like sheep," he continued. "American society tells them to do something and they do it without question. They think there is no difference between themselves and the boss."

"That's not true," I interjected. "I worked in an auto parts factory last summer and the workers there were involved in a campaign to defeat a new job speed-up. And believe me, they know the difference between them and the boss."

"Okay, so they fought a speed-up plan. Big deal. What are they doing to stop the war?"

"First of all it is a big deal," I continued. "If you worked there you would understand why it was so important to stop the job speed-up plan. And about working to stop the war, a bunch of unions have formed a Labor for Peace organization." I had heard one of the working-class SDS members mention that two days earlier.

"And what are they doing? Passing resolutions? That's a big help," he said sarcastically, his left eye twitching so violently I thought it was going to pop out of his head.

"It's a start," I continued. "That's the first step in building stronger worker opposition to the war. When workers in key industries understand what the war is really about, they can hinder war production."

"You've got to be kidding! That will never happen." Now both eyes were twitching.

"It's already happening," I continued. "Dockworkers in Europe, Australia, and in San Francisco have refused to load ships with war material bound for Vietnam." I had learned about that in the radical and anti-war newspapers that I read. "I just read about some US sailors – one was an electrician, who were on a ship bound for Vietnam with napalm bombs and who commandeered the ship and diverted it to Cambodia to stop the bombs from going to Vietnam." I knew these events were few in number, but I hoped they increased in frequency.

"I haven't heard about that," he said looking a little startled. He quickly recovered his know-it-all attitude: "Even if it is happening, it's too little too late. The Vietnamese don't have time to wait for American workers to oppose the war. They're dying now."

"Look, students and the rest of the anti-war movement can't stop the war by ourselves," the guy in the Army jacket said. "We have to reach the majority of Americans. The majority of voters are working people," he continued. "If we reach them and they turn against the war, that will send a message to the politicians that they must oppose it if they want to get re-elected."

"The politicians don't give a shit about what workers think or anyone else," the guy with the twitching eyes said. "The politicians do what their corporate sponsors order them to do, regardless of what the voters say. The electoral system is rigged and you're wasting your time going there!" Now his body was twitching. I wondered if he was on speed.

"Well, there has been enough public opposition to force Nixon to pull out a lot of the troops," I continued.

"Yes, but he's sent in more bombers. The Vietnamese don't care if they are killed by soldiers on the ground or by bombers in the air. They're dead either way."

"Of course," said my friend in the Army jacket. "But we must stop the war effort however we can. Getting the government to pull out US troops is a good thing. Now we have to keep building the size and strength of the anti-war movement to stop the bombing. But it's going to be harder to do that with you and your Weathermen friends attacking the American people. We need to win the public over, not turn them off to us."

"It's a waste of time," the Weatherman supporter exclaimed. "They're not even listening to us. They've sold out to the system. The Weathermen are right. The only thing to do now is to reach out to revolutionary youth and blacks – people who don't have a vested interest in protecting this system, and who are ready for revolutionary action."

"Ready for revolutionary action?" my friend asked in a loud voice. "How many people are ready for revolutionary action? What percentage of the American population does that constitute? A very small percentage," he said emphatically.

"The Black Panthers are ready."

"Yes, and they are getting killed. We need to reach many more people," my ally continued.

"There isn't time."

"There isn't a choice," I chimed in. "There won't be any fundamental change in this country unless many more people are involved."

"But we're not alone here," the Weathermen advocate proclaimed. "We are aligned with the Vietnamese liberation movement, and all other national liberation movements all over the world. That makes us the majority."

"The majority?" I asked sarcastically. "Where? Not in the US. Our job is to win over people here, large sections of people, to a more progressive position *inside* the US. For most of them, that is getting them to oppose the war."

My friend in the Army jacket interjected. "Stopping this government from waging war against the Vietnamese and others will do more to help those national liberation struggles than small bands of Weatherman zealots running amok in the streets here screaming about fighting the police and revolution."

"Your problem is that you refuse to give up your white skin privilege," the Weatherman supporter shot back. "You want to hide behind your white skin so you don't have to risk anything. You have to be willing to fight the pigs in the streets."

"What, are you crazy?" my friend continued. "Most people aren't going to risk anything in a nutty, losing adventure like that. And that will give the government the excuse they need to crack down on all dissent. Ruling classes everywhere have provoked disorder and street battles so they'll have an excuse to arrest anyone who protests, and then erode democratic rights. That's how fascist dictatorships have come to power. You should know that. You're playing into the hands of the ruling class. We need to build a much larger movement – that is the number one goal. That's why we're going to have a RYM II chapter here at UB."

"The Weathermen will build a revolutionary movement by setting a revolutionary example," he said in a rising voice. He was almost jumping around now. "Youth and blacks will join us when they see us taking on the pigs in the streets and doing material damage to the ruling class and war machine. You people are either cowards or stupid. You don't have to be a genius to see which way the wind blows!"

"Please, spare me the rhetoric" my friend answered. "The SDSers from Wisconsin got it right about the Weathermen: you don't need a rectal thermometer to know who the assholes are."

"Fuck you!"

"What are you going to do about it?" asked my friend in the Army jacket as he leaned toward twitching eyes until their faces were about two inches apart.

"You've got three of you and one of me."

These other guys will stay out of it." He clenched his fists and brought his right had up about chest high.

"Yeah, like I'd trust you. Your buddies would jump in." He turned and walked away.

"No they won't. It's just you and me," my friend yelled after him. He kept walking.

"What is it that they want?" I asked. It was depressing to see people who were against the war act so crazy.

"They want to turn our national action in Chicago into a street battle with the Chicago Police."

"Yeah, I've heard about it. That's the Days of Rage actions, right?" I asked.

"Yeah. When it was first being planned, our goal was to carry out a series of marches and actions with other groups – like the Black Panther Party and the Young Lords. We want to reach out to workers who are battling abuses at work, and to minorities to make the connections between racism, poverty, the exploitation of workers, injustice at home, and the war. You know, money spent on the war is money not spent on jobs, or education or health care, or for affordable housing. We also want to make it a spirited street march through working-class and third world communities to show blacks, Latinos and whites marching together, and so people will see how all these issues are connected. Then this small minority group in SDS that became the Weathermen decided that they wanted to turn it into street battles with the police. That's their idea of the slogan: 'Bring the War Home.' Like they're going to open up a new front in the war on the side of the Vietnamese right here in the US by attacking the armed might of the state. Some of them come from very rich backgrounds, and they openly attack working people, like that guy who was just here at the table. They're so out of touch with most Americans that they don't believe they can be organized. So they've come up with these hair-brained theories. They're nuts. And they've created this big split in SDS and it threatens to do serious damage to the movement."

"Do you think the split is permanent," I asked. "Or can it be fixed?"

"I doubt it. They seem to have made up their minds to go through with this crazy action in Chicago. RYM II is planning our own, separate demonstrations. You should come with us."

"Is the Buffalo SDS solidly a RYM II chapter?"

"Yep. There are a few people here who are pushing the Weatherman line – like that guy who was just here, but the big majority want it as a RYM II chapter."

"What else does RYM II believe?"

"The main thing is to reach out to the community, to working people and others to get them involved in the movement. That means going out to support their causes. Like we did with the South Buffalo Railroad workers who were on strike earlier this year. We manned their picket lines when the courts got an injunction against the union to bar the workers from doing mass picketing."

I remembered hearing about that. I wished I had known about the picketing beforehand – I would have joined them. "I totally agree with that. Is there anything to read that talks about the differences between Weathermen and RYM II?"

"Yeah, read this." He handed me a document from the SDS literature table titled: "The Debate Inside SDS: RYM II vs. the Weathermen."

I took the document home and read it. It was loaded with quotes mostly from Mao and other revolutionary socialists and communists, along with their pictures. While many of the passages seemed to make sense, at least for revolutionary China, I was concerned that there was too little in the document about conditions in the United States. I also didn't think the prominent display of these revolutionary leaders would do much to win over many Americans, and in fact, would probably turn them off. None-the-less, of the two factions of SDS, the RYM II faction was more sensible than the Weathermen. And while there were a couple of Progressive Labor Party members in Buffalo, I saw their open call for communist revolution as totally out of touch with most Americans.

The Buffalo SDS chapter, which did align with the RYM II group, had presented an excellent agenda of demonstrations and conferences for the fall 1969 semester. So, I decided to go to Chicago with the Buffalo RYM II contingent. The dates were October 8-12. I then planned to leave Chicago on October 11 to go to a big demonstration at Ft. Dix in New Jersey on October 12 to support soldiers who were protesting against the war at the base. I was going to use some of the money I received from the accident to my hand to cover travel expenses. When I returned, I would get ready for the Vietnam Moratorium in Buffalo, set for Wednesday, October 15. October was going to be a very busy month.

While the SDS chapter at the University of Buffalo was a RYM II chapter, some of its leaders and others in the movement had a reputation for being tough. A number of them were working-class guys who had worked in factories or other blue collar jobs and some were war veterans. Some were used to fighting in their neighborhoods, in bars, and in Vietnam, and they brought that culture to the university.

I had heard stories about some SDS and movement leaders and activists getting into fist-fights with right-wingers and pummeling them. If it was done in self-defense, I understood that. But I also heard and saw some of these movement leaders intimidate others who were in the movement, including punching them over some disagreement.

That bothered me. That type of behavior was completely wrong. It was an affront to the individual being attacked, and it hurt the movement. It was too bad because some of these aggressive movement leaders had strong leadership qualities. They gave people confidence when they stood up at a rally and announced that we were going to fight for what was right. But I'm sure their abusiveness toward others kept many, many people from getting involved in the movement. I had heard that this abusiveness had taken place in other organizations and in other parts of the country as well. I also had heard and believed that some of this abusive behavior was by undercover police agents who were trying to disrupt these organizations from the inside. But I also believed from my own observations that some people in the movement were abusive because that's who they were.

Some had a political explanation for this behavior. Some of those who proclaimed themselves revolutionaries believed that a small vanguard of very dedicated revolutionaries could spark and lead a revolution in the United States and they wanted to recruit other like-minded people. Some would prod and goad the less militant people to get them to act tougher and commit to revolutionary activity now or in the near future. "Are you ready to pick up a gun," some would challenge.

Others in RYM II believed that the most important thing was to build a mass movement around popular demands that would improve life for people. Some in RYM II who believed in revolution felt this was essential before any revolutionary activity could take place. RYM II wasn't promoting armed revolution in 1969. That was good news, I thought. But some RYM II members said that some day in the future we should be prepared for armed revolution. I hoped such a day was a long way off, and I redoubled my efforts to build a powerful enough movement to bring about fundamental social change as peacefully as possible. Talk of armed revolution in the United States in 1969 seemed suicidal to me. But the broad social upheaval of the period and increasingly militant protests created an atmosphere where one thought, 'if this spreads to large groups of people, maybe it's possible.' The RYM II demonstrations planned for Chicago were organized and announced as completely legal and peaceful. That was reassuring.

However, when I arrived in Chicago, the city looked like an armed camp. There were many hundreds, maybe thousands, of riot-clad police with guns everywhere. They were out in force for the Weathermen's march, I figured. Our RYM II group gathered in a park to get ready for our march, and the Chicago riot police lined the streets, almost surrounding us. There seemed to be more of them than us. I thought, didn't the police get the word that we were the peaceful, law abiding faction of SDS, and not the crazy, violence-prone Weathermen faction? Apparently not. That was not a good feeling. Several thousand people gathered and we started marching toward the Federal Courthouse where the Chicago 8 conspiracy trial was taking place. Those were the anti-war leaders who were arrested and charged with conspiracy to riot at the Democratic National Convention the summer before. We stopped there for a rally where speakers denounced the trial as an attack on the anti-war movement and urged freedom for all eight defendants.

Then we went to the large International Harvester factory to show support for workers there who were struggling for justice at work. Along the way we picked up another thousand community people from largely black and Latino neighborhoods that we marched through, so now our march was very multi-racial. RYM II activists had been working in these neighborhoods for months, along with the

Black Panthers and Young Lords, so the people knew what we were advocating. We then marched to Cook County Hospital to demand money for health care and not for war, support for the health care workers and patients, and for a universal health care system. Many of the health care workers gave us the thumbs-up and the "V" for peace, and some joined our rally and spoke at it. We carried signs and chanted slogans for multi-racial solidarity, for jobs, good education, decent housing, and an end to the war. The response from the public was overwhelmingly positive. I felt like we were going in the right direction. This was by far the largest gathering over the four days of activities in Chicago.

Things didn't go so well for the Weathermen, however. According to reports from some of our RYM II people, the Weathermen had perhaps 300 people show up for their first event – they expected thousands, and their plan was to run through the streets and physically attack the police with clubs and other weapons. It was bizarre. Despite all their talk of being in alliance with and supporting black and Latino revolutionaries, their group was almost all white. Many wore helmets, the report continued, and they rampaged through the streets of Chicago in well-to-do neighborhoods smashing windows, cars, and attacking innocent pedestrians and the police. I completely disagreed with these tactics. As part of their strategy, these activities turned out to be not such a good idea. Many of the Weathermen were beaten pretty badly by the police and some 200 were arrested. While they did injure some policemen, they were on the losing end of the battle, according to our RYM II reporters, and their ranks were so depleted that they were crippled for the rest of the weekend. Not a great start for the revolution. Even the Black Panthers, who advocated armed self defense, knew these street battles were suicidal and the Panthers had nothing to do with the Weathermen actions.

We disagreed so strongly with what the Weathermen were doing that any thought of reconciliation was impossible. It was hard for me to believe that the two groups had, until very recently, been a part of the same organization. When a group of Weathermen were under attack by the police and were being arrested near one of our rallies, one RYM II person near the scuffle told the police, who thought we might be with them: "we don't know 'em, they're not part of our group," and he turned away to listen to our speaker. The cops arrested the Weathermen and left us alone.

Leaders of SDS, the Young Lords, and the Black Panthers addressed our rallies. I saw Fred Hampton, the dynamic chairman of the Illinois Black Panther Party, and heard his moving speech about the oppression of blacks and poor people and how they had to organize to achieve freedom. These three organizations presented an image of a national coalition of radical blacks, Latinos and whites, working together to promote the demands of low and moderate income people, minorities and workers, and calling for an end to the war, racism, poverty, and ultimately, capitalism, and for socialism. A guy standing next to me at the Fred Hampton rally commented half out loud: "This ought to send a chill down the spine of the ruling class." I thought he might be right.

Even though we were the saner SDS faction, the political atmosphere in Chicago was very tense. I, for one, felt some threat to our safety, though I didn't admit it to anyone. It wasn't good to show fear.

The Buffalo RYM II group stayed in a church in a poor working-class community along with other RYM II contingents from many other cities. There were so many people there that our sleeping bags were one right next to the other. I saw Jim there, my red-headed friend from UB, one afternoon and asked him if he had heard anything more about the Weatherman actions.

"Yeah. They've been a disaster," he explained. "We heard that they ran through a couple of Chicago high schools yelling 'jailbreak,' pushed around some teachers, and did some property damage, but the students attacked the Weathermen and threw *them* out of their school."

How could one-time movement leaders come up with such a counter-productive program, I wondered?

The SDS/RYM II alliance with the Black Panther Party and the Young Lords seemed like a big step forward, and was in many ways. We were uniting the most militant leftist groups in the black, Latino and white communities. That was huge. Building multi-racial unity was very important to me. But the more I thought about it, the more questions I had about our political approach. Could this group reach out to and connect with much broader sections of the American public and influence them? I saw this as essential. While many people in these groups were smart, bold and politically progressive on most major issues, the people who were arrogant, undemocratic and abusive hurt us and the entire movement.

I thought about the people I worked with at Standard Mirror. They might agree with many of our demands, but would they follow us? I highly doubted it. I felt we were too extreme. A number of people in all three organizations advocated violent revolution. That scared most Americans. I felt more attention had to be given to working with people where *they* were at politically and around issues that *they* identified as important to them. Once that was done successfully, then we could evaluate whether it would be possible to move on to more politically advanced demands and activities that required a higher level of political consciousness and organization.

We also needed to better define what a new society would look like. Would there be full democratic rights for all? Freedom of speech? The rights of due process, even for those holding minority viewpoints? Would our Bill of Rights remain intact? I sure hoped the answer was "yes" to all these questions. But I didn't hear much about these issues discussed in this movement. I wondered, what if, eventually, some of the people leading this movement actually came to power? I didn't feel very comfortable with that. I thought it was important for a political movement to live by the ideals it professed for the new, more just society.

On October 11, a day before the SDS RYM II actions concluded, I left Chicago for Ft. Dix, New Jersey. I felt good that day. One, I was getting out of the tense atmosphere in Chicago. Two, I heard that a Gallup Poll had reported that 57% of the American people wanted Congress to pass legislation to get *all* American troops out of Vietnam by the end of 1970. While I favored immediate withdrawal and believed the end of 1970 was way too long to wait, I saw this sentiment as a step forward, since up to that point, a majority of Americans had still been supporting the war. And three, I was heading to Ft. Dix to support anti-war soldiers. *That* was very important to me. It's hard to conduct a war when soldiers resist fighting.

Chapter 35

Fort Dix Demonstration

I was spending so much time organizing against the war that I took a reduced course load at school in the fall of 1969. And, like many other anti-war activists, I had been sharing apartments or houses with other fellow activists so we could divide the rent between us. I was living in a small house with three other people, so my rent was one-fourth of the total, or $75 a month. I could earn that working three or four days at day labor. That left me a lot of time for studying and organizing. Our living conditions were a little crowded, but I wasn't home that much. Sometimes I had a steady part-time job that paid the bills, and that left me a lot of time for school and the anti-war movement too. I also had cut my living expenses to the bare essentials, primarily rent and food. Since I knew I was going to be doing a lot of traveling in October, I worked extra days at day labor in September to cover the costs, and I used some of the money from the settlement from my factory accident.

On October 12, 1969, the civilian anti-war movement came to Fort Dix, New Jersey to support a group of anti-war GI's there who were facing serious charges, and to support the burgeoning anti-war movement there and throughout the Armed Forces. I thought this anti-war GI movement was very important and I wanted to be a part of it. Ft. Dix was a good choice for the demonstration because it housed a major U.S. Army Basic Training program and a major Army Personnel Center to process troops for overseas duty. Many of the draftees from the Buffalo Draft Induction Center were sent to Ft. Dix. A mock Vietnamese village was set up inside the base and soldiers received training for combat in Vietnam, and that's where many were sent. Located about 15 miles southeast of Trenton, the base covered over 30,000 acres, making it one of the largest military bases in the country.

The goals of the demonstration were to reach out to the soldiers to support those already opposed to the war, support those facing criminal charges for a protest riot that took place there months earlier, and to help convince others that going to war in Vietnam wasn't the right thing to do. The hottest issue was to support the soldiers facing criminal charges. I had read about the case in the

Guardian, the American Servicemen's newspaper *The Bond,* and other anti-war publications.

Earlier in 1969, many soldiers were put in the stockade at Ft. Dix for opposing the war and the abuse of authority by some officers. Tensions increased all over the base. On June 5, 1969, over 150 prisoners housed in the stockade, rioted and took over three buildings and fires were set. Thirty-eight soldiers were arrested and charged with arson and inciting to riot. Among the 38 were several leaders and activists of the American Servicemen's Union. I and other members of the Buffalo Draft Resistance Union had been handing out anti-war leaflets and *The Bond* almost daily to draftees at the Buffalo Draft Induction Center throughout the year. I remember handing out issues of *The Bond* which covered the case of the Ft. Dix 38. For all these reasons, I felt a personal connection to this case and the GIs at Ft. Dix. I wanted to be there to show my support for these courageous soldiers and their Defense Committee. This act of resistance at Ft. Dix was not an isolated rebellion. Scores of sit-ins, work stoppages, riots and other forms of protest had taken place on US military bases since 1967, and they were increasing in number every year.

I had heard about a meeting place that had been set up by anti-war organizers near the base, the Wrightstown Coffeehouse, to provide a safe place for soldiers to come and relax and talk about the war and other issues of concern. Similar coffee houses had sprung up outside many military bases across the country. Many Ft. Dix soldiers learned about the history of Vietnam at the coffee house, as well as the growing GI opposition to the war. There were anti-war newspapers, leaflets, and articles, speakers and movies there, and the soldiers developed camaraderie with one another. Since the coffeehouse played such a central role in organizing anti-war activity among the soldiers, that was where we were going to gather before our march to the base.

I had tried to get some of my anti-war friends from Buffalo to come with me, but none of them could. So I went alone. As I flew to Trenton, I thought about how the anti-war movement had grown inside the military. I had read that many anti-war activists believed the GI resistance movement began at Ft. Hood in Texas in 1966 when three courageous GI's, James Johnson, Dennis Mora and David Samas, refused to go to Vietnam, calling the war immoral. The Ft. Hood 3, as they were called, were court-martialed and spent time in prison. But their action spurred the formation of a defense committee that fought for their freedom and publicized their case far and wide, and now those seeds of resistance were bearing fruit.

Before we landed, I read again the leaflet I had with me announcing the demonstration. It demanded the freedom of the Fort Dix 38 and all political prisoners, an end to the stockade system as a repressive method to snuff out anti-war sentiment, and an end to the war in Vietnam. The coalition that called the demonstration was very broad politically, including the Wrightstown Coffee House, the Catholic Peace Fellowship, the American Servicemen's Union, and the Black Panther Party, to name only a few.

When I arrived, people were already gathering outside the Coffeehouse. It looked like a thousand people were there, with huge banners reflecting the three main demands. Several of the organizers told the crowd that our goals were to go onto the base to show support for the soldiers, try to talk to them, and to explain why the war was wrong. We were to be completely peaceful, and we were not to get into altercations with any of the soldiers or police. When the last speaker finished, the crowd started marching across Highway 68 toward the base in a demonstration that stretched out for a quarter of a mile. That was quite a sight in that quiet, sparsely populated rural area.

People were chanting, "Free the Fort Dix 38," "Big Firms Get Rich, GI's Die," and "End the War Now."

As we approached the base, we could clearly see the buildings and groups of soldiers standing about while others were driving military vehicles. There was also a line of Military Police with rifles, bayonets, helmets and gas masks for as far as I could see. It looked like thousands of them. I thought I had left this behind in Chicago.

The head of the march started crossing a large open field and we all followed. A contingent of military police quickly cut us off and an officer approached in a military vehicle holding a bullhorn.

"You are trespassing in violation of fedcral law. If you do not leave, you will be arrested," the officer announced.

The marchers slowed for a moment and then continued. Within seconds, three troop carriers arrived and hundreds of armed soldiers jumped out in full battle gear, and took up positions flanking us. Army helicopters circled overhead. It looked like Vietnam. I thought if this were Vietnam, we might just be machined-gunned to

271

death, and the official government announcement that the mass media would dutifully report would be: 'Thousands of Communist Invaders Wiped Out in Assault on US Army Base.'

In many places we were right next to the soldiers, in fact, only a few feet away from them, and people in the crowd started talking to them.

"We are with you," a young girl next to me yelled over the din of the helicopters swirling overhead. "We know you're ordered to be here. It's the Nixon Administration that is to blame for the war."

"You are on US Army property," an officer bellowed through his bullhorn. "You must leave immediately, or you will be arrested."

The crowd began chanting: "Free the Fort Dix 38, end the war now." Over and over, and the increasing volume partially drowned out the officer's orders.

All of a sudden a helicopter swooped down toward the crowd. The roar of its engine was so loud that it sounded like the copter's runners could take our heads off. People ducked and some started running.

"Don't run," a march organizer yelled through his bullhorn. People stopped running and rejoined the large throng of people.

Some young guy about 30 feet from me started yelling at the soldiers:

"You are murderers! You will be killing children and babies!"

I wondered if this guy was an undercover police agent who had infiltrated the demonstration to undermine our message and turn the soldiers against us. I had heard that similar provocations by undercover cops had taken place before.

I looked over at a march organizer who was holding a bullhorn at his side. He was standing about ten feet from me just watching. I rushed over to him.

"We can't let that guy say those things," I implored.

He looked at me with a pained look on his face and then mumbled, "but what can we do?"

"Let me have the bullhorn," I said as I reached for it. He gave it to me.

"Soldiers. We are here with you today," I yelled through the bullhorn, completely drowning out the guy who was yelling at them. "We are in solidarity with you. We know that many of you were drafted into the Army. We know that many of you joined because you were told that we had to fight to defend freedom. That is admirable. But we have not been told the truth about the war in Vietnam. We have not been told about the elections that were called off in 1956 in Vietnam that would have reunited the country and put an end to the war then. We have not been told that the person we are supporting there, General Ky, said that his only hero is Hitler. We have not been told how badly the Vietnamese people were exploited under General Ky, until millions finally rose up to win their freedom, just like we did from Great Britain in our American Revolution. We have not been told about how big corporations in our country want to get the cheap raw materials and cheap labor in Vietnam so they can increase their profits, while we risk our lives." The guy who was yelling at the soldiers was drowned out and gave up.

Just then three explosions ripped the air and tear gas canisters rocketed into our ranks. Several people fell to the ground. Others started coughing, wheezing and running. My nose and eyes started burning and watering, and we retreated from the base and headed back to the coffeehouse.

When everyone had gathered there, a coffeehouse organizer addressed the marchers. "We've scored important victories today. I learned from some of the servicemen at Fort Dix that the brass was so worried about this demonstration that they released 365 prisoners from the stockade."

A loud cheer went up from the crowd.

"The brass didn't trust its own MPs either. They brought in MPs' from Fort Meade."

The crowd cheered again. Just then we saw a busload of Fort Dix soldiers go by. Through open windows some flashed victory signs and raised fists showing their support for our demonstration.

The crowd roared again.

After the last speaker had finished, we returned to the busses to go back to Trenton. I felt good about the work we did at Ft. Dix. It was clear that the anti-war movement was alive, well and growing inside the US military.

AUG. 23 ANTI-WAR DEMONSTRATION

BUFFALO N.Y. NIAGARA SQ. 12:30 P.M.

BUFFALO COALITION TO END THE WAR IN VIETNAM
884-0426 • 882-2109

buffalo draft resistance union • peace & freedom party • clergy & layman concerned about vietnam • students for a democratic society • urban action association • buffalo rights action group • women's international league for peace & freedom • quaker peace committee • youth against war & fascism • cause • 1969

I designed this flyer to help advertise the anti-war march in Buffalo in the summer of 1969. Many thousands were passed out across Buffalo.

I spoke at an anti-war demonstration in front of the Buffalo Draft Board, August 23, 1969, demanding an end to both the draft and the war.

Students for a Democratic Society demonstrate August 23, 1969 in front of a major bank in downtown Buffalo to protest the role of banks in financing and supporting the war.

Anti-war protestors on August 23, 1969 demonstrate outside the Erie County Social Services Building. A speaker from the Buffalo Welfare Rights Organization decried the billions of dollars spent on the war instead of on social services.

This print was a gift to me from a member of the Vietnamese independence movement at a meeting with US anti-war leaders and activists that I attended at the University of Windsor in Canada, September 1969.

Teachers from the Vietnam independence movement teach classes in rural areas in South Vietnam.

I was among over 1000 protestors who went onto the Ft. Dix military base in New Jersey on October 12, 1969 to support the Ft. Dix 38-soldiers charged with felonies stemming from protests against abusive officers and the war.

Shakedown was an anti-war newspaper published by the soldiers at Ft. Dix and their supporters.

Growing numbers of soldiers wore the peace sign, and refused to fight.

Paul Krehbiel

EXTRA!!
THE SPECTRUM

Campus and city police battled students here for at least three hours last night, resulting in at least 17 arrests and several injuries. Campus police entered Norton Hall shortly before 9 pm, scattering occupants of the main floor, and making two arrests. City police surrounded and eventually invaded the student union an hour later. City and Erie County police remained on campus throughout the night.

A partial list of those arrested includes: Tom Kearns, 3rd degree assault, disorderly conduct; Terry Keegan, disorderly conduct; Barry Koran, possession of a dangerous weapon; David Shaw and Lawrence Harris incitement to riot. Lawyer Willard Myers, who was posting bail for the jailed students, was charged with first degree riot.

A high-level administrative meeting in Acheson Hall early this morning resulted in Acting President Peter F. Regan calling for an investigation into the evening's events. No one, however, would admit to giving the campus police the first order to evacuate Norton Hall. Administrative sources indicated that it was the campus police who exercised their perogative to call for city re-inforcements, in cases of violence.

Rallies and forums are scheduled for today. Classes have not been cancelled as of this writing.

INVASION!

A special edition of *The Spectrum,* our student newspaper, covered the police assault on students in Norton Union after a student sit-in on February 25, 1970. My friends are in these photos: Ron (top photo), is holding the chair, and Jim is standing next to him. Terry Keegan (bottom photo) is being beaten and arrested by police. I was standing near the photographer who took the top photo. Ron, Jim and I got away. This attack led to the student strike.

Over 4,000 students packed Clark Gym and called for a campus-wide student strike, sparked by the police attack on students on February 25, 1970. Several days later, the university was virtually shut down. One of our strike demands was for the university to cease all military activities on campus. I am behind the right shoulder of the guy with the long scarf.

University administrators responded to the student strike by calling in the Buffalo Police to occupy the campus. Here, the police block entry into university buildings.

Demonstrations sometimes resulted in confrontations with the police. On the evening of March 12, 1970, Buffalo police clashed with students in front of Hayes Hall. Bruce Beyer and I were chased by a police car across the front lawn of the campus and into a dead-end alley.

Clashes often resulted in arrests…   and beatings.

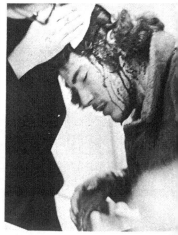

On Sunday, March 15, 1970, 45 UB faculty members slipped into Hayes administration building and staged a sit-in to demand that the police be removed from campus. Acting UB President Peter Regan responded by having the professors arrested. Here, the professors are being led from Hayes Hall into a Buffalo Police Van and taken to jail.

The *Courier-Express* found a willing organization, the VFW, to call on New York State Governor Nelson Rockefeller to crush our student strike.

Paul Krehbiel

The killing of students at Kent State (OH) and Jackson State (MS) in May 1970 led to more protests at UB and at 400 other colleges across the country in what became a National Student Strike. I was among students in Buffalo who built a barricade across Main St. (above) to stop the police from attacking us as we protested these killings and stepped up our demand to end the war on Vietnam.

Police respond to our protests by firing teargas at us on Main Street near the university. I was in this crowd of students.

I helped start a local labor newspaper, *New Age*, in 1970 to support workers' rights and connect labor to the anti-war, civil rights and women's movements. In November 1970 (above) we wrote about unions opposed to the war, and in April 1971 (below), about a local labor women's anti-war march, and labor support for the April 24th peace demonstration in Washington D.C.

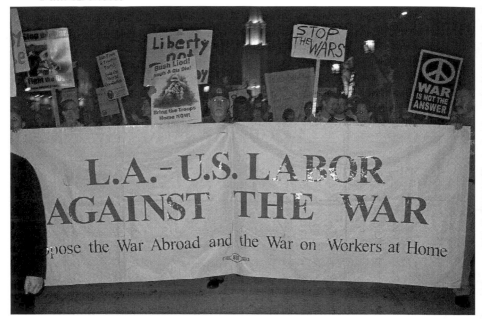

I joined with millions to protest Bush's 2003 war on Iraq: (above) with the Los Angeles Chapter of U.S. Labor Against the War in January 2005, at the World Peace Forum in Vancouver, Canada in June 2006 (right), at the Pasadena Doo Dah Parade in November 2006 (below), and with the Iraq Moratorium in February 2008 (lower right).

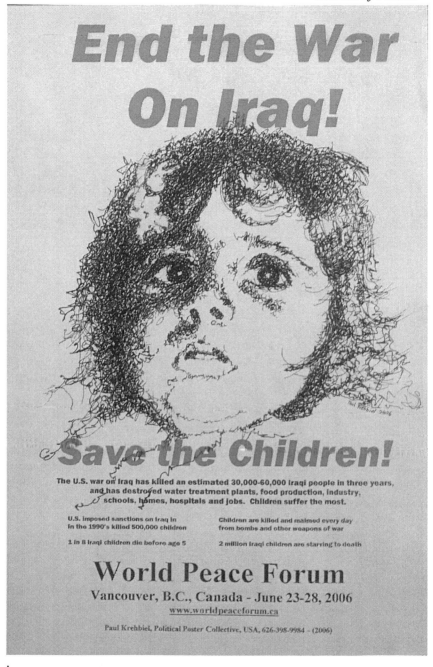

I made this poster for the World Peace Forum, held in Vancouver, Canada in 2006 and attended by 5,000 anti-war leaders from around the world. Hundreds of copies of this poster were distributed to people from many countries.

285

Chapter 36

Shopping and Chicken Wings

After all this political activity, I needed a break. Maybe not a long one, but something. Especially after the craziness in Chicago. I looked at the newspapers that had collected at our house when I was away and was amazed at the wide-spread support that had materialized for the Vietnam Moratorium. Church groups, elected officials, heads of colleges, union leaders and even business people in Buffalo had endorsed the Vietnam Moratorium, and the calendar of events seemed to have doubled in size.

I was in front of our house late one afternoon after returning from Ft. Dix when the neighbors came out. They were a young couple a few years older than me. I didn't know them very well but we were becoming friends. John was a Buffalo Bills fan like me, so we hit it off well. I had watched a game on TV at his house. His wife, Mary, was very sweet and they seemed very much in love. They knew I was a student at the University. I once mentioned something about an anti-war demonstration, but they didn't seem interested so I dropped it and never brought it up again.

"Hi, Paul," John said from his driveway. "We had a beautiful day today."

"Yeah, we did," I responded. When the sun comes out in Buffalo, people notice. "The leaves look great, don't they?" It was October and the fall leaves were turning red, orange and yellow and the bright streams of sunlight made them sparkle. John had a big maple tree on his front lawn and it was brilliant.

"I'll say. I've got some raking to do but it's worth it. What are you up to today?"

"Not too much. I'm going shopping for a new shirt, and then I was going to go out and get some dinner.

"That's what we're doing too," John replied. "Did you have a place in mind to eat?"

"Somebody told me about the Anchor Bar and some new dish they have there; chicken wings I think they said."

"We were thinking of going there too," John exclaimed. "You want to join us?"

I thought about it for a moment. We weren't good friends. But I thought spending a little time with some nice people who weren't involved in politics would be good. Get away from all the political infighting and politics in general. I thought how lucky John and Mary were to have each other. Thoughts of Donna and my past failed relationships crept into my mind, but I pushed them out.

"Okay, sounds great," I said.

We took their car and when we got to the Anchor Bar we took a table near a front window.

"You asked about the chicken wings," said John. "They're right here on the menu," he pointed. "We really like them."

"What are they exactly?" I asked.

Just then our waitress approached.

"Tell him about your chicken wings," John said to her.

"They're the hit of the restaurant. They're the wings off chickens. And we serve 'em with our special hot sauce, and with celery and blue cheese dressing. People love 'em."

"I heard something about them, but never had them before. Where did they come from?"

"Right here in our kitchen several years ago," she said.

"Tell him the story," John said.

I looked up at the waitress.

"Well, it happened on a weekend night," she began. "We had a real big dinner crowd and had served everything in the restaurant. Later in the evening a group came in after a night out on the town and they were hungry. We knew them – they were regulars. But Frank told them we were out of food. They pleaded with him to find something. So Frank went into the kitchen and the only thing he saw was a platter of chicken wings. They had been cut off the chicken dinners we served that night and we normally threw them into the soup pot. Since that was the only food in the restaurant, he and Teresa cooked 'em up and made a special hot sauce to put on 'em. Our customers loved 'em and they've been on the menu ever since."

"We'll have an order of wings," John said.

"They are good," the guy at the next table added. "We get 'em every time we come here."

"Okay," I said. "I'll have the chicken wings too." We also got a large order of french fries, onion rings and cokes. Shortly the wings were served and they *were* good. When we finished eating we left for shopping.

287

John and Mary were talking quietly and smiling at each other in the front seat. I couldn't hear what they were saying but I felt like an intruder in a love affair. *I Saw Her Standing There,* an early Beatles love song, was playing on the radio and thoughts of Donna and Molly came to me and how I wanted someone special in my life. I was a little jealous of John and Mary, but I was happy for them.

We arrived at the Boulevard Mall, parked and went inside.

"I want to look at some lace, John," Mary said.

"Sure," he responded, and I followed them into the fabric store.

"I'd like to get some material for the curtains," she continued.

"That's a good idea," John agreed.

Mary picked up several pieces and slowly turned them over in her hands. She went to several other isles and repeated the process. John and I followed. Then she returned to the first isle.

"What do you think about this lace," Mary asked as she held up a piece of the white delicate material.

"That's nice," John responded.

"Do you like it better than this off-white piece?"

"They're both nice," John continued.

"But which one do you like better?"

"I like them both," he said with conviction. "Which one do you like better?"

"Well, I think the white would go better with the colors in the living room. But I'm concerned it might be too bright for the dining room. And I think I like the pattern better in the off-white one."

"Okay, let's get the off-white one," John responded.

"But I'm not sure the off-white will go that well with the wall paper," Mary continued thoughtfully.

"I think it will go just fine," John said. "Let's get it and go." I could see he was starting to get impatient. "Wait. Maybe we should consider a whole different color arrangement," Mary said with renewed confidence. "If we got the green table cloth, we could get the beige lace. That would go with the curtains, and I think it would be okay with the wall paper. But I'm not sure it would go with the carpet."

For Christ's sake, I thought, will you get something. How much longer are we going to be in here?

"I think it would go fine with the carpet, dear," John strained. I could see he was trying to remain calm.

"Which one?" she asked, clearly in a quandary again. "The green table cloth and beige lace? Or the off-white lace with what we have now?"

"Either one, honey," John continued. "They all look fine. Let's just pick one. If we don't like it we'll return it." Mary didn't notice the veins sticking out of his neck as she turned some more material over in her hands.

"But I want to make sure it looks good. You know, Joan and Sam are coming over next week, and I want it to look good when they're here. You see what they've done with their house."

"Fuck Joan and Sam," John blurted out. "I'm tired of competing with them. We've been here for forty minutes. I want to get some beer and get home. I'm tired."

"And I still have to get a shirt," I whispered to John.

"And Paul has to get a shirt yet." He looked at me and said quietly: "Why don't you go and get your shirt and meet us back here. How long will it take?"

"Only about ten or fifteen minutes. I don't take long to shop."

"Okay, I'm sure we'll still be here," he said to me. We both looked up and Mary was on the verge of tears.

"I'm sorry, honey." He went over to comfort her, and I quickly left the fabric shop.

When I came back, Mary was somber and distant and refused to speak. John was still apologizing without much success. It was a quiet and awkward drive back home.

I was surprised that John got so mad, and felt bad for them both. John seemed so mild mannered, and they both seemed so well matched. I guess Mary hit a nerve with the Joan and Sam thing. And she was taking forever to pick out some fabric. But I learned something. Even regular people, who are very nice and who are in love, can have problems too. Living a quiet private life doesn't guarantee marital bliss. Both John and Mary seemed oblivious to a war that was tearing our country apart. She was focused on the color of fabric, and John on beer and football. And they weren't the only ones. Maybe the majority of people lived in this kind of world. How would we reach them with our message about the war, or on any other issue, I asked myself? The Vietnam Moratorium was about to take place, and I wondered if they even knew about it. I wasn't going to bring it up now.

I had thought that I wrecked my relationships with Donna and Molly because I was getting interested in the anti-war movement and they weren't. I thought that if I hadn't gotten so involved, maybe I could have saved my relationship with one of them. But would it have meant turning my back on the anti-war movement? I couldn't do that. The war was tearing me apart. Even if I had not gotten involved in the anti-war movement, things still may not have worked out in either relationship. Look at John and Mary. I had spent a couple of hours with them, my nice normal neighbors, to get away from the craziness of politics. Now, I felt like I was in a different kind of craziness. What's the difference between craziness in private life and craziness in politics? I wanted a break from all of it. When we got home, Mary was still not talking to John. I quietly thanked them for a nice evening, and excused myself. We never got the beer.

Chapter 37

Vietnam Moratorium Day

Two weeks before Vietnam Moratorium Day, October 15, 1969, all signs pointed to a huge display of anti-war sentiment. The snowballing of events called into the Moratorium office were beyond our expectations. Both little and big events were being planned in seemingly every part of Buffalo and Erie County. We started typing up schedules of events and additions were made almost daily. At 6:30 am, people were going out to various worksites to hand out anti-war leaflets. By 8:00 am, several peace breakfasts were set to begin. At 9:30 am, a peace tree was to be planted at the Salem United Church of Christ at Garfield and Calumet streets, sponsored by the church and the Women's International League for Peace and Freedom and other groups. At 10 am, Vietnam Moratorium teams would go out to Buffalo area high schools to participate in educational forums. Peace activities were planned throughout the day at the University at Buffalo and other area colleges, and many schools planned to cancel classes to accommodate Moratorium activities. At 12 noon, a rally and march would take place in downtown Buffalo sponsored by a large coalition of various groups. Participating churches agreed to ring their church bells at 12 noon in support of the Moratorium.

At 1:00 pm, an Ecumenical Service was scheduled for St. Paul's Cathedral on Shelton Square, sponsored by the Council of Churches of Buffalo and Erie County. Prominent city leaders were scheduled to be the main speakers. A growing number of other Moratorium events were set throughout the afternoon at numerous locations across the county, including by research scientists at the famous Roswell Park Cancer Institute. At 7:00 pm a candlelight march was to take place beginning in Delaware Park, sponsored by the students from Rosary Hill College, the all-women's Catholic university. At 7:30 pm, a memorial service was scheduled at Temple Beth Am, a large Buffalo Jewish synagogue, which was sponsored by the Temple's Youth Group. At 9:00 pm a Moratorium program and rally was set for the Unitarian Church at Elmwood and W. Ferry.

George, Howard and I were at the university one day looking at the most recent schedule of Moratorium activities.

"This is great," I said. "Look at all the events. Which ones are you guys going to?"

"I think I'll go to some of the events here at the University during the day," said George," and go to the march at noon and the candlelight march at night."

"I was planning to do the same thing," said Howard.

"I'll do that too," I said, "but I'm going to do some leafleting early in the morning and then go to Bennett High School around ten for the program there. Did you hear? We're having the Moratorium forum in the high school auditorium. And it will be an official school function, approved by the principal."

"That's good," said Howard. "The Moratorium is really taking off. And in a lot of other cities too, I heard. Nixon won't be able to claim that the anti-war movement is just a bunch of radical students on university campuses anymore."

As the Moratorium gained support among large groups in the political mainstream of Buffalo, city leaders came on board. The Common Council, which is our city council, passed a resolution in support of the Moratorium. On Friday, October 10, Buffalo Mayor Frank Sedita announced that he was proclaiming October 15, 1969 as Vietnam Moratorium Day in Buffalo and he urged residents to participate in Moratorium activities. Sedita was no radical anti-war activist. He was a mainstream Democratic Party politician who was careful not to go out on a limb on highly controversial issues. If he was coming out against the war, the anti-war sentiment among the public must be widespread. This was huge for the peace movement

The next day, Saturday, October 11, the conservative morning newspaper, the *Buffalo Courier-Express,* wrote in a rambling editorial: "The so-called moratorium in many of the nation's normal daily activities on Wednesday is directed specifically at Richard Milhaus Nixon's failure to respond to the will of the American people..." That same day, New York State Democratic party chairman John Burns, urged "fellow Democrats" to support the Moratorium.

Also on Saturday, former Vice President Hubert Humphrey who served under President Johnson, came to Buffalo to boost mayor Sedita's re-election campaign, and he did it with gusto. No mayor in the nation, Humphrey said, "has a greater sense of public duty and public service" than Mayor Sedita, he proclaimed. Humphrey, apparently caught up in the mushrooming support and excitement for the Moratorium, then proclaimed that he too supported the objectives of the Moratorium. That was startling, since Humphrey had supported the war throughout Johnson's presidency and failed to take a firm stand against the war in his razor-thin loss to Nixon for the presidency in 1968.

On Sunday, October 12, The Reverend Hugh Carmichael, a canon at St. Paul's Cathedral warmed up parishioners for Wednesday's Moratorium by asking: "How can we consider ourselves seeking to uphold, maintain and protect principles of democratic government when we continue to support a sham puppet regime (in South Vietnam) which could never be elected by the popular vote of the Vietnamese people?" All of this was reported in our morning newspaper.

The *Courier-Express* also reported in the same issue that major national organizations and prominent leaders had endorsed the Moratorium, including the Southern Christian Leadership Conference – the famous civil rights organization; John Cardinal Dearden, representing the 1.5 million Roman Catholics in the Detroit Archdiocese; and Dr. John Knowles, the general director of the Massachusetts General Hospital who was heading a special Moratorium medical committee, to mention only a few.

Perhaps most remarkable was a quote in Parade Magazine, the Sunday insert in the *Courier Express* which also appeared in hundreds of other newspapers across the country. In the "Personality Parade" section on page two, the magazine answered a reader's question about Ho Chi Minh who had just died in September 1969 and who was the US government's arch enemy in Vietnam: "Throughout most of Vietnam, North and South, Ho Chi Minh was and is regarded as the George Washington of his country," Parade Magazine wrote. "He was its most beloved, respected and admired figure. His singular commitment was to the independence and unity of his country from which he expelled the French, (and) fought the U.S. to a standstill…" I was amazed. Other people in very influential positions knew this information. They just needed the official "okay" to say it. The huge groundswell of support for the Moratorium provided that. I was thrilled with these developments.

The newspaper also reported that the presidents of 79 private colleges and universities sent a letter to President Nixon and Congress in conjunction with the Moratorium urging a "stepped-up timetable" for withdrawing from Vietnam. It also reported that practically every city in the United States was planning Moratorium activities.

On Monday, October 13, the newspapers reported that Niagara County Community College in near-by Niagara Falls would be holding a series of all-day Moratorium events, featuring a talk by the dean of the college, Dr. John O. Hunter. The mayor of Niagara Falls, who had the misfortune of being christened with the surname, Lackey, also announced support for the Vietnam Moratorium on behalf of his city.

On Tuesday, October 14, the *Buffalo Evening News* ran a banner headline across the top of page one: "Millions Prepare to Join War Protests." A sub-headline read: "Most Colleges in State to Hold Anti-War Events." The article began: "The Vietnam Moratorium will be observed at most colleges and universities in New York State tomorrow with events ranging from speeches to anti-war films and plays, prayers, marches and periods of silence." The article went on to say that endorsers ranged from former New York State Democratic Governor and U.S. diplomat Averill Harriman to the Republican Senator from New York State in the US Congress, Charles Goodell. Both papers published schedules of Moratorium events.

A number of big labor unions including the United Autoworkers (UAW), Teamsters, and Chemical Workers unions, representing over four million workers, broke with the very conservative AFL-CIO chief, George Meany – who supported Nixon and his war, and instead supported the Moratorium. I knew that just because the leaders of a large organization opposed the war and supported the Moratorium, that didn't mean that all the members did. But I was still blown away as I read all these articles because the number and size of the groups opposing the war was way beyond any previous public opposition.

The Vietnam Moratorium created a safe public forum for millions of people to speak out for peace for the first time. Nixon's claim that the "silent majority" was behind him and his war drive was shattered by the Moratorium because a big chunk of this so-called "silent majority" was supporting the Moratorium. I was ecstatic.

I got up early on Wednesday, October 15, and joined several other Moratorium supporters in handing out anti-war leaflets to UAW members at a General Motors plant. The UAW had a reputation for many decades as being a liberal union so we hoped the reception would be good. It was. Most of the workers took a leaflet, and many thanked us and said they were supporting the Moratorium. One middle-aged man told us to go back to Russia, but three others asked if they could take additional leaflets in to pass to their co-workers.

After leafleting, I stopped at a restaurant to get breakfast and look through the morning newspaper. There were numerous pages of news about the Moratorium. One article featured interviews with four Buffalo university students. It was great to see the anti-war movement given such extensive space in the media. This was rare. I glanced over the article quickly between mouthfuls of eggs and toast. One student was a UB leftist, Dan Bentivogli, of Youth Against War and Fascism, who spoke forcefully against the war and the system that fosters it. I knew Dan and agreed with much of what he said. But he criticized political leaders who were supporting the moratorium, believing that they were insincere and just being opportunists. I was glad they endorsed the Moratorium. If they said they supported it, then we could press them to take the next step which was to vote to cut off funds for the war. Also, their public support would help us win others to an anti-war position.

A second student was a black basketball player at Canisius College, Roger Brown, who said he was so busy with school and basketball that he didn't have time to protest. But he noted critically that black protest against the war was largely ignored while the protests of whites were more often covered. A third person, Barbara Clinton, a student at Buffalo State who described herself as a liberal and who supported the Moratorium, gave her take on it: "The 'silent majority' is shrinking, but I wouldn't say it is moving to the left." I thought the first part of her statement was true, but I wasn't so sure about the second part. I thought that people were moving slightly to the left of where they had been. That may not have put them on the left, but moving away from a conservative position and even slightly towards the left was a good thing.

The fourth student was the most revealing. He was Bruce Marsh, a student at UB, who said he was the "president of the Young Republican Club, which is the nearest thing to a right-wing organization there is on campus." He said he wasn't supporting the Moratorium, but did say "I am in sympathy with many of the aims of the radicals – all of us are against the war – but I disagree with their tactics. That's why I feel the moratorium will accomplish nothing…" Astounding, I thought. Even some very conservative people are against the war. That's great. Nixon's base was crumbling. I finished my breakfast and headed to Bennett High School.

Along the way, I heard on my car radio that Nixon had announced smugly that he wasn't going to pay any attention to the Moratorium. Funny, I thought, everyone else was.

When I arrived at the school auditorium, I saw Bruce Beyer. He was a graduate of Bennett and the former leader of the Draft Resistance Union and now a convicted member of the Buffalo Nine. He was going to be a featured speaker on the panel. I went over to greet him. Other people were standing with him.

"Did you hear," he began, "half the school boycotted classes today to support the Moratorium and protest against the war."

"No, I didn't," someone responded. "That's incredible." We watched large groups of students file into the auditorium and it soon filled up. "But the rest of them will be listening to us," I commented. Bruce smiled.

There were three people from the Vietnam Moratorium on the panel and one teacher who was going to take the government's position. Before the discussion started, I handed out the Moratorium leaflets which I had written originally for the Draft Resistance Union. The Moratorium speakers gave a brief history of US involvement in Vietnam that showed clearly why we shouldn't be there. Bruce then talked about the second Buffalo Nine trial.

"The Buffalo Nine were arrested and charged with felonies for protesting against the illegal and immoral war in Vietnam," Bruce explained. "We need your support. We are having demonstrations at the courthouse every day the trial is in session. The government couldn't convict all of us in the first trial, so they are holding a second trial. Come down and join us." The students applauded.

The pro-government speaker said that he, like President Nixon, wanted peace in Vietnam but it had to be an "honorable" peace. There were some boos and catcalls from the students, and the school administrator admonished them, asking that they show respect for all the speakers. But the pro-government speaker was so weak that we easily defeated his arguments, and in the question and answer session, the students largely ignored him. They asked us questions about the strength of the anti-war movement, how strong anti-war sentiment was among soldiers in Vietnam, and several asked how they could get out of going. We told them they might be eligible for legal deferments from the draft, and that we would talk to them after the forum. Several students came up to us as we were leaving and gave us their names and telephone numbers.

As we walked to the parking lot we all agreed it was a big success. When we got back to the university we heard that other Moratorium teams who went to other high schools had a similar experience.

I felt exhilarated. We were getting out the truth about Vietnam to thousands of draft age kids. Many would receive draft notices at the end of the school term and many would receive orders to go to Vietnam. Hopefully, we gave them information that would help them choose other options.

At about 11:30, I met up with George and Howard, and we left to go to the march downtown. I told them about my experiences at General Motors and Bennet High, and they told me about the Moratorium programs they attended at the university. When we reached Niagara Square, the gathering place for the march, we saw what looked like several thousand people. Organized by a broad coalition of organizations, speakers included Reverend Donald Brown of the Presbyterian Churches of Western New York, Ellicott District City Councilman Charles Black, Bruce Beyer and others. People from all walks of life were present, including a group of 100 scientists from the Roswell Park Memorial Institute, the cancer research center. Dr. Irwin Olsen, an organizer of the Roswell Park Scientists Against the War, and other scientists had gathered signatures on a petition calling for an immediate end to the war.

The march started and we walked up Court Street and turned onto Main Street carrying signs and chanting "Stop the War Now!" and "Free the Buffalo Nine." Passersby honked and waved. We marched to the Selective Service office where the Draft Board was housed, chanting, "Hell no, we won't go, end the war now!" We saw a hand-made peace symbol displayed in one of the windows in the Draft Board, and some employees waved to us and gave the peace sign as we passed by. Workers at the Draft Board were supporting us! It was an incredible feeling. I knew the anti-war movement was now really spreading into mainstream America.

The march then headed toward the Federal Courthouse where the second Buffalo Nine trial was underway. We started chanting, "Free the Nine, the trial is the Crime!" We had conducted these protests for the Buffalo Nine before. Now, prominent Buffalo leaders were also calling for their freedom.

When the march ended, Howard, George and I went back to the university. We learned that a little earlier that day a group of radical antiwar protesters broke into the Air Force ROTC office on campus and destroyed files and equipment.

Two days latter, the student newspaper, *The Spectrum*, ran a front page article about the destruction of the ROTC files under the headline: "Nixon, are you listening now?" While this clearly wasn't part of the Moratorium calendar, it was a sign that some people were so frustrated with Nixon's continuing war that they resorted to the destruction of military property. There were some debates about the attack on the ROTC program, but most people focused on the broad support for the Moratorium activities that took place all over the city that day.

That evening, George, Howard and I attended the candlelight march in Buffalo. This was the big public event of the day. An estimated 10,000 people participated, making it the largest anti-war march ever in Buffalo. Whole families were there, with husband, wife and their children marching together. We marched through Delaware Park, carrying candles. The long line of flickering lights, representing many thousands of extinguished lives in Vietnam, was emotionally moving. It was a public mourning for the dead, marked by long stretches of respectful silence, quietly broken with soft-voices singing hymn-like, "Give Peace a Chance."

The march got to the Unitarian Church around 9 pm and hundreds of people filled the pews for an anti-war program. I was one of the speakers and by the time I got there, the church was packed. I had a fairly standard speech by now. I talked about the Geneva Agreements and how the US called off the election in 1956 and why, the quotes from government and business leaders about getting raw materials from Southeast Asia, how American youth would kill or be killed while corporations profited. I called for an immediate end to the draft and the war.

I also said the Vietnam Moratorium had broken new ground, and that we had to continue to reach out to broader sections of the community to build an even stronger anti-war majority. People cheered. As I looked out at the audience, I was surprised to see my old neighborhood bully, Carlton, whom I hadn't seen in years. He was just sitting there watching me speak, with a look on his face like he was lost but wanted to be a part of this growing movement. I looked away, and scanned other faces in the audience, and then finished up. Other people spoke and then the rally ended. A number of people came up to talk with me and the other speakers. Then, behind me, I heard a familiar woman's voice. It sounded like Donna. I was startled but excited and my heart started pounding. I turned around to see her and was thrilled that she was interested in the anti-war movement. But it wasn't her. It was another young women talking to her boyfriend. Memories of Donna and I together came back to me.

The sanctuary was clearing out, and I looked back to the row where Carlton was sitting. He was gone. Everyone was making their way toward the door, and I was alone with my thoughts as I gathered up my papers. When I was younger, I dreamed of one day getting even with Carlton for all the times he had humiliated me and physically attacked me. But I never did. The image of him looking up at me in the pulpit while I spoke to hundreds of people about building a political movement for peace, was justice for me. But I also thought about Donna. I wondered where she was. Was she paying attention to the anti-war movement, and especially to this widely publicized Vietnam Moratorium? I didn't know. I thought again about trying to locate her to see if her thinking about the war had changed. But that would have to come later. I closed my briefcase and left the church. I was tired, but felt the Moratorium was a huge success.

I read later in both the commercial and anti-war newspapers that an estimated 2 million or more people took part in Moratorium activities all across the country in thousands of cities, towns and villages, making it the largest display of anti-war sentiment ever in the history of our country. Massachusetts was a good example. In Boston, 100,000 people turned out on the Commons. But Moratorium activities also took place in large and small towns and villages across the state, including Sudbury, Concord, Ipswich, Marblehead, Newburyport, Woburn, Wayland, Watertown, Lexington and many others. In many small towns and rural areas, these were their first anti-war protests. In Lexington, the Republican Governor Francis Sergeant told the crowd, "This war is costing America its soul."

In New York City, Republican Mayor John Lindsay heartily endorsed the Moratorium and scheduled 15 personal appearances. It was estimated that 40,000 of New York's 60,000 high school teachers cancelled classes in support of the Moratorium, and 90% of the 276,000 high school students didn't come to school. The School Board announced there would be no discipline for teachers or students who boycotted classes for the Moratorium. Fifteen off-Broadway shows shut down, and 7,000 businessmen held a rally on Wall Street at Trinity Church in support of the Moratorium. North of the city, in White Plains, 4,000 people picketed the local Draft Board, and that evening, 15,000 people heard Averell Harriman, US negotiator at the Paris Peace Talks, speak at a big Moratorium rally at East Meadow, Long Island. Scores of other Moratorium activities took place all over New York.

In Washington, D. C., there were many Moratorium activities, including a silent anti-war protest on the steps of the capitol by 1,500 Congressional staff workers. A growing number of Congressional representatives endorsed the Moratorium, as did some of the children of Nixon's staunchest pro-war supporters. One of those was the 14-year old daughter of Vice President Spiro Agnew, Kim, who was barred by her father from participating.

In Manchester, New Hampshire, home of the right-wing and fanatically pro-war *Union Leader* newspaper, 4,000 Moratorium supporters marched through town. At the University of Vermont, Governor Philip Hoff called for bringing the troops home. In New Haven, Connecticut, Mayor Richard Lee denounced the war at a Moratorium rally. In Paterson, New Jersey, workers at Life Manufacturing Company – makers of bullet-proof vests and body bags for the troops in Vietnam, took time off at lunch to join a Moratorium peace rally at City Hall.

There were wide-ranging activities in many hundreds of cities, towns and college campuses across the country, including peace marches and rallies of 75,000 in Cleveland; 50,000 in Pittsburgh; 15,000 in Madison, Wisconsin; 10,000 in Chicago; 10,000 in Minneapolis; 7,000 in Evanston, Illinois; 5,000 in St. Louis; 5,000 in Salt Lake City; 4,000 in Seattle; and 2,500 in South Bend, Indiana, to name only a few.

The genius of the Moratorium was that it invited millions of Americans from all walks of life to express their opposition to the war in *their* own words and acts, in whatever way they felt comfortable. That was hugely important. It made millions of people feel that *their* thoughts about the war were important, were valid, and deserved to be heard. When the Vietnam Moratorium received the endorsement of nationally known and respected leaders, that opened the doors for millions of Americans to step forward. Prior to the Moratorium, Nixon claimed that the "silent majority" of Americans backed him and his war policies. After October 15, 1969, this myth was shattered. It was now okay to be publicly against the war. I was thrilled with the results.

One of the most important things about the Vietnam Moratorium was that it showed Congressional Representatives that a large and growing segment of voters in many Congressional Districts were against the war. When a large enough number of constituents in a Congressional District turned against the war, *that* Congressional Representative would feel tremendous pressure to oppose it too. Politicians want to be re-elected. Many saw the shift in public sentiment. A growing number of Representatives now voted to end the war, but not enough. Others dragged their feet, so many in the anti-war movement turned their attention toward convincing those Congressional Representatives to vote "No" on the war. Our two major demands were to (1) cut off funds for the war, and (2) to vote to bring our troops home. It didn't mater to me if they were Democrats or Republicans, liberals or conservatives. I knew when enough Congressional Representatives voted the right way on these two issues the war would end. But strengthening the mass movement was the key to make this happen.

While the Moratorium was a huge break-though for the anti-war movement into mainstream America, there were still a lot of people who were confused about the war, uncommitted, or in support of the president's policies. Most people had repeatedly heard Nixon's views, and ours only recently, so they didn't have enough information to know why the war was wrong.

I knew we had to build on the gains of the Moratorium by continuing to reach out to the broader community. And we had to talk to those people who still supported Nixon, to convince them that Nixon was wrong, and to undermine his base of support. I didn't know it at the time, but I had an opportunity to do that almost immediately, right in the heart of Buffalo.

Chapter 38

Teamsters and Freight Docks

Right after the Moratorium I got a job as a freight handler at Universal Carloading and Distributing Company near downtown Buffalo. I wanted a job that paid better than day labor and had regular hours. My part-time student status brought me onto the campus for classes on Mondays, Wednesdays and Fridays, so I could work full eight-hour shifts on Tuesdays and Thursdays. Fortunately, the company needed the extra help so they agreed to give me those two days a week, and while the Teamsters union was reluctant – for good reasons – they went along.

The first day on the job I was introduced to my supervisor and some of the workers and my job was explained to me. There was a long loading dock with railroad cars on one side and trucks on the other. Our job was to transfer freight from one truck or train to another so the freight would get to the proper destination.

One of the first things I noticed was a little old man who was bent over, pushing a two-wheel dolly loaded with boxes. I don't know how old he was – maybe in his 50's, but the sight of this crippled man loading and unloading trucks was jarring to me. I thought that maybe he became bent over from many years of doing this work. The Teamsters union represented all the workers on the dock, and they protected him. I saw some of his union brothers pitch in and help him if he was struggling, and I heard that they stuck up for him when the company had tried to push him to work harder. The Teamsters had a pretty tough reputation. If a company was messing with Teamster members, they had been known to rough up people or damage property to make their point. Their message was: 'if you mess with us, we're going to make you pay for it, so lay off.'

I wondered if the company got rid of this crippled guy, would he become homeless? Homeless and crippled. What a way to live out your final days. I thought that he should be home on some sort of disability benefits. Maybe he didn't qualify, or perhaps it wasn't enough to live on. Anyway, he came in to work every day, and bent over as he was, did his job. I thought our industrial system was pretty cold and heartless.

When I started, I wanted to do a good job, so I was careful not to let the boxes fall off my two-wheel dolly. I tilted it way back and carried the weight on my arms, shoulders and back. That made a long and exhausting day. An experienced worker, Mack, showed me how to balance the load on the wheels, taking the weight off my arms. With a little practice, I got it. It sure made the day easier. We had to load many of the boxes onto the railroad cars and into trucks by hand, so by the end of the day I knew I had been working. It was interesting seeing the names of hundreds of cities and towns all over the country where these packages were sent, and I felt good about my small contribution in helping get products to people who wanted and needed them.

When we had our breaks and lunch I sat in the lunchroom with the other guys. Since I was new on the job, I didn't say too much and mostly listened. Some days, the guys would talk about something that was in the news. There were a lot of anti-war activities that fall and some of it made the newspapers. The Moratorium got good and widespread coverage because of the involvement of prominent city leaders and moderate organizations. But the mass media largely ignored educational anti-war events, and focused on confrontations or property destruction which they then denounced. A number of the latter events happened at UB .

One day as we sat down to lunch Mack opened the newspaper and stared at an article about damage done to the ROTC office.

"Look at those radical students at UB," he said, throwing his newspaper on the table. Mack was a huge man, standing about 6'3" and weighing 250 pounds. He was stocky and had hands like catcher's mitts. He was about 35 and had wavy black hair combed back. They guys looked up to him. "They're tearing up the university, and for what? I'd give my right arm to be able to get an education like that."

"Yeah," Louie agreed. "They don't know how good they have it."

"Look at this," a third guy said pointing to the newspaper article. "They wrecked some buildings up there, and they're against our military. The cops ought to arrest 'em and throw 'em in jail."

"Or draft 'em," said a big guy with a nasty six inch scar across his face. "That would fix their asses."

Some of them had heard that I was a student at the University. They had been pretty friendly and helpful to me on the job, but now Mack looked over at me.

"What do you think about all this?" he asked. "You're a student up there aren't you?

"Yeah, I'm taking some classes up there," I said hesitatingly. I was caught off guard and wondered where this might be headed. Louie glared at me like he wanted to tear my head off. I was a little nervous, but knew I couldn't show it.

"The newspapers don't always tell the whole story," I said.

"There was a bunch of stuff about that anti-war Moratorium in the newspaper," Mack said. "There were pages of it. Why can't people just give Nixon a chance? He's got a plan to end the war."

"Well, a lot of the anti-war people believe Nixon hasn't told the American people the whole truth about the war."

"Yeah," growled Louie. "Like what?"

"Well," I began, "they found out that the main reason we're over there is so big corporations can get cheap raw materials from that area. You know, so they can make bigger profits. The government and the newspapers don't tell us about that." I figured I had to present this to them in terms they could relate to.

"That's no surprise," scarface spit out. "The big corporations always want to make more money."

"Yeah, but the way they want to do it is by really taking advantage of the workers in Vietnam," I continued. "You know, they don't allow unions there, and people are getting only starvation wages. When they rebel, the government arrests them, throws them in jail or shoots them. That ain't right."

"No, that isn't right," Mack agreed. "But why are those students tearing up the University?"

"The University is helping the US government keep the Vietnamese workers in their place."

"How they doin' that?" he asked.

"Well, the University is training pilots in the Air Force ROTC program on campus," I explained. "The US military is trying to keep a real anti-union dictator in power, General Ky. He said one time that his only hero is Hitler"

"He did?" Mack asked with a surprised look on his face. "How do you know that?"

"It was in the British newspapers. The US newspapers didn't print it."

"Where did you see British newspapers?" he said with a big grin of disbelief on his face.

"At the University. They're in the library."

"You get British newspapers at the University?" Mack asked.

"Yeah, they get newspaper from all over the world up there. And that stuff gets written about in books which are up there too."

"But why are they wrecking the University?" Mack asked.

"Well, the students have tried talking to the University Administration about these things for years, and the Administrators just ignore them. Some of the anti-war students were in the military in Vietnam and saw how corrupt it is over there, and they're frustrated that no one is listening to them."

"So that's an excuse to tear up the place?" Louie asked with anger in his voice. "They're anti-American! I still say arrest 'em and send their asses to Vietnam!" I clearly wasn't winning over Louie so I ignored him and looked at Mack. He seemed a little more open.

"Well, don't workers in this country get frustrated sometimes when management doesn't listen to us when we have legitimate complaints?" I continued. "And if the problems don't get fixed, sometimes it leads to strikes or other actions. And if the bosses call in the police to break up our picket lines, then sometimes violence breaks out. I mean, you guys don't let management push you around if you're on strike, right?"

"No one pushes Teamsters around," scarface growled.

Just then the buzzer sounded for us to return to work.

Mack got up from his chair and turned to face me. He was towering over me and paused a moment. "I never thought about it like that. You made some good points." He patted me on the back. "Let's get back to work." I'm sure I didn't win over Louie and I didn't know about scarface, but I believe Mack started thinking about what I had said. Not that I had won him over with that one short conversation. But he was thinking. That was a good first step. He was kind of a buddy to me after that, which was a good feeling. He was certainly the kind of guy you didn't want to be against you. I also noticed that some of the other guys didn't get so worked up about the student radicals anymore. That was good.

I knew from other friends who were working that these kinds of conversations were going on at other work places around Buffalo. And I had heard that some members of SDS in all parts of the country were getting jobs in factories to do this kind of work. I hoped that with enough of these discussions workers would understand that the war was wrong and begin to oppose it. After all, workers and the sons of workers made up the overwhelming majority of the soldiers fighting in Vietnam, and they were bearing the sacrifices. I knew we had a long way to go, but if enough workers spoke up, and their unions spoke up, the anti-war movement would receive a tremendous boost. Not only do many workers vote, but they also are strategically located in the economy. If they engaged in strikes or other job actions, it could hinder the war effort. Some people believed that such actions would never happen. I believed it would be hard work, but that it was possible. I thought about the slowdown we did at Standard Mirror to stop the new quota. What if workers did slowdowns that slowed down war production? That would be huge.

Outside of work my immediate goal was to talk to people who were already against the war about going to Washington for the November Moratorium. I spoke with my friends at the Buffalo Draft Resistance Union and my friend Howard. The November 3rd speech by Nixon didn't seem to negatively impact any of them. They were going to Washington. That was a good feeling. Buses were rented and scheduled to leave from the University for Washington, and people started lining up carpools. I was hopeful that the turn-out would be good.

Chapter 39

Washington, D. C.

In the weeks after the October 15, 1969 Moratorium, many of us heard that the National Moratorium Committee was still recovering from the first Moratorium, and the key organizers were exhausted. We learned later that many of the campus Moratorium organizers couldn't keep up the pace of organizing every day and going to school full-time. Many were falling behind in their classes and they were concerned about their grades. Since many of the more radical students, including myself, had cut back on the number of courses we took, and some had dropped out for a semester or more, we had more time for daily anti-war organizing.

Honestly, it didn't seem very important to me or many of my anti-war friends if we graduated with our class, or even if we graduated at all with the terrible killing going on every day. I, like many others, was consumed by the war and with building a stronger and more effective anti-war movement. So, many of the more radical students played a more influential role in organizing the November Moratorium activities.

In many places, the New Mobilization Committee to End the War (called the New Mobe) filled the vacuum. The New Mobe had called months earlier for mass demonstrations in Washington D.C. on November 15, and after some lively discussion within the Moratorium Committee, both groups agreed to hold the New Mobe march together with Moratorium activities on both the 14th and 15th. A west coast march was set for San Francisco. The alliance of the Moratorium and the New Mobe was a big step forward for the anti-war movement. The more moderate Moratorium Committee leaders had great contacts with huge mainstream organizations and leaders across America, while the more committed anti-war activists in the New Mobe provided much of the organizing muscle.

I was still learning about some of the leaders of the National Moratorium Committee and their ties to large, influential organizations. I knew that Sam Brown, the national coordinator, was a former officer of the National Student Association and former national student coordinator for the Eugene McCarthy presidential campaign in 1968. I now learned about some of the other leaders too.   David Hawk, who was working for the National Student Association and was a former staff worker for the staunchly anti-war New York State Congressman Allard Lowenstein, was also a national Moratorium leader.   Hawk was also a draft resister, though the Moratorium Committee wanted that played down.   David Mixner, who was on the George McGovern Commission to reform the Democratic Party after the debacle at the 1968 Democratic National Convention, was also a national Moratorium leader.   The McGovern Commission's reforms helped the strongly anti-war McGovern get the Democratic Party nomination for president in the 1972 race.   I was happy to see those reforms take place in the Democratic Party because it opened it up and made it more democratic.   Other Democratic Party supporters of the Moratorium included party chairman Fred Harris, other leaders of national stature like Massachusetts Senator Ted Kennedy and many, many others. The Moratorium had even broken into the ranks of Republicans, and won support from influential Republicans like Oregon Senator Mark Hatfield.   These were all heavy hitters with very broad connections into every major institution of American society.

The New Mobilization Committee activists were comprised of many of the best organizers, intellectuals and leaders of the anti-war movement.   They included some of the brightest lights in the universities and the broader community, people like Boston University History professor Howard Zinn, who tirelessly spoke and wrote about the sordid history of US involvement in Vietnam; Sidney Peck, a professor at Case Western Reserve in Cleveland; and Sidney Lens, a labor organizer, anti-war leader and writer.   The alliance of the Moratorium and the New Mobe was very important and the results were incredible.

I went to Washington, D. C. with a group of my anti-war friends from Buffalo.   We got there Friday afternoon and saw the "March Against Death."   This lead-off event had begun Thursday evening, November 13, and was still going.   There was a long line of people marching solemnly in silence from Arlington National Cemetery past the White House, each person carrying a placard bearing the name of an American serviceman killed in Vietnam or a village destroyed in Vietnam.   The 46,000-plus marchers represented the number of Americans killed in Vietnam to that date.   I learned later that day that a row of drummers led the column – like the drummers that lead the American Revolution, tapping out a slow funeral march, followed by the wives and other family members of fallen American soldiers.

We heard there was going to be a march that evening to the South Vietnamese Embassy, beginning at DuPont Circle in the heart of Washington, D. C. We knew the leaders of the South Vietnamese government were corrupt and brutal, and hated by large sections of the Vietnamese population, so this was a good target. Some of the people in our group were tired and wanted to rest, so Howard and I decided to go. As we approached DuPont Circle, it was cold and dark, but the circle was lit up with an array of lights from neon signs, streetlights, and the police. There were at least 1,000 people there, and we saw signs denouncing the South Vietnamese government as a "puppet government," and demanding that all US aid and support to it be cut off. I agreed with all those sentiments.

The throng began marching toward the embassy, but as we got about a block away, lines of riot police blocked our path. Howard and I were in the middle of the march so we couldn't see what was happening up front, but I saw our friend Jim ahead of us. I called out to him, he turned and saw me and waved for us to come up to join him. But all of a sudden we heard a loud commotion in front of Jim, and people in front of us turned and ran back toward DuPont circle. Teargas canisters whistled overhead and into our ranks, and we were swept up in the quickly moving crowd. My heart beat faster and I looked over my shoulder to see if the riot police were near me. I didn't see them. But when we got back to DuPont Circle I saw the police wading into the march behind us and along the right side of the crowd, and rioting broke out.

"See that bank," I heard a guy near me yell to his friend as he pointed to a big building to my left. "They're profiting off the war!" I couldn't see the name of the bank, but I saw a rock sail toward one of its huge windows. There was a loud crash, and big sheets of glass smashed to the ground. More windows were broken in other banks and corporate offices around DuPont Circle.

We could see the police moving toward us, beating and arresting people along the way, so Howard and I got out of there. We made our way onto darkened streets, and we headed back toward the White House. In the distance we saw a long silent line of marchers with candles. It was the March Against Death. They had been walking for 24 hours straight.

It was an eerie but moving sight watching thousands of small flames flickering and weaving along city streets, each light representing a human life or a Vietnamese village that was needlessly extinguished. We watched for several minutes and then followed the line to its destination near the White House. As each marcher passed in front of the main entrance, they read aloud the name of a dead soldier or a bombed village, continued down Pennsylvania Avenue and dropped their placards into one of a long row of coffins. A chill went up my spine; I didn't know if it was from the cold November night or the sight of this funeral procession. Howard and I then went to where we were staying for the night.

Saturday morning, before the big march, I got up early and went out to a nearby café to get donuts and coffee. I noticed the guy in front of me, who looked about my age, reading a rumpled copy of *The New York Times*. I glanced over his shoulder and caught the first part of the headline of what looked like a full-page ad. In bold black letters it said: "We are 1,365 active-duty servicemen. We are opposed to American involvement in the war in Vietnam." That got my attention. Just then he folded the paper up and put it under his arm. I asked him if I could look at it for a moment, and he handed it to me.

It was an ad in the Sunday, November 9, 1969 edition calling for an immediate end to the war, and urging other GI's to join them in Washington on November 15 for the Moratorium. The entire first column and part of the second contained the names and rank of servicemen in Vietnam. I was ecstatic. Nixon's November 3rd speech didn't deter these soldiers. I thought of the soldiers at Ft. Dix and wondered if some of them had signed this ad, or better yet, were here. I took out a pen and made notes on a piece of paper so I could tell Howard and the others about it, and returned the paper to its owner. I learned later that these anti-war GI's were stationed at over 80 US military bases all over the world. I saw them as the real heroes.

I met up with our group and we headed toward the Washington Monument to gather for the main march. While we were still blocks away, the streets were so packed people were hardly moving. Eventually, I saw a huge grassy area around the monument, and couldn't believe the sea of humanity spread out before us. We heard the organizers initially hoped for 70,000 to 100,000 people to attend. As people poured into Washington D. C., the organizers increased their estimate to 250,000. Now, they were saying there were over 500,000 people and more were still coming. Final estimates put the crowd at 750,000 or even 1 million. The size of the crowd was beyond anyone's dreams. Nixon was on the ropes now, I thought.

There were banners and signs everywhere, from every imaginable organization. Miraculously, Howard and I saw a familiar banner in a sea of rainbow colors, "Free the Buffalo Nine." We made our way through the crowd to the banner and joined our friends from Buffalo.

I saw a mop of frizzy red hair and spotted Jim.

"Hey, how are you doin'?" I asked.

"Good," Jim replied. "I lost track of you at DuPont Circle last night."

"Yeah. We were standing next to a guy who took out a huge plate glass window in a bank, and the cops came after him. So we got out of there. Where did you stay last night?"

"I was at someone's house with people who were taking copies of Seymour Hersh's article on the My Lai Massacre to area newspapers," Jim exclaimed. The My Lai Massacre took place a year and a half earlier, but had been covered up by the government and the media. Over 500 unarmed Vietnamese, mostly women and their children, were massacred by US troops in May of 1968. I was sickened when I read about it in the anti-war newspapers. A US soldier tried to expose the massacre after it took place, but was ignored. Hersh finally got his article published in 30 newspapers on November 12, just before the November Moratorium marches. Then it was picked up by news media all over the country. The expose was a major blow to the US government and its war effort, and coupled with the expanding anti-war movement, polls now showed increasing numbers of Americans were turning against the war.

I felt even more strongly about how important the anti-war movement was now and was proud that I was a part of it. I thought about the soldiers that committed the Mai Lai Massacre. Were they following orders? I wanted to believe that such atrocities were committed by a small minority of our troops – which is still no excuse for it, and that the majority of soldiers were in Vietnam simply because they were drafted or lied to, and they were trying to get through it the best they could. But it was chilling to think that Americans – any Americans, could commit such horrible crimes. That's not the way we were raised in our families or school system, and those weren't the values of the American people. I thought that war could radically change people and their behavior, leading them to do things that they would never imagine doing in peace time.

The march began at about 10:30 am. It slowly moved through the streets of Washington. People carried signs, sang songs and chanted slogans. There were people from all walks of life: students from high schools and universities, veterans and soldiers and their families, parents and their children, religious groups and community organizations, elected officials and teachers, civil rights groups and unions, including a large contingent of hospital workers from Local 1199 from New York City all wearing their distinctive 1199 hats.

There were scores of anti-war banners and signs, including American flags with the peace symbol in the area where the stars normally are. I didn't see this as anti-American, but rather as a statement saying it's patriotic to be for peace. I agreed. When we got near the rally site we were so far away from the platform, that we could hardly hear the speakers. But I didn't care that much. The important thing was the size of the march. I heard people in the group next to us say it was the largest march ever in the history of our country.

By 4:30 pm, many people were leaving the rally and we heard that a group was going to march on the Justice Department. That was the office of the widely hated Attorney General John Mitchell, a major architect of the repression against the anti-war movement, so it seemed like a good place to continue our protests. I saw John Mitchell as anti-American. Howard and I and the group we were with from the Buffalo Nine Defense Committee joined the large throng that was festooned with hundreds of anti-war banners. Some people were carrying red flags, which I saw as a symbolic call for a revolution to drive Nixon and Mitchell from power.

As we approached the large building at Constitution Avenue, we saw rows of police in riot gear. Someone ran an NLF flag up the flagpole in front of the building, and someone else threw red paint, signifying blood, at the building. The police responded with a barrage of tear-gas. We were among thousands of demonstrators that retreated north into a shopping district. The police were in pursuit and shot more tear gas canisters at us. But, by now, we were intermingled with many hundreds of shoppers and other innocent bystanders, and everyone was tear-gassed by the police. The cops waded into the crowd and started arresting people. We heard later that about 200 people were arrested, including many people who were simply shopping, and who weren't part of the march. Over-reaction by the police drove many passive supporters of the peace movement and the uncommitted into vocal critics of the war and the Nixon Administration.

I heard later that Mitchell had watched the march from a fifth floor office in the Justice Department and declared to his wife that "it looked like the Russian Revolution going on."

Some in the movement expressed different opinions about whether the march on the Justice Department was productive or counter-productive, especially since violence broke out. I didn't think about it one way or the other. For me, we were all protesting the war and that's what counted. I understood the anger and frustration of those who marched to the Justice Department and I joined them. I didn't go intending to cause any violence, but tempers flared, and it happened. What was more important to me were the nearly one million people from all walks of life who participated in the main march. That, I thought, should really send a message to the government and the media.

I left Washington with a feeling that the totality of all of the activities on November 14-15 made the two days hugely successful. We reached out to broader sections of the American people, drawing to the march some who hadn't publicly demonstrated before. We helped win over many people who watched it on TV. And a group of thousands warned of increasing social unrest if the war wasn't stopped.

Perhaps, most importantly, we learned years later from a report by Seymour Hersh, that these Moratorium demonstrations likely stopped Nixon from using nuclear weapons in Vietnam. The devil's mentality all along was to use increasingly more heinous forms of mass death and destruction in an effort to get the Vietnamese to surrender. When this didn't work, Nixon contemplated using nuclear weapons in the fall of 1969, but he changed his mind after seeing the huge and growing Moratorium protests. Nixon was concerned that an escalation of the war with nuclear weapons would really tear our country apart, isolate him even more domestically and internationally, and risk his presidency and his career.

Nixon had a long history of being reckless, right-wing and vicious, and had worked closely for decades with the most conservative big corporations. He was first elected to Congress in 1946 by waging a dirty campaign against his Democratic opponent by falsely charging that she was pro-communist. He willingly assisted Senator Joe McCarthy in his anti-communist witch-hunts of the 1950's, which drove honest and hard-working people out of their jobs as teachers, union leaders, Hollywood actors and many other professions. Nixon raised millions of dollars from conservative and right-wing organizations, and worked attentively to help major weapons manufacturers, oil companies and many other giant corporations receive huge government contracts and other benefits.

When the Buffalo contingent returned, many people had changed. Tom, Beverly and a couple of other BDRU members were now much more radical after being in confrontations with the police, and they started to work with SDS. That was fine with me. I was working with SDS too. But these formally moderate people, who once warned me about not bringing my radical SDS ideas into the BDRU, now threw themselves into SDS work and abandoned the BDRU. A couple of them said they felt the BDRU wasn't radical enough because it wasn't espousing socialism or revolution.

I didn't agree with their reasoning. The main goal of the BDRU, from my perspective, wasn't to be "radical" in that sense. It was to reach draft age youth and convince them that they shouldn't go to war in Vietnam. Getting them to understand that the war was wrong was more important to me than getting them to understand the flaws of capitalism and the benefits of socialism. I didn't see any contradiction between being a radical and appealing to other people at whatever political level *they* were on. If they were moderate in their thinking, as many were, we needed to be moderate in our approach when talking and working with them. Being too radical would turn many of the moderates off to us, and end our chances of influencing them.

Some people have asked what we meant by the word "radical." The word "radical" means going to the root or source of something. That is a good thing. Going to the source of something helps us learn the truth by understanding how and why things happen as they do. That is why I studied philosophy, to learn methods that would help me arrive at the truth. When I applied that method to the war, I began by studying the history of Vietnam to learn what really happened. Then I wrote a leaflet explaining that history. I tried to write it in words and a tone that would appeal to a broad range of people, and would convey the truth. I was doing radical work, but I was not being too radical.

The word "radical" can also mean advocating fundamental or extreme change. Some problems are so deep and serious that a fundamental or extreme change is needed to correct them. We needed an extreme change in policy and action to end the war. Since many people have difficulty accepting any change, much less extreme change, it is important to organize in a way that helps people take small, comfortable steps along a path of acceptable changes that will ultimately bring about the fundamental change that is needed. The Vietnam Moratorium was doing that. As people went through various experiences and found that their interests or moral beliefs were thwarted, denied or repressed, many became more radical, meaning they understood that big, fundamental changes were needed to correct the problems and to achieve justice. It was necessary to put building blocks in place to create a foundation before you could get people to see the bigger problems, or bigger solutions. It's like building a house. You must build the foundation before you can put up the walls and roof. Some radicals wanted to skip over these steps and rush people to adopt a viewpoint that they were not comfortable with. I disagreed with that approach. Pressuring, threatening or forcing people to take a position or action that they didn't agree with was and is morally wrong and politically counter-productive. At some point, people will feel resentment and turn against the person doing the pressuring, and in some cases withdraw their support from the good cause as well. I think that is what some people meant when they said some political activists were "too radical." In 1969, growing numbers of Americans were turning against the war, and some were learning so much that they were making big changes in their thinking. Many called themselves "radicals." Some were moving to the left, though for most this change in their thinking didn't seem too extreme to them. It seemed logical. That was the process that I went through. Nixon, conversely, became more isolated, more desperate, more hostile and more repressive. That was a recipe for an explosion.

Part 5: Students Strike, Protests Spread

Chapter 40

Repression

December 1969 and January 1970 were slow months for the movement in Buffalo. We wondered if the National Moratorium Committee was still in business or winding down. Part of the lull was the holidays, and for us in Buffalo, the cold and snowy winter weather was rolling in and had some impact.

But anti-war, anti-racism and labor actions were taking place around the country, and increasing in number and intensity. There wasn't much about this in the commercial mass media, but I read about it in *The Spectrum, The Guardian,* and other movement newspapers. Unfortunately, this increased activism seemed to bring about more repression from the authorities, and this, in turn, fueled more activism. One very brutal act of repression particularly shook my friends and me and many others both inside and outside of the movement.

On December 4, 1969, Fred Hampton, the Black Panther leader I had heard speak in Chicago less than three months earlier, was shot and killed in his sleep by the Chicago police, along with fellow Panther, Mark Clark. I was shocked, as were others I spoke with. Over 80 shots were fired into his apartment at about five in the morning. At first, the mass media reported that the Panthers shot at the police, but after an investigation, it was shown that the two men didn't take any shots as they were asleep in their beds. I was outraged. This was a cold-blooded assassination. I knew blacks bore the brunt of repression in the US, and now it was getting more blatant and worse. But I wondered if whites who protested against the government might not also receive worse treatment.

We continued to organize against the war in Buffalo and to expose the system causing it by holding a demonstration at Cornell Aeronautical Laboratory on Genesee Street near the Buffalo Airport on December 13. That was our local Vietnam Moratorium activity for December. Two weeks before Christmas is a hard time to get people to protest anything since most everyone is preparing for the holidays. But, in keeping with the Moratorium's schedule of protests every month, we went forward. SDS, the BDRU and other groups working under the umbrella of the Vietnam Moratorium Committee printed a hand-out titled: "Vietnam is a stake not a mistake." The article explained that the goal of the US government and its corporate backers was to gain control of Vietnam so they would be in a position to control all of southeast Asia with its abundance of raw materials, cheap labor, and new markets. The piece was written by the Committee of Returned Volunteers, ex-Peace Corps volunteers who became radicalized by the suffering and repression they saw working in poor countries.

I was at the demonstration at Cornell Lab with friends and we marched in front of the building in the snow carrying signs and passing out this newssheet. We had a crowd of about one hundred people, considerably smaller than we hoped for, but at least we were keeping the Moratorium going. That was the positive message I and others put forward.

Cornell Lab was chosen because it was a major research center in the Buffalo area for developing bombs, chemical and biological warfare, intercontinental nuclear missiles and an array of weapons used in Vietnam and elsewhere. We argued that money spent on work at Cornell Lab diverted money that could be used to improve education, health care, housing, jobs, the economy and other needs and services. We pointed out that some weapons made from Cornell Lab's research could be used domestically against the anti-war movement, poor and minority communities, striking workers and anyone else who protested US policies. I thought Cornell Lab was a good target for our protest, but I was disappointed at the low turnout.

In January 1970, repression increased against Buffalo anti-war activists. Nineteen people, mostly students at UB, were charged with crimes in connection with a raid on the campus Air Force ROTC office on October 15, 1969 when military files there were destroyed. Sixteen people were arraigned in County Court on charges ranging from burglary, inciting to riot, riot, criminal mischief and tampering, and conspiracy. Many were student leaders of the movement. The pro-war forces were, of course, very angry at the destruction of military property, but a significant number of peace activists also opposed it. They argued that destroying anything, even military property, hurt the anti-war movement

317

because it turned off large numbers of people. Those who defended the destruction of military property argued that many years of peaceful protest had not ended the war and that the destruction of military files was nothing compared to the destruction of human lives in the war. Furthermore, they argued, the destruction of military files made it a little harder for the military to continue its operation. I understood the arguments of both sides. For my part, I wanted to focus on what ever would help increase the number of people who opposed the war. According to public opinion polls, we still had a little less than half the population on our side. At any rate, this case kept the issue of the war on the pages of our student newspaper.

Some people thought all anti-war actions, including the destruction of military property, moved others to get more involved in peaceful protests. The destruction of military files showed that some anti-war activists were willing to risk arrest and imprisonment to try to end the war, so it made legal and peaceful activities seem easy to do in comparison. I thought there was some truth to that argument.

But I also believed that it turned others more strongly against us. Some of the more radical students argued that it was good to polarize society so we knew clearly who was for us and who was against us. I never felt like that was a good approach. I was concerned that we would become isolated, and easier to ignore or crush. It didn't make sense to harden the opposition against us.

We needed to develop a well-thought out strategy. If we could isolate a small core of the worst pro-war people or organizations, or those who were pushing other politically reactionary policies, then we could launch an aggressive campaign against them. We could put a spotlight on them with the goal of weakening or defeating them, at least politically, and doing it in a way that would win over many others to the anti-war movement, including those who were previously pro-war or somewhere in the middle. The campaign against Dow Chemical and its production of napalm was a good example. We had to find creative ways – both bold and subtle – to reach people not currently with us and win them over. That was key.

I also thought it was important to do everything possible to build a peaceful movement. But I knew we didn't have complete control over that. If the opposition used violence, it was natural for people to do what ever they could to protect themselves. Usually, when our opposition used violence against us, it drove many more people into our ranks. If we could build a large enough movement for peace and justice, there would not be enough people on the other side to use violence against us, or they would see it as a losing strategy. That's why working to educate people to the truth was so vitally important.

Years of organizing and education on the UB campus were paying off, and that accounted for a large increase in student interest in social and political issues. Students had been demanding more relevant classes for many semesters and the university established experimental colleges. They were interdisciplinary and allowed students and teachers to develop the courses. This was a very big and important reform. By January 1970, the popularity of these courses increased dramatically. One of the most popular courses was "Conflict and Change in the Local Community," offered by College A. This course focused on combining the study of social sciences with community activity – merging theory and practice. The demand for this class was astounding. Over 500 students signed up for it and another 500 wanted to sign-up. A similar course, "Social Change in America 302," signed up 900 students in 45 separate sections and more wanted to enroll.

I enrolled in both classes. In one class I was studying and participating in draft resistance activities through the BDRU, and in the other one I was studying and participating in organizing the broader anti-war movement. These were the only two classes I enrolled in for the spring 1970 semester, so I was essentially a full-time organizer. George and Howard also signed up for these courses. University Administrators were worried and tried to limit enrolment, but it was too late. Student demand for these classes was expressed daily, reaching the level of an ongoing campaign. The clamor was so great that the Administration opened additional sections. Nearly 2,000 students were enrolled just in these two classes which encouraged involvement in social and political issues on the campus and in the community. There were other similar classes in many of the other Colleges, and even in some regular departments, so it was estimated that least 3,000 students – and maybe many more – were involved in some type of social and political activity and getting college credit for it. The UB student movement was growing into a very powerful force.

I read in *The Spectrum* about strong student movements at other colleges. They were also fighting for educational reforms, and against the war, racism and discrimination against students, workers and the poor. SDS, as a national organization, played a huge role in initiating and building many of these movements, since there were hundreds of SDS chapters on campuses across the country. I read about students at the University of Detroit who staged two days of sit-ins to protest Navy recruiters on campus. At MIT in Massachusetts, hundreds of students lead by SDS occupied the University President's office for two days demanding an end to military research on campus and the dropping of disciplinary action against students involved in earlier protests. At Duke University in North Carolina, students and university hospital workers occupied the office of a hospital official demanding an end to discrimination against the workers and recognition of their union. Many of those workers were Black. I didn't see any of these stories in the commercial newspapers.

University Administrators disliked *The Spectrum*. Since it was completely student-run, they had no control over it. So, the administration started their own newspaper in January 1970, *The Reporter,* to give their views on the issues of the day. But it was much smaller, came out only once a week, and was no where near as lively as *The Spectrum*, so it was no competition for the student newspaper.

While protest demonstrations were heating up on campuses across the country, things were heating up in Buffalo too. It began with trials of 19 students charged with disrupting Air Force ROTC drills on campus in the fall of 1969. Charges were brought in City Court downtown and before the Student Judiciary on campus. These trials were attended by hundreds of students who were there to support the anti-war student defendants.

On February 19, 1970, the news media reported that Congressional critics of the war blasted Nixon for secretly bombing liberation forces in Laos, the Pathet Lao, who were fighting against a right-wing government there. Many of us were concerned that the war might expand into Laos. I hoped this new aggression would spur the anti-war movement to launch new anti-war activities. I spoke with my friends in the movement in Buffalo and everyone felt the same way. We started talking about organizing another round of demonstrations.

That same day, Judge Julius Hoffman sentenced Chicago 8 defendants to 19 years in prison for contempt of court during their trial on conspiracy to riot charges stemming from the anti-war protests at the 1968 Chicago Democratic National Convention. We shifted our attention to organizing a march to protest these harsh prison terms. Tens of thousands of people in other cities felt the same way. The nation exploded in demonstrations opposing these sentences and the expanding war. Big marches took place in Chicago, Berkeley, New York, Seattle, San Francisco and many other cities. Buffalo SDS and other groups planned a big march in downtown Buffalo for Friday, February 20. Tom Hayden, a founding national leader of SDS, was one of those convicted in Chicago and sentenced to prison, so we felt this was an attack on both SDS and the entire movement.

About a thousand people showed up in downtown Buffalo. We gathered at Niagara Square, in front of City Hall, and began marching up Court Street. I was in the front, behind the Buffalo SDS banner, which read, "Year of Solidarity with the Vietnamese," and "All Power to the People." In the center of the banner was a large fist inside a red circle, and the words, "Buffalo, SDS, RYM II." A banner several rows behind me read: "Free the Chicago 8." As the march left Niagara Square, we started chanting, "Free the Chicago 8, End the War Now." Our march wound through downtown streets and when we started a second round, we marched in the opposite direction. Police cars zoomed into the crowd to break up our demonstration, confrontations broke out, some shop windows were broken, and nine people were arrested. *The Spectrum* reported on the march and arrests, the war in Vietnam was still raging, and anger was mounting back at UB.

Chapter 41

Police Assault

Several days later, on the evening of February 25, 1970, Howard and I were at an anti-war meeting in Hass Lounge in Norton Union to discuss how to respond to the most recent arrests. About 100 people were present, and I saw a number of friends there, including Jim, and Ron – a guy I knew who worked at Standard Mirror. Suddenly, someone burst into the room.

"The black basketball players are holding a sit-in on the court at Clark Gym, and they're asking for support," a young student with long wavy black hair announced as he gasped for air. It was a Wednesday evening, about 7:30 pm, in the dead of a cold, snowy Buffalo winter. There were about 100 of us, mostly white, and mostly radical.

I was aware of the situation with the black players. Most of us were. It had been publicized by *The Spectrum.* A number of the players had complained that they hadn't received scholarship money that was promised to them for coming to UB to play intercollegiate basketball. They were very good players and having a good intercollegiate basketball team was important for the prestige of the University. Equally or more importantly, it helped the University get sizable donations and endowments. The dispute over the scholarship money had dragged on for months, and now the players had finally had enough.

"That's bullshit!" declared Arnie, the six foot tall amateur boxer and leader of SDS. "And it's bullshit for us to be meeting here when this action is going on. Let's go over to Clark Gym to support the players."

I heard chairs scrapping the floor and some comments of agreement as people got up and put their coats on. There was no discussion or vote. But it didn't matter too much to this group. They were eager to support just causes. I would have liked to have had at least a brief discussion and vote, but democratic processes were often brushed aside as taking too much time, or being too "liberal," which was a bad thing because we were "radicals." I thought getting the sense of the group was just a good idea, and had little to do with what was liberal or radical. But if there had been a vote, I and likely everyone else would have voted to end the meeting and go over to the gym to join the sit-in.

Howard and I joined the large group of students which began walking to the gym on the other side of the campus. It was dark outside and almost deathly quiet, except for the loud crunching of snow beneath our feet.

When we arrived, we saw police officers and people in street clothes milling around under tall sidewalk lampposts. Their breath looked like megaphones of silver mist in the cold night air. We went through the main door of Clark Gym and brushed past the table where startled ticket-takers just stared at us. We entered the gym and saw about fifteen players, most of whom were black, in their uniforms sitting on the gym floor. They had been joined by about ten to fifteen supporters. The stands were still filled with people and they were talking and yelling things. A guy near us yelled: "Get off the court, you assholes! If you don't want to play, go!" Men in suits, along with a handful of campus security officers were trying to get the protestors to end their sit-in.

"If the people on the court do not leave the court immediately, you will be arrested," came an announcement over the loudspeaker.

We walked onto the court and spread out over the entire playing surface and stood there. About 100 of us. Some sat down. The boycotting players and their supporters cheered, and smiles spread across their faces as they gave us the thumbs up. A man in a suit standing near me was still trying to get a protester to leave the court. When he saw we weren't moving, he mumbled to himself, "Oh great. This must be the SDS communists." He shook his head and left. With 100 more people on the court, the University officials gave up.

"The game scheduled for this evening has been cancelled," came another announcement over the loud speaker. We cheered along with the black players and their supporters. "Everyone please leave the building. You have five minutes to vacate this building, or you will be arrested." People from the stands were leaving. "The Buffalo Police are here and they are coming in to arrest anyone who does not leave."

I joined two other guys to look out a window. Sure enough. There were a large number of cops outside. And not just the regular Buffalo police. It was the Tactical Patrol Unit, the elite of the Buffalo Police Department, usually called the TPU. They were specially trained for riot control and other dangerous large-scale operations, and had a reputation for being tough, and even brutal. They wore thick leather jackets with a lighting bolt on it – reminding many of us of a similar uniform worn by Hitler's Storm Troopers. "Here comes the SS," a protestor next to me commented.

"Who the hell called them," an SDS leader shouted angrily. "We had an agreement with the University that they would convene the Joint Student-Administrator Committee before police were called on campus. Let's go over to Regan's office to find out what happened." Peter Regan was the Acting President of the University, and had on past occasions shown himself to be quick to over-react to student protests.

With the game cancelled, we got up and started towards the doors. As we were leaving the gym, the TPU guys were entering. They were decked out in full riot gear: helmets, face shields, tall black boots, three-foot long clubs, teargas and guns.

We started marching toward Hayes Hall, the Administration Building where Peter Regan had his office. Hayes Hall was a beautiful old stone building covered in ivy, located near the front entrance to the University near Main Street. It was a perfect picture of a place where deep intellectual thought takes place.

When we got to Hayes Hall, an SDS leader told the security guards at the door that we were there to speak with Mr. Regan.

"He is not available to meet with you tonight," a guard announced through the glass door.

"This is an emergency," the SDS leader continued. "We want to know why the Student-Administrator Committee wasn't called to meet to discuss the sit-in at Clark Gym before the Buffalo Police were called. The police aren't supposed to be called until that committee meets to discuss the situation."

"Mr. Regan is not here," the guard answered.

"Yes he is. We just saw him in his office. His light is still on in there."

"I'm sorry. You will not be able to meet with Mr. Regan tonight," the guard continued. "Come back in the morning and speak with his secretary. Every one has gone home for the night."

Normally, all of the administrative offices closed at 5:00 pm. But this night, some were still open. Several people claimed they saw Regan in his office. We went around to the side of the building where his office was located and I saw the light on in his second floor office.

"Regan! Come down and meet with us," a student shouted.

"Why did you call police?" another one yelled.

"All pigs off campus!" another hollered.

I didn't feel comfortable calling people "pigs." I knew some cops were nasty, but many weren't. For many of them, it was just a job. Mike's dad was a Buffalo policeman and he seemed like a nice guy. I didn't think personal insults would help us win public support. But I still felt relatively new to all of this, and I figured the folks who had been around longer must have had more bad experiences with unresponsive University administrators and the police and were so frustrated and angry that the epithets just poured out.

"Hey look! The pigs are coming over here!" another voice yelled from the crowd. I looked to my left and saw the TPU cops marching toward us from the gym. They were about 200 yards away. I could see the light from lampposts gleam off their shiny white helmets and clubs, which they were holding with both hands in front of them.

"Those bastards," someone else grumbled.

Suddenly there was a crash. I looked up and saw a hole in Regan's office window. Someone had apparently thrown a rock or an ice ball. Was it a student protestor, or an undercover police agent sent into our ranks to spy on us and provoke confrontations? I had heard stories of police agents doing that. But I didn't know. It was so dark along side the building, it was heard to see who threw it.

Students started moving away from Hayes Hall toward Norton Union. We were closer to Norton than the police were, but the cops turned toward us. Students broke into a run and Howard and I joined them. I looked back and saw that the cops were running too. We passed the big fountain just outside Norton Union and ran into the building. A group of students rushed into Hass Lounge and dragged chairs and tables out to barricade the doors. Someone pushed an oversized stuffed armchair toward me and I shoved it in front of the glass doors. Smaller chairs came toward me and I hoisted them onto the tables and couches already stacked there. Other students were doing the same thing.

All of a sudden I saw the TPU guys through the glass doors. They swung their clubs and the glass shattered, whole sheets falling to the ground. I ducked as glass went flying over my head, and I scurried along the barricade toward Hass Lounge. The cops pushed the barricade out of their way and chairs and tables crashed to the ground right behind me. I looked back over my shoulder and saw the cops clubbing everyone in sight, protester and non-protester alike.

I saw three TPU guys grab Terry Keegan, a fellow Philosophy student and friend. They clubbed him in the head and kicked him, and then arrested him. Other cops moved down the hallway, grabbing and clubbing students who couldn't get out of the way in time.

Then four cops grabbed Tom Kearns, another friend who I had worked with in the BDRU, and threw him up against a wall. They surrounded him and clubbed him in the head and arms and shoulders, and his glasses went flying. He fell to the ground in a ball, blood gushing from his head. Students were screaming and throwing things at the cops. I picked up a broken table leg and threw it at the officers who were beating Tom, aiming high so as not to hit my friend who was now slumped on the ground. They looked around to see where all the objects were coming from. They held one arm up in front of their faces and dragged Tom with the other into a hallway to get out of the line of fire. I heard glass breaking everywhere, as whole chairs and furniture parts crashed through windows and glass showcases.

The cops kept moving through the hallway toward the doors at the other end of Norton Union, and then left the building on the east side where the Tower dormitories where located.

We were stunned. No one expected such a brutal assault from the cops. I looked around for Howard, but couldn't find him. Arnie, the SDS leader, got on the public address system about 9:15 pm.

"People should stay inside the building," he advised. "The pigs are still around the building and they are beating and arresting people who go outside. Go to Hass Lounge so we can meet and discuss our next steps." I was worried that Howard may have gone outside and got caught.

"Oh no, were trapped in here," said a brown-haired girl who was standing next to me. She was practically in tears.

"Let's go into Hass Lounge so we can figure it out," I said to several students. I was standing in the foyer area in front of the Lounge watching to see if students followed this advice. Some did, but many stayed in the hallways.

"What are we going to do if they attack again," asked a slightly built guy with short hair and thick glasses, and a biology book under his arm. He was clearly terrified. "I just came over here to buy a book. I'm not part of this," he whimpered. There were a lot of students in Norton Union who were not part of the protests. The Student Bookstore was in Norton Union, right across from Hass Lounge, and various student clubs held meetings in Norton.

"You are now," remarked a beefy, tough-looking guy in a black motorcycle jacket who was passing. He didn't look like a student, but it was hard to tell these days. He stopped for a moment and looked at both of us, and then revealed a pair of brass knuckles. "Here's my answer for those pigs." He quickly slipped them back into his pocket, and moved on into the crowd. The biology student turned white. I thought he was going to faint. I wasn't feeling too good either. How were we going to get out of here, I wondered? Brass knuckles were hardly a match for three-foot long clubs, mace, guns and face shields. I hoped somebody had a better strategy than Mr. Hell's Angel.

Since so few students went into Haas Lounge, we didn't have a meeting. I think people were more afraid of being trapped in one room than trapped on the first floor of a building. There were two main entrances to Norton Union, one at each end of the long hallway. We didn't know if the cops were at both sets of doors or not.

Leaders of the Student Association broadcast appeals for people who witnessed acts of police brutality to come to the Student Association office on the second floor to make notarized statements. I was standing in the foyer area in front of Hass Lounge about twenty feet from the set of doors that were smashed in, when suddenly I saw students running toward me in a panic

"The cops are coming!" they screamed. Behind them were rows of TPU cops from wall to wall sweeping down the hallway clubbing everyone in their path. My friend Ron, from Standard Mirror, grabbed an overstuffed chair and ran a couple of steps down the hall toward the cops to throw it at them. He was about thirty feet away from them and twenty feet in front of me. I didn't wait to see the outcome of that confrontation.

I turned and ran toward the doors behind me. My heart was pounding in my chest. I was among the first eight or ten students to get there, and went through the smashed opening in the center and onto a large porch that was enclosed by a railing in front of us. On my right and left were stairs leading to the ground. Out of the corner of my eye I saw a club crash down on the head of a guy near to me. It made a loud cracking noise, and blood gushed down his cheek. The cops had set us up. One group of cops chased us down the hall toward the fountain side doors, and another group of cops hid in a row outside the building along the wall next to those doors so they could club us as we came out. When I was on the outside landing I made a sharp turn to the right to go down the ten steps in front of me. To my right, I could see the cops clubbing everyone that passed them. I was on the outside of the crowd, near the railing, so I escaped. But I saw other people being clubbed, falling and screaming and blood was everywhere.

I jumped down the last three stairs and ran along a diagonal sidewalk toward the fountain. There were some shrubs and bushes there, with rocks a little smaller than baseballs in the shrub beds. I stopped to pick them up. A couple of other students picked up rocks too. I looked back at Norton, and the police were still clubbing students, so we threw the rocks at the cops. There were lights over the doors that illuminated the cops so I could see them well, and within seconds a hail of rocks sailed into their ranks. Rocks bounced off their helmets and face shields and bodies, distracting them so more students could get out unharmed. Then, I saw a cop raise his nightstick over his head to club a kid running by, and I threw my rock. Several rocks hit him at the same time, and he slumped to the ground before he could swing his club.

There was another group of students on the other side of the fountain throwing rocks too, so we had the cops in a cross-fire. They retreated along side the building for protection, and the rest of the students poured out of the building unhurt. A cheer went up from the crowd and people dispersed in all directions. All my senses were on high alert and I could feel the adrenalin rushing through my body. I was in a fight or flight mode.

I waited for a few minutes to see if the cops would reappear to look for us, but I didn't see them, so I worked my way around the building keeping in the shadows. When I got to the front of Norton Union I saw that the crowd had swelled to five hundred people, as students spilled out of the dormitories and people called their friends to come to the campus to join us. I scanned the faces of the crowd for Howard, but didn't see him.

"Pigs off campus! Pigs off campus!" the crowd chanted in a deafening roar.

Everyone was in a frenzy now. Suddenly, a group of cops charged a section of the crowd that had ventured too close to their ranks. People scattered in all directions, slipping and sliding on the ice and mud. Some made it back into the Tower dormitory, about 100 yards from Norton Union. Somebody slipped and fell and three cops were on him immediately, clubbing him repeatedly. Another hail of rocks rained down on the cops, who brought their arms up over their heads to protect themselves.

A loud scream pierced the air. I looked toward the wail and saw a girl being dragged by a cop down the steps of Tower Dormitory by her hair. A boy on the steps jumped on the cop to help her, and two more cops nearby swung their clubs at him. I could hear a cracking noise as the wood hit his skull. This only incensed us more and we threw rocks at those cops.

Five more cop cars came screeching up the street in front of Norton Union. Students hurled rocks at the cars, smashing the windows. The first two cars kept going to escape our assault, and the others turned back.

On the side of the Tower dormitory, I saw flames and smoke pouring from what looked like a cop car.

The police were now trying to pick off people standing alone and away from the crowd. Some were simply bystanders. I saw two students arrested in front of Norton, and an individual who witnessed the arrest was also arrested. This infuriated the crowd even more.

"Pigs off campus! Pigs off campus!" the students roared, and another wall of rocks hit the cops and their cars.

The battle raged for three hours Wednesday night. Seventeen people were arrested, including my friends Tom Kearns, who was charged with 3rd degree assault – apparently for smashing his head into a policeman's club, and Terry Keegan, who was charged with disorderly conduct. One person was charged with possession of a deadly weapon – I don't know if that was the guy with the brass knuckles. Two people were charged with inciting a riot. And our attorney, Willard Myers, was charged with first-degree riot while simply trying to post bail for the arrested students.

Scores of people suffered injuries and some were hospitalized. Most were students, but some were cops. Janet Cohen, the girl dragged down the steps by her hair, was sent to the hospital with a slipped disc in her neck and facing possible surgery.   When things calmed down Wednesday night, I finally left campus and went home. I found out that Howard made it out safe too.   In one evening, our university education was changed forever.

Chapter 42

Students Strike at UB

The next morning, Thursday, I got up early and hurried to the campus. It wasn't to get to my classes, but to see what our next steps would be. As I entered Norton Union, I saw windows and showcases boarded up. But the student union was alive with activity. Many students were already there, and many were reading a special edition of *The Spectrum*. I picked up a copy. This paper was distributed all over the campus earlier that morning to the over 25,000 students, teachers and campus workers.

It was a special one-page Extra! edition with a huge one-word headline: "Invasion!" There were photos of the Buffalo police breaking through the barricade in Norton Union that I helped build the night before, police beating students, arresting Terry Keegan, and rushing down the hall toward Ron, who was getting ready to throw the overstuffed chair at them. Next to Ron, with a partially blacked out face, was my friend Jim. I wasn't in the top photo, but I had been standing right near the photographer who had taken it.

SDS leaders had posted signs in the Student Union and around campus urging students to attend a rally at 1:00 pm in Hass Lounge to protest the police assault the night before. I spent the morning talking to friends about what had happened and strategizing about what to do. I saw my friend Jim and went up to him. We were in a class together. He was easy to spot in a crowd with his mop of curly red hair. He was with Michael, the guy I had met at the Buffalo Nine demonstrations.

"Did you go to class this morning?" I asked Jim.

"Naw. Plato's *Charmides* doesn't seem quite as interesting today as it did on Tuesday," he responded. *Charmides* dealt with questions of moderation in life.

"Yeah, I know what you mean," I said. "Did you hear that Regan started up his Rumor Control Center again?"

"Yes, and a fine idea it is," broke in Jason, a wisecracking student in the Theater Department who had been walking by. He was a tall skinny guy with long black hair. Today, he was dressed in a black cape with red lining, a bright yellow flower print shirt, black pants, and a red and purple bandanna around his head.

"In fact," he continued, "we want to help Mr. Regan so we've been calling in rumors all morning. We told him there was an invasion at the far end of the campus by a big potato. Then we told him that all the water facets in Clark Gym were turned on and all the drains were plugged up so water was flooding everywhere. Then we told him that the art students are tripping out on LSD that someone put in the eggs at breakfast this morning and they are now pouring paint all over the instruments in the music department."

"Did you talk to him in person?" Michael asked sarcastically.

"No. He's too busy leading us in these turbulent times, so we just left messages with his secretaries," Jason said nonchalantly. "Lots of them."

"Well, that'll probably be the last we hear of the Rumor Control Center," I added. We all chuckled. Jason wandered off into the crowd. I had gotten to know Jim and Michael through meetings and events that SDS organized. I liked them both. I learned that both had working-class backgrounds, both were Irish-Americans, and most importantly, both had a pretty level-headed approach to radical politics, which was not always the norm.

"Well, things are on a whole new level now," Jim commented.

"Yeah," I agreed. "People are really angry, so this is a good opportunity to build the movement." The news about Wednesday night had spread across campus like wildfire. The Extra edition of *The Spectrum* sure helped. A lot of students didn't go to class that day in what began as a spontaneous boycott of classes.

As 1:00 pm approached, there were nearly 1,000 students packed into Hass Lounge and the corridors throughout the student union. The students were angry and wanted to do something about the police brutality. We got a sound system so students up and down the halls could hear.

Arnie, the SDS leader, took the microphone: "There was a police riot on campus last night and the pigs broke in here and busted a lot of heads." He went on to describe what had happened and talked about how students fought back. Students started lining up at the microphone to speak.

"I can't believe all the boarded up windows," said one student who hadn't been on campus last night. "How did that happen?"

"We were attacked right here in the student union and we had to defend ourselves!" another student responded. "The pigs smashed in the glass doors and attacked us with their clubs, and we responded by throwing rocks and furniture at them."

Andy Steele, a Student Association officer, reminded the crowd that "the confrontation didn't start with rock-throwing students, but rather was a result of the war and the University's long involvement in Air Force ROTC and Project Themis to support the war, and the suppression of the Colleges." Radical students had been elected to many of the positions in the Student Association – the student government, and the Graduate Student Association, and were on the staff of *The Spectrum,* so that helped in building the movement.

I agreed with Andy. We needed to continually put the disturbances on campus within the larger context of the war and the University's complicity in it. The actions of the students were in response to this horrible and unjust war and the police brutality.

Another student reminded us that US planes were dropping bombs every day, "including as we are meeting right now! More and more Vietnamese are being killed for a war based on lies! That is the horror that we are trying to end!" The crowd cheered. Yes, I thought, we must keep that focus.

John, an officer of the Graduate Student Association, explained that the University was just one cog in the "military-industrial-university complex," and the entire machinery was set up to "advance and protect capitalism and imperialism. They use repression to crush our movement, but that only angers more students who join us. We have to demand pigs off the campus, and the firing of Regan!" A cheer went up in the crowd. I agreed.

The focal point for organizing was now the police assault on students and the continued police presence on campus. But the war was ever present in people's minds, and that was at the root of the crisis. If the university would have severed all its connections to the war effort, that would have gone a long way toward curtailing the crisis on campus. But the university did not cut its military activities.

The rally ended with shouts for a march to the Hayes Administration Building to continue our protests. I joined a group of students who headed for the doors. Once outside, the crowd began to swell behind two banners that called for an end to the war and an end to political repression. When we arrived at Hayes Hall, we opened the big double glass doors and marched inside.

Chants of "End the war now, pigs off campus," echoed throughout the building. "We want Regan. Regan must go!" reverberated off the walls as we marched through the halls. Suddenly there was a loud ringing noise. A fire alarm had been set off. Office doors opened and people streamed out, pulling on their coats as they left the building. There was snow on the ground and temperatures hovering in the 20's. Regan was nowhere to be seen.

The marchers then headed toward the campus police office on Winspear Avenue, still angry about the beating they took the night before. "Pigs off campus!" they chanted. When we approached the building, people started throwing rocks and ice. Windows were smashed in the building and in some police cars, yet there were no police seen anywhere.

The crowd, giddy with excitement over what one protestor called a "victory" against the police, headed toward the Project Themis site, which was still under construction. This was the military project that would test a soldier's ability to conduct military operations under water. I remembered reading that a week and a half earlier, US and South Vietnamese forces killed 145 of the "enemy" near Danang, a city near the coast. Would Project Themis help the US military kill more effectively in Vietnam, I wondered? The killing in the war was relentless; it went on and on no matter what we did to protest it. This insanity made us mad – some so mad that they felt we must escalate our protests to physically hinder the war effort.

Students were chanting "Stop Project Themis!" and "Pigs off campus!" as we approached the fenced off area. A group of students leaned on the fence, and the force of the crowd bent the poles over until the fence was flattened. People walked over it and onto the site, and more windows were broken in the Themis construction shack. A truck was set on fire, and flames and thick black smoke poured into the air. A loud cheer went up from the crowd. The police were still nowhere in sight.

Anger changed the way I felt, especially when I was with a crowd and a cause that I identified with. Some primordial emotion took over inside me, and I was willingly propelled into this wild rebellion. I suspect others felt something similar. If someone had asked me six months earlier if I advocated protests that destroyed property or caused violence I would have said no. When I look back on it, I can see how soldiers or victims of abuse could change from peaceful, law-abiding citizens into purveyors of violence. All the more reason to talk and negotiate and try to find some resolution to differences. But, in February 1970, things had gone beyond the talking stage.

I thought the university administration figured they over-reacted Wednesday night by calling in the riot police so quickly, so they were keeping the cops out of sight on Thursday in hopes that our anger would subside with a limited amount of damage. That wasn't happening.

The crowd now headed for the Air Force ROTC office, located in the basement of Clark Gym. Students smashed windows in an empty police car parked next to Diefendorf Hall along the way, and then gathered in front of the military office.

A student with short hair and a tie and who looked like a ROTC cadet stood on the steps of Clark Gym near the ROTC office, and shouted out, "Please, stop breaking the windows! I'm sick of all this destruction." He's concerned about the destruction of windows in a building, I thought, yet he's being trained to destroy human beings by dropping huge bombs on Vietnam. I was with a group of students who drowned out his plea with the sound of rocks crashing through the ROTC office windows. There were no cops at the ROTC office either.

Deep down it was exhilarating. The sound of glass breaking in a military establishment felt like we were breaking down the war effort, the racism and all the other inhuman things in society. It felt like, for a brief moment, we had power. All of the forums, and leaflets, and meetings and arguments we made had won over the students, but were ignored by administrators. Now they would hear us. Now they would take us seriously. This was the politics of anger and frustration, and I was swept up in it.

As we began to head back to Norton Union, we spotted a group of about 50 cops, decked out in full riot gear, gathering on the ROTC drill field. We were still so enraged and feeling so invincible that we turned and headed toward the police. As we approached their line, students broke into a run toward them, throwing rocks into their ranks. I felt a surge of strength, but also a streak of fear. Momentarily, I realized that if the cops turned and attacked us with clubs and maybe even guns, we would have suffered many casualties. But the police retreated off campus. The crowd was ecstatic. The fear evaporated in me and I felt like superman again. A roar went up among the students, and people started chanting "pigs off campus." We then marched back to Norton Union triumphantly.

But our euphoria was short-lived. The University and police had finally had enough. They called in reinforcements. Hundreds of fully equipped riot control police came onto the campus. They had tear-gas, grenade launchers, and riot guns. The K-9 corps was called in, along with the TPU, and police helicopters began circling overhead. Cops were seen taking off their name badges. At 3:30 pm, Norton Union was cleared of everyone and closed.

Our ranks had grown and there were now over 1,500 students protesting outside. The battle lines were drawn. A confrontation now seemed inevitable. All of my senses were in a state of alert. The fear crept back but I didn't want to show it. Would the police charge us like they did Wednesday night, I wondered? I felt more protected being outside and in a much larger crowd than I did trapped inside Norton Union. How far could we push them without a physical response? I hoped the size of the crowd might make the police think twice about attacking us again.

We were between Norton Union and Tower Dormitory, a distance of about 300 feet. There was a small parking lot between the buildings, and the area was landscaped with sidewalks, grass, trees and shrubs. About thirty students had gotten on the roof of the dormitory with stockpiles of rocks, and looked down on the area where the students were congregating. The heavily armed police started arriving in the area. There was a standoff. The students chanted, "Pigs off campus," and "End the War Now."

Then we saw a stout, middle-aged man with white hair and glasses approach the police. It was Dr. Siggelkow, University Vice President for Student Affairs. I didn't know what to think. Would the cops bludgeon us in front of a vice president of the university? He talked to the cops for a few minutes, and the police began moving away from the area toward the front of the campus. The crowd cheered.

"Dr. Sigglekow," a neatly dressed, shorthaired and clean-shaven student yelled out as he approached to within about 25 feet of him. The police were standing about 75 feet behind Dr. Sigglekow. "Who called the police on campus last night?"

"The Administration, including me, was responsible for calling the police," he responded.

"Do you know that students were hurt last night during the police assault?" the student continued.

"Yes," Dr. Sigglekow answered. "It's unfortunate, but it was necessary to stop the destruction of the buildings."

"One window was broken," another student yelled back. "That doesn't justify clubbing every student in sight. And when we came onto campus this morning, we saw the cops here again, dressed in full riot gear. That's like throwing gasoline on the fire."

"Yes, I know that tensions run high when the police are on the campus, but we have no choice."

"Yes you do," a third student yelled. "Get the military off campus, stop supporting the war in Vietnam, and get the police off campus." The crowd cheered. I agreed completely with these sentiments. That was the solution to the unrest on campus. We weren't rampaging just for the hell of it, or for some mindless youthful rebellion. After the crowd quieted down, everyone was looking at Dr. Sigglekow.

The standoff with the police had gone on for over an hour. Since there was no more rock throwing or destruction of property during this time, the police had no reason to attack us, though reason didn't always over-rule emotion in decision-making – on either side. Also, even though they were better equipped, they were heavily outnumbered and they saw that the students weren't afraid to fight.

The police started moving away from Norton Union towards the end of the campus, and we followed them from a distance, chanting all the way. Finally, they left campus and a great cheer arose from the students. Thursday was definitely our day.

Before we broke up that evening, I attended one of several small informal meetings that took place among the radical student leaders.

"I say we continue with more guerilla-war type actions, like we did today," whispered Steve, one of the militant students that had been pushing for more confrontational tactics.

"I think we have to reach out to the rest of the student body and the community," I said, "and explain why we're doing what we're doing. We have to keep educating people about why the war is wrong, and how the University is supporting the war, and how past efforts to get the university to stop supporting the war have been ignored. If we don't do that, people will just see the protests and violence at the university as mindless destruction, and turn against us."

"So what," said Robert, a radical student in the English Department. "We've tried educating the public and they just don't give a shit."

"Let's organize a student strike," my friend Jim said. "People understand strikes. It's our way of saying we aren't going to participate in the traditional business of the university until action is taken to stop the war." Jim had worked at the big General Motors plant in Tonawanda and knew about strikes from the labor movement. His friend Michael, who had worked at Bethlehem Steel, agreed.

"Yes. A university-wide strike would get people's attention and dramatize our demands," I added. "And it would allow us to continue to reach out to students and faculty and the Buffalo community." I also thought a well organized strike could help curtail the violence, *and* could be effective in stopping or at least slowing down the military training and research on campus. If enough other campuses did the same thing, perhaps that would put enough pressure on the government to end the war.

"And it would allow us to continue to attack ROTC and Project Themis and the power structure on campus," Steve added.

No one challenged Steve. I think we all realized that after the police busted people's heads Wednesday night things had changed. Years of teach-ins, forums, and articles in the student newspaper, leaflets, marches, rallies and demonstrations had gotten us just so far. We had built widespread support from the students and many faculty members on campus, but still had not moved the university administrators or the larger society. The Vietnam Moratorium was important, I thought, for reaching large numbers of people in the community, but the one day event in October and the two-day marches in November weren't enough. We brought the real history of the war to a number of community residents then, but only a small minority. Those efforts were excellent, but they should have continued.

Our little group agreed: a university–wide strike was the way to go. We talked to other informal gatherings of students and learned that others were talking about organizing a strike too, so we couldn't claim credit for the idea. A strike had been attempted last year, but fizzled out. But this year seemed different. There were many more students involved, they were more determined, and they were angry over the police riot on campus. We agreed we would come to campus early Friday morning to talk to other students about joining our boycott of classes and build momentum for a university-wide strike.

On Friday morning, we set up picket lines at the entrances to classroom and administrative buildings to spread the boycott. We also handed out a leaflet announcing meetings that day to discuss the crisis on campus. The majority of students we spoke with were receptive. The anger at the university and cops for what they did Wednesday was so widespread that other students joined us on the picket lines.

But not all the students agreed. I was in front of a classroom building when a shorthaired guy wanted to go in.

"We're asking everyone to join our boycott of classes to protest the police brutality on campus," I said as the guy started to walk past us to enter the building.

"I'm here to get an education," he said.

"Do you know about what the police did here on Wednesday night?" I asked.

"Yeah, I heard about it. But I'm not part of your protests, so it doesn't concern me."

"Yes, but people who were not a part of the protests were clubbed by the police too. Doesn't that concern you?" I continued.

"Well, what were they doing up here Wednesday if they weren't protesting," he countered.

"All sorts of things," I went on. "Going to class, buying books at the bookstore, eating in the cafeteria, going to club meetings. I saw people getting clubbed that had nothing to do with the protests. You could have been one of them."

"Well, I wasn't, and I'm going to class. I don't agree with your protests. I agree that we should end the war in Vietnam, and Nixon's doing that, but I don't agree with protesting. That cuts into my education." There were four other striking students standing in front of the two-door entrance and no one moved.

"But Nixon isn't ending the war," I continued. "It's true, he's pulling out ground troops, but he's sending in more bombers. I understand your point about the protests cutting into your education. But when bombs are dropped on innocent people in Vietnam, that cuts into their lives. They are killed. Innocent men, women and children are being killed every day in our name, and what are we doing to stop it? Our university is supporting the war effort by training Air Force pilots to drop those bombs. We can't continue with business as usual. The university hasn't stopped its support for the war, so now we have to stop the university. That's the only way we're going to end the war. What's more important? Your and my education for a few days, or stopping the killing of innocent people?"

As I was talking, a couple of the student strikers went in a side door and looped the legs of a chair through the emergency exit bars of both doors, so the chair was braced against the metal door divider, effectively locking the doors from the inside. Since the doors were glass, you could see the chair had pinned the doors shut.

When our friend saw this, a look of defeat crossed his face and he walked away.

"Hey, don't worry about it," I called after him. "No one is going to class today."

Friday was normally a lighter classroom day and many students didn't come to campus after the rioting that took place Wednesday night and Thursday. Teachers who were a part of the movement or sympathetic to the students cancelled their classes. Other teachers cancelled theirs when so few students showed up.

The University administrators wanted to stop this development quickly. They went to the State Supreme Court and got a restraining order barring demonstrators from any action that would disrupt the normal operation of the university, or was viewed as a possible threat to persons or property. Notices of the order were published and placed at literature distribution sites around campus. The restraining order listed 13 individuals by name, mostly SDS leaders, but also some students who were just in the crowd. My name wasn't on the list but I knew many of those who were. Students didn't seem too concerned about the restraining order. Many copies just sat where they were placed. Others were thrown out. I walked by a group of students who had just thrown a stack of them into a trash can and set them on fire.

"Fuck the courts," one of them howled as he threw in another handful of court orders onto the blazing flames.

"Yeah. No court is going to stop us," another added. I didn't say anything and kept walking. It was a liberating feeling watching the court orders go up in smoke. The boldness and defiance of some of the students emboldened many others, including me. Obviously, burning a court order wouldn't make it go away. But it showed that students were angry, strongly against the war, and determined to not let legal orders intimidate them.

More meetings were held throughout the day, by student groups, faculty members, and in various academic departments. On Friday at noon, I attended a meeting of over 700 students in Hass Lounge. It was organized by a hastily formed group calling itself the Student Strike Committee and was made up of many leaders of SDS and others in the anti-war movement. The goal was to unify the strike effort and further refine our list of demands. Many of the demands were the same as those made during earlier protests and demonstrations, and during the short-lived student strike attempt last year.

They included abolition of ROTC and Project Themis, the firing of Acting University President Peter Regan with the new President to be democratically elected by faculty and students, removal of all police from campus, the dropping of all disciplinary charges against students involved in political demonstrations, independence for the Colleges, an open admissions policy at the university to encourage minority and working-class youth to attend, support of the Black students demands regarding the school's athletic program and the introduction of courses on Black History, and the demands of the Engineering students who were already boycotting classes over departmental policies regarding curriculum and the hiring and firing of professors.

As soon as our meeting was over we headed down the hall to attend a meeting in the Fillmore room called by Bill Austin, the politically moderate president of the Student Association, and other moderate students. They were concerned that the more radical students were running the strike, and the Austin group opposed blocking classroom doors as well as the violence on campus. Over 1000 students packed the Fillmore Room, and both moderate and radical students were in attendance.

The moderates were running the meeting and they proposed the appointment of "student marshals" who would keep order on campus to prevent further acts of violence. This idea was met with a chorus of boos, as the radical students outnumbered the moderates in the audience. I agreed. I thought students shouldn't be snitching on each other. I was concerned that politically moderate student marshals might see something they didn't agree with and, under questioning from the police, give testimony against their fellow students. That would definitely disunite the student body and undermine building a solid, unified strike.

"It's not our job to finger students who may be doing something that somebody thinks is too militant," said a radical student from one of the microphones on the floor. "Where do you draw the line? Why aren't people more upset about the real violence and coercion that is being committed against the Vietnamese people every day by our government?"

People applauded. The proposal was never put to a vote.

Elaine Kolb, a student leader in College A – the student and faculty run program that encouraged students to work in the community, took the microphone and warned the crowd that some student leaders "will try to co-op the strike like they did last year, and dissipate our energy into teach-ins." Teach-ins are fine, she said, but now the main focus must be on organizing the strike. "College A is scheduled to have a large meeting in Clark Gym on Monday at 3:00 pm and that would be a good forum to try to get student support for a strike."

People applauded. I joined the long lines of students who gathered at the microphones that had been set up in the audience.

"I agree with Elaine," the next speaker began. "We should make leaflets and invite everyone to attend the meeting at Clark Gym on Monday to discuss a possible strike."

The next speaker added: "We should call that meeting a strike meeting. That should be where students vote for or against a strike. So we should get out leaflets to the entire student body inviting them to attend. We'll have to do that Monday morning." There was more applause. An ad hoc committee was formed to produce the leaflet.

I agreed. We had to make sure the leaflets got out to all the students so people could have their say. I didn't want a situation where only the radical students knew about the meeting, showed up and then voted for a strike. The more moderate students would then say that they didn't have a voice in it. And if we didn't have support from a majority of the student body, the strike wouldn't be successful. I felt the movement had done enough education on campus, through regular articles in *The Spectrum*, almost daily leaflet distribution, forums, rallies and marches to win a strike vote. I committed to being on campus early Monday morning to help insure the widest distribution of the leaflet as possible.

The moderates tried to resurrect the issue of not blocking classroom doors.

"We shouldn't be stopping those students who want to go to class," a student wearing a big arctic coat said into the microphone on the floor.

"But we must enforce the strike if it's going to be real, like labor unions do," the next student at the microphone countered.

"This is a university where learning takes place," another student said. "We're not a union, and we can't impede the learning process. Let those who want to strike go on strike, and let those who want to go to class go to class."

"More learning has gone on over the last three days on this campus about how our system really works than most people learn after years of classroom study," a radical leader of SDS exclaimed. "And this strike movement is about winning our demands to abolish ROTC and Project Themis and the other demands."

Bill Austin tried to bring order to the contentious meeting several times.

"Okay. Let's have a vote on whether or not to block students from attending classes," he announced over the microphone.

"No, no," people shouted from the audience drowning him out.

"Why are they shouting him down?" a blonde haired girl ahead of me in line said to her friend. "We should vote on that."

"That isn't something we want to have a public vote on," I commented to the girl. She turned around and looked at me a little startled.

"But people shouldn't be stopped from attending classes if they want to go," she responded. "I don't agree with using force."

"Well, I understand your point," I answered. "But sometimes, there is a fine line. Students on a picket-line might be able to make good enough arguments to convince someone not to go class and to support the strike. Someone else might interpret that to be a form of force, when in fact, none was used or intended to be used."

She didn't respond. Other discussions were taking place all over the room, and there was a low din of noise and commotion.

"People, can I please have your attention," Bill Austin pleaded. But no one was listening. Side discussions continued and people broke up into small groups and headed for the exits. The meeting ended without a vote on how to approach students who wanted to go to class. My goal was to build such a strong strike movement that it would become a moot point.

It was clear that the radicals were in charge, even at a meeting called by moderate student leaders. It was a great feeling being a part of a political movement that was by far the most powerful political force on campus, and that was building towards shutting down one of the larger university's in New York State and the nation to protest the war in Vietnam. That was a far cry from my life a year and a half ago when I felt very alone in my opposition to the war as an art student in Canada.

That evening another meeting was held in the Goodyear Dormitory cafeteria. Hundreds of students were present. The main topic was to get our attorney's opinion of exactly what the restraining order meant.

"This restraining order is intended to stop the movement on this campus," said Bill, one of the movement attorneys. "It was based on sworn affidavits from University administrators and the police who cite certain incidents beginning with Wednesday night. While there are a number of misstatements of facts, it is likely to stand. The main thing to understand about the restraining order is that it shortcuts the normal procedures of our legal system. For example, anyone seen trying to prevent another student from attending class, or disrupting a class in progress, could be arrested and charged with contempt of court, brought before a judge, and immediately sentenced to 30 days in jail. We can appeal, but it obviously is intended to stop the organizing activity and could remove an organizer from campus."

"But if they do that, it could also backfire," I said. "If they arrest someone, it could just make more students angry and make the movement even stronger." People applauded.

"That's true," Bill responded. "I'm just telling you what the legal ramifications are. You'll have to decide how you want to proceed."

"This is bullshit!" another student yelled out. "We're not going to be intimidated by this University Administration or the courts. We're going to organize a strike here, and they can all go to hell!" People clapped and cheered. Few of us had faith in the courts, especially after what happened to the Buffalo Nine and the Chicago Eight.

Another hand went up in front. "The key thing is to organize in a way that they can't pin-point any one or two leaders. Organize into small affinity groups of three or four close friends who you can trust, and then do what ever you can to build the strike. If this gets big enough, they can't arrest everyone." I had heard a couple of the radical students talk about affinity groups earlier. They said the reason for organizing an affinity group was for protection. Many students believed that undercover cops, posing as radical students, were attending our meetings and infiltrating our organizations. We were concerned that they not only knew our plans beforehand, but would try to lead us into illegal activities so we could then be arrested. By forming a small group of two or three trusted friends, every one in that tiny group could feel secure and protected from police informants. That made sense to me. The group agreed, restraining order or not, we were going to organize for a strike.

I attended another meeting on Saturday evening where we went over the plans for Monday. I sat next to a friend, Ken, whom I had met my first semester at UB, and had gotten to know from attending meetings and rallies together. He was a tall, muscular working-class guy with long wavy light brown hair and light blue eyes who wore his emotions on his sleeve. I found we had agreement on a number of issues and we became friends. He was from Buffalo and worked at Kaufman's bakery, a large commercial establishment just off Main Street about half-way downtown. He was a good looking guy, despite some acne scars, and he described himself as an anarchist. He thought leaders were too easily corrupted by power and then they corrupted the organization, so he didn't join any of them – except his union at work. I understood his position but felt we needed some type of organization. He was smart, practical, and committed, and was a staunch supporter of the anti-war movement, the Vietnamese people and their right to independence, workers, and anyone else who was exploited or oppressed.

On Monday morning, Ken and I went with a group of students to distribute leaflets at several classroom buildings. Many were already half or three-quarters empty. The boycott of classes among students and teachers in most of the social sciences departments was especially strong; so strong that most of those classes had been cancelled. Many of the leaders of the movement were from the departments of Philosophy, Sociology, History, Economics, Psychology, Social Work, Anthropology and American Studies, as well as the Division of Arts and Humanities, which included English and the fine arts. It seemed to me that there were more radicals in the Philosophy and English Departments than the others. I was proud to be in the Philosophy Department, and my long-time friend Howard was in the English Department.

Ken and I went to other buildings where students were still going to classes, such as the math and science buildings. While not traditionally areas of protest, there were some student and faculty strike leaders in Math, Biology, Chemistry and Physics, and the response we got from the larger body of math and science students was encouraging.

At about 2:45 pm on Monday, we started heading toward Clark Gym. Students were coming from all over the campus. By 3:15 there were over 4,000 students and teachers packed into the gym. We were astounded. I and others never expected such a large turnout. It felt good that all the work we had done was paying off.

College A had agreed to turn over the entire agenda to the question of a university-wide strike. From the conversations I overheard as people entered the gym, most were strongly for a university-wide strike. The main topics on the agenda were to discuss the issues, formulate our demands, take a vote on whether to go on strike, and how to organize a strike – if it was voted for. Speaker after speaker spoke passionately in favor of a strike. Many cited the repeated efforts students and faculty made over several years to get administrators to make changes, only to be ignored or rejected by the administration. When the strike vote was taken, it passed overwhelmingly to a deafening roar of cheers. I was ecstatic. We then discussed setting up picket-lines at the entrances to every building, and agreed we needed strike signs and leaflets to explain to other students that we were on strike.

When the meeting in Clark Gym ended, groups of students got together to produce signs and leaflets. I helped make "On Strike" and "End ROTC" signs. It was a liberating feeling. We were now taking matters into our own hands to stop the functioning of a small but important component of the war effort on our own campus. Clearly, what we were doing at UB wouldn't stop the war by itself. But we saw ourselves as part of a much larger anti-war movement. With students on hundreds of other campuses opposing their ROTC programs and other military projects, along with growing public opposition to the war, and the growing anti-war movement among soldiers and veterans, together, collectively, I believed we could make a difference.

Chapter 43

Week One, Two and Beyond

I attended meetings over the next two days to formulate our demands. In 1969, after students occupied the Hayes administration building, students listed five demands. None of those demands were granted, so they were listed again as strike demands, and new ones were added. The demands included self-determination for the Colleges, such as College A; abolishment of ROTC at UB; abolishment of Project Themis and all military research and military work at UB; the establishment of a Workers College at UB for Buffalo-area working families to be controlled by them; support for the demands of the Black Student Union which included ending racism in the Athletic Department and throughout UB; support for a racially integrated workforce to build the new UB campus in Amherst (SDS, the BSU and other progressive students and teachers wanted the new campus built in downtown Buffalo but ground had already been broken in Amherst); establish an open admissions policy to UB, especially for low income families, workers, blacks and other "Third World peoples" and Vietnam veterans; the removal of Acting President Regan and a new President to be elected democratically by students and faculty; the immediate lifting of the injunction; and the dropping of all charges against students and others engaged in political activity on campus. As time went on new demands were added, including a free day care center for UB students and employees who have young children. The strike demands were printed on leaflets and distributed all over the campus.

Every morning at 7:30 am, we set up picket lines at every door to every building. Many students joined the strike immediately and more classes were cancelled. Some students were hesitant at first, but joined as the strike picked up momentum. As this took place, several interesting things happened. The confrontations and violence that marked the first two days prior to the strike vote were almost completely gone. In its place was a university community alive with self-directed activity in support of the strike demands and to empower students, teachers and community residents. I supported all of the strike demands, and committees were organized to advocate for each demand, and where possible, to implement them whether the university administrators agreed with them or not.

I was on the Student Strike Committee as a representative from the Buffalo Draft Resistance Union, and I now joined the committee to establish a Workers College at UB. I saw this college as a good way to reach out to the community, and especially to Buffalo's large labor movement. This college was to be among the newly formed colleges, like College A. I talked to Ken about joining this committee and he said he had already decided to do so. When we went to the first meeting, I saw a number of people I knew who worked in Buffalo-area factories or other workplaces and who were also students at UB. I felt right at home with this group. I also saw people on this committee who I had worked with or saw at campus events, and Ken and I started working closely with one of them, Ira.

Ira was about my size and had long black hair and a full black beard. I knew him from a variety of activities, including from the Student Strike Committee, where he represented his organization, People Against Racism. His group's politics were similar to those of SDS. Ira was from the New York City area and was a pretty savvy guy. He had an infectious smile and great rapport with people. I don't know if he had a working-class background or experiences, but he was interested in building a college for workers. The three of us started working and spending time together.

The Workers College committee invited workers and union leaders from the community to meet with us. We wanted to develop a college that would address the needs of working families, and ensure that workers were involved in planning the college from the beginning. It was exciting to be involved in such a project. I always believed that if the public had access to *all* the information about an issue, and had a forum where they could study and discuss it, they would be able to come up with a good policy. Establishing this Workers College was a good first step in that process and an excellent way to really deepen democracy. While I attended some meetings of a number of the other committees, building a workers college was one of my major priorities.

On Wednesday, March 4, 1970, Acting University President Peter Regan was called to appear before a "People's Judiciary" made up of student strike leaders to answer charges of complicity in "war crimes and illegitimate management." Even I was sometimes surprised at the creativity and boldness of some strike leaders. I'm sure no one really expected Regan to show up for such a trial, but the order to appear before a "People's Judiciary" put things in a completely different perspective. Reagan and the other supporters of the war were the ones who should be put on trial, not anti-war protestors.

Regan had a different idea. He suspended twenty student leaders for their role in campus anti-war activities and for organizing the strike. This just stirred up more anger from students. I wasn't on that list either, but I knew most of the people on it. I purposely tried to play a more behind the scenes role. I was concerned that as outspoken leaders were being expelled from school or brought up on serious legal charges, others had to stay out of the limelight in order to keep the political organizing going.

I began working with a group that demanded that the twenty students be reinstated, and that President Regan be fired. First, we argued, the students were suspended without due process, which was against university policy. Second, some of the suspended students weren't even students – a couple had left the university a semester earlier. This, we pointed out, was one more example of the incompetence of the Regan Administration.

The Spectrum responded with an editorial on its front page of March 6, in bold letters: "Suspend Regan!" permanently, and wrote that "Regan has proven himself incompetent almost beyond belief."

The Black Student Union issued a list of demands, which included cleaning up the mess in the Athletic Department and treating the black athletes fairly, getting the police off campus, and the resignation of Regan if he didn't adequately address all their demands. They later demanded the formation of a Black Studies Program. All of these were included in the strike demands. The strike spread throughout the university, and campus organizations and academic departments had meetings with students and faculty to discuss their views on the strike.

One professor, who I was good friends with, told me that their union, the American Association of University Professions, was going to issue a statement condemning Regan's actions, and they were going to ask their national union to investigate him.

"That's great," I responded. "We really appreciate that. It's important to show that students and faculty are united, at least on that issue, and are supporting each other. If any faculty members come under fire, let us know, and we'll do what we can to support you." He thanked me. This was very important. The more groups we could get to support us the stronger our movement would become. I knew the faculty union wasn't prepared to issue a statement in support of all our demands. And they didn't call for Regan to be removed as Acting President, as we did. But that was okay. It was a start and I welcomed it. For me, the important thing was that they expressed some degree of support for us. That initial unity was something we could build on.

Many of the academic departments followed suit, and I was happy about all of their statements. The Faculty of Arts and Letters and the Anthropology Department voted a lack of confidence in Regan, and the Biology Department voted to support an elected group to assume the executive function of the university.

The School of Social Welfare voted to support the boycott of all classes. And the Anthropology Department urged the phasing out of ROTC and Project Themis. Every time I heard about another academic department publicly condemning Regan, and supporting any of our strike demands, I was ecstatic. I could see that the strike was gaining strength, and that would help us win more of our demands. Protesting wrong-doing was important. But being involved in a campaign that could win substantial gains was even better. I also found the creative, self-directed activity not only exhilarating, but essential in creating a new and better world.

Teaching assistants founded their own Teaching Assistants union. The Puerto Rican organization on campus, PODER, met with organizations in the Puerto Rican community to draw up plans for a Puerto Rican Studies program on campus, and to immediately recruit at least 500 Puerto Rican, Mexican-American and Native American students to attend UB.

I joined hundreds of other students and attended "Liberated College" classes that were held off campus by many of the progressive faculty members and teaching assistants. These were often more informal and we were able to talk about things that were more directly related to our lives. We discussed the strike, strike strategy, new models for university governance, methods of expanding democratic rights, and strategies for strengthening the anti-war movement. Course titles included "The Strike" by Robert Cohen, one of my philosophy teachers; "Racism," by Ira's organization People Against Racism; "Strike Issues," by Jane Swigart and others; "Community Organizing," by Tom Rainey and Bunnie Small; "Imperialism," by James Lawler, another one of my philosophy professors; and "The Feminine Mystique," by Liz Kennedy, a teacher and a leader of the Women's Liberation Movement on campus and in Buffalo.

My own involvement and development was growing. I felt like we were beginning a process to really humanize society and I was excited to be right in the middle of it.

"All the work we've done has finally paid off," Jim said to me one day while we were on the picket line. "Remember all those days of handing out leaflets and talking to students and getting the same 100 people to attend a meeting. And now this. It's amazing. Probably 80% of the university is shut down."

"Yeah, I remember," I responded. "This is a good example of how dialectics works." I had studied dialectics in one of my Philosophy classes. "You know, heating water one degree at a time, and then finally at 212 degrees it boils and is transformed into something new. We raised the temperature one degree at a time with every leafleting and forum and demonstration, but didn't see any change in people's thinking or behavior until last Wednesday. When the cops busted into Norton Union, that pushed the temperature to 212 degrees, and people really changed. Hundreds, even thousands of people, who before this didn't seem to be hearing anything that we were saying, are now talking about ending the war, getting rid of Regan, and empowering themselves in the process. It really is amazing. Marx was right."

Many of the radical student strike activists attended the meetings of their departments to argue for our demands. Howard attended meetings of the English Department and they adopted one of the strongest statements. It urged support for *all* the students' demands, and stated that no negotiations could begin until all twenty suspended students were reinstated, the injunction lifted and all police removed from the campus.

I attended meetings of the Philosophy Department, which had a reputation as the most radical department at UB, especially because of its graduate student teaching assistants. These meetings were attended by hundreds of students and faculty members. We passed the most far-reaching resolution of any department at the University. In addition to supporting all of the demands of the student strike, our resolution stated that "we condemn the arbitrary and dictatorial powers Acting President Regan has assumed..." and vote "no confidence in the Regan Administration and call for the immediate resignation of that Administration." The statement also charged that "President Regan and the powerful corporate and political interests he represents have chosen to meet by brutal and repressive force the legitimate issues the University community has raised."

Our resolution went on to support the open admissions strike demand "which would open up new educational possibilities to working class and third world people," and praised the formation of the "Workers' College which would serve the interests of the people of Buffalo..." It stated that "by opposing ROTC and military research at State University of Buffalo, students have made clear that they want taxpayers' money to go to meet the genuine needs of the community and not the interests of the monopoly-military-educational complex." It further urged all "faculty to cancel their regularly scheduled classes and ask that students boycott classes which are not cancelled."

I was proud to be a Philosophy student! I supported the entire statement. It contained many of the ideas that the most progressive students and faculty had been advocating from many different departments across the university.

Even departments not normally involved in social issues supported the strike. The Mathematics Department, for example, issued a statement condemning the police presence on campus and stated that their department will "not conduct classes until the police are removed and until the University Administration initiates discussions with the students on the substance of their demands."

After many individual departments came out in support of the strike and against the police presence on campus, entire academic Faculties and Divisions met and issued its own statements. The Faculty of Arts and Letters, made up of the departments of English, Art, Music and Theatre went on record to "urge the complete and immediate abolition of ROTC," and stated that "Arts and Letters will no longer recognize it (ROTC classes) for credit..." Because of the university's complicity in the war in Vietnam, that Faculty demanded the immediate abolition of all contacts between the university and the Department of Defense. The Arts and Letters Faculty went on to demand the immediate reinstatement of the twenty suspended students pending full due process under the law, support for a Black Student Union resolution urging the creation of a Black Dance Workshop and Black Theatre Ensemble, and support for the strike.

The Provost of the Faculty of Social Sciences and Administration, and the chairman of its fifteen departments – including the Department's of History, Political Science, Economics, Sociology, Philosophy, Anthropology, Geography, Psychology, Social Welfare and even the School of Management issued a statement urging reinstatement of the suspended students until due process determines their guilt or innocence. This was the largest Faculty at the university, and it also urged Acting President Regan to "condemn violence by police as well as students," and convene a University-wide conference where all the issues of the strike would be discussed, with the goal of negotiating a settlement of these issues.

Regan's response to the mushrooming opposition to his rule was to call in 400 more riot police on Sunday, March 8. Regan's action reminded me of Nixon. When we returned to the University early Monday morning, we were outraged. As I headed to my picket site, I could see through a thick fog that blanketed the campus the hazy images of heavily armed riot police everywhere. I had leaflets to hand out to students and faculty about the week of strike activities that were planned, including more forums, marches, teach-ins and rallies in support of our demands and for removal of police from the campus. The strike was so successful that the entire university was shut down. Now, with armed riot police patrolling the campus, tension was rising. I sensed another confrontation.

I checked in at my picket site and found four other students already picketing. No one was trying to enter the building. We spoke for several minutes about the riot police on campus and what we thought our next move should be. I volunteered to go to the Strike Office in Norton Union to find out what other students were thinking and then report back. The others agreed.

When I arrived at the office, there were ten or fifteen student leaders there and they were angry.

"Regan can't get away with this," one student exclaimed. "He thinks he can intimidate us by calling in more cops. We need to respond to this, and respond hard." Everyone agreed. We decided to issue a deadline to the University to respond to our demands by Thursday, March 12, at 8:00 pm. That was a good date because we had a big rally set for that evening on campus featuring anti-war soldiers from the American Servicemen's Union. So far, the Administration had ignored all our demands.

There were also some other big events set for that week. All of it would help energize students to increase pressure on the administration.

On Tuesday, March 10, 1970, Yippie leader Jerry Rubin came to speak at UB. He was out on bail from his conviction at the Chicago 8 Conspiracy trial in Chicago. A Yippie was a left wing, politically active hippie.

I believed that every one of the Chicago 8 were framed on conspiracy charges and that all of them should be set free. I didn't necessarily agree with every thing each one said or did, but that wasn't the point. The war was the real crime. I thought Jerry Rubin was funny, irreverent, creative, entertaining, and he represented and would appeal to a significant wing of the anti-war, youth, counter-culture and revolutionary movements. But I also thought some of his crazy antics and speech did as much to alienate large segments of the public from us as to win over others. But there was no question that he had a big impact on a large number of disaffected and rebellious students and youth, and that was a group that we wanted supporting the strike.

Ken, Ira and I planned to go together. I think they felt the same way about Rubin as I did. But I figured it would be good to get an insiders view of the Chicago Eight trial, get together with our friends in the movement to strategize, probably be entertained, and see Rubin's crazies get revved up.

When we got to Norton Union, the place was jammed. Over 1,200 people packed the Fillmore Room, and another 3,000 watched via closed-circuit televisions throughout the building.

Rubin was in fine form. He was dressed in a long-sleeve tie-dyed T-shirt, and had a scraggy stubble of a beard. His colorful headband did little to contain his unruly mop of curly black hair. He began by describing his occupation as "inciting to riot," which was the charge that was brought against him and the other defendants in the Chicago trial.

"Our crime was bringing the evils of this country to the surface," he charged. "We won in Chicago, because maybe now no one will take the court system seriously."

"That trial was a circus," I whispered to Ken,

"Yeah," he whispered back. "Hoffman was totally out of control."

Judge Hoffman took the bait every time Rubin and some of the other defendants created a ruckus in court. The Judge screamed at them, scolded them, and handed out years of jail time for contempt of court, and in the process, turned off millions of people who heard or saw the Judge's over-reaction.

"The government tried to use the conspiracy law as a deterrent to riots," Rubin charged, "but because of our trial there have been more riots than we could ever have organized."

Then Rubin launched into an attack on the liberals on the jury. "I'm not concerned with the eight jurors who really wanted to convict us. I'm pissed off at the four liberals who didn't want to convict us, but who caved in to the right and voted with them. The greatest threat is not with the right wing, but with the liberals who compromise with the right wing."

The crowd cheered and applauded. This audience was going to applaud almost anything Rubin said. I understood his feelings. But I didn't agree that the liberals were our greatest threat. The biggest threat to our country was from the rightwing – they were the ones promoting the most anti-human policies and practices, including the war. While they were in a minority, they lied to the public and won over many others to support them, so on some issues, they had a majority. The radical anti-war activists constituted perhaps 5% of the entire population, though a considerably higher percentage on the campuses. And liberals, who constituted about half of the society, opposed the war, so we had to work with them and convince them to stand up for what they knew was right. I also believed we had to reach out and win over some of the conservatives and pro-war people, which I thought we could do. But I truly believed that many liberals were good and decent people. George was just one of many. I thought it was self-defeating to attack liberals – they had to be our allies. But Rubin was on a roll.

"We don't respect the world that our parents built because it's built on racism and military power," Rubin continued. I couldn't identify with that either. My parents didn't support racism. And my father, who was a veteran, believed there were times when we had to use military strength, like we did against Hitler in WWII. I agreed with my dad on that. My dad didn't believe in racism or militarism or in using military power to get our way. My mother was strongly against violence. And many of my friends' parents didn't support racism or militarism either.

Rubin then said: "We're motivated by brotherhood, love and conspiracy. Everyone in this room is a conspiracy. We want to be a conspiracy."

Brotherhood, and he should have added sisterhood, and love, yes. But conspiracy? I understood his point. He was making fun of the absurdity of the conspiracy charge. If anti-war demonstrators who traveled to the Democratic National Convention in Chicago to protest against the war called a friend in another state to join them, they would be guilty of committing a conspiracy. If a multi-state organization held an event that voiced criticism of the government, and some disturbance broke out, it would be guilty of conspiracy too.

Such talk by Rubin was fine for this group, I thought, and it maybe even helped draw people together. But calling us a 'conspiracy' fed the fears of the broad public who were either not sure about anti-war demonstrators or didn't like them – people who I felt very strongly that we had to talk to and win over.

Maybe some of the liberals weren't so quick to embrace the radical left because the liberals believed the road we were going down was fraught with many more dangers than we saw or admitted to. I knew that we radicals didn't have all the answers and that we made mistakes too.

Jerry Rubin's appearance was an example of the strengths and weaknesses in the movement, and Rubin embodied both, like most all of us.

Clearly, Rubin did have a following. But I also wondered how much of it was created by the mass media that gave so much attention to Rubin's wacky antics and proclamations, while ignoring more serious and sensible anti-war leaders.

On Wednesday, I saw George in Norton Union.

"Are you going to the ASU meeting tomorrow night?" I asked.

"I don't think so," he responded.

"Why not? This is an important meeting. It's also the deadline for the University to respond to our strike demands."

"I know," he said. "I agree with what you guys are doing. But this is getting pretty serious. What if the Administration doesn't respond? Then what? More rioting? I just don't know if that's the right way to go? What if we're not successful?" He had a point. But I didn't know what else to do. I felt we were on a freedom boat that was cast out on a stormy sea and there were no other viable boats around.

"George, you know how wrong this war is and how much suffering its causing," I pleaded. "Why not work hard now to try to end it and then move on with your life. You're right, I don't know where this is heading either, but the administration has heard our voices for years and still they do nothing to try to end the war."

"Well, we can keep trying," he said. "But we also have to think about out own lives. Why not just try to make the people around you happy and have a good life."

I was silent for a moment. "I can't just have a good life with all this suffering and pain around me, especially since it's caused by *our* government with *our* tax dollars," I said quietly. "It tears me up. I can't concentrate on anything else. If everyone helps just a little, it will make a big difference. And I'm not advocating rioting. But we have to do something." I could see I was making him uncomfortable, and I didn't want to do that. George was a close and dear friend. I also knew that he was still in love with his high school girlfriend, Leslie, who had moved out to California with her father after her mother had died. Maybe he was thinking about his future with her, about having a family and a career. I had to respect that.

"Look, I support what you are doing," he said, "but I just can't get as involved."

There was more silence. I was hurt. We had been best of friends since high school. We went through a lot of things together. It wasn't a lack of courage, I thought. George was fearless on the soccer field and stood tough in the face of adversity. He was such a smart, thoughtful guy who had so much to offer. He could excel in almost anything he chose.

"I understand what you're saying," I continued. "There are risks. And I'm not trying to pressure you. Everyone has to make up their own mind, and I'll respect what ever you decide."

He thanked me and we parted.

Even if he wasn't going to get more involved, I still appreciated his support of the anti-war movement. There were a lot of people like George. They played a role. Many talked to other middle-of-the-road people in their own quiet way and were often quite effective. While George and I didn't see each other as much, we still hung out together when there was time, and we remained friends. That was important to me.

Chapter 44

March Madness

A little later on Wednesday I was still in Norton Union when I saw Mary, a woman who was very active in a number of causes on campus, including the Women's Caucus of the Strike Committee.

"Hi, Paul," she said with a big smile on her face. "The Women's Caucus set up the Day Care Center and we're asking people for financial contributions and to volunteer time. Can you help?"

"Sure," I responded, reaching into my pocket to give her some money. "I can give you this now, and let me check my schedule as far as volunteering." I didn't feel comfortable volunteering because I knew nothing about taking care of small children. This was an excuse since I could have learned. "How is it going?" I asked to change the subject.

"Pretty good. People have been real supportive. We want to ask the University for financial support."

"Absolutely," I said. "That's a good idea. When did you open and where is it located?"

"We just set it up. It's in Clement Hall, and we're open from 8:00 am to 6:00 pm. It's free, and we have a lot of volunteers."

"Great," I said. I hoped that meant I could feel less guilty for not volunteering. "Who is using it?"

"Everyone. It's for the children of all university faculty, staff and students. You know, every employer should provide child care for its employees," she continued.

"I agree. That's important work that you're doing. How is it being run?" I asked.

"We want the parents to have the major say in how it's run, so we're setting up periodic short meetings with them to get their ideas."

"That's great," I added.

"Gotta run," she said. "I got to talk to some more people." She blended into the crowd of students going into Hass Lounge.

Mary was part of the Women's Liberation movement in Buffalo, a fairly recent development that was picking up a lot of support. Seeing her and the work she was doing made me think about this new social movement. I knew that men had dominated almost all organizations, nations and the world since the earliest days of human civilization. This continued into the 1960's, even within the anti-war movement and New Left. But I also saw that was about to change.

Growing numbers of women at UB and elsewhere were speaking up. They demanded that they be given the same respect that male leaders received, and in some cases, they started up their own all-women's groups. It was a trying time for women and men on many levels. Some men didn't want to give up any of their power. Other men believed there should be equality between men and women, but how that played out in organizations, in class, on the job and in relationships was often tricky and confusing.

I agreed with the idea of equality between men and women and tried to be supportive, but I'm not sure I was always as conscious of these dynamics as I should have been. I had always been in classes, from elementary school on, with girls and women who were very smart, so I saw men and women as equals in intelligence. When men and women worked in the same organization or political movement together there was often another relationship at work. I thought about the Day Care center. My guess was that mostly women set it up, and I felt guilty again about putting Mary off when she asked if I wanted to volunteer. And personal relationships were confusing to me. Did women's equality mean treating women just like men? In terms of rights and opportunities, absolutely. But personally, with someone I loved, that was a different dynamic. If I gave flowers to a woman I liked, would that be seen as a form of paternalism – an effort to buy her affection, just like some men from older generations – and younger generations had done? Or would it be seen as a genuine reflection of love? If I didn't show personal affection, would the woman think I wasn't interested in her when I was? I didn't know the answers, especially to the last set of questions. But deep down I thought it was okay to give flowers to a woman I loved.

Just then, I saw Howard enter the building.

"Hey, Howard," I called out to get his attention.

"Hi Paul," he said as he made his way toward me.

"How are you doin'?" I asked.

"Good. Did you hear, the graduate students in the English Department are pushing to allow students to have an equal say with faculty in decision-making in the department?" he exclaimed. "It looks like it might happen."

"Terrific!"

"And 300 Teaching Assistants organized the Graduate Student Employees Union to bargain with the university administration over wages and working conditions for all teaching assistants."

"Yeah, I heard about that."

I knew Howard was interested in labor issues. He grew up in a union household. His dad was a union electrician. And Howard had worked at Anaconda Brass Company on Buffalo's west side where he was a member of the United Steelworkers union.

"A lot of good things are happening around here," I exclaimed. "The strike and the movement are having an affect. Did you hear, the Day Care Center has been set up and is in operation? I don't know if the administration formally agreed to that demand, or if people just did it. I just saw Mary and she told me about it."

"I heard something about it," Howard responded. "That's great."

"And a special committee of the Faculty Senate just released a report recommending the abolishment of ROTC. We've got classes going in the Workers College now, and more leafleting is taking place at high schools and factories and at other university's around the state. The ecology movement folks are hooked up with a national campaign to organize something called Earth Day, sometime in April. And a Provisional Revolutionary Government made up of everyone who is working on any of the strike-related issues has been set-up here on campus to help facilitate and coordinate all of this." Our 'Provisional Revolutionary Government' got its name from the Provisional Revolutionary Government that was set up by independence forces in South Vietnam. I'm not sure how much we knew about how the Vietnamese PRG functioned. We believed it was democratic and fair, and it was resisting US aggression so we supported it.

Of course, our PRG was hardly a government, and no one saw it that way. But we wanted to project a vision of what a really democratic, participatory government would look like, one that would empower students, faculty and staff, and foster peace, cooperation, fairness, and equality. We were trying to create elements of a new society, either building upon existing structures or creating new ones.

"Yeah, it's pretty incredible," Howard added. "But, unfortunately, Nixon seems oblivious to all of it – the war is still raging."

"Yeah, I know," I said with a noticeable drop of enthusiasm in my voice. Back to the real world, I thought, or at least the one that Nixon is ruining. "But the movement is increasing its strength," I said with renewed conviction. "Eventually it has to get to him and the members of Congress. There are demonstrations and strikes going on all over the country."

"Yeah, a lot of stuff is going on," Howard agreed. "I've got to go to a meeting. I'll see you tomorrow."

I left Norton and ran into Ira near the fountain.

"Hey, tomorrow is a big day," he said.

"Yeah, that's right," I responded. "Have you talked to Ken?"

"Yeah. We'll meet in Haas Lounge before the ASU program begins. Then we'll stick together."

"Good. I'll see you then." We both left.

Thursday, March 12, 1970 was going to be a big day. The Strike Committee had given the University Administration a deadline of 8:00 pm Thursday to respond to our demands. Representatives from the American Servicemen's Union were set to speak on campus that night. They were a very militant group doing difficult but heroic work building a union inside the US military to fight for better treatment of soldiers, and to demand the immediate pullout of all US troops from Vietnam. The ASU knew about our campaign to abolish the ROTC program at UB, and titled their talk: "The GI's Case Against ROTC." Andy Stapp was the chairman of the ASU and he had been thrown in the brig while a soldier for organizing the union and refusing to fight in Vietnam. He was quoted on the leaflet: "If the students want to show the GI's that they're on their side against the war and the brass, they should smash these officer training schools on their campuses..." No beating around the bush with this group.

I had heard Andy Stapp speak in Buffalo months earlier about the growth of the ASU and he told me then that our leafleting at the Buffalo Induction Center had brought him members Now, ASU activists were in Buffalo to speak at an anti-war rally during our student strike. We were building solidarity between anti-war soldiers and anti-war students. It was a great feeling.

On Thursday evening, I went with Ken and Ira to hear the ASU speakers. We had agreed earlier that the three of us would form an affinity group to watch each other's backs. We agreed that we would stick together during demonstrations, marches and other events. If the police attacked one of us, the other two would try to defend him. If one of us was arrested, the other two would be witnesses for our accused friend.

Some affinity groups attacked military targets, but they and they alone did the action when no one else was around. And since each affinity group operated independently of other affinity groups, if one group was arrested or broken up, the other affinity groups could continue to operate. We didn't realize it at the time, but we were developing a common type of secret or underground cell that many liberation movements developed and used quite successfully. While our affinity groups did help prevent undercover cops and police informers from framing protesters, the affinity group didn't always work.

Ken, Ira and I were among the 1,000 students and faculty members who attended the ASU rally. The first ASU leader spoke about the horror of the war, the terrible killings and the importance of strengthening the anti-war movement. The second soldier explained that ROTC programs were essential to the functioning of the military because the majority of officers came from ROTC programs. Without trained officers, the war effort would be crippled, he said. He commended us on our fight to shut down ROTC at UB. This brought a roar of approval from the crowd. SDS had put out a national pamphlet on the key role of ROTC in the war effort and urged SDS chapters all over the country to build a movement to remove ROTC from their campuses. The anti-ROTC campaign was also strongly supported by other groups, such as Youth Against War and Fascism – which had close working ties with the ASU. We learned about many of these anti-ROTC struggles on campuses across the country through the SDS national newspaper, *New Left Notes,* as well as from *The Spectrum* and the *Guardian.*

The third ASU organizer talked about the growth of the ASU in Vietnam. When soldiers learned about the real history of US involvement in Vietnam, or were abused by their officers, they often refused to go into battle, he said. Some of the anti-war soldiers were then retaliated against by being forced onto the front lines in suicide missions, he continued, which sparked a war between the soldiers and their officers. This battle ultimately resulted in "fraggings," he said, where US soldiers threw hand grenades at their own officers or shot them. He also talked about the fierce repression of the ASU, but said the union and anti-war movement among soldiers continued to grow. The crowd cheered wildly.

"I always believed that if we could get the soldiers who were fighting the war to see how wrong it was they would eventually refuse to fight," I told Ken as the cheering died down.

"I agree," he said. "The ASU is doing great work. But I don't know how widespread the opposition is among soldiers because the media doesn't cover it."

"Yeah, I know," I responded. "But I have read about GI's refusing to fight, in *The Bond,* and other anti-war papers. It's happening. Maybe not everywhere, but it's happening."

"I've heard about it too," added Ira. "A lot of black soldiers are involved, especially because of the racism in the military."

"This GI movement is one of the most important developments in the anti-war movement," I said. They both nodded in agreement.

The ASU speakers finished about 9:30 pm, and the crowd was revved up. A strike leader announced that the University Administrators had still not responded to our demands and the anger exploded. The crowd surged out of the Student Union and set out to trash the ROTC office again, chanting, "On Strike, Smash ROTC," and "Pigs off campus, End the War Now." Ken, Ira and I stuck together and when we got to the ROTC office there was a small group of Peace Patrol members lined up between the angry students and the police who were guarding the building. The Peace Patrol was a self-appointed group of faculty and students who tried to keep the peace between police and students.

Some antiwar students yelled at Peace Patrol to get out of the way, but they didn't move. Then rocks sailed over the Peace Patrol and police officer's heads and crashed through the ROTC windows again. The police moved towards us, roughing up Peace Patrol members along the way. Part of the crowd stayed there to keep the police at bay, and another part of the crowd that Ken, Ira and I were in marched over to Project Themis near Bailey Avenue where a fence was broken down and more windows were smashed at the Themis site. Several patrol cars from a line of cop cars parked along Bailey Avenue sped to the Themis site, and officers jumped out and started chasing the students. Two officers caught one student and knocked him to the ground, viciously clubbing him repeatedly on the head and back. Students responded by throwing rocks at the cops. Ken, Ira and I were still together. Just then, other cop cars that had been parked on Bailey Avenue started their engines to join the fray, but they were met with a contingent of students who bombarded their cars with rocks before they could leave the curb.

The crowd then went to the Hayes Administration building. Two officers in riot gear drove to the entrance of the building, and jumped out, brandishing their nightsticks to frighten the students. But rather than run away, about fifteen students rushed the cops and knocked them to the ground. Ken, Ira and I were with another group of about ten students that hurled a wall of rocks at the cop's car, smashing out every window. As students rocked the car back and forth to turn it over, a line of police cars raced to the scene, hitting students who couldn't jump out of the way in time. People scattered in all directions, and I got separated from Ken and Ira.

I then saw Bruce Beyer and walked toward him. As I neared him, I heard over a police radio: "Get 'em!" One of the cop cars turned sharply and headed right for us. We both turned and ran down the lawn in front of Hayes and toward Main Street, slipping on patches of snow and ice. I looked back and the police car had jumped the cub and was coming after us. We ran between trees that were close to each other, hoping the cop car would crash into one of them. I looked back to see the car swerve around the trees and zero in on us again.

My heart was pounding as we approached Main Street, and I could hear the cop car racing behind us. Bruce was just in front of me and as we turned left onto the sidewalk we ran about 30 feet to a driveway. First Bruce and then I hooked our left arms around a pole and used it to make a 90-degree turn so we could run up the lane. As soon as I made the turn I saw that we were going to be trapped in a dead-end alley. There were buildings on each side of us and one at the end of the road. I heard tires screeching as the cop car made a sharp turn and I could feel it closing in on us. As I passed one wing of the building on my right, I saw a row of cars parked there. I quickly jumped between two parked cars. My heart was exploding through my chest. I'm trapped in this alley, and these cops could kill me and no one will even see it, I thought. I had lost Bruce and saw the cars headlights on the pavement in front of me. I clutched the rock I had in my hand, and turned to face my attackers. I figured if they slammed on the breaks of their car, as soon as the guy on the passenger side jumped out, I would charge him and throw the rock at him as hard as I could, and run back down the driveway to Main

Street. If I failed, they could kill me right in that alley, or at least beat me to a pulp. The glow from their headlights got bigger and the front of their car zoomed into sight, and they kept going. I couldn't believe it! As soon as they passed I ran out into the driveway and back to Main Street. I was sweating profusely -- even in the cold winter night air, my chest was still heaving. I breathed a sigh of relief and then disappeared into the darkness. I didn't know then if they had caught Bruce. I learned later that they didn't. Apparently, there was an exit at the other end of that driveway and Bruce got away. He was sought by authorities after a federal judge revoked his bail on his conviction of assaulting federal officers in the Buffalo Nine Case. That was the last time I saw Bruce. Facing additional felony charges, Bruce fled the country and received political asylum, first in Sweden, and then later in Canada. I sympathized with him. The country seemed to be veering to the right so sharply under Nixon that many of us thought that he was leading us to fascism. Once the government had anti-war leaders and other government critics in jail, they might keep them there indefinitely. Any of us could be next. Yes, Nixon really was the devil. It was a scary time.

Chapter 45

The Faculty 45 and Legions of Old

Students came to campus on Friday furious about the police attacks the night before. The university administrators still had not responded to our demands, other than to call more police. We responded by organizing a big march of a thousand students that paraded around campus. More meetings were held and we made plans for more demonstrations the following week.

Over the weekend, unbeknownst to most of us, 45 members of the faculty slipped into the Hayes Administration building on a quiet Sunday morning, March 15, and staged a sit-in to demand that the police be removed from campus. Many of the professors also supported many of our strike demands. They issued a statement saying they wouldn't leave until the police left. Acting University President Regan's answer was to arrest the professors and charge them with "criminal trespassing." We learned about it later that day on the news. The professors were hauled away in a Buffalo Police Department paddy wagon and taken to jail. The students were angered and rallied to their defense, demanding that they be set free and all charges dropped. The 45 professors were adamant in their stand, and issued a statement charging UB Acting President Regan with defying the Faculty Senate. That was the faculty governing body that had repeatedly criticized the Regan Administration for mishandling the crisis on campus, for over-reacting by calling in the police, and failing to deal seriously with the strikers' demands. Their case became known as the Faculty 45.

That was a pretty remarkable action by those faculty members. Many were leaders in their departments and on various university committees. Most were published authors, and some were known nationally and internationally as top scholars in their field. Most were full tenured professors at a major university, and they all were putting their careers on the line. They were from all disciplines: Social Sciences, Arts and Letters, Mathematics and the Natural Sciences. I was proud to see that a number of my professors were among the 45. I joined many other students and professors in supporting the Faculty 45 Defense Committee that was formed to help them.

Our movement was clearly picking up momentum.

On March 17, 1970, the Faculty Senate at the University voted 229-92 to accept the report of the Special Committee on the Future of ROTC. The report called for ROTC to be abolished, but it could be reconstituted as classes on the "spectrum of military phenomena." What the hell did that mean, I wondered? Did the study of "military phenomena" include training military officers? We didn't know. We weren't happy about that part, but the report did urge the dismantlement of ROTC as it currently existed. That was a beginning. Also, even though the Faculty Senate vote was not binding, it increased pressure on Acting President Regan to do something about ROTC. Regan's response was to hold tough and hunker down and arrest more leaders of the movement, just like Nixon was doing, as opposition forces swelled and encircled both men.

The next day, Don Sherman, a Vietnam veteran and one of the ASU speakers at UB, and Dan Bentivogli, chairman of YAWF and a student leader at UB, and several other protesters were arrested and charged with rioting and other felonies. This angered students again and was like throwing gas onto a fire.

Those in positions of power, both locally and nationally, knew they had lost the support of most students, many youth, and growing numbers of soldiers, so they did everything they could to appeal to the general public. They had powerful allies in the major news media.

In Buffalo, the morning *Courier Express* and the *Buffalo Evening News* really got lathered up over the protests on campus. Both papers gave extensive coverage, for example, to two right-wingers on the Buffalo Common Council, our city council, who ranted and raved about the upheaval at UB. Fortunately, these two council members were outnumbered by the largely moderate to liberal city government, but the toleration for physical confrontation and property damage at UB by the majority on the local governing body was wearing thin. The problem was that the larger community outside the campus did not know why the protests at UB were becoming so volatile. From what I could see, government leaders from Buffalo made little effort to learn why the students were so angry. There was little or no coverage by the mass media of the educational forums, expert speakers, scholarly studies, the positive programs that students and faculty had initiated, nor the informative leaflets and reports about Vietnam and other issues that would have explained why the protests at the university were so intense. Nor did the media talk to the striking students to get *their* side of the story.

In all honesty, by the time the strike began, many students believed that the mass media was so biased against UB students that many wouldn't have spoken to the media, fearing that they would be seriously misrepresented. That was based on past bad experiences with the media. The students were so cynical about the mass media that it had lost its credibility with many of them. Most of the public, however, knew only what they read or saw from the mass media. A very large majority of community residents had no access to the information we had, and the media repeatedly ignored our story. The latest "missed" news was the story and explanation for why the Faculty Senate voted to weaken ROTC. But criticisms of the anti-war movement at UB, or even a whiff of confrontation garnered front page headlines. Conversely, both papers gave regular coverage to conservative and right-wing voices in the community.

The same morning of the important Faculty-Senate vote on ROTC, the *Courier Express* ran a front-page banner headline: "Crush UB Sedition, VFW Urges." The main article was about a plea that the area Veterans of Foreign Wars made to New York State Governor Nelson Rockefeller to bring about "an immediate cessation of the anti-American activities being perpetrated on the campus of the State University of New York at Buffalo."

There was a large photo right under the headline of hundreds of students standing in long thick columns on the snow covered lawn in front of Clark Gym, home of the ROTC program. The caption read: "Vanguards of protesters prepare to charge, as legions of old, at Clark Gym."

I was in one of those columns. Terry Keegan, who was very creative and funny, had thought up that idea. We were trying to find new ways to keep people involved in the strike and support for our eleven demands. Terry suggested that we call a rally on the field in front of the gym and line people up in columns, like soldiers did in ancient Rome, and that we march them through some maneuvers. I think his idea was to poke fun at the military and liken the suicidal military strategies of ancient times to the equally suicidal military adventures in Vietnam. No one had any other idea so we agreed. There was no plan to attack the building.

When the newspaper took this picture, Terry was yelling out incoherent military drill maneuvers through a bullhorn and people were marching back and forth and bumping into each other. We all laughed at how silly it was. There never was an attack on Clark Gym. Yet, the *Courier Express* headline and photo implied that an attack took place that day by those radical menaces to society at UB on the hapless Clark Gym.

I was angry at the deception but not surprised. I also found it funny because of the lengths the paper would go to smear us. I also had mixed feelings about the coverage. On one hand, being on the front page of the morning newspaper showed that we were getting attention. But I was also concerned because I knew that these kinds of articles were poisoning the minds of the one and a half million people that populated metropolitan Buffalo.

In many ways, those of us at UB were an island of anti-war activists and progressive thinkers – maybe 10,000-20,000 strong, surrounded by a community of over a million people, most of whom were much more politically moderate. While growing numbers of people in Buffalo opposed the war, as evidenced by the large involvement in Vietnam Moratorium activities, their knowledge of the underlying causes of the war was limited. The devil's November 3rd speech to the nation confirmed that. And while there were some progressives in the larger Buffalo community who understood what we were doing at the university and why, they were a small minority.

Since we knew that most of the people of Buffalo had little idea why we were so angry, we had tried to get our point of view into both major daily newspapers, but aside from an occasional letter to the editor or a quote in an article, we were ignored. We couldn't even buy ad space – the papers refused our ads. The power of the mass media was so great it was scary. It could shape the way people thought.

I wondered why the mass media was so biased against us and the anti-war movement, as well as against workers and unions, people of color and others. I had heard people refer to the mass media as the "corporate media." I did some research. A friend who had worked at the *Buffalo Evening News* told me that the paper was owned by the Butler family, one of the richest, most elitist and most powerful families in Buffalo. Mrs. Edward Butler sat on the Board of Directors of Buffalo General Hospital, owned WBEN TV and radio stations, and had large stock holdings in American Airlines and other corporations. The family and the paper supported the Republican party, and often the more conservative leaders in it, like Nixon.

The *Courier-Express* was also owned by a well-to-do business family, the Conners, for most of its existence. Politically, it usually supported the Democratic party, though more often the conservatives in the party – the very Democrats who were still supporting Nixon's war in Vietnam. However, when Democratic Buffalo Mayor Sedita endorsed the Vietnam Moratorium of October 15, 1969, the *Courier-Express* gave broad and fair coverage to the event. This pleasantly surprised many of us since the paper routinely ignored, attacked or ridiculed practically every other type of anti-war protest. I understood why critics referred to both papers as the "corporate media." Most, but not all, businesses saw the war in Vietnam and our government's goal of establishing a bought-and-paid for client state in Vietnam, as good for business. Both Buffalo daily newspapers, along with the local TV stations – which were owned by ABC, CBS, and NBC, were a part of this pro-war business community.

Learning this made me think that the anti-war movement, and students and teachers should build alliances with all the other groups who were also misrepresented by the major meida, like labor and the black community, and start our own newspaper of TV station. But I had no idea how that could happen. Obviously it would take a lot of money, likely much more money than these groups had. At some point, creating a national alternative to the corporate media must happen or the American people will be at the mercy of the corporate media slant on every thing. That's why I felt that our leafleting in the community was important, even as limited as it was.

A two-week spring vacation was about to begin, and the Strike Committee met to discuss how we would keep the strike going after spring recess. Going into the break, some students were starting to worry about what grades they would get in all the classes that weren't being held, or if they would even get credit for taking these classes at all. Thousands of students needed these classes for graduation or to move from one grade to the next. We'd been on strike now for over a month.

I wasn't thinking about moving to the next grade. I was thinking about how I could cut down the number of days I was working so I would have more time for organizing. I heard of a really cheap apartment at 1528 Main Street at West Ferry in an old, red-brick building. The apartments were above a pharmacy owned by a high school friend's dad. Other radicals lived in that building and in nearby buildings, so I thought this would be a good move. The place was run down, but was big and roomy and had three bedrooms. And the rent was only $60 a month. I got a roommate, and sometimes had two, so that cut my portion of the rent to $30 or even $20 a month. Also, the building was condemned, so the landlady came around for the rent usually every other month, so that cut my rent to $15 or even $10 a month! I could earn that in one day at day labor. So I was virtually a full-time political organizer. That was the good news.

The bad news was that my personal life was virtually non-existent. I was so involved in the anti-war movement, the student strike, the Workers College and the Strike Committee that I had no time for anything else. When thoughts of Donna or Molly crept into my head, I pushed them out by getting busy with political work. But I did take time out to get together with friends and socialize at Maxl's, a bar across the street. Unexpectantly, Maxl's turned out to be more than just another bar.

Chapter 46

Maxl's Bar & Grill

Maxl's was kitty-corner across the street from where I lived. Main Street was the dividing line then between the black community and the white community. I lived on the west side, or white side of Main Street, and Maxl's was on the east side. The bar was owned by blacks and most of its clientele were black.

My apartment was in a neighborhood with about ten or fifteen white radicals, all against the war, and all living in close proximity to each other. Some were students and some were workers. There was my roommate, Steve – not the Weatherman Steve from UB but a young radical worker employed at Republic Steel. Then, across the hall lived Wayne and Carl, both a few years older. Wayne was a coke oven worker at Bethlehem Steel and a veteran, and he took classes at UB. Wayne and I had great discussions about philosophy, the war, the labor movement and Karl Marx. Carl worked at Allied Chemical. Around the corner on West Ferry, radicals lived in a couple of apartments in The Fenton. Across Ferry were several more apartment buildings where more radicals lived.

Wayne and I went over to Maxl's one day to get some beer. The front entrance to the bar was about ten feet across and was on a 45 degree angle to the street. It looked like someone had cut off the corner of the building and put the front door where the corner had been. Around the door was some interesting wood molding that had been painted bright green decades earlier, but was now faded and peeling. There was a small vestibule just inside the front door, and a second door to let you inside the bar. That little room kept out the cold and snow in the winter.

When we entered, we heard rhythm and blues on the jukebox, saw people laughing and having a good time. Pitchers of beer were on many tables along with baskets of free peanuts. People were eating the peanuts and throwing the shells on the floor. It wasn't inconsiderate – that was expected. As we entered, I felt like I was walking on a carpet that crunched. We went to the bar, ordered a couple of beers and took a table. The patrons were about 90 percent black, with a couple of other whites at the bar. People said hello or nodded to us so we felt welcomed. We noticed posters on the walls advertising jazz and blues on certain evenings, and we talked about coming back on entertainment nights. Others from the white side of Main Street had also gone to Maxl's. We shared this new location with other friends and soon a bunch of us were going over there.

I wouldn't say I got to know the regulars there real well, but I learned that some of them worked in area factories and were union members. We talked about the job, the bosses, the union, beer, women and girlfriends, and about the neighborhood, poverty, lack of decent housing and jobs, unemployment, racism, police brutality, how they hated Nixon, and opposed the war. When they talked about poverty and poor housing, we could see it right around Maxl's. There were blocks of old wooden houses, many battered and broken.

None of the bar patrons had anything good to say about Nixon, and more than one heaped scornful abuse on the evil man with the horns. One favorite epithet for Nixon was "jive-ass motherfucker." We agreed. I didn't get the impression these guys were political, like the Black Panthers or even civil rights groups. But they had a gut-level street sense about the world and how it operated and how blacks were given the short end of the stick at just about every turn.

As we got to know the owners and some of the patrons better, we went into more detail about our views about society, especially about the war and racism. They agreed with us, so we hit it off with them. Some radicals with connections to radical film-makers asked the owners if they could show films in the back room. They explained that the films were about the war and how bad it was, about the evils of racism, about worker and community struggles for improvements in working and living conditions. The owners agreed and said that Sunday afternoon would be a good time for it because things were slow in the bar then.

We put the word out to our other radical friends around the city, and on the first Sunday film showing thirty white radicals showed up. We invited the regulars to join us. A couple did, but the rest stayed in the big front room where the bar was.

One Sunday after the big Saint Patrick's Day parade in downtown Buffalo, I headed over to Maxl's for the film showing. When I entered the backroom, I saw my friends Jim and Michael sitting at a table with some of our other friends. We were all there for the film, and of course, the beer and peanuts, and to socialize. This was the Michael I met during the protests to free the Buffalo Nine. He was a friend of Jim's, so that's how I got to know him better. He was from

373

a Catholic family in St. Teresa's Parish in Irish South Buffalo and had helped organize a contingent for the Saint Patrick's Day parade.

The Saint Patrick's Day Parade was one of the biggest events in Buffalo. Hundreds of thousands of people would come out to watch the festivities, which featured the Mayor, marching bands from area high schools and Irish clubs, and even some bands from Ireland, and it was often broadcast on television. I went over to join them.

"Hey, sorry I missed you guys at the parade," I said as I pulled up a chair and sat down. "Did you guys make it?" I had planned to joined Michael and the other radical Buffalo Irishmen under the banner of the James Connolly Brigade. James Connolly was one of the leaders of the Easter Rebellion in Dublin in 1916 for Irish independence from the British. He was also a trade union leader and a Marxist. The Rebellion was crushed by Great Britain, and Connolly and his comrades were executed in prison by a firing squad. This act of brutality inflamed the Irish people and sparked a revolutionary movement that succeeded in winning independence for 26 of Ireland's 32 counties. Only 6 counties in the north, Northern Ireland, remained under British control. Most of the people in the Buffalo James Connolly Brigade were Irish, and since I had those McClearys on my mom's side of the family, I figured I could pass for Irish as well.

"Yeah, we were there," Michael replied after taking a couple of swallows of cold beer. "What happened to you?"

"I had to do an errand for my mom and I was late."

"Ah, you missed a good time, laddy," Michael said with a smile and a put-on Irish brogue.

"Oh yeah. What happened?"

"Well, everything started out good. We got the group together an hour before the parade, but we didn't have any signs. So we went to Danny's house and borrowed his mom's window shades and made them into signs. We wrote 'Brits out of Ireland,' and 'US out of Vietnam.'"

"You wrote that on her window shades?"

"Yeah. Danny said it was okay, right Danny? They were old ones." Danny was a little younger than us, as Irish as the green shamrock, and was drawn to the freedom movements here and in Ireland.

"Yeah," Danny responded, but he looked uneasily at the floor.

"What did your mom say?" I asked.

"She's pissed. She kicked me out of the house."

"Yeah, he'll be sleepin' in the garage tonight," Michael laughed.

"Maybe she'll let you back in the house tonight," I suggested.

"I hope so," Danny mumbled.

"Anyway, we got the signs and went down to the parade and took our place on the side street where the various contingents were lining up," Michael continued.

"So you got permission to be in the parade."

"Well, sort of. I'm not sure they knew who we were, but we were in." He took another swallow of beer, cracked a couple of peanuts, and tossed the shells on the floor.

"Actually, we got in as guests of the Community Action Corps," Jim added. His frizzy red hair looked like cotton candy in the light from a ceiling lamp. The Community Action Corps was a neighborhood-based organization that worked on improvement projects in poor, working-class and minority neighborhoods. A number of radicals had worked with them.

"So, then what happened?"

"Well, one of the parade marshals came by and asked us who we were and how we got into the parade," Jim continued.

"We told him we sent in our application and our money and that we were accepted," Michael explained. "He looked at the roster of entries and said he couldn't find us on it. Then he saw our signs and told us to leave. I asked to see his roster and he refused. He was wearing one of those big top hats and a funny green suit. He looked like a clown. We told him we were staying and marching for the freedom of *all* of Ireland. He started yelling something about you damn radicals and communists and IRA-lovers and we don't need the likes of you to ruin the annual Saint Patrick's Day Parade."

Jim leaned forward. "I told the guy that the people who went around dressed up like that in Ireland were the landlord's agents who evicted the poor tenants from their homes. He started fuming again, and then just left. So, we planned to stay and march. But then the police came over and forced us out of the parade. So we rolled up our window shades and left." We all laughed.

"It got even more interesting after that," Michael explained. "The cops who told us to leave were just regular Buffalo cops. But as we walked down Allen Street to our cars, we were approached by a group of TPU's." That was the unit that crashed into Norton Union at UB clubbing everyone in sight and that started the student strike.

"Ah, that's our version of the Black and Tans," I commented. The British Black and Tans terrorized the Irish.

"Exactly," said Michael. "Anyway, they told us they were going to shove the window shades up our commie asses," he continued. "A couple of them grabbed the window shades and started hitting us with them, so we jumped into our cars and took off. They got into their cars and came after us. As I went down Virginia Street, I saw their lights flashing, signaling us to pull over. When I stopped, they came up to my window and announced that they needed to do a vehicle safety inspection on my car. I couldn't believe it. I would rather get whacked with the window shades than have my car inspected 'cause that would cost me money to get the repairs. You know what a wreck my car is."

"But they were looking for something more than motor vehicle violations," Michael continued. "They asked us for our identification, and then asked 'where's Arnie?'" Arnie was the leader of our SDS chapter, but he wasn't with the group. "Then one TPU told me that I had a broken tail-light and to get it fixed. I said it wasn't broken, so he smashed it with his nightstick, and said, 'now it is.' So, all in all, it was a pretty normal day in Buffalo." We all laughed again.

Wayne and Carl had come in during the middle of this story and had taken a table next to ours and they heard the second part of it. Wayne leaned toward us. "That's standard. If they can't find evidence, they'll create it." We all nodded.

"So our efforts to influence the thinking of thousands of our Irish brothers and sisters and the general public of Buffalo fell a little short," I commented.

"Well, not completely," Michael corrected me. "The parade officials and a couple of other contingents saw our signs." People laughed again.

Then I heard a woman's voice asking people to quiet down in the bar.

"Can we have your attention please. We're going to begin this evening's film. It's about the recent strike of oil workers in Richmond, California. Next week we'll be showing one on the Black Panther Party." I figured that would draw a good crowd from the regulars.

"I hear this is pretty good," Michael whispered to me. "I'd like to see them make a film about the struggle in Ireland. We'd show that one right in South Buffalo." The lights dimmed and the movie started. What a great set-up this was, I thought. Great movies, great friends, beer and food, and all in a bar across the street from where I lived.

Chapter 47

Counterinsurgency

I was in Norton Union one day during a slow period in the strike when a guy I had seen at many of the demonstrations, but who I didn't know, came up to me with a package under his arm. He looked around quickly and asked if we could step into Hass Lounge. I agreed and we did. It was late in the afternoon and not many people were in the building. He was holding a brown paper bag about the size of a notebook.

"You need to see this," he said quietly, as he looked around the room. I was near a wall that shielded me from the view of most everyone in the area.

"What is it?" I asked as I took the package from him. It felt like a book with a hard but flexible cover on it.

"It was taken from Hayes Hall last year during the student takeover," he whispered. "But don't look at it here," he warned. He turned and quickly left the building.

I looked around to see if anyone was watching and everyone within my vision seemed to be going about their own business. I thought about the student take-over of the main administration building last year and remembered seeing students rifle through administrator's files.

What could this be, I wondered? I didn't want to wait until I got home to look at it. I held the bag tightly under my arm and went to the back corner of the lounge. I sat in a large overstuffed armchair that had its back to the wall. Its sides curled around me and I felt pretty safe. I could see everyone in the lounge as they were all in front of me. I sat motionless for a minute or two slowly surveying the large room. No one was paying any attention to me. The nearest people were thirty feet away, a young couple wrapped up in each other's arms on a couch. They were clearly more interested in each other than in me.

I opened the bag and slowly slid out what looked like a thick report. It had a light greenish-gray hard cover on it, and a title in black letters: "Study Material: Counterinsurgency, Volume One." At the top of the cover, there was printed in smaller letters: "Naval Air Basic Training Command." At the bottom: "U.S. Naval School,

Pre-Flight, U.S. Naval Air Station, Pensacola, Florida." I looked around the room and still no one was paying any attention to me.

I opened the cover and the first page contained a letter from the Head of the Education Department of the Naval War College, based in Newport, Rhode Island. The letter explained that the book was to be used as a primary text for the course, "Counterinsurgency." I had heard the Naval War College trained high-ranking military officers in military planning, and CIA officers and other operatives made presentations there.

I turned to the table of contents and read the topic headings for each chapter and the authors' names: "On Guerrilla Warfare," "Guerrilla War and U.S. Military Policy," "Theory and Practice of Insurgency and Counterinsurgency." What! That chapter was written by Albert Somit, a vice president at our university! A chill went down my spine. On the first page of Somit's chapter he was listed as "Professor A. Somit, Staff, Naval War College."

So here it was. The smoking gun. A direct connection between high-level military planners working to crush the independence movement in Vietnam – what they liked to call an "insurgency," and top level administrators at our university who were also trying to crush the student and anti-war "insurgency" in Buffalo. Counterinsurgency was the effort to crush the insurgency.

Somit's chapter, which was presented as a lecture at the War College, talked about the characteristics of an insurgency. He explained what it was, how it was organized, how to identify people who are engaged in "insurgent" activities, and how to stop them. He wrote several things that caught my attention. "Guerilla warfare," he wrote, "is a dirty business and the military have always had a very high sense of ethics as to how warfare should be conducted." A high sense of ethics? What was he talking about? The United States military was using napalm, anti-personal weapons, torture, massive carpet bombing, flame-throwers, defoliants like Agent Orange and more in southeast Asia, and had incinerated hundreds of thousands of innocent people in Hiroshima and Nagasaki in 1945 by dropping the only two nuclear bombs ever used on humans.

He also wrote that many insurgencies are against colonial powers. He mentioned that the Boers, Irish, Cypriot Greeks and Burmese, to name a few, had rebelled against the British, and then wrote, "as you can see, the British have a distinguished colonial record." A distinguished colonial record? This guy is sick. He then warned that "present day insurgency has an international aspect to it. The insurgent is not fighting simply by himself but as part of a general international effort. If things go too badly for him, he can expect that the 'heat' will be turned on somewhere else, and our attention and efforts distracted or diverted...Traditionally insurgency has been a national problem aimed at a given government. Today it is part of a world-wide struggle and pressure is increased or relaxed as dictated by the strategy of this struggle."

Here was a version of the well-worn theory about an international communist conspiracy. Somit didn't understand that people rebel because they have just grievances, and that other people act in solidarity with them because it's the moral thing to do – like Europeans who hid Jewish families in their houses to protect them from the Nazi Holocaust, or Americans who were trying to stop the genocidal war against the Vietnamese people.

Part of what he said was true. I did want the anti-war movement in the United States to get so big and so strong that it would divert energy away from the war against the Vietnamese. I wanted our movement to undermine the US war effort so that the US military would have to get out of Vietnam. Somit seemed to see everyone who rebelled against US government policy as enemy insurgents. He ended his chapter by saying: "Do unto your enemy what he would do unto you, but do it first!" This, from a vice president of our university! I felt the hairs stand up on my neck. What kind of people were running our society, I wondered? I looked around again to see if anyone was watching me. They weren't.

I didn't read any more there in the student lounge, but slipped the book back into the paper bag and left. When I got to my apartment, I turned on the lamp next to an old overstuffed chair and sat down to continue reading. I was the only one at home. It was getting dark outside, the wind was blowing and it was cold, but I was warm and I opened the book.

I skimmed the Table of Contents and then began with the first article.

It was titled, "On Guerrilla Warfare," and was by Brigadier General Samuel B. Griffith of the US Marine Corp. Written in 1961, he began by saying that there would likely be growing numbers of guerrilla wars. History had proved him correct. But his explanation caught my attention. He wrote: "A potential revolutionary situation exists in any country where the government consistently fails in its obligation to ensure at least a minimally decent standard for the great majority of its citizens..." That made sense. That is exactly what happened in Vietnam under 100 years of French colonialism and now under the rule of the US. He continued:

"People who live at subsistence level want first things to be put first...land, tools, fertilizers, something better than rags for their children, houses to replace their shacks, freedom from police oppression, medical attention, primary schools. Those who have known only poverty have begun to wonder why they should wait passively for improvements. They see – and not always through Red-tinted glasses – examples of peoples who have changed the structure of their societies and they ask, 'What do we have to lose?'" I had read elsewhere that 200,000 to 400,000 Vietnamese died of hunger and preventable diseases *every year* before the country achieved independence in 1946. This guy sounds like *us,* though I knew he wasn't. But he understands why people rebel.

He wrote that "guerrilla warfare was not invented by the Communists; for centuries, there have been guerrilla fighters. One of the most accomplished of them all was our own Revolutionary hero Francis Marion, 'the Swamp Fox.'" He went on to say that "Marion's guerrilla activities in South Carolina soon told heavily on the British, especially Cornwallis...Operating with the greatest speed from inaccessible bases, which he changed frequently, he struck his blows in rapid succession at isolated garrisons, convoys, and trains. His information was always timely and accurate, for the people supported him. The British, unable to cope with Marion, branded him a criminal..."

Incredible. This Brigadier General just laid out the similarities between our own Revolutionary War and the Revolutionary War of the Vietnamese. Something that I had done in my arguments with pro-war people. Both groups of revolutionaries waged a similar type of guerrilla war, both were fighting against a powerful colonial master which sought to exploit the colony, both were fighting a foreign aggressor who had invaded their homeland, both were fighting for independence, both had widespread support from the people, both had to fight homegrown puppets of the colonial power who were seen as traitors by the people, and both were branded as criminals by the colonial aggressor. Why couldn't our military and government leaders see that the Vietnamese were simply struggling for independence, just as our ancestors had done, and support the

Vietnamese revolutionists? Perhaps some did, but they kept it to themselves. The answer, I thought, was because these guys were benefiting by being part of an exploiting colonial power.

Brigadier General Griffith wrote about China prior to the Chinese Revolution when Mao and the Chinese Communist Party organized and led a huge popular revolutionary movement: "The peasant was fair game for everyone," Griffith wrote. "He was pillaged by tax collectors, robbed by landlords and usurers, at the mercy of rapacious soldiery and bandits…" Furthermore, he wrote, "An external factor had for almost a century contributed to the chaos of China: the unrelenting pressure and greed of foreign powers."

Amazing! That is exactly what we in the New Left were saying about the US in Vietnam. Was the Brigadier General sympathetic to the Chinese peasants? If so, why not Vietnamese peasants too?

Griffith went on to explain that Mao went in 1926 to Hunan to organize the peasants to wage a campaign for "land reform." He continued: "…the problem was how to get rid of the gentry landowners who fastened themselves to the peasants like leeches and (who) …kept the people constantly impoverished." The more I read the more this guy sounded like a communist revolutionary, though I was certain he wasn't one.

I was surprised. I didn't expect to see such insights from a high-ranking military leader, and presented so honestly. That wasn't the explanation they gave to the US troops, or the American people. I wondered if other contributors saw things the same way. I skipped through the book and found this from Chester Bowles, a Special Representative to President Kennedy. His contribution was originally published in the Department of State bulletin, March 5, 1962:

"More than a billion people in Asia and Africa have won their freedom since World War II. Since 1945, 44 new nations have been born. These newly independent peoples, joined by millions more in newly awakened Latin America, are now dreaming great dreams. Suddenly they have come to see that their ancient afflictions – disease, injustice, illiteracy, hunger, and poverty – are not part of God's plan for the unfortunate but evils to be fought and overcome…These people now know that the means exist by which their lives can be improved, and they are determined to improve them." I was stunned by this.

"The revolution of rising expectations is not a Communist plot," Bowles continued. "Had there never been a Marx, a Lenin, a Stalin – or even the idea of communism itself – there would still be this natural flow of pent-up desires…"

What was terrifying was that these military and political leaders who knew the truth, disregarded it, and threw themselves into the fight on the side of tyranny, oppression and injustice! And these were the people leading our country. This wasn't the country I grew up believing in. I saw these people as traitors, willing to destroy our country's reputation for personal wealth and power.

I knew what was at the bottom of it. I wondered if they would admit it. I found it in several other articles. In one, dated 1962, titled "Guerrilla War and U.S. Military Policy: A Study," Peter Paret, a military researcher at Princeton University and a former military intelligence officer, and John Shy, a history professor at Princeton and a West Point graduate, revealed the real reasons for US military involvement on the side of tyranny and war. They wrote:

"Only now, when guerrillas in Laos, Cuba, the Congo, and Algeria have directly touched our national interests, do we seem to be awakening to the full range of military possibilities." *Our national interests.* That's it! Major US corporations and banks have financial holdings, investments, and money-making enterprises in these foreign countries. When these businesses, which make such huge profits from the cheap natural resources, cheap labor, and new markets and military bases in other people's countries, feel that they are threatened, then the line has been crossed. They want to protect the possessions they've laid claim to. They want to send a message to the world that *they* are boss and they will have their way. That's capitalism. It's like a local neighborhood bully – like Carlton.

It was also striking to me that a large number of counterinsurgency experts who contributed to this book worked for major universities. In addition to Albert Somit at the University of Buffalo, and Peter Paret and John Shy at Princeton University, Charles Burton Marshall was at John Hopkins University in Washington, D. C., George A. Kelley was at Harvard University, Hans Kohn was a Professor of History at City College of New York, and Merle Kling was a Professor of Political Science at Washington University in St. Louis. SDS was right. There is a military-industrial-education complex, and it was revealed in the government's own Counterinsurgency book.

It's okay to have right-wing counterinsurgency experts working for the universities, with some holding top administrative positions, but Marxist, anti-war and other left-wing professors and activists were scrutinized, and some were fired.

Some authors were blunt and brutal. Charles Bohannan, a retired Lieutenant-Colonel in the Army with experience combating guerrillas in the Philippines, and a former anthropologist, wrote that there were four basic approaches to anti-guerrilla operations. The first one is "extermination or resettlement of the civilian population." That was exactly what the US military was doing in Vietnam, *exterminatng the civilian population!* It is madness! It is insanity! I remembered that US General Curtis LeMay said that the US should bomb the Vietnamese "back into the Stone Age." Those barbarians are behaving like Nazi war criminals, I thought.

Bohannan and a number of other authors in *Counterinsurgency* also talked about the importance of using informers and infiltrating the opposition movement to gain information about their activities, fingering activists to be arrested or wiped out, and to create internal mayhem, suspicion and internal fights. *That* had been going on in the movement in Buffalo. It was frightening. I wondered how far those in power would go to repress us. We New Left activists weren't guerrillas, but the government was using some of these same tactics – on a lesser scale – on us. The Black Panthers were bearing the brunt of it. I remembered the cold blooded police assassinations of Fred Hampton and Mark Clark, killed while asleep in their beds.

Just then I heard a noise at the back of our building. I quickly turned off the light and sat motionless in the dark, listening. My heart was pounding. Beads of sweat formed on my forehead. Does somebody know I have this document and followed me home? I got up slowly and felt my way along the walls toward the sound. Little streams of muted light filtered through the window shades, creating weird shadows across the floor. When I got to the back of the apartment, I looked out the window. There was a light from next door that partially lit up the area behind our building. I peered out from behind a curtain and carefully scanned the entire area. I didn't see anything. I looked and waited. Still nothing. After fifteen minutes, I figured no one was there and I went back to the front of the house, turned on the lamp, and resumed reading.

It was revealing to see that what these experts said among themselves was completely different from what they told the

American people. The US government line to the American people was that we were defending the rights and freedoms of the people of South Vietnam. Our government tried to play on the lofty ideals held by most Americans to get them to support a war based on lies.

There was more. Franklin A. Lindsay, a vice president of Itek Corporation and the former Chief of the United States Military Mission to Yugoslavia, wrote an article originally published in *Foreign Affairs* in January 1962 that was reprinted in the Counterinsurgency book. He referred to counterinsurgency operations which crushed independence movements years earlier in Malaya and the Phillipines, explaining that "...the side which uses violent reprisals most aggressively will dominate most of the people, even though their sympathies may lie in the other direction." That was exactly what the US was trying to do in Vietnam. Lindsay then wrote that in 1962, the independence forces – which he called Communists, were on the verge of victory in South Vietnam *then!*

That's not what the US government told us. The American public was told in the early 1960's that things were looking very good for a quick victory over the communists. I remember reading optimistic reports in *Vietnam! Vietnam!* I took the book from my shelf.

Defense Secretary Robert McNamara was quoted in *The New York Times* on May 12, 1962: "After 48 hours in South Vietnam Mr. McNamara was tremendously encouraged by developments...'I found nothing but progress and hope for the future," he said."

In October of 1963, McNamara announced to the public: "The major part of the U.S. military task can be completed by the end of 1965. In October 1965 the war was much worse, but McNamara managed this fairy tale for the American people via the mass media: "We have stopped losing." Now, five years later in 1970, Nixon said he had a secret plan for peace, but the war was worse than ever.

I realized that all this was simply to fool the American people into supporting the US war effort, and coaxing more young American boys to sign-up for flag and country and promises of military glory in a war that the Vietnamese liberation forces had already won.

I thought that if only someone like Brigadier General Griffith, who wrote the first article in the counterinsurgency book, would have stepped forward to tell the real story before we got involved militarily, maybe the war could have been avoided. Fifty-eight thousand Americans and *two million* Vietnamese could have lived. But he didn't. Or if he tried, he was silenced.

I thought about another Marine Corp leader, Major General Smedley Butler from the early 20th century, who did have the courage to tell the truth. I looked through some of my history books and found it in *Labor's Untold Story*. Major General Butler wrote: "I spent thirty-three years and four months in active service as a member of our country's most agile military force – the Marine Corps. I served in all the commissioned ranks from second lieutenant to major-general. And during that period I spent most of my time being a high class muscle man for Big Business, for Wall Street, and for the bankers. In short, I was a racketeer for capitalism.

"Thus, I helped make Mexico and especially Tampico safe for the American oil interests in 1914," Butler continued. "I helped make Haiti and Cuba a decent place for the National City Bank to collect revenues in. I helped purify Nicaragua for the international banking house of Brown Brothers in 1900-1912. I brought light to the Dominican Republic for American sugar interests in 1916. I helped make Honduras 'right' for American fruit companies in 1903. In China in 1927, I helped to see that Standard Oil went its way unmolested." Similar deceptions were used in all those other wars by our government to get earlier generations of Americans to support war – 'we just want to help the suffering people of those poor countries' was the common refrain. It was sickening to think about the millions of people, here and abroad, who were sacrificed for lies.

I had to get this information out to people, I thought. But how? I couldn't just have copies of the book printed and hand them out in the Student Union. People would wonder where I got the book, and I was certain the authorities would be even more interested. I had to get the information out in a way where it couldn't be traced to anyone. I decided to talk to a couple of trusted friends in the movement for their thoughts.

But things were spinning out of control quickly. The leadership of SDS and the movement was under attack. Three Buffalo SDS leaders had recently fled the country to avoid arrest on numerous felony charges. Others were laying low. I decided to make an anonymous leaflet and quote heavily from the book, and leave stacks around campus and in the community. I wanted to use another typewriter so the leaflet couldn't be traced back to mine.

But I didn't have time. The next level of repression was right around the corner.

Chapter 48

National Student Strike

I was walking down the stairs with Ken and Ira from the second floor strike headquarters in Norton Union on Monday, May 4, 1970, when John, another strike leader stopped us on the stairwell while hurrying upstairs.

"Did you hear what happened?" he asked breathlessly, obviously agitated.

"No," I responded.

"Four students were just killed at Kent State by the National Guard. They were protesting against the war."

"What? When did it happen?" I asked.

"Just a little while ago," John replied. "We need to call a mass meeting to protest this." He was tall and lanky and turned and leapt up the stairs two and three steps at a time.

I looked at Ken and Ira. We all were silent for a moment.

"So, it's come to this," Ira said. "Everything is on a new level now. They've decided they *can* kill us. They couldn't snuff out the anti-war movement with lies, suspensions, arrests, beatings and firings, so now they've decided to kill us."

"Well, it's terrible, but what's the surprise," said Ken. "We know they are vicious, brutal bastards!"

"Look at what they've been doing to the Vietnamese for years," I added. "We hoped this day would never come, but it has. They don't see us as any different than the Vietnamese. Except we're exposing their rotten system right in their own backyard, and putting up roadblocks to their war efforts right here at home. Let's go back to the strike headquarters." I was outraged at the killings and could feel the adrenalin rushing through my body.

We turned and went back upstairs.

There was pandemonium. Strike leaders were pouring into the office and plans were made to have an emergency meeting.

Students started massing in Norton Union where strike leaders were screaming through the sound system denouncing the government. Through a national telephone tree we had set up with radical students on other campuses, we started getting reports of other Universities going out on strike. We had been on strike since February.

Dan Bentivogli, out on bail from his felony arrest, and other leaders of Youth Against War and Fascism, put up long sheets of butcher paper from the ceiling to the floor in the main hallway in Norton Union with the heading: "Schools on Strike." I helped them letter the names onto the paper of new schools that were joining the strike movement as we learned of them. The school names were in big black letters three inches high. Soon one sheet was full and we started another. Students gathered around the sheets and cheered every time a new university's name was added to the list. We often got information about what the striking students were doing at these schools, and took it down in notes. Some of these notes got transferred onto leaflets.

Ken, Ira and I, along with many others, helped hand out leaflets announcing another large mass meeting on Tuesday. Small group meetings took place in every nook and cranny that afternoon. Old affinity groups reactivated themselves and new ones formed, and Ken, Ira and I met quietly in a darkened classroom to plan our activities for the evening. As the darkness of night fell, our group and other small affinity groups slipped out into the night. Every military and administrative target on campus was attacked. Area banks had their windows smashed. Our group slipped in and out of the shadows, while police cars raced throughout the university district with sirens blaring trying to find the mini guerilla units.

On Tuesday, May 5, three thousand students gathered on campus for another rally at mid-day, and then surged onto Main Street and started marching toward downtown to the Military Induction Center and the Draft Board. We took over the entire street, our feet stomping on the ground in a cadence, row upon row, stretching from one curb to the other curb. I had been to the Draft Induction Center many times before to hand out leaflets against the war and the draft. Today things might get more intense down there. I was thinking of how we could block the entrance to the building to stop the induction of young men into the war.

But the Buffalo Police were out in force. They were lined up across Main Street at Hertel Avenue, along with police cars, K-9 trucks and other riot control equipment to block our march. They probably heard from their informers that we were headed for the Draft Induction Center. We approached the viaduct before Hertel

Avenue and stopped. Main Street went under a viaduct that carried railroad tracks overhead. There were concrete walls lining the sides of the viaduct from where we stood all the way to the other side where the police were, about 500 feet away. Traffic had been diverted from this section of Main Street, so it was just us and the cops.

I was up in the front with Ken and Ira. While I was angry, I still had my wits about me.

"If we go down there, the cops could send reinforcements over the railroad tracks and come around behind us and trap us down there and attack us," I said to both of them, "like they did at Norton Union." Others also saw the potential danger of advancing.

So, we headed for the sides of the railroad tracks. We were joined by other students and we started dragging old railroad ties, discarded furniture, boxes, rolls of paper, rocks, bricks, boards and tree branches that littered the railroad right-of-way into the street. We stuffed old newspapers, cardboard boxes and ripped off sheets from the paper rolls into the barricade and set it on fire. More wood and furniture was thrown onto the barricade until it was five or six feet high in some places. Flames leapt into the air and black smoke billowed under the viaduct and curled up the sides by the railroad tracks.

With the cops effectively cut off from us, students went back to the campus and attacked the military and Administrative targets again. It took the cops an hour to clear away the barricade and get back to the university, but by then we were gone. When the cops arrived, we had already gone out the other side of the campus into University Plaza where windows were smashed in the Manufacturers & Traders Trust bank.

By Wednesday morning, a student strike wave was sweeping the country. The National Student Association called for a National Student Strike and a National Strike Information Center was functioning at Brandeis University. That became the central location for people to call if their school was involved in strike activities, and the one center we could contact to get the most comprehensive list of striking schools. Within the week we learned that many major universities were closed in what was becoming a national student strike. What struck me was that there must have been months and likely years of educating, organizing, protests and anti-war actions on these campuses before the events of May 4, similar to what had been going on at UB. It was also noteworthy that many university and college professors joined this strike wave.

Many of the smaller colleges and community colleges and even some high schools joined the strike. In western New York, strikes took place at schools where there had been little anti-war activity before. At Alfred University and Alfred State Agricultural and Technical College, located in a rural area of upstate New York, students went on strike and thousands went into town and shut down traffic and business for hours.

The Faculty Senate at Brockport State College voted to support the national student strike and 1,000 students marched through that small peaceful village and staged a sit-in demonstration in Main Street. Strike votes were scheduled at Niagara County Community College in Niagara Falls, and at Fredonia State College, located about an hour drive southwest of Buffalo on the way to Erie, Pennsylvania. We had distributed or sent anti-war leaflets to students at the last two colleges many months earlier.

Over 3,000 students from all the colleges in the Albany area marched on the state capitol Wednesday in support of the national student strike. At the capitol, the students burned President Nixon in effigy and lowered the American flag to half-mast. Two propane gas tanks exploded on one Albany area campus.

Stony Brook students joined the nation-wide strike and 500 students staged a two-hour sit-in in the street in front of the local draft board to stop the induction of new soldiers into the military.

At Cornell, in Ithaca, 3,000 students held a rally at the ROTC building and ripped down a sign commemorating the Department of Defense's contribution to the construction of the building.

The University of Syracuse closed after fires broke out across campus Wednesday night. Classes were cancelled at St. Lawrence, Skidmore, Potsdam State, Clarkson, Canton Tech and Wells College along the St. Lawrence Seaway in support of the national student strike.

Students occupied two buildings at New Paltz near the Hudson River in support of the strike, and students staged a sit-in in the Administrators offices at Cortland State University College.

In New York City, every college and university was on strike or conducting strike activities, and many high schools were shut down in support of the strike.

In Austin, Texas, the University of Texas was on strike, and 2,000 students stormed the State Capitol and were dispersed by tear gas. The state capitol was evacuated by the Texas Rangers.

At the University of California at San Diego, 200 students occupied the fifth floor of the Science Building for ten hours to protest war-related research on campus, the Kent State killings and the war.

Mass protests closed Boston University, Brown, Princeton, and Tufts.

In Madison, students at the University of Wisconsin were on strike, and students occupied the Administration building after 4,000 people held an anti-war rally. The National Guard was called in to subdue the students, rioting was widespread and 21 students were arrested.

Protestors at Washington University in St. Louis burned down the ROTC building on campus.

Over 1,000 students at the University of Illinois in Chicago marched to the ROTC building, forced their way inside and smashed windows and furniture.

At the University of California at Berkeley, 2,000 students rioted for hours in the university district and attempted to burn down the ROTC building there.

Protestors at the University of Kentucky destroyed the ROTC building there by fire.

On May 7, over 1,500 students at West Virginia University smashed windows and destroyed other property at the ROTC office there.

That same day, students at the University of Michigan at Ann Arbor occupied the ROTC building for 24 hours and then set fire to it.

During the first week in May, 30 ROTC buildings were burned or bombed on campuses across the country, and the National Guard was dispatched to 21 campuses in sixteen states.

On May 7, black and white students at New York University (NYU) protested the killings and the war, and then held a $6 million computer system ransom and demanded $100,000 to pay bail for jailed Black Panthers who they said were framed on false charges.

On May 8, hundreds of student protestors occupied the Student Union at the University of New Mexico and were forcibly evicted from the building by police and National Guard. One hundred and twenty-two protestors were arrested and nine were stabbed with bayonets and were hospitalized.

At Colorado State University in Fort Collins, students destroyed a building with fire to protest the war.

On May 8, at Concord Teachers College in Illinois, protests resulted in $100,000 damage to the Administration Building.

On May 9, in a hastily organized demonstration, over 100,000 people swarmed into Washington D.C. to protest the war.

That same day, 200 students at Southern Illinois University at Carbondale were arrested for curfew violations, and 9,000 national guardsmen were on stand-by throughout the state.

On May 11, over 1,000 angry students and police rioted at the University of Southern California in Los Angeles. Students ransacked the administration building protesting the Kent State killings and the earlier arrests of anti-war demonstrators on that campus.

That same day, ROTC offices at Occidental College in southern California were firebombed.

Also that same day, a student at the University of California at San Diego died ten hours after he set himself on fire to protest the war in Vietnam.

The next day, on May 12, students ended a two-day occupation of the ROTC building at San Diego State after police roughed-up and arrested 32 people.

That same day, riots broke out between student protestors at the University of South Carolina at Columbia with police and National Guardsmen where 45 students were arrested and many were beaten.

On May 13, police with dogs evicted 100 anti-war students from a building they occupied overnight at Virginia Polytechnic Institute.

On May 14, police opened fire on black students at Jackson State University in Mississippi who were protesting against the war and the killings at Kent State, killing two and wounding ten. National Guardsmen had been patrolling the area in Armored Personnel Carriers, and the police were armed with carbines, submachine guns, shotguns and other assault weapons. After the shooting, investigators counted over 460 rounds shot at Alexander Hall, a women's dormitory. Police claimed they thought a shot came from the dorm but no evidence was found. I was outraged, as were many others across the country, and the protests escalated. Now, many of the protestors cited the dead students at Jackson State and added those murders to their list of grievances.

The University of North Dakota was on strike and organized an anti-ROTC rally on May 15, when the governor visited to review the ROTC corp.

On May 20 a confrontation between police and students at the University of Santa Cruz in California broke out when protesters blocked a bus carrying draftees for military service.

That same day, riots broke out between students at Fresno State in California and police, in part, over the firing of eight popular ethnic studies faculty members. In response to the repression, a computer system worth $1 million was destroyed.

Even the University of Idaho joined the national student strike, with support from the university's vice president and the city's mayor.

The student strike was so powerful in California that Governor Ronald Reagan was forced to shut down the entire California university system, involving nearly 300,000 students on 28 campuses. The student strike was so strong in Pennsylvania that the entire state university system of 18 campuses was also closed. Much of the New York State university system was shut down, as well as those in Illinois, Massachusetts, Minnesota, Wisconsin and other states.

In early June, five days and nights of protests at the University of California at Santa Barbara resulted in 622 arrests.

While such confrontations garnered headlines, completely legal and peaceful protests took place on even more campuses, including on many considered politically conservative. Those protests also stopped the normal functioning of many of those universities, at least temporarily, and sent a message that anti-war sentiment had permeated the majority of higher educational institutions in the US. At many of these universities, administrators either supported their students, or at least did not over-react to their protests.

The government lost credibility in the eyes of a majority of students, youth, and many of their teachers. You cannot sustain a country when its brightest young people and much of their generation, have lost faith in the system. What made matters worse for Nixon was that large and growing numbers of Americans from all walks of life, including leaders of a broad cross-section of organizations and institutions, began to speak out against the war and the Nixon Administration. This sea change in public consciousness and action would have a profound impact on the nation over the next two years.

On June 13, 1970, Nixon convened the President's Commission on Campus Unrest, headed by former Pennsylvania Governor William Scranton. When the report was completed, it began: "The crisis on American campuses has no parallel in the history of the nation." It went on to say: "We utterly condemn violence. Students who bomb and burn are criminals. Police and National Guardsmen who needlessly shoot or assault students are criminals...We must declare a national cease-fire." All well and good, I thought, but what about US presidents who carpet bomb, napalm, and slaughter millions of people in Vietnam and other countries? That makes Presidents Johnson and Nixon criminals according to Nixon's own report. I saw them as war criminals who should be prosecuted just like Nazi war criminals were prosecuted at Nuremburg. If the president's Commission "utterly condemns violence" and calls for a ceasefire at home, how about an immediate ceasefire in Vietnam where the killings and maimings were taking place on a level a million times greater than in the US. The hypocrisy of the US government was glaring and sickening, and Nixon's credibility among the public was plummeting.

The report went on: "The violence must stop because it is wrong. It destroys human life..." Yes, that is what the anti-war movement had been saying for years about the destruction of human life in Vietnam. "It (violence) must stop because no nation will long tolerate violence without repression." Yes, we saw that. 'Keep up these protests and there will be more Kent States and Jackson States,' or worse, the government was warning.

Top government officials were stunned by the magnitude of the national strike. Henry Kissinger, the chief advisor to President Nixon on the war, admitted this years later in his book, *White House Years:* "The very fabric of government was falling apart. The Executive Branch was shell-shocked. Their children and the children of their friends took part in the demonstrations." That's true. Defense Secretary Robert McNamara's son Craig, for one, was a student anti-war protestor at Stanford University.

Over two million students at over 400 colleges and universities across the country went on strike against the war and the repression of students. Over four million students, comprising over half of all college students, participated in some form of anti-war protest in connection with the national student strike. In 1970, the FBI recorded 1,785 student demonstrations against the war, including the occupation of 313 buildings, and the arrest of 7,200 students for protest activity. It was by far the largest general strike of students, supported by many teachers, in the history of our country and it deeply shook those in power.

After two straight days and nights of protests and rioting at the University at Buffalo, Acting President Regan announced that no academic penalty would result if students chose to leave campus, bringing the semester to an official close. We had been shut down for almost the entire semester.

During the strike at UB, the top four administrators all resigned: Acting President Regan, Vice President Warren Bennis, Vice President Richard Siggelkow, and Assistant to the President Theodore Friend. World renowned sociologist Edgar Friedenberg, a strong supporter of many student activists, resigned in disgust at the Administration's terrible handling of the crisis.

"The university now exists in a vacuum," said Harold Segal, professor in the Faculty of Natural Sciences and Mathematics. "We are without administrators." Dr. Segal, a sympathizer of the students, also resigned his position on the Faculty Senate Executive Committee.

On the third night of rioting, people in unmarked cars – we believed they were Buffalo police and right-wing vigilantes, started shooting at us. I was there that night and heard the gunfire. An unmarked car roared near us with a gun sticking out of the window, and Ken, Ira and I ducked into some thick bushes. It was terrifying. I thought of the horrors that the Vietnamese people faced daily, and for many years. If spotted, we would have been easy targets. We had no guns with us, and even if we did, we would have been no match for the armed might of the Buffalo police. We also saw Buffalo police cars speeding through campus, and heard more gun shots. We got out of there as quickly as we could. Twelve students were wounded that night.

That was the last night of rioting at UB. Everyone realized that if the protests continued, people would likely be killed. We all went back to the drawing board to figure out how to take our message into the community to organize pressure on the government from new and larger constituencies.

In June of 1970, I worked with other anti-war activists on an underground youth and counter-culture newspaper that was begun in Buffalo called *Cold Steel.* I was the principal author of a four- page feature article describing US involvement in Vietnam. I used all the history and facts I had studied and written about before, and it was a powerful indictment of US policy and action in Vietnam. We published 50,000 copies of that article as a stand alone piece and distributed them at high schools, colleges, worksites and in neighborhoods. But I didn't feel comfortable with the direction and tone of *Cold Steel.* It started to glorify violent revolution, drugs, and even criminal behavior – excused because the system was so criminal itself. I disagreed with this. Our country may be run by criminals, but it was important to me that we hold ourselves to a higher standard of moral principles. I spoke with other anti-war activists who felt the same way. Many were workers and union members, or had experience in the working world and with unions, so we made plans to publish a different type of newspaper.

I left *Cold Steel* after one month, and in July, I became a founding member of a new newspaper called *New Age*, which was written by and for working families in the Buffalo area. It was named after a similar newspaper that was published in Buffalo in the early years of the 1900's. While most of us were former UB students, the majority of its founders had been or were currently workers in Buffalo. My friends, Jim and Michael, for example, got involved in this project.

One of our goals was to help make the labor movement more politically progressive and activist. We saw organized labor as a very powerful political force, one that could apply tremendous pressure on the government to end the war, eradicate racism and other forms of discrimination, and win significant improvements for workers and the entire society. We would do this by reporting on labor struggles in Buffalo and elsewhere, and work to build solidarity between the labor movement, the anti-war movement and the civil rights movement. There were hundreds of thousands of union families in western New York, a huge and powerful constituency if informed, organized and aroused. I believed that if we could move significant numbers of workers and their unions to oppose the war, elected officials who relied on the votes, money and volunteer hours of working people would be forced to cut off money for the war.

The strike at UB produced some remarkable victories. ROTC was abolished on our campus. Similar struggles elsewhere led to the abolishment of ROTC at over 40 other colleges and universities nationwide, crippling the officer training program. ROTC trained and supplied half of the officers for Vietnam, so the closing of so many ROTC programs meant a serious shortage of leadership on the battlefield. This undermined the war effort and forced Nixon to withdraw more troops. I was ecstatic. Our work had an effect on changing government policy.

The Day Care Center was formally approved. Graduate teaching assistants had established their own permanent union. The multi-disciplinary and community-oriented Colleges were institutionalized and grew from one College to ten over the next couple of years, teaching and training many thousands of students in community organizing and providing a deeper analysis of the problems of society. While the Workers College wasn't approved as an official college, many of its courses were incorporated into the very progressive Social Sciences College and several other colleges. I later got very involved in Social Sciences College, and in 1975, I became an instructor there.

Other gains from the student strike included the establishment of the Women's Studies College, a Black Studies Program, a Puerto Rican Studies Program, a college to study ecology and other important topics. I heard that similar programs were also started at many other colleges across the country. Earth Day was born nationally during this period and helped launch a massive environmental movement to stop polluting our land, water and food. That movement expanded greatly over the decades, and by 2000 was working to save our planet from the dangers of global warming.

The National Student Strike not only served as an example of the big gains that could be made from such a powerful political movement. But it also opened the floodgates of opposition to the war and injustice from people from all walks of life, and from every corner of our country. This opposition came even from organizations that had been staunch supporters of the war.

In the decades since the 1970 National Student Strike, it is remarkable, but not surprising, that those with great wealth and power have effectively eliminated this unprecedented protest from the history books and the public's collective memory. And for good reason. It terrified them. They don't want another generation of young people to learn about, and possibly emulate, an incredible social and political movement that empowered a generation.

Chapter 49

National Anti-War Movement

People from various backgrounds had protested against the war for years, but except for students, mostly in modest numbers. After the tumultuous National Student Strike of May 1970, peaceful protests were now seen as acceptable by millions of people. In fact, respectful and peaceful protests looked good compared to the riots and rebellions that took place on hundreds of college campuses.

Now, doctors, lawyers, university presidents, religious leaders, union leaders and members, ethnic and racial minorities, community residents, business people, politicians, military personal, government leaders, and millions of ordinary people added their voices of opposition to the war.

One of the most important and influential organizations to speak out was Vietnam Veterans Against the War (VVAW). Formed by Vietnam veterans in 1967, they captured the attention of the American people through public forums, marches and demonstrations. I worked with a number of Vietnam veterans in Buffalo, including Al Donohue and Dan Amigone, who were active in the UB Vets Club and who became members and leaders of the Buffalo Chapter of VVAW. They, along with other Vietnam veterans provided leadership for many veterans in western New York and nationally. VVAW played a huge role in helping to build the anti-war movement inside the military, and winning over large numbers of Americans to the anti-war cause.

On May 16, 1970, in the midst of the massive National Student Strike, coordinated anti-war protests by thousands of active duty servicemen took place at seventeen military bases across the county, including at Fort Bragg, North Carolina; Fort Hood, Texas; Fort Riley, Kansas; Fort Meade, Maryland; Fort McClellan, Alabama; and Fort Benning, Georgia. This was the largest anti-war protest by active-duty GI's do date, stunning the military officer corps and the Nixon Administration.

Combined with the draft resistance movement, these actions, and the increasing numbers of soldiers in Vietnam who were refusing to fight, were crippling the US military. During the spring of 1970, for example, the draft resistance movement was so strong that it was hindering military recruitment in many areas of the country. At the University of Berkeley alone, over 2,500 students turned in their draft cards and said they wouldn't go.

But the anti-war movement spread into the mainstream of society, with important leaders of well established institutions voicing opposition to the war. In May of 1970, during the National Student Strike, the presidents of 37 major universities and colleges, including many of the elite centers of learning, sent a letter to Nixon demanding that he end the war immediately.

Opposition to the war inside the government was spreading at all levels. Later in May, more than 250 State Department and foreign aid employees signed a letter that was sent to the Secretary of State criticizing the war.

In June of 1970, the US Senate voted 58-37 to cut off money for training US troops to fight in Cambodia. While it didn't pass, it marked a large increase in the anti-war sentiment growing in Congress.

Feeling the heat from the National Student Strike in May and the broader anti-war movement, Nixon publicly announced in June that 50,000 US troops would be withdrawn from Vietnam by October 15, leaving 150,000 there. That was a good first step, but Nixon secretly increased bombing runs over Vietnam in an attempt to "change the color of the corpses," as the anti-war movement charged.

Also in June of 1970, a national rank and file labor organization was founded in Chicago, Trade Unionists for Action and Democracy, by over 800 trade unionists from over 50 unions. Workers from the Buffalo area attended. One of their goals was to end the war in Vietnam, marking a sharp break with the pro-war George Meany leadership of the AFL-CIO. I was thrilled with this development.

Also in June, two national anti-war coalitions were organized with hundreds of affiliated organizations representing millions of students, seniors, trade unionists, women, workers, civil rights organizations, religious groups, professionals, community organizations and others. One became the National Peace Action Coalition, and the other the People's Coalition for Peace and Justice. The later was the largest peace coalition ever formed in US history up to that time. The major goals of both coalitions were to immediately end the war, stop the bombing, and bring home all the troops. Our anti-war movement in Buffalo affiliated with PCPJ and I was among those in the local leadership group.

In August, the US Chief Negotiator attended his first session of the Paris Peace Talks, set up to end the war.

On August 29, 1970, over 25,000 people marched through working-class neighborhoods in East Los Angeles in the Chicano Moratorium to protest against the war. Students and workers and community residents and their families participated. The police attacked the march, and a popular antiwar journalist, Ruben Salazar, was shot to death. The community was outraged and even more people turned against the war and the government.

In the summer of 1970, a group of commissioned officers formed the Concerned Officers Movement; one of their goals was to end the war. Hundreds of black and white anti-military, anti-racist and anti-war GI's pressed their demands that broke out in riots at foreign military bases, including at the Nellingen, Bad Hersfeld and Neu Ulm bases in Germany.

In the summer and fall of 1970, thousands of students and other anti-war activists turned their attention to the upcoming congressional elections in November and threw themselves into the campaigns of strong anti-war candidates.

By September of 1970 I was back at work at Standard Mirror, and our progressive workers' group put out our first issue of *New Age* that month with an article denouncing Nixon's war on Vietnam and Cambodia, and articles supporting auto workers and chemical workers who were on strike in Buffalo. We published 10,000 copies and distributed them at the work places we wrote about, steel mills, auto factories, arms manufacturing companies, hospitals, at government buildings and other businesses in western New York, and started making contacts with workers who were against the war.

In October, Nixon asked the North Vietnamese and the National Liberation Front in South Vietnam to agree to a ceasefire and proposed negotiations to work out a plan for the withdrawal of all US military forces. Unfortunately, he also attached other demands that were unacceptable.

In November 1970, a group of some of the most progressive and staunch anti-war candidates ever were elected to Congress with help from the anti-war movement, including Bella Abzug, a founder of Women's Strike for Peace in New York, and Ron Dellums, an anti-war Berkeley City Councilman in California. The strategy was to beef up the anti-war representatives in Congress to get Congress to cut off money for the war.

From September 1970 through January 1971, I wrote five of seven feature anti-war articles for *New Age* (at least one anti-war article appeared in each issue), including articles about US corporate war profiteers and the need for US and Vietnamese worker solidarity, the history of US involvement in Vietnam, unions who were against the war, and articles about workers, women and students who were organizing against the war.

With cutbacks in US ground troops and more soldiers refusing to fight, liberation forces in South Vietnam scored impressive victories throughout the later half of 1970. This further weakened the moral of US and South Vietnamese troops and pro-war supporters. Nixon relied more and more on bombing as US troops were pulled back to safer areas. Protests continued in the US.

On January 1, 1971, the US Congress voted to forbid the use of US ground troops in Cambodia and Laos, marking a big set-back for the Nixon Administration.

Also in January, South Dakota Senator George McGovern announced his candidacy for the presidency; a major plank in his platform was to end the war in Vietnam.

From January 31 – February 2, 1971, VVAW held a riveting forum in Detroit called the "Winter Soldier" Investigations where Vietnam veterans gave public testimony about atrocities that they and other US soldiers committed or witnessed against the Vietnamese people. The veterans made an urgent plea to end the war. This hearing was covered in the anti-war press and ignored by most but not all of the commercial media. Many supporters of the war and fence-sitting moderates who heard about the hearings now turned against the war.

Also early in 1971, Business Executives Move for a Vietnam Peace opened an office in Washington, D. C. and began lobbying Congress to end the war. Founded several years earlier by Henry Niles, Board Chairman of Baltimore Life Insurance Company, the group attracted 1,000 business executives. They were very effective lobbyists in Congress, influencing moderate and conservative pro-business Representatives and Senators to oppose the war.

On February 22, 1971, both houses of Congress initiated legislation that would forbid any support for South Vietnamese government military action in North Vietnam.

On April 19, 1971, Vietnam Veterans Against the War began a five-day protest in Washington, D.C. They came in wheelchairs and on crutches, and they marched and lobbied representatives in Congress, and then testified before congressional hearings. On April 23, over 1,000 Vietnam veterans filed past the White House and threw their Vietnam medals – Silver Stars, Bronze Stars, Purple Hearts and others – over the fence. This was one of the most dramatic anti-war protests ever. This was covered by the national media and was witnessed by many millions of Americans watching television news. Public opinion grew stronger against the war.

On April 24, between 300,000 and 500,000 protestors held a massive anti-war rally in Washington, organized by the National Peace Action Coalition, under the banner "Out Now!" Over 150,000 protested in San Francisco – the largest ever demonstration in that city up to that date.

On May 5, 1971, tens of thousands of anti-war protestors engaged in sit-ins and other acts of civil disobedience in the streets of Washington D. C. Initiated by Rennie Davis, a former SDS leader and convicted defendant of the Chicago 8, this massive protest was supported by many people and organizations active in the People's Coalition for Peace and Justice. The slogan for the demonstration was, "If the government doesn't stop the war, we'll stop the government." I helped publicize both the April 24th and May 5th demonstrations, in part, through articles I wrote in *New Age,* and we helped organize groups of workers from Buffalo to go to Washington. Protestors shut down government buildings on May 5, and over 12,600 people were arrested while blocking streets and the entrances to government buildings. It was the largest number of people ever arrested in our nation's history in one day.

In May 1971, there were 250 independent anti-war newspapers published in cities and towns all over the country with a circulation estimated at between 4-6 million. They were distributed to students and youth, soldiers and veterans, trade unionists and non-union workers, teachers, nurses and other professionals, Blacks, Latinos, and Asians, seniors, and to churches, community organizations, elected officials, government workers, the mass media and the general public. *New Age* was one of them.

On May 15, 1971, the day anti-war soldiers called "Armed Farces Day," there were anti-war demonstrations on 19 US military bases.

In June 1971, a former Marine Colonel wrote in the *Armed Forces Journal* that "the morale, discipline and battle-worthiness of the U. S. Armed Forces are, with a few salient exceptions, lower and worse than at any time in this century and possibly in the history of the United States."

On June 3-4, over 300 delegates attended the Emergency Summit Conference of Asian, Black, Brown, Puerto Rican, and Red in Gary, Indiana to plan increased anti-war organizing among people of color.

In the June 1971 issue of *New Age,* I wrote an article about how the Oil Workers union (OCAW) broke the story of how major US oil companies, including Mobil, Esso (later Exxon), Gulf and others, were planning to carve up the coast-line around six southeast Asian countries to explore for oil. Gaining control of Vietnam was key to their strategy. Our headline read: "Are Our Sons Dying Because of Oil?" Ten thousand copies were distributed to union workers at Bethlehem Steel, General Motors, Ford, several oil refineries and other big corporations in Western New York where young workers were being drafted for military service in Vietnam.

On June 13, *The New York Times* began publishing the government's secret history of the war in Vietnam that had been leaked to the paper by a high-level government war planner, Daniel Ellsberg, who had turned against the war. Called the Pentagon Papers, *The Washington Post* and many other newspapers also started publishing sections of this document, and television stations across the country, including in Buffalo, carried the story. This coverage went on for the rest of the year. The Pentagon Papers confirmed what the anti-war movement had been saying about the war for years. The government's credibility was in tatters as more supporters of the war, including those high in the government, now turned against it.

On July 1, 1971, feeling the heat from the anti-war movement, Congress reduced the legal voting age from 21 to 18. We had loudly criticized the government for forcing young men 18 and 19 years old to fight and die in Vietnam without giving them the right to vote. It felt great to have been part of the movement that brought this change.

Also in July, 1971, women's rights activists Congresswomen Bella Abzug and Shirley Chisholm, along with Gloria Steinem, Betty Friedan, Myrlie Evers and others – many were strong anti-war activists, held the founding convention of the Women's National

403

Political Caucus to help elect women to political office. The organization was successful, and many of the women they helped elect added to the growing anti-war block in Congress.

In August, Clergy and Laymen Concerned held a national conference in Ann Arbor, Michigan, attended by 500 religious leaders, to step up their protests against the war and to target Nixon's relentless and indiscriminate bombing campaign.

On August 21, 1971 five anti-war activists broke into the Buffalo Draft Board to destroy draft files and were arrested at gunpoint. The following day, 28 protestors, mostly Catholic priests and lay people, were arrested in Camden, New Jersey after a raid on the Draft Board files there. The Group in Camden had been infiltrated by an undercover FBI agent who set them up. Over 35 Draft Board offices had been broken into and over one million files had been destroyed since 1967.

That fall, over 1,000 active duty soldiers signed an anti-war petition circulated by VVAW.

On October 2, 1971 a referendum was held in San Diego after months of intense anti-war organizing asking voters if the U.S.S. Constellation war ship should leave San Diego for Vietnam. Eighty-two percent of civilians and 73% of servicemen who voted in the referendum said "No," and nine sailors refused to sail and took sanctuary in a San Diego church.

Also that fall, sailors organized the Stop Our Ship movement, and sailors on the USS Coral Sea ship, departing from San Diego, secretly defused bombs that were on board and headed for Vietnam.

On November 19, 1971, the U.S. National Conference of Bishops endorsed a forceful resolution opposing the Vietnam War, stunning the Nixon Administration, as large influential former allies deserted the war effort.

By the end of 1971, growing numbers of troops weren't fighting, and government figures showed that for every 100 soldiers, 17 went AWOL and seven deserted. Desertions from the military had risen to almost 90,000, double what they were in 1967.

In January 1972, I was one of three delegates from the Buffalo Chapter of the People's Coalition for Peace and Justice to attend the PCPJ National Coordinating Committee meeting in Boston to plan the year's anti-war and pro-justice activities nationally. Over 300 delegates attended from cities and towns across the country. A full calendar of peace and justice activities was approved for the year.

On January 13, 1972, Nixon responded to the growing pressure of the anti-war movement and announced the withdrawal of 70,000 more US troops within the next three months, leaving 69,000 troops still in Vietnam. Under unrelenting pressure, Nixon had been forced to withdraw 400,000 US troops since taking office. The anti-war movement continued to charge Nixon with conducting a massive bombing campaign that was indiscriminately killing tens of thousands of Vietnamese men, women and children.

I joined millions of people from all walks of life to work in the campaign of the strongest anti-war presidential candidate, the Democratic Senator from South Dakota, George McGovern. Anti-war sentiment was so widespread, that other major Democratic presidential candidates felt compelled to come out against the war, but not as forcefully as Senator McGovern, and he won the Democratic Party nomination for president. During the general election campaign, the Nixon Administration waged a dirty tricks crusade against McGovern, trying to scare the public by painting him as an irresponsible radical who would destroy our country.

In February, representatives from most US peace organizations, many student and youth groups, unions, civil rights organizations, church groups and others were among 1,200 delegates from 84 countries in Versailles at the World Assembly for Peace and Independence of the People's of Indochina, further isolating the Nixon Administration internationally. It seemed that the entire world had come to Vietnam's defense against the devil in the White House and his corporate allies.

On April 1, 1972, ten thousand people marched in Harrisburg, Pennsylvania to protest the trial of the Harrisburg 7, anti-war leaders framed on wild charges, including conspiracy to kidnap Nixon's war advisor, Henry Kissinger. One of the defendants was Reverend Philip Berrigan, a well-known Catholic priest who was among the leaders of the anti-war movement. Their defense attorney was Ramsey Clark, former Attorney General under President Johnson, who had turned strongly against the war. In nearby York, several days earlier, executives at American Machine and Foundry, makers of 500-pound bombs for Vietnam, announced that there had been "sabotage" in their factory when they found that Vietnam-bound bombs had been disarmed by workers.

Also in April, a GI based in Hawaii told VVAW that the Nixon Administration had nuclear weapons targeted on Hanoi. Out of

405

desperation, it looked like Nixon was considering the nuclear weapons option again. Protestors responded immediately with mass leafleting, marches, occupying buildings and student strikes in scores of cities across the US. PCPJ called for an emergency demonstration in Washington, D. C. on April 15, and the National Student Association called for a national student strike for April 21, both events to protest the threatened use of nuclear weapons, and to demand an immediate end to the war. No nuclear weapon was used.

On April 17, three thousand students in Madison, Wisconsin marched on the ROTC building, while in California protesters shut down the Alameda Naval Air Station and an Air Force Recruiting station, and others in Connecticut blocked the entrance to an aircraft plant.

On April 19, 1972, eight Ivy League University presidents issued a joint statement condemning the bombing of North Vietnam and supporting peaceful anti-war demonstrations.

On April 21, 1972, students at over 150 colleges and universities went on strike, shutting down many campuses, and disrupting ROTC programs and work on military projects.

On April 22, 1972, hundreds of thousands of people marched against the war in cities all across the country: 100,000 marched in New York, 50,000 in San Francisco, 20,000 in Los Angeles, and many thousands more in Chicago, Detroit, Cleveland, Pittsburgh, and other cities. I helped organize a march in Buffalo. Nixon announced that another 20,000 US troops would be withdrawn from Vietnam in May and June.

By May 1, 1972, the number of US troops in Vietnam was now down to 66,000, from over 500,000 only two years earlier.

On May 8, 1972, in an act of desperation, Nixon began mining the ports of North Vietnam, causing an international outcry against the US as ships from other countries were at risk of being blown up. A wave of anti-war protests swept the US resulting in clashes with police. Over 1,800 anti-war protesters were arrested from San Jose to Boston. Police used wooden bullets and tear gas in Berkeley. Over 1,000 student protestors were arrested in Florida. Three policemen were shot and wounded in Madison, Wisconsin, and 715 National guardsmen were activated to quell rioting in Minneapolis.

On May 9, 1972, US Senate Democrats passed a resolution "disapproving the escalation of the war in Vietnam," voting to cut off funds for the war.

On May 10, 1972, protests and disturbances were so massive in Saigon and other areas of South Vietnam that they threatened the regime of South Vietnamese dictator Thieu. He responded by declaring martial law – the first time since the 1968 Tet offensive rocked the country.

On May 19, 1972, the Weather Underground set off a bomb *inside* the Pentagon's Air Force section to protest the bombing of Vietnam, destroying a computer that was assisting the US air war. The Weather Underground bomb hurt no one, in sharp contrast to the bombing by the US military that routinely killed and maimed hundreds and thousands of people in Vietnam. Nixon and the military generals were deeply shaken by this infiltration of the command center of the US military by militant anti-war activists.

On June 3, 1972, a thick report on the My Lai Massacre, where 504 Vietnamese civilians were killed, was made public by the Pulitzer-prize winning reporter Seymour Hersh. Hersh found that the entire command structure suppressed information about the massacre.

On June 19, 1972, veteran war correspondent Kevin Buckley called the My Lai massacre "trifling by comparison" to the many *thousands* of other innocent Vietnamese civilians that had been killed under the guise of the US "pacification" program.

That same month, burglars hired by the Committee to Re-Elect the President (CREEP) broke into the Democratic Party headquarters at the Watergate Hotel in Washington, D. C. in an effort to find anything to use against anti-war Democratic presidential candidate George McGovern.

On June 23-25, 1972, Labor for Peace was founded at a convention in St. Louis by 1,200 delegates from 32 states and representing 4 million workers. Workers from Buffalo attended, including some who had been influenced by *New Age*. National leaders of a number of unions were involved. It was the largest labor gathering ever held against the war.

On July 14, 1972, six national leaders of the 25,000-member Vietnam Veterans Against the War were charged with conspiracy to incite armed rebellion at the Republican National Convention.

On August 22, 1972, 5,000 anti-war demonstrators protested against Nixon and the war at the Republican National Convention in Miami. I helped organize support in Buffalo for these demonstrations. Hundreds of protesters were arrested in tear-gas filled Miami streets.

Throughout the fall of 1972, I joined tens of thousands of anti-war activists in campaigning against Nixon and for McGovern, and I wrote articles and leaflets against the war. Nixon scared voters by saying there would be continued chaos in the streets if McGovern was elected president. Nixon was causing the chaos, not McGovern.

On November 7, 1972, Nixon's fear campaign worked and he was re-elected by a large margin. However, McGovern received nearly 30 million votes on a strong anti-war campaign platform, and anti-war candidates gained seats in Congress, showing that anti-war sentiment had permeated the entire society and was growing. Voters in most major cities with Democratic majorities and influential anti-war movements, like Buffalo, New York City, Boston, Philadelphia, Cleveland, Detroit, Chicago, St. Louis, San Francisco, Los Angeles and many others cast majority votes for McGovern. Unfortunately, it wasn't enough. Yet, the anti-Nixon forces were so strong that a movement began to impeach Nixon for the break-in at Watergate Hotel and for his prosecution of the war in Vietnam. Anti-war sentiment continued to spread, along with demands for a peace settlement at the Paris Peace Talks.

By the end of 1972, many peace organizations had grown dramatically in size: the Fellowship of Reconciliation increased by one-third to 23,000 members since 1969, and Another Mother for Peace skyrocketed to 236,000 members.

In December 1972, in a final act of desperation, Nixon escalated his bombing frenzy of North Vietnam, bombing hospitals, civilian neighborhoods and foreign Embassies in one of the cruelest crimes of the war. These war crimes murdered and maimed thousands of civilians, in blatant violation of most international laws having to do with the conduct of war. The amount of bombs dropped in this Christmas bombing, in one week from December 18 to December 24, equaled half of the total tonnage dropped on England in all of WWI, or 20 times the tonnage of the atomic bomb dropped on Hiroshima. Americans from all walks of life and foreign governments all over the world protested this savage assault and Nixon halted the bombing of North Vietnam on December 30.

On January 27, 1973, the Paris Peace Agreement was signed, bringing an official end to the war. That same day the US government also gave in to the anti-war and anti-draft movements and announced the end of the hated military draft. I was ecstatic. The Buffalo Draft Resistance Union and all other anti-draft and anti-war organizations achieved an important victory.

When the draft was abolished, 8,750 young men had been convicted of draft resistance. Some served prison sentences. But anti-war sentiment was so high that 570,000 other draft offenders were never prosecuted. It was estimated that more than 16 million young men had found ways to avoid the draft. I was proud that I had played a part in helping to fuel this huge and crucial act of resistance to the war.

On March 29, 1973, the last US troops left Vietnam.

On June 4, 1973, both houses of Congress passed a bill to cut funds for further US military activities in Indochina. Unfortunately, some US tax dollars continued to go to prop up the Thieu dictatorship. Fighting continued in Vietnam, as Thieu struggled to hold on to power. The movement in the US to remove President Nixon from office gained support among the public and in Congress.

In July and August of 1973, approximately 150 people staged an anti-war protest *inside* the White House when they broke away from a tour group. They denounced continued US support of Thieu and were arrested.

On October 26-28, 1973, a conference was held in Germantown, Ohio, initiated by the Indochina Peace Campaign, to form the United Campaign to End the War. Its goal was to set up a massive lobbying campaign to convince Congress to cut off *all* funds for the Thieu regime, and to support the impeachment of Nixon. The Indochina Peace Campaign was founded by Tom Hayden, a founder of SDS and later a California State Legislator, and his wife at the time, actress Jane Fonda.

In March of 1974, the United Campaign and the Coalition to Stop Funding the War, received the endorsement of the US Conference of Mayors and other major organizations.

In early April 1974, the House of Representatives voted down Nixon's request for additional aid to Thieu.

On April 27, 1974, ten thousand people demonstrated in Washington, D. C. in the first mass impeachment demonstration. Growing numbers of Congressional Representatives joined the impeachment movement.

In the summer of 1974, my father and I reconciled and our family was brought back together. It happened one afternoon when he and I went out to lunch together and we talked. We had had very little contact with each other for five years. We agreed that we would not argue about the war, and we arrived at a new level of respect for each other. I was very happy that we achieved that understanding.

On July 30, 1974, Congress voted to impeach President Nixon.

On August 9, 1974, Nixon resigned due to the intense public outcry, the first president in our nation's history to be forced from office in the middle of a term. The anti-war movement was credited with playing a major role in Nixon's downfall.

Throughout 1973 and 1974, the South Vietnamese military continued the war to protect its corrupt leaders in Saigon, but without support from the US military and dwindling financial help, they were losing. The anti-war movement continued to demand that *all* US funds be cut from the Saigon regime.

I returned to UB as a full-time student in January of 1974 and joined the staff of *The Spectrum.* I wrote numerous articles throughout 1974 and early 1975 demanding that Congress end all funding of Thieu. I was also a member of the Western New York Peace Center, and we regularly lobbied Congress to stop funding South Vietnam. Little by little, Congress continued to reduce US funds until Thieu's government practically collapsed. This corrupt creation of the US government lost control of all areas of South Vietnam and the liberation forces swept across the country.

On April 30, 1975, liberation forces entered Saigon and overthrew what was left of the South Vietnamese government and the war ended. People all across Vietnam and all over the world rejoiced that peace had had finally been achieved. Saigon was renamed Ho Chi Minh City. There was no "bloodbath, as pro-war advocates warned throughout the war.

Vietnam earned the highest respect and admiration from people around the globe for standing up to the US empire-builders and war-mongers, fighting against incredible odds, and winning its independence.

As remarkable as this accomplishment was, the horrible suffering and loss of life should never be forgotten. The magnitude of the killing in Vietnam was staggering. Two million people or more were killed in a country of 44 million – that's one death for every 22 people. If that same ratio were applied to the US, that would be like having four to eight people killed on every residential block on every street in every city and town and village in every state in the United

States by a foreign aggressor. It is estimated that upwards of 1,000 Vietnamese were killed *a week* by the US military. Many millions more Vietnamese were wounded, many crippled for life, and people are still being killed and crippled as I write this in 2007 from previously unexploded US cluster bombs and US Agent Orange.

With the war finally over, the Vietnamese had to overcome the legacy of centuries of oppressive colonial rule that held back the development of the country in practically every field. Yet, Vietnam has made important strides to develop its economy, political, social and cultural life. Our government has yet to provide the reparations to Vietnam – with no strings attached – that she so rightly deserves and needs.

The war against Vietnam was foisted on the American people with a campaign of lies. Our government and its corporate supporters did not represent the interests or desires of the American people. The war was a betrayal of the best qualities that we stand for as a nation and as a people – freedom, independence, democracy, respect and compassion for others of all races and nationalities, and the sanctity of human life.

I am not a pacifist, and I believe that if any nation or people are truly threatened, they have the right to defend themselves. But we don't have the right to impose our will on others. That's what our government did in Vietnam, and unfortunately, what it has done to many other countries around the world.

The anti-war sentiment in the US in the 1960's and 1970's was so powerful that it lived for decades and still has significant influence today. It created a political atmosphere that gave others, in the US and in other countries, the courage to stand up for their rights. As a result, throughout the 1970's and into the 1980's and beyond, movements for national liberation, freedom, independence and progressive programs won or made significant advances in many countries all over the world, especially in Africa, Asia and Latin America. Those in power in the US dared not to interfere, or at least not so openly, brazenly and brutally as they did in Vietnam. While many problems continue to exist, Laos gained independence from a long colonial rule, the Nicaraguan people overthrew the murderous US-backed Somoza dictatorship, and the African National Congress freedom movement in South Africa dismantled apartheid and created a progressive, democratic republic, to name only a few.

But some of those elite corporate executives and bankers in the US who lost power and privileges during those years, or who felt threatened by the freedom of others, worked to turn back the clock of time. They wanted to return to the old days, when they could bully others with impunity to enrich themselves at the expense of millions of people. By 2000, they were ready to strike.

Chapter 50

From Vietnam to Iraq

In 2000, Republican Party leaders George W. Bush and Dick Cheney were elected president and vice president of the United States in a very close election marred by vote fraud in their favor. A number of investigators believe they were not elected, but rigged the vote by disenfranchising large groups of traditionally Democratic Party voters in Florida, particularly African-Americans. Both men were very conservative to right-wing politically, and both had been top executives in oil industry companies. They were the most visible men in a larger group of wealthy and privileged corporate executives who determined that the time was ripe for them to throw their weight around in the world again. Their immediate goal was to significantly broaden their hold on the world's major energy source – oil, which would allow them to increase their domination of the world. Many in this group are members of a very conservative, semi-secret organization called the Project for a New American Century. To those who followed the machinations of this group, it was clearly a group intent on building a world empire. And it would be brutal and ruthless.

They set their sites on the Middle East, an area that contains 65% of the known oil reserves in the entire world. They already had significant influence in Saudi Arabia, the country with the largest known oil reserves, but now wanted to control the country with the second largest known oil reserves, Iraq. But their one-time friendly relationship with the long-time Iraqi dictator, Saddam Hussein, had deteriorated in the 1990's. So they decided to overthrow him to get control of Iraqi oil.

But they needed a reason to overthrow Hussein, something big that they could sell to the American people to win our support. After the Vietnam debacle, the American people were skeptical of any US government leader who hinted that he might want to go to war over anything short of a very serious threat to our country, and this corporate crowd knew it. On September 11, 2001, the media reported that terrorists hijacked American planes and flew them into the World Trade Center in New York, and the Pentagon in Washington, D. C., killing nearly 3,000 people. The American people were stunned and rightly outraged at this attack, and President Bush said the government had information that the terrorists were members of Al Qaeda, based in the Middle East. Bush announced to the nation that the perpetrators of this crime would be punished, and that the US would track down, jail or kill the top Al Qaeda leadership, headed by Osama bin Laden, and destroy their organization.

The Bush Administration decided this terrible event could be used as a pretext to invade Iraq. The only problem was that there was no connection between Al Qaeda and Iraq. So they made one up.

Here was the line of reasoning that the Bush Administration presented to the American people: Al Qaeda is a terrorist group that killed nearly 3,000 Americans. All terrorists are a threat to the United States because, according to Bush, terrorists hate democratic, peace-loving countries like ours. Finally, terrorists are so nasty that they use any type of weapon they can get their hands on, including "weapons of mass destruction." Iraq has weapons of mass destruction, Bush claimed, and Saddam Hussein is harboring terrorists. Therefore, Saddam Hussein is a threat to the United States, so we have to take him out. And to do that, we have to use military force. We will tell our young people, especially those who are poor, black and Latino and those whose future looks dim, that it is patriotic to join the military, and by invading Iraq they will be protecting our country, and maybe even be war heroes. Most importantly, they will be enticed with promises of money for college and other benefits, which may or may not be given to them. Furthermore, the war with Iraq would be short and with limited suffering because the Iraqi people would welcome us with open arms as liberators.

The only problem with this line of reasoning is that *none* of it was true. Here are the facts.

Scott Ritter, a US Marine Corps officer, a Republican, and the chief weapons inspector for the UN in Iraq, said in March 2002 that Iraq was disarmed – a *full year before* the US invasion. He also stated that there was no connection between Iraqi leader Saddam Hussein and Al Qaeda and the attack on the World Trade Center. Bush continued saber-rattling anyway.

On February 14, 2003, one month *before* the US war began, Dr. Hans Blix, head of the United Nations inspection team reported to the US Security Council that his team had found no weapons of mass destruction in Iraq. Between February 20 and March 15, I joined thousands of others to organize peace marches, and I was among an estimated 15 million people who marched in over 100 cities in the US and other countries to oppose the coming war.

President Bush ignored all of this and on March 20, 2003, launched a massive air strike on Iraq, called "shock and awe," which was a criminal mass murder. He claimed he was launching a war on terrorism. But there never was a threat from Iraq toward the US. Over the next several months US troops and inspectors searched Iraq for weapons of mass destruction. They found none. This was reported to the nation. Faced with this evidence, President Bush admitted that there were no WMDs, but he claimed that the war was justified because Iraq was harboring terrorists. After more investigation, that turned out to be false too. The Iraqi people did not welcome US troops as liberators, and a war has raged in Iraq from 2003 to the time I am writing this in late 2007. And the killing and suffering has been horrendous.

In October of 2006, researchers at John Hopkins University reported that over 650,000 Iraqi's, overwhelmingly civilians, have been killed in the war, and many more seriously injured for life. By 2007, over 3,000 US troops have lost their lives and more are injured. All for a war based on lies – just like in Vietnam.

Children have suffered the most. According to the United Nations, the US government-led economic sanctions begun against Iraq in the 1990s crippled Iraqi society, resulting in the death of one in eight children before his or her fifth birthday. Since the war, things have gotten worse.

Paul William Roberts, a Canadian journalist, was in Iraq when the war began. He wrote a book, *A War Against the Truth,* detailing the terrible suffering that he witnessed. In Tikrit, he saw a young girl about six years of age lying in a hospital bed who "had lost both legs...and her left arm from the shoulder." He learned that she had picked up what looked like a toy in the rubble of her school and it exploded. It was a US cluster bomb. These cluster bombs contain up to two thousand time-delayed bomblets that are scattered over a wide area and explode when picked up or bumped. These were the same, now "improved," cluster bombs that the US government used against the Vietnamese 35 years earlier. Roberts wrote that the US and Britain dropped "thirteen thousand cluster munitions" on Iraq in the first nine months of the war. The goal in Iraq, as it was in

Vietnam, is to so seriously maim such large numbers of civilians that the nation will be paralyzed with fear and horror and they will surrender. That *is* "shock and awe," and *that* is terrorism. The US mass media, which is owned and controlled by the same corporate and banking interests which seek to benefit from a US client state in Iraq, has virtually blacked out this story.

Young US soldiers were then sent into battle zones believing they were going to stop bad people from doing bad things, and then witnessed these US-caused horrors. The result is that growing numbers of US troops are turning against the war in Iraq, just as they did in Vietnam. Darrell Anderson of the Army's 1st Armored Division in Baghdad said, "I was willing to die for my country. I thought I was going over there to defend my country. But that's not what I was doing there... Innocent people are being killed every day." Echoes of Vietnam veterans 35 years later.

Ehren Watada, an Army first lieutenant, refused deployment to Iraq and said, "the wholesale slaughter and mistreatment of the Iraqi people is not only a terrible moral injustice...but a contradiction to the Army's own Law of Land Warfare." He has been charged with seven violations and faces eight years in prison if convicted.

The US torture at Abu Ghraib further hurt our reputation in Iraq. Rather than renouncing torture, President Bush shockingly proclaimed to the nation and the world that some forms of torture were acceptable.

It was no surprise that Iraqi resistance to US troops increased dramatically. The blatant lies turned US public opinion against the war and polls have shown repeatedly that a majority of the American people want the war to end. By late 2007, that number is at 70 percent. Bush and his strongest supporters ignore the will of the people and continue the bloodletting.

The US corporate quest for more Middle Eastern oil is so strong that the Bush crowd arrogantly dismisses the growing hostility of former allied nations around the world toward our country, greatly harming our reputation. Just like in Vietnam. The US quest for Iraqi oil is not new. It has gone on for over 80 years. It's just more brutal under the Bush Administration.

Oil has been very good for top US leaders and they are awash in it. Vice President Dick Cheney, for example, was the CEO of Halliburton, where he has $8 million in stock options and still receives $1 million a year. Cheney loves his power, wealth and lifestyle and wants to protect it at any cost – including the impoverishment, starvation and murder of hundreds of thousands of people. In March of 2001, six months *before* the attack on the World Trade Center and two years *before* the US invasion, Cheney set up a Task Force on Energy to study geological maps of Iraq to identify the most lucrative Iraqi oil fields. After 9/11, he dusted off his maps, and started planning how to take control of Iraqi crude.

The war on Iraq, like the war on Vietnam, is illegal, immoral and repugnant to the values we hold dear. It is a crime against the Iraqi people, the American soldiers and people everywhere, and it must be ended as quickly as possible. Fortunately, a large and growing anti-war movement is leading the drive to end the war. Just like in Vietnam. A significant number of the leaders of the anti-war movement to end the war on Iraq are the same people who helped build and led the anti-war movement to end the war on Vietnam. They have been joined by many others, of all ages, races and nationalities. But we must involve more people, increase the pressure everywhere, support the soldiers who refuse to fight, and get Congress to cut off funds for the war, now. We can build an anti-war movement that had the political clout of the movement to stop the war in Vietnam. If everyone pitches in with what ever contribution they can make, it can be done.

Epilogue

When I look back over the past 40 years, my active participation in the movement to stop the war against Vietnam, and now the war against Iraq, stand out as the most important things I have done in my life. The chain of events that took place in my formative years from 1966-1970 changed my entire life. I could no longer remain in my own private world. I became socially and politically aware and active. More importantly, a similar transformation took place for millions of other people.

While we didn't end the war in Vietnam nearly as quickly as we wanted, what we did accomplish was incredible. The activists in that cause built a massive grassroots political movement unlike anything our country had experienced since the Civil War. From a small group of anti-war activists in the early 1960's – constituting a tiny fraction of 1% of our population, they overcame the daily barrage of anti-communism, opposition by every major organization in the country in the early years, two gung-ho war presidents, almost the entire Congress, lies from government leaders, the mass media and the business community, misleadership on the war issue from many top officials in the labor movement, and repression from the state. I joined this movement in the middle of it, at a time when it was growing by leaps and bounds. Nine years after the war in Vietnam began, anti-war sentiment was embraced by the majority of Americans. While it took too long, we finally got our government to withdraw US troops, and ultimately to cut off money for the war.

When President Bush began making speeches in the later part of 2002, threatening to go to war against Iraq, the anti-war sentiment from the Vietnam years emerged among millions of Americans and huge demonstrations against the war took place, even before the bombing began.

Many hundreds of organizations came forward to protest in early 2003. The largest anti-war grouping is a coalition of groups called United for Peace and Justice. It mushroomed in size from a relatively small number of organizations in early 2003 to embrace over 1,400 organizations by 2006. Anti-war sentiment was much broader after one year of organizing against the war on Iraq than it was after three years of organizing against the war on Vietnam. In many ways, the anti-war movement today is standing on the shoulders of the anti-war movement of the 1960s and 1970s.

When I was 18, I asked myself two questions. Why do wars happen? And are they an uncontrollable fact of life? Within a couple of years, I had answers to both. To the second question, the answer is an unequivocal "No." Wars are started by people, they can be ended by people, and be prevented by people.

The answer to the first question is a little more complex, but there is an answer. Wars are not an uncontrollable fact of life. When the needs of all people in every society are satisfied, and when social relations are based on fairness, respect and justice, wars can be eliminated. This may seem impossible but it is not. We have the resources, knowledge and compassion to accomplish this.

In most cases, war begins when one party wants something that another party has. That can be oil or other natural resources, land and water, the exploitation of labor, or the ability to control these resources and people, including a military presence to secure and protect these gains. Those seeking the resources of another may turn to war if they don't get what they want on the terms they want. Real or imagined injustices by the targeted party are cited to justify war and rally the people to fight, but the quest to take the resources of another is almost always the root cause.

People everywhere, of every race and nationality, men, women and children, want and deserve to be treated with dignity and respect. They all want and deserve to have good jobs, adequate food, housing, medical care, education, freedom of speech and of the press, freedom in every aspect of their lives, meaningful participation in a fully democratic society, security, peace, and control over their lives. People also want to respect the rights of others, and to live in peace and harmony with all people on earth. They want what is fair, honorable and morally correct – in a word, they want justice. All this is achievable.

Justice, however, isn't achieved in one fell swoop. It rarely takes place along a steady continuum. There are starts and stops, small and large gains, and setbacks. Unfortunately, people suffer along the way, even those not involved in any aspect of a dispute. I wish no one had to suffer, ever. As more and more people of the world join social justice movements, the suffering will be progressively lessened. Unfortunately, the price people have paid for war has been horrific. Millions upon millions of people lost their lives needlessly. Millions more were wounded and crippled, physically and mentally. Economies and nations and civilizations have been destroyed, and others harmed so severely that people still suffer many decades, even generations after the war is over.

For my part, I paid a price of sorts, though it was small compared to the price paid by so many others. But to me, it was significant. The war in Vietnam ruined my relationship with Donna, the young women I was so much in love with. It also harmed my relationship with my parents, especially my father. And it diverted me from a life as an artist.

But the destruction of my relationship with Donna was the worst loss. For years after Donna and I broke up, I still thought about her. I thought about our life together before the war – how beautiful it was, so bright and innocent, and with so much promise. When the war destroyed that, I sunk into depression. But I held out hope, sometimes fleetingly, that somehow we could get back together. In the early or mid 1970's I heard that Donna and her family had moved away from Buffalo. I thought about trying to find her. I went to her house and stared at it, and tears came to my eyes. I saw her running down the front steps with her smiling eyes and jumping into my car and leaning over and giving me a kiss. But it was a mirage, a memory. A beautiful memory, but a memory.

The first love is special. I thought about going up to the door and asking the new owners if they knew where Donna's family had moved to. But I didn't. I was paralyzed. I went back several times, and the same thing happened each time. The war had changed everything. Me, her, and us. The war made everything that was beautiful ugly. Each time I drove away, I was left with a profound feeling of loss. Sometimes that loss would hide in the recesses of my soul, lying dormant while I was frantically doing something else. But when I had a lull in my life, that loss woke up and reminded me that it was still there. That loss stayed with me – for years.

But life goes on. It must go on. My new life direction propelled me forward. There was some inner drive that pushed me to help organize the anti-war movement and other social justice movements, some force that seemed to be outside my control. Like my love for Donna. Working to build the anti-war movement was important to me. It was essential to my being. It made me feel like I was alive and doing something good. But it wasn't all smooth sailing. People are imperfect. There were many frustrating meetings. Things didn't always go as I thought they should. Mistakes were made, opportunities missed, and the ball was dropped too often. But, overall, we had an impact. A very big impact. I saw with my own eyes that the work for justice advances. It makes gains and wins victories.

Most of the time, justice is won in little bits and pieces, one or two small improvements at a time. Each person's effort to end the war in Vietnam was like placing one building block upon another, or for an artist when they place one layer of paint upon another, creating a mosaic of colors. When millions of people took many small and large steps for justice, on many levels, and in a rich variety of activities, the accumulation of all these activities produced big results. In drawing or painting, the variety of shades enriches the art. In life, the variety of activities enriches the social justice movement, and in both art and life, many shades are needed.

That was why the Vietnam Moratorium was so successful. The variety and sheer breadth of activities, from people of all walks of life, greatly expanded the anti-war movement. This was a great example of the many shades of justice coming together to create a force much larger than the sum of its parts. Once this expansion started, it kept spreading. It finally embraced so many Americans that it put enough pressure on the entire nation to act, encouraging and supporting the soldiers who refused to fight, disrupting and fraying the normal course of our lives, pressuring Congress to cut off funds for the war. The US anti-war movement, in all its diversity, played an important role. When it became large enough, an important step toward justice took place. It can and will happen again.

Of course, we can't overlook the central role played by the Vietnamese people. Their resistance to the aggression of the US government and corporations was the principle factor in ending the exploitation, the killing, and the war. The Vietnamese people deserve the lion's share of praise, and the world stood humbly to honor them for their steadfastness, sacrifices and achievements in their century-old quest for freedom from foreign domination. The Vietnamese people set an example for the whole world. They showed that a small nation of very proud people can overcome incredible odds in the struggle for justice over a much larger immoral force. They showed that justice can prevail. They showed that when a people take up a noble cause, they will be supported by millions of other people all over the world.

The most important lesson I learned was that a mass movement, democratic in nature and organized from the bottom up, is what makes positive social and political change. Experts and people in positions of influence can help, and under the right circumstances, they can play a big role, including helping to provide leadership at many levels. But, so often, they are restrained by forces that have a vested interest in keeping things as they are. The mass movement is what motivates the decision-makers to act. Building a mass movement is the single most important component in changing the world. One of our goals should be no empires, not in the US nor any where else.

There is also another benefit to building a mass movement for social justice, and it isn't a small benefit. That is the positive impact this work has on us, as individuals. When I work for peace and justice, I feel good about what I'm doing and good about myself. It is life-affirming. It embraces and advances humanity. I feel it is the most important thing I can do on earth. It is the greatest gift we give to each other. Ultimately, it makes us human.

The End

Appendix A

Steps in Organizing for Social Change

1. **Identify the problem and publicize it.** You want to publicize it - by word of mouth, in letters, leaflets, emails, articles in newsletters or newspapers or any other means, in order to inform others about the problem and find people who agree with you.

2. **Bring people together who agree.** It's hard to solve problems by yourself, so gather others who agree with you to help. Even a group of two or three or four is better than trying to solve problems by yourself.

3. **Determine what your remedy is – what do you want to happen to resolve the problem?** It is important to have a remedy and to ask that the remedy be granted and implemented. You might want to have a short-term, partial remedy, and a long-term more complete remedy.

4. **Develop a campaign of activities to pressure decision-makers to fix the problem.** A campaign might include handing out leaflets, organizing a letter-writing campaign, holding public educational forums, having a march or rally, or doing many other creative things. Throughout the campaign, you will likely have to continually do all four of the above steps: keep publicizing the problem, keep recruiting more supporters, keep making your demand for change, keep putting pressure on decision-makers and increase the pressure at each step if possible and feasible.

Photo Credits

276	(top)	Author's collection
	(bottom)	Democratic Republic of Vietnam
277	(left)	Authors collection
	(right)	UPI/Corbis
278	(top)	*Buffalo Courier-Express* (Buffalo State College Archives and Special Collections)
	(bottom left)	Author's collection
	(bottom right)	New Mobilization Committee to End the War in Vietnam
279	(page)	*The Spectrum*
280	(entire page)	*1970 Buffalonian* SUNY at Buffalo
281	(entire page)	*1970 Buffalonian*
282	(top)	*1970 Buffalonian*
	(bottom)	*Buffalo Courier Express* (Buffalo State College Archives and Special Collections)
283	(top)	Buffalo Anti-war Movement
	(bottom)	*Midnight Oil* SUNY at Buffalo Milliard Fillmore Night School
284	(entire page)	*New Age* (Author's collection)
285	(entire page)	Author's collection

Paul Krehbiel

About the Author

Born in Buffalo, Paul Krehbiel was one of many leaders in the peace movement of the late 1960's and early 1970's to end the war in Vietnam. He was a union auto parts worker and aspiring artist. He earned BA and MS degrees from the State University of New York at Buffalo in the mid and late 1970's where he wrote for the student newspaper and taught in Social Sciences College at SUNYAB.

In the early 1980's, while working as a Teamster, he was active in the Colorado Coors Boycott which helped win a $1.2 million jobs creation program for blacks and Latinos. While involved in the Nuclear Freeze movement, he worked on a campaign that ended nuclear weapons production at a major arms manufacturer in Colorado. In 1985, he became the managing editor of the *Furniture Workers Press,* national newspaper of the United Furniture Workers, AFL-CIO, in Nashville, and assisted union organizing in the south.

In the early 1990's, he worked as a Senior Assistant to the Majority Whip of the Assembly in the California Legislature. He was also president of Los Angeles Health Access, and a founder and vice president of Health Care for All, California's state-wide organization working for universal single-payer health care.

In 1998, he went on staff with Service Employees International Union, Local 660, in Los Angeles County, where he organized work-site Stewards Councils. He was also the chief negotiator for over 5,000 Registered Nurses, and helped lead a campaign that improved hospital staffing. He was elected president of United Union Representatives of Los Angeles for five consecutive terms.

Since 2003, he has been active in the campaign to end the war in Iraq, working with the Coalition for World Peace, US Labor Against the War, and the Iraq Moratorium.

He is one of 70 authors of *A Troublemaker's Handbook 2* (2005), a guide for employees seeking to improve their working conditions.

In 2007, he became a local coordinator for Step it Up, a national environmental organization working to stop global warming.

He lives, works and writes in southern California. *Shades of Justice* is a coming-of-age memoir.

Paul Krehbiel